DESIRING EMANCIPATION

SUNY series in Queer Politics and Cultures
————
Cynthia Burack and Jyl J. Josephson, editors

Photograph of Claire Waldoff and Ottilie von Roeder. Reproduced with permission of Peter Finckh.

DESIRING EMANCIPATION

New Women and Homosexuality in Germany, 1890–1933

MARTI M. LYBECK

Published by State University of New York Press, Albany

For information, contact State University of New York Press, Albany, NY
www.sunypress.edu

Production by Ryan Morris
Marketing by Michael Campochiaro

Library of Congress Cataloging-in-Publication Data

Lybeck, Marti M.
    Desiring emancipation : new women and homosexuality in Germany, 1890–1933 /
Marti M. Lybeck.
        pages cm (SUNY series in Queer Politics and Cultures)
    Includes bibliographical references and index.
    ISBN 978-1-4384-5221-0 (hc : alk. paper) 978-1-4384-5222-7 (pb : alk. paper)
    1. Lesbianism—Germany—History—19th century. 2. Lesbianism—Germany—
History—20th century. 3. Lesbians—Germany—History—19th century.
4. Lesbians—Germany—History—20th century. I. Title.

    HQ75.6.G3L93 2014
    306.76'630943—dc23   2013029946

                    10 9 8 7 6 5 4 3 2 1

Contents

Illustrations

Acknowledgments

This book would not have been possible without the generous support of the Berlin Program for Advanced European Studies at the Free University Berlin, which supported the original research, and the Institute for the Humanities at the University of Michigan, which funded time for the initial writing of the dissertation on which it is based. I thank the staffs and boards of both agencies for supporting my work. I am also grateful to the German Historical Institute, Washington, D.C., for recognizing the work in its earlier form with the Fritz Stern Dissertation Prize in 2008. The Institute's Transatlantic Seminar in 2005 and a fellowship from the University of Michigan Institute for Women in Gender also provided valuable opportunities for presenting sections of the work, as did the Workshop for Comparative History of Women, Gender, and Sexuality at the University of Minnesota, the Yale Research Initiative on the History of Sexualities, and the Rethinking German Modernities Workshop, organized by Geoff Eley and Jennifer Jenkins.

I thank the many archive personnel who helped me navigate and use their collections. Heino Rose of the Staatsarchiv Hamburg and Ute Schumacher of the Institut für Stadtgeschichte Frankfurt deserve special mention for making me aware of the disciplinary case files that became chapter 4. Thanks to the Frankfurt Institut, the Geheimes Staatsarchiv Preussischer Kulturbesitz, the Lou-Andreas-Salomé-Archiv Göttingen, and the Münchner Stadtmuseum for granting permission to use illustrations. Special thanks to Peter Finckh for his enthusiastic support of the project and permission to use the photograph, from his family collection, of Claire Waldoff and Olly von Roeder for the book's frontispiece. While doing research in Germany, I received much appreciated assistance from Claudia Schoppmann, Kirsten Plötz, Alf Lüdke, Dorothee Wierling, and Annelie Schalm.

The work owes a great debt to my dissertation advisers at the University of Michigan, Geoff Eley, Kathleen Canning, Scott Spector, Kerstin Barndt, and Nancy Hunt. Each in his or her own way supported, encouraged, challenged, and pushed. I'm especially grateful for their continuing interest in my work and welfare. I'm also indebted to my mentors and friends in Arizona, Doug Weiner and Susan Crane, who encouraged and helped with the very earliest versions of chapter 5.

I thank my colleagues at the University of Wisconsin La Crosse for their interest and support, especially those who are part of the History Authors Writing Group—Victor Maciás-González, Jodi Vandenberg-Daves, Jim Longhurst, Jennifer Trost, Heidi Morrison, Tiffany Trimmer, Gerry Iguchi, Gita Pai, and John Grider. Their comments on book chapter drafts have been invaluable. I also thank the anonymous readers for SUNY Press, whose comments significantly improved the final manuscript.

Although many supportive friends have contributed along the way and deserve thanks, I hope Roberta Pergher, Mia Lee, Karen Lybeck, and Rick Lybeck feel my deepest love and gratitude. Thanks for being there when I needed you.

Introduction

The collar-and-tie-wearing, bicycle-riding, and cigarette-smoking New Woman was a prominent international media figure of the 1890s. German writer Frieda von Bülow, one of several younger novelists who might be considered new women themselves, probed beneath the New Woman's surface image of alternately alluring and dangerous modernity. Her story "Just Let Me Forget!" portrayed a relationship between two characters—the conventionally feminine Gunhild and the often cross-dressed, radical Senta—that represented potential strategies for aspiring new women.[1] Gunhild keeps a worried eye on the excesses she sees in her friend Senta's embodiment of New Woman ideals. Their fictional interaction may be read as Bülow's attempt to think through the limits of emancipated behavior.[2] The crux of the problem these characters try to sort out is the relationship between femininity and heterosexuality. Senta rejects the conventional forms of both based on her critical feminist convictions, while Gunhild defends the boundaries of acceptable emancipation using rubrics of love and normality.

The same defining elements that were in play for Bülow—emancipation, femininity, sexuality, and women's relations with one another and with men—are the focus points of *Desiring Emancipation,* an account tracing historical new women in late-nineteenth- and early-twentieth-century Germany. In Bülow's stories, as in this book's discussion, emancipated femininity could not be thought through without coming to terms with the double import of sexuality: sexuality as the basis of the heterosexual social order and sexuality as an element in individual subjectivity. The latter aspect is the thread that pulls the diverse research landscapes of the book together. How did women seeking emancipation strive toward sexual subjectivity in and through their individual life experiences? To answer this question, *Desiring Emancipation* addresses the broad historical problem of how change happens at the level of the individual.[3] How did historical subjects such as those represented by Bülow decide to fight the powerful forces of social continuity and cultural

1

construction? Although Senta and Gunhild are fictional creations, I use them here as composites that express central questions in the reworking of the New Woman's sexuality carried on by individuals and groups in the era.

A scene early in the novella depicts Senta and Gunhild arguing angrily over the nature of femininity. Senta sees Gunhild's mooning over a male lover as incompatible with emancipationist goals. "You are just like the others!" she accuses Gunhild bitterly. Gunhild defends her emotions as normal for women, implicitly smearing Senta's idiosyncratic appearance and behavior as abnormal and adding, "Abnormalities belong in formaldehyde." Senta cries, "Yes, if only there were such a thing as a normal woman! . . . What we are today is man-made work- and pleasure-slaves. . . . To develop according to our nature, we must not be put in fetters and surrounded by countless obstacles. . . . The normal woman belongs to the future."[4] Senta's robust defense of disturbing, seemingly "abnormal," experiments in female existence and her passionate desire for emancipation from "man-made" femininity give this book its title and signal its argument that seeking autonomy was the core animating motivation for new women.

The argument scene also evokes other important themes developed in the book. Gunhild's rebuke expresses uneasiness with Senta's bold appropria-tion of masculine privileges in her bodily habitus and relations with other women. Senta wears knee pants, short hair, and a cap and carries a whip. She speaks forthrightly, smokes, sits straddling her seat, and does "gymnastic stunts" in the drawing room. Men do not suffer Senta's attention-grabbing presence for long. And Senta complains that she has had few opportunities to see Gunhild without "annoying boring men" always hanging around.[5] Gunhild is perturbed to observe that there is "something of the practiced courtier or ladies man in the way [Senta] interacted with women." In Gun-hild's disapproving analysis, Senta has "jumped into her trouser role so completely" that she "felt herself as a young man in relation to women and acted accordingly." Her flattery and gallantry succeed in working "a curious enchantment on women."[6] Gunhild condemns Senta's female masculinity, erotic effect on women, and preference for female company as emancipation taken too far. Late-twentieth-century readers might have interpreted Senta's characteristics as signs of lesbian subjectivity and desire. These and other possibilities will be considered and further deconstructed in the course of the book. Here it is sufficient to make the point that female masculinity and female same-sex relations raised crucial questions for New Women writers wrestling with emancipation in the late nineteenth century.

The scene's cutting exchange between friends reflects tensions among his-torical new women—tensions that often hinged on questions of respectability and sexuality. Gunhild's alarm is not a reaction to suspicions of homosexuality; instead, it expresses the fears of many new women that placing themselves too far outside the norms of social order might make them irrelevant. These fears were complex, varying from individual to individual, yet they often erupted into rage directed at one's intimates rather than at superiors, men, or social norms in general. Bülow's novel had Senta fall in love with a man and simultaneously begin to feminize her appearance, restoring her to the heteronormative gender order. But such neat plot resolutions were not available to actual historical women. Conflicts among groups of friends and co-workers sometimes became toxic, ruining the liberating potential of new lives and subjectivities. Attention to the substance of these conflicts prevents this history of emancipation from following an uncomplicated trajectory of liberation. Finding a usable emancipated identity was generations in the making and was far from completed when the new Nazi state radically changed the conditions for asserting female identities in 1933.

Finally, Gunhild's use of the word *normal* points to the medicalization of sexuality, then becoming increasingly familiar to the German reading public. Early sexologists often explained the entire New Woman phenomenon as an effect of abnormal sexuality. Concepts of the homosexual person and his or her deviant desires circulated in explanations of sex aimed at professional, elite, and popular audiences. Encountering these, twentieth-century new women had to define their sexuality and intimacy with other women. Sexological theories never succeeded in becoming completely hegemonic, but they did play a mixed role in the emergence of homosexual identity among women. *Desiring Emancipation* recovers the complex interaction between medical discourses and historical subjects in this formative period.

The emergence of New Woman figures, not only in novels but in representations and debates in many media, signals the onset of a change in the gender order that gradually came to define gender roles and relations that persist into the present. One aspect of the new norms involved recognition of desire as formative of gender and sexual relations. Another was the growing determination of women to become autonomous persons in the social sphere. As Senta put it, "We can only be freed from the curse of our present existence when we learn to seek and find the center of our being in our selves."[7] To what extent did Senta's quest represent the concerns of actual young women of the era? While that is a difficult question to answer, it is clear enough from the testimony of eyewitnesses that at least a noticeable proportion of younger women, first in the United States and Britain, soon across Europe and in Japan and China, adopted what might be called emancipationist attitudes toward existing gender arrangements.[8] These early seekers of emancipation were the cutting edge of the women's movement and the forerunners of generations of career women, professional feminists, and eventually women who claimed homosexual identities. Numbers of women fitting the description increased over the period to encompass women of all social classes. In Germany, the term *neue Frau* continued to designate a particular kind of modern young woman in the interwar period. This study uses the term expansively to bridge the boundary between imperial Germany and the Weimar Republic—a point of rupture often replicated in analyses of women's movements and female emancipation in German history.[9]

Desiring Emancipation applies a new analytic lens to the intersection of women's emancipation and theories of homosexuality.[10] Its analysis begins with a fundamental claim of queer theory: normative assumptions defining the relation between gender and sexuality are unstable fictions enforcing social order. From this theoretical starting point, sexuality can be investigated in all of its problematic complexity without taking any labels, positions, or acts as givens. Radically disaggregating the phenomena associated with the New Woman and the female homosexual opens the possibility of recovering how historical subjects perceived them. In a second move, meanings can be interpreted in the context of individual lives, public discourses, and same-sex social environments.

The following pages trace the genealogy of women's emancipation and its relationship to female homosexuality. They reveal the struggles of diverse women writers attempting to represent women's claims to sexual subjectivity. In addition, the judgments of observers, whether voyeuristic, bemused, outraged, embarrassed, or sympathetic, form a counterpoint of broader context for reception of women's new identities. In both kinds of sources, emancipation, homosexual identity notions, and women's claiming of sexual subjectivity develop alongside of and intertwined with one another. *Desiring Emancipation* follows this triple helix—emancipation, homosexuality, and subjectivity—through a historical era when the three strands became interrelated and increasingly effectual in defining individual lives. It argues that the emerging problematic of female sexual subjectivity developing here continues in the "DNA" shaping our present understanding of and contentions over gender and sex.

Emancipation

The arguments developed in *Desiring Emancipation* depend on a clear definition of "emancipation." The term derives from post-Enlightenment legal emancipation of previously restricted categories of persons, especially serfs, slaves, and Jews. Recognition of women as equal persons before the law lagged behind. In the upheaval generated by nineteenth-century industrialization and conflict over political representation, newly polarized concepts of gender worked to stabilize the family as the source of order. Instead of overturning legal gender inequality, the Enlightenment enhanced it in the near term.[11] In response, feminists campaigned for the amelioration of women's legal disabilities. However, the "emancipation" in *Desiring Emancipation* has a different meaning. As activist movements have recognized, formal and legal emancipation must be accompanied by emancipation within stigmatized subjects. Remaking the self as an autonomous and self-regulating subject—subjectivity formation—is the connotation intended in the book's arguments about emancipation.

Like most objects of desire, emancipation was, and is, a chimera. Trying to achieve it involved women in a struggle that brought as much bitterness, anger, and resentment as satisfaction. The book tells stories of middle-class women's difficult paths toward their dreams of emancipation. As social space for independent women's lives widened dramatically in the decades surrounding World War I, more and more women of diverse backgrounds engaged in this everyday struggle.

The New Woman figure changed with the times, facilitating public discussion of the social changes she represented. The 1890s figure was often a means to ridicule and attack feminist women. Women's autonomy appeared to threaten the entire social order of family and reproduction. Yet the active and confident figure was also a model and point of identification for women who desired the self-possession she represented. The gender transgressions of 1890s New Woman images coincided with an explosion in avant-garde cultural critique of bourgeois ideals, including gender polarization, the rigid sexual double standard, and the erasure of sex from polite discourse. In Germany, the transfer of power from Chancellor Otto von Bismarck to Kaiser Wilhelm II in 1890 might seem remote from the intimate lives of women. However, the end of the Bismarck system of rule with its antisocialist laws had a revitalizing effect on organization and reform across the political spectrum. New discursive spaces for challenging imperial and bourgeois norms emerged in satire, organizations, critique, and theatrical presentations.[12]

A generational dynamic shaped social rupture in 1890s Germany. The generation that participated in the 1848 movement for democratization was succeeded by the self-satisfied and successful generation of the unification period.[13] Their complacency generated scorn and envy in many of their children. Products of an affluent society, they nevertheless criticized it savagely, spurred on by reading Zola, Ibsen, and Nietzsche. The radicals of the era styled themselves as self-consciously modern enemies of the hierarchies and hypocrisies of bourgeois respectability.[14] At the same time, rapid urbanization facilitated many young people's escape from family responsibilities. Bohemian "scenes" and artists' circles in larger cities provided a stimulating context for independent living. New opportunities to train for teaching or the arts offered girls an additional semi-sheltered first step toward autonomy.

Historical new women of the 1890s were children of elites, primarily the professionals and civil servants of the German *Bildungsbürgertum*, which based its status and position on education and service to the state. Their chances of living independently were slim.[15] A few women supported themselves or were supported by indulgent families. Most who lived on their own were orphaned or had lost their fathers. Without a father to veto their plans, and perhaps with a small inheritance or income, they traveled, studied, or tried their luck as writers, actresses, or painters. Many 1890s new women wanted to make a difference intellectually, culturally, or socially. They transformed the ideals of service and purity they were raised with to apply to the broader public sphere. Sexuality was a sensitive issue for them. A very few preached and practiced sexual freedom. Others had discreet affairs with men. Yet female honor, defined as virginity prior to marriage, remained hegemonic. Only transcendent love could justify their becoming sexually active. Emancipatory rhetoric depended on the ideal of female purity.

The 1920s New Woman was even more a discursive construction than her turn-of-the-century counterpart. She was no longer perceived as a harbinger of change, but as a typical expression of the times, ubiquitous in advertising, journalism, the cinema, and on the street.[16] Whereas the 1890s New Woman had been criticized for inappropriate seriousness and ambition, the 1920s version was dangerously frivolous and self-centered. Of uncertain class origins, she pursued consumption, entertainment, and adventure. She was assumed to be sexually active, perhaps promiscuous, and heartless toward any poor man in love with her.[17]

The belief that a shift toward sexual activity among young unmarried women had occurred since the turn of the century had some basis in fact.[18] The flapper figure, in Germany as elsewhere, reflected a noticeable increase in the number of young women moving more freely and confidently in public places. However, the social phenomena and conditions contributing to this presence and image were complex; historical actors did not conform to the image nor can they be grouped easily together. Differences of class origins, relative economic security, social and political outlook, family ties, and locality make it impossible to specify a single historical 1920s New Woman.

The best fit for the image was the young chic urban woman. A number of progressive intellectuals pursued this lifestyle. In 1920s Berlin, homosexual experimentation became part of their sexual and style repertoire. Marianne Breslauer remembered the fashionable style of her friends: "We were all very similarly dressed, masculine, with short hair, got up 'in the lesbian' [*auf lesbisch*] so to speak, but in no way really so!"[19] Though a number of women in Breslauer's circle were known to have had affairs with each other, she was probably accurate in that women of these sophisticated circles did not form identities using sexological labels. For them, passion might be directed toward anyone who attracted and fascinated. Fashionable cross-dressing in the interwar period has complex cultural resonances; however, in Weimar Germany, it lent erotic ambiguity to sexual desire and attraction.[20] While 1890s observers had assumed that androgyny hindered sexual attraction, Weimar's erotic atmosphere often drew on ambiguously gendered interplay of desires and attractions.

This book's examination of sexual subjectivity in the 1920s leaves aside the experimentation of elite women such as Breslauer in order to concentrate on "ordinary" women in new professional careers and in the homosexual movement. The latter group included mostly urban petit bourgeois and declassed women for whom an identity based in sexual preference made sense. Homosexuality, as a preferred alternative to heterosexuality and the family, was useful to them as a technology of the self.[21] Joining homosexual clubs, reading homosexual publications, and participating in homosexual events facilitated social contacts and explained their position in the otherwise lonely and atomized metropolis. Identity work—accumulating knowledge, imagining scenarios, and narrating one's own life story—became a site of mastery and pleasure in itself. (Fig. I.1)

Anxieties about women's reproductive roles were crucial to both New Woman debates, but this did not lead to widespread suspicion that all emancipated women were pathological deviants. Class competence and comportment continued to determine women's social acceptability, while prostitution and promiscuity were far more prominent in morality politics than homosexuality. When forced to confront evidence of homosexuality, mainstream society did reject and stigmatize the conceptual or perceived homosexual. However, the members of the general public seldom applied the label using the symptoms suggested in medical literature. Still, as new women struggled to define the parameters of self and sexuality in times of abrupt change and social uncertainty, "homosexuality" became a category significant to the process.

Fig. I.1. Reading as a technology of the self. Advertisement for *Das lesbische Weib,* by Franz Scott. Rep. 77, Tit. 2772, Nr. 11, Bd. 1. Reproduced with permission of Geheimes Staatsarchiv Preussischer Kulturbesitz, Berlin.

Homosexuality

Organized and visible large groups of women defining themselves as homo-sexual first appeared in Berlin in the mid-1920s. Their mass membership clubs owed their existence to similar organizations of men that formed soon after World War I. This emergence of homosexual identity and community among second-wave new women was part of a longer history of homosexual theorizing and activism in German-speaking Central Europe. The notion of a unique type of individual came into being both among the men who so defined themselves and among doctors describing their legal and medical cases. In the 1850s and 1860s, as the separate German states moved toward unification, men in states with no legal penalty for male same-sex acts feared that the Prussian legal code, with its criminal sanction, would be adopted for the new national state. One of these, Karl Heinrich Ulrichs, published pamphlets arguing that same-sex sexual acts usually resulted from a man's innate character and should not be punished as criminal. He posited a biological category of individual who had a female soul within a male body, using the term *Urning* for them, and a parallel term, *Urnind*, to denote a woman with a male soul. Ulrichs's terms and ideas influenced doctors who were then categorizing same-sex phenomena as symptoms of psychiatric disorders.

Medical reports on same-sex phenomena have been traced to mid-century cases published by Berlin doctors Johann Ludwig Caspar and Carl Westphal. The former interpreted homosexual acts as caused by a constitutional tendency he termed "mental hermaphroditism." Wesphal linked the cases of a woman suffering from "a mania for loving women" and a man who "felt a pressing need to put on women's clothing" under the diagnosis "*konträre Sexualempfindung*" (contrary sexual feeling).[22] Richard von Krafft-Ebing integrated the concepts of contrary sexuality and the natural occurrence of the *Urning* into the categorizing scheme of his foundational work *Psychopathia sexualis*.

Early in his career, the prominent German sexologist and theorist of homosexuality Magnus Hirschfeld borrowed another of Ulrichs's terms, "the third sex," in his publications for a general readership. Through World War I, *Urning*, with its conflation of gender character and same-sex desire, remained the dominant term used in medical discourses. Hirschfeld's eventual switch to "homosexuality" led to its common usage in Germany, especially in the 1920s. "Homosexuality" as a preferred term of the 1920s movement signals that some men wanted to separate same-sex sexuality from effeminacy. Women, on the other hand, found the notion of innate masculinity useful in their appropriation of new social positions and sexual subjectivity.

Female case studies notwithstanding, the process of naming was carried on by men in relation to a masculine object. They assumed that same-sex phenomena among women were a mirror image of those observed among men. While men who claimed the category were able to influence doctors' conceptions, evidence of women's intervention in naming has not been documented.[23] Sophisticated discourses referring to love or eroticism between women used the terms *Sapphismus, Tribadie*, and *lesbische Liebe*, imported from Latin and Greek. These terms connoted a practice, preference, or taste rather than an identity. As sexological ideas spread, they gradually began to shape the perceptions of subjects in the direction of identifying essential types. Anna Rühling's 1904 speech, "What Is the Interest of the Women's Movement in the Solution to the Homosexual Problem?" an early statement by a woman explaining female homosexuality, used the terms *Urninde* and *homosexuelle Frauen* interchangeably, clearly referring to a subset of women marked off by an essential difference.[24]

Given the international historical importance of homosexual theorizing and activism in Germany, it is surprising that no English-language scholar has updated James Steakley's 1975 monograph, *The Homosexual Emancipation Movement in Germany*. The few treatments of German female homosexuality in English include Claudia Schoppmann's work on repression during the Third Reich as remembered by individuals and her essay on female homosexuality in Nazi ideology.[25] Lillian Faderman's references to female same-sex love in Germany provide useful starting points for research.[26] The first book-length treatment of the 1920s women's subculture in Berlin appeared in 2004 in Germany; Kirsten Plötz's short 1999 book on female homosexuality in the provinces was an important forerunner.[27] German published work has tended to have a limited documentary focus rather than attempting a broad analysis.[28]

Although the main argument of *Desiring Emancipation* focuses on connections between sexuality and emancipation, the book also provides English-language readers with an in-depth account of the 1920s homosexual movement in Berlin and its connections to earlier feminist activism. By the end of the nineteenth century, circles of same-sex–oriented women can be documented in urban settings among working-class women, prostitutes, bohemian subcultures, and aristocratic adventurers in the United States, Britain, much of Europe, and Japan.[29] The form of each community was shaped by its context—female couples in Britain and the United States, sexual and artistic avant-gardes in Paris and New York, middle-class urban women in Berlin. Numbers and types of sources available limit our ability to analyze these early social formations. The homosexual movement's publications provide a significant set of sources qualitatively different from those available for other earlier and contemporary national contexts.

Historians of lesbianism have engaged in heated debates about sources and definitions. Lacking documentation similar to court prosecution of male homosexuality, where does a historian "find" lesbianism? Early on, researchers looked for historical actors who could be claimed as lesbian foremothers. Uncertainty in these claims generated formative questions for the field. Is sex necessary? Did the historical subject have to identify herself as sexually different? What is the significance of gender in erotic attraction? If we look at women broadly, do we lose the specificity and meaning the designation "lesbian" is meant to provide? If we limit our criteria, do we disqualify relevant, but historically different patterns of same-sex relating?[30]

Some scholars have claimed to intuit an essential lesbianism even if it cannot be defined. Martha Vicinus suggests the term *lesbian-like* to encompass a broader range of women's loving relationships and to avoid getting bogged down in definitional issues. She urges scholars to focus on the ways such appearances trouble and challenge the existing sexual and gender orders.[31] Valerie Traub selects one particular aspect—the erotic—and asks how it reveals and shapes social and discursive relations within a particular historical conjuncture. In *Between Women*, Sharon Marcus argues for attention to women's same-sex relations and desires that may or may not have anything to do with lesbian sex. When we analyze same-sex phenomena, Marcus claims, we impoverish the discussion with a singular focus on lesbian sexuality and its transgression against male-dominated compulsory heterosexuality.[32]

I am indebted to the innovative scholars who have emphasized the poverty of the heterosexual/homosexual binary as a tool for understanding erotic cultures and identities in the past. Taking a deconstructive and queer approach to sources and phenomena allows me to consider a wider range of voices, choices, and meanings. I place women's stories within the context of historical norms and practices to reveal the ways they, purposefully or not, upset existing notions of women's sexuality. But I do not ignore the many ways that historical subjects sought to maintain faith with gendered norms and values they had inherited. Changes in women's sexuality could not proceed outside of normative cultural and structural boundaries. Both rupture and continuity are essential features of the story of emancipation.

An ancillary problem for scholars is choosing terminology that avoids subtly imposing upon the past meanings and assumptions from contemporary cultures. Using familiar terms to name what we see risks obscuring differences between the past and present or between one location and another. Short of inventing a new language, which seems likely to obscure as much as it clarifies, scholars of sexuality are obliged to declare their choices, usages, and compromises. In my case studies from before 1900, historical subjects did not have any term that referred to homosexuality in the modern sense. "*Urning*" and "*Homosexualität*" began to appear widely only after 1900. In the interwar period, the organized movement chose adjective combinations: "homosexual woman," "homoerotic woman," or "same-sex-loving woman." The common informal term among women was "*Freundin*" (girlfriend), used not only to mean a partner, but also in the plural for the community in general. According to Mel Gordon, a whole insider's argot for different styles, types, and roles developed within less respectable subcultures.[33] The adjective *lesbisch*, was common in mainstream publications to describe women or relationships; however, some of the women in the Berlin movement rejected this term because it connoted decadence and perverse pleasure.[34] The term *schwul*, equivalent to "gay," dates at least back to the 1920s, but was not used in the organized movement.

Of all these possibilities, it seems to me that the words *homosexual* and *homosexuality* offer the most clarity while fulfilling the multiple functions I need my analytical term to encompass. Its clinical connotations led gay activists in the later twentieth century to reject it as a term of identification. Accordingly, scholars have found it a more neutral descriptor for same-sex phenomena. Its common use across the twentieth century and in both the German and American contexts connects most of my subjects and readers. This choice still risks collapsing the meaning of the term, obscuring what it connoted in the earlier period. But more time-specific words such as "invert" or "third sex" also have connotations that leave out some of the diversity I strive to capture.

A gender-specific term such as "lesbian" might reflect the gender focus of the analysis. I decided against it partly because some of my historical subjects found it objectionable. More importantly, I find that "lesbian" is still too intimately invested with the power of identification. Debates about the term continue to be bound up with definitional and ownership struggles. I find the danger of essentializing "lesbian" more insidious than that possible with "homosexual." I try not to use "homosexuality" to denote individuals' sexuality, focusing instead on subject formation through identity claims, narratives, life choices, emotional relations, self-presentation, and desires.

Subjectivity

Encounters with gender emancipation and homosexuality led to social change as women individually and collectively began to conceive of themselves differently. In order to probe this process, *Desiring Emancipation* takes methodological and conceptual inspiration from literary and queer studies, as well as ethnography. The concepts of subjectivity and subject formation supply theoretical grounding for the book's arguments. Although many of the women in these pages were feminists and pioneered new careers and lifestyles, I put their desires to become, and to be recognized as, autonomous subjects on center stage. The historical subjects were socialized to value the devotion to love and sacrifice expected of wives and mothers.

Self-definition had only been possible in relation to men and to family. The fight to change assumptions about femininity may be better understood as a belated Enlightenment project of refusing male tutelage rather than an outcome of expanding political rights. In my analysis, the feminist goal of participation in the public sphere is secondary to claiming and cultivating autonomous subjectivity. Beyond that, claiming *sexual* subjectivity was one of the most fraught and threatening aspects of this kind of gender emancipation. Throughout the book, women seeking emancipation policed their own and others' actions to make certain that unleashed desire would not compromise their desired autonomy.

The following chapters address these broad changes on the level of the human being. The ideas and methods of Judith Butler and Eve Kosofsky Sedgwick on performance, narrative pattern, and subjectivity inform the analysis.[35] While Butler and Sedgwick use subjectivity to work with intellectual and literary texts, I apply the concept to the broader range of sources commonly used by historians.[36] To answer the questions posed earlier in the introduction, I approach archival sources, as well as journalism, scientific discourse, and popular literature as elements in and sites of struggle where usable subjectivities were constructed. In the process, subjects articulated positions in relation to history, politics, and morality. The central theoretical insight is gained by acknowledging that the subject's unity and coherence are illusions. Subjects struggle to overcome their splits, contradictions, and incoherently combined influences using story and action. Their unstable and incomplete attempts to gain the autonomy offered by a newly defined subject position provide the historian with an opportunity to see the process at work and to make some historical claims about it.

One example of the troubled work of subjectivity formation is a book self-published by schoolteacher Anna Philipps. In it, Philipps relates her first encounter with the concept of homosexuality. She experimented with it as a way of understanding relationships among her co-workers. When her colleagues suggested that she also used the term to explain her relationship with one of her older students, the school authorities were forced to investigate. Several years later, she produced her book to bring her story to the public, asking for support of her demands that she be found innocent of suspicions of inappropriate advances toward a female student.[37] As her tentative assertion of identity led to accusations in the school setting, the once-liberating idea became Philipps's lever of revenge against her former friends. In desperate attempts to preserve an emancipated yet innocent sense of self, she revalued "homosexuality" from an intriguing potential erotic identity to a perversion uniting a sinister cabal threatening the state.

Since my work takes groups of historical women like Philipps and her co-workers as its object of study, it is a social history of gender and sexuality. Investigation of women's aspirations and desires, their messy personal relationships, their struggles with gender constraints, and their social self-positioning provides new texture to our understanding of women's changing lives. As cultural history, my analysis traces the corresponding development of knowledge and public discussion of the New Woman and of the female homosexual as each figure came into use. My focus is less on knowledge production than on its strategic mobilization, contestation, and internalization. Subjectivity provides the conceptual terrain for bringing together women's experiences of gendered subject positions and their reception and internalization of discourse.

The sources for researching subjectivity, genres of personal expression such as memoir, fiction, and essay, cannot be taken as giving transparent access to the individual's interior process. However, close reading using literary strategies provides the best means of deconstructing and reconstructing what we can of it. Explicitly personal genres circulated women's narratives of the self to reading publics of the late nineteenth and early twentieth centuries. Narrating and describing oneself in the world became an important way of making the confusion of modernity legible and navigable by the individual. And as it gave meaning to individual lives, it anchored lonely selves within broader social formations.

Fictional treatments of the New Woman and her sexuality in both periods are indispensable sources for probing subjectivity because sexual topics were difficult for women to claim personally and address publicly. I do not read them as lightly disguised representations of actual occurrences but as thought experiments deploying a variety of new practices, critiques, and other elements of a self-consciously "modern" period. Aimée Duc's novel *Are These Women,* for example, certainly takes emancipated women the author observed at university around 1900 as its models.[38] Its narration brings to the surface the erotic and love connections that the characters keep from public view. Without enabling claims about how the models for the characters actually acted, thought, or felt, the novel displays one way of making sense of puzzling new phenomena and indicates that the problem of how to define emancipated same sex-loving-women was pressing for the author. Nineteen-twenties periodical fiction explored the implications and meanings of homosexual identity in a similar way.

Four of the following chapters reconstruct actions, interactions, aspirations, and emotions among specific groups of emancipating women. Chapters 1 and 2 focus on the new women of the fin-de-siècle in two overlapping circles: the first generation of women university students in Zurich and radical feminist activists living in Munich. Although archival sources are drawn on when available, most of the sources relating the intimate details of lives are from novels. In that period, novels by writers such as Bülow, Käte Schirmacher, and Lou Andreas-Salomé, themselves women experimenting with emancipation, provide the best access to writers' public attempts to cope with the implications of sexuality for female emancipation.

Chapters 4 and 5 investigate two very different types of new women that emerged in the conditions of the Weimar Republic (1919–1933). Chapter 4's civil servants in Hamburg and Frankfurt embodied a professional type very different from the New Woman image of the 1920s. Chapter 5 focuses on the self-described homosexual women who became visible in Berlin in the 1920s. As female homosexuality became a concept for wider circles of the public, a much broader range of sources supports the analysis in these chapters. As a bridge between the two sets of microhistorical case studies, chapter 3 interprets significant changes in the visibility and meaning of women's sexuality and female homosexuality between 1900 and World War I in popular sexology, scandal journalism, law reform debates, and New Woman texts. In these sources, historical women contested cultural construction of the New Woman or homosexual woman as perverse and deviant.

As research into women's historical agency has expanded, it has become clear that many if not most women preferred to live within socially approved gender roles and assumptions. In times of change, they longed for a return to the imagined protection of invented pasts and lent their support to the most conservative and reactionary political initiatives. In women's new lives, the hard reality of betrayal, disappointment, and overwhelming emotion was as significant to subject formation as ideals, courage, and aspiration. My research takes all of these phenomena seriously as important indicators of the unexpected ways that subjects combined and reshaped received notions. The multiple sides of self-making cannot be separated.

As a historian, my eye remains closely focused on empirical detail. Feminist research has done much to explain women's movements, political and legal struggles, and the influence of gender on cultural constructions from war and politics to science and sexuality. How women come to desire new lives, identities, and sexualities, however, often remains assumed rather than probed. Neither uncomplicated agency nor disembodied structure is adequate to explain gender change. My claim and hope is that the powerful theories from gender and sexuality studies can be extended, reinvigorated, perhaps even challenged by using them in conjunction with readings of a broad range of sources in historical context. Ultimately what this research seeks is the historian's goal of explaining how change happens.

"Are These Women?"

University Students' Quest for a New Gender

The title of the 1901 novel *Are These Women? A Novel about the Third Sex* immediately focuses the potential reader's attention on the gender "problem" represented by a certain "type" of woman. These women, female in biology but masculine in ambition, are depicted in the novel's characters, gathered in university towns where some of them are students. The characters struggle to link their studies to the cause of proving to science and society that their "type" is natural and deserves acknowledgment. The novel's central character, Minotschka, heatedly explains why she has given up medical studies: "Are not doctors our worst enemies, because they don't expose the truth publicly in the light of science?" She challenges her companions to alter knowledge itself. "Would you dare to present a doctoral dissertation based on scholarly evidence that provides positive proof of the existence of a third sex?" she asked. "Would you?"[1] The answer was obvious: not if you want to get a degree.

As the students and their friends discuss questions of gender in this scene of the novel, they bring up many of the issues of social change that surfaced in the late nineteenth century, some reflected in the figure of the female student. The characters' focus on biological knowledge and proof represents the contemporary trend toward using biology to solidify the threatened gender system of nineteenth-century bourgeois Europe. Minotschka's hostility toward doctors as perpetrators of orthodox knowledge about femininity anticipates much late-twentieth-century scholarship plumbing the influence of doctors on women's perceptions and practices. Doctors were clearly leaders in claiming that study at the university level would be harmful to society and to women students themselves. Why was a woman student such a potent challenge to the existing gender order? Why were students with academic goals seen as masculine or non-woman rather than simply eccentrics and exceptions?

Duc's title describes her sympathetic New Women characters as a "third sex." As Duc defines it, the term reveals how fused normative gender roles and biological sex had become. Women who gave up, or at least subordinated, love, children, and family for some other life goal could not be imagined as biologically normal; a whole new gender category was necessary to understand them. In the book, the characters themselves are the experts who explain the "nature" of the "third sex." At this turn-of-the-century moment, other writers on gender and sexuality were using the phrase "third sex" to make the new concept of homosexuality legible to the broad public. This use of "third sex" drew on inversion theories that conflated gender style and sexual object choice. Magnus Hirschfeld adopted it to express his theory of homosexuality (for both males and females) as an intermediate point on a gender continuum. Writers in Hirschfeld's circle conceptualized homosexuals as constituting a third sex distinguishable from the conventionally understood two. Hirschfeld eventually discarded the concept, but the ambiguous term appeared in the titles of a diverse array of books meant to enlighten the public about either New Women or homosexuality in the first decade after 1900.[2] Duc's book also suggests this second meaning in its portrayals of romantic attachments between such ambitious masculine women.

The novel's dialogue also uses terms such as "perverse" and "Krafft-Ebinger" to demonstrate how the characters align themselves with emergent sexological theories. The students and their friends in the novel adopt the notion that gender is the primary determinant of character, but revise its emphasis to claim masculine privileges for themselves. As one character puts it, "We must stand our ground again and again and not let ourselves be forced to retreat or be categorized as sick. . . . We must demonstrate that we are representatives of a combination, a human species, that has a right to be recognized—that has appeared without exception as an intellectual elite."[3] These declarations closely resemble the campaign rhetoric of the homosexual rights movement of the time, which claimed that gender inversion or role transgression was a property of especially highly gifted individuals. As members of the third sex, women deserved emancipation that need not be extended to "normal" women, while sex between men was justified as natural to their feminine nature.

Parallel to the novel's development of the proposal that the "Woman Question be put on a different track, not as a Woman Question, but rather as a question of the third sex," the plot follows the love story of Minotschka and Marta. As an aside to an assertion that intellectual women must avoid marriage, the narrator confides that the two main characters "had developed an intense passion for one another."[4] The novels' conjunction of these two "third sex" implications led to the portrait of this fictional group of emancipated women being interpreted as important evidence of proto–lesbian feminist or homosexual identity among emancipated women at the turn of the century.[5] However, close reading of the novel calls this assumption into question. The portrayal of the love affair is disconnected from and in tension with the characters' interpretations of their gender. The discussions, highly critical of heterosexual marriage, leave it implicit that a better alternative might be (same-sex) relationships of equality in status and sameness rather than difference.

Ironically the resolution of the love plot removes the lovers from the assertive circle of homosexual friends, emancipated achieving women, and female students to the private space of a remote estate. The withdrawal of the couple to private space and the very instability of the original student group suggest the fragility and defensive position of women's single-sex relations and lives. Furthermore, what seems at first glance to be mutually acknowledged same-sex desire, on closer reading turns out to be repressed or secret desire. Minotschka and Marta conceal the romantic side of their friendship from their circle by addressing each other in the formal *Sie*. Toward the end of the novel the reader finds out that Marta and Minotschka's courtship was idealized and nonsexual for a long time until "their hearts found each other" and they "completely belonged to each other" on a vacation trip.[6] What the novel leaves unaddressed is how their "passion for one another" fits in with their theories of gender, except as a *faut de mieux*, reinforced by both women's regret over their heterosexual marriages.

Still, the novel does present characters knowledgeable about theories of sex and gender difference, working toward a new model of identification, and carrying on love affairs with one another. To what extent were women students' milieus in the late nineteenth century sites for investigation of these phenomena and then for adopting homosexual identity? Additional evidence comes from the lives of feminists from the period such as Anita Augspurg, Franziska Tiburtius, Käthe Schirmacher, Ella Mensch, and Joanna Elberskirchen. Each lived with a female partner after her studies. This fact too hints that study in Switzerland might be a productive site for investigating the origins of female homosexual identity.[7] However, the rich sources generated by the unusual presence of women in higher education in this period reveal that the causative link must be reversed. University attendance was a consequence rather than a cause of radical feminism, "masculine" ambitions, or close emotional attachments between women.

Swiss universities were not a hotbed for discovery of homosexual identity and proliferation of relationships defined by that term. Except for *Are
These Women,* sources produced by women students make no reference to
sexological theories and show no evidence of familiarity with them. However,
these sources were important sites of the reconstruction of gender for some
middle-class women in response to nineteenth-century social and cultural
modernization. We might hypothesize that exploring new opportunities,
new knowledge, new spaces, and new forms of female sociability fostered
awareness of same-sex attractions—attractions that were not, however, connected to discourses of sexual deviance. But the evidence points to a third
conclusion where students are concerned: women students gave priority to
study and achievement, consciously avoiding passionate entanglements with
either sex. They worked at constructing new subject positions that were not
limited by gender. They explored new ways of relating to both men and
women—models that were based on an ideal of genderless mutual recognition between human subjects on an equal plane.

The hesitant ambivalence toward sex in Duc's development of Minotschka
and Marta's love relationship was characteristic of feminist struggles to define
and rethink morality and sexuality. As bourgeois girls, students had been
socialized to regard sex as a lower and dangerous component of the spectrum
of human functions. Control of desires and passions was fundamental to class
identity and differentiation. Shame was the woman's proper response to intrusions of the sexual. This automatic experience of emotional discomfort had
to be overcome through ideology or avoidance. In addition, feminism that
emerged in response to German classical education stressed self-cultivation
toward becoming a moral subject.[8] Emancipation desires were thus embedded in
conceptions of moral autonomy and responsibility for the moral improvement
of society. The women students' overdetermined concepts of sexual morality
inevitably contributed to their motivation to seek emancipation by challenging the barriers against women's higher education. They hoped to use their
new knowledge and qualifications to improve the state of morality in society.

Because almost all European women were excluded by custom and lack
of preparation from university study, the terms *woman* and *student* seemed
radically incompatible.[9] Yet late-nineteenth-century feminists were determined
to open higher education to women. Both proponents and opponents of
the regular admission of women to degree programs recognized that lack
of university degrees barred women from positions in the two of the most
privileged preserves of German middle-class masculinity: the professoriate and
the civil service. As feminists concentrated their efforts on access to higher
education, defenders of male privilege analyzed, ridiculed, and stigmatized
women's desire to study.

Scholars of German women's and institutional history have carefully documented and analyzed feminist educational campaigns within a historiography of Germany's problematic progress toward legal gender equality and access to the public sphere.[10] My analysis concentrates on the deeper motivations for study rooted in self-fashioning and the desire to reshape the entire gender system. Self-making came before, accompanied, and responded to women's inhabiting subject positions previously gendered male. Sexuality (in the Foucauldian sense of the truth of the self) emerged in and through thinking and performing a new iteration of femininity.[11] Intellectual women wanted to contribute to German society and culture through the force of their minds, talents, and personalities. They reacted angrily to assumptions that they were imitating or trying to compete with men. They wanted to be recognized as autonomous human subjects, an impossible goal given existing gender assumptions. On both conscious and unconscious ideological levels, students' experiences incited an urgent revision of the meaning of gender—and of sexuality, which served as the primary referent of gender difference in contemporary discourses.

Patricia Mazón argues that women students pursued a strategy of rethinking gender that enabled them to inhabit the category of student as women.[12] My argument builds on Mazón's work to investigate "woman student" memoirs and novels as a site of gender construction for new women of the era. Attention to sexuality in the process of self-fashioning adds a significant new dimension to the history of feminism and gendered sociability. New women students were not simply battling traditional restrictions; they were also consciously laboring to inhabit new gendered subjectivities. At university, women sought to deepen the philosophical underpinnings of their social and political ideas. Self-formation occurred in and through rethinking society, morality, and politics.

The students who represented their experiences in writing were all members of the same social milieu and of a particularly influential generation born between 1855 and 1865.[13] Most women students were significantly older than their male counterparts. The individuals discussed here were between twenty-three and thirty-five when they began their studies, while male students typically came direct from secondary school at eighteen or nineteen. All came from wealthy families in rural or provincial settings.

Frieda Duensing's (1864–1922) path to the university in Zurich is exemplary of women for whom the university was a late choice following a period of doubts and difficulties. Her struggles and anxieties are clear in the collection of her letters and diary entries published by friends after her death.[14] Ella Mensch (1859–1935) earned one of the first doctorates by a woman in literature, in 1886.[15] Her novel *On Outpost Watch: Novel of My Student Days in Zurich* was published in 1903, probably at least partially as an intervention into the debates on women's access to German universities.[16] Ricarda Huch (1864–1947) came to Zurich in 1887, earned her doctorate in history in 1892, and stayed on for several years in Zurich to work as a teacher and librarian. The emphasis on freedom as the hallmark of student life and relationships in her 1938 memoir *Spring in Switzerland* can be read as a camouflaged protest against the Nazi regime.[17] Käthe Schirmacher (1865–1930), one of the most colorful figures in the German women's movement, studied in Zurich between 1893 and 1895 and published a pamphlet in 1896 describing and defending women's study there.[18] Her novel *Die Libertad* was inspired by her experiences as a student at the Sorbonne in Paris during the 1880s; her autobiography also touched on her experiences in both Paris and Zurich.[19] Another notable member of this cohort was Anita Augspurg (1857–1943), who earned her law degree in 1898. Even more so than Schirmacher and Duensing, Augspurg had a well-established life before she began her studies at the age of thirty-five.[20]

Already in the 1880s, Zurich had become the symbolic backdrop for the widely circulated cultural figure of the woman student. As a relatively new university in a liberal city, the University of Zurich was the first in Europe (except the Sorbonne) to admit women as regular students.[21] For German women especially, Zurich was attractive as an accessible German-speaking city.[22] Crossing the international border meant that women's student experiences unfolded in a space outside of their own national context. Zurich's relative smallness and isolation allowed women to live and socialize in ways that might have been difficult in a cosmopolitan city such as Paris. Memoirs by Huch, Schirmacher, and Duensing reflect the exhilaration of exchanging local and family social embeddedness for social ties based on mutuality and intellectual affinity. Once a critical mass of women students were present in university towns like Zurich, the conditions were in place for formation of new, if temporary, forms and sites of both hetero- and homosociability. But in the context of public controversy over the implications of women's university studies, women students' gendered subjectivities took shape between response to stigma and space for creative gender performance.

How Can These Be Women?

Outside observers were keen to interpret the growing number of women students as a variety of the 1890s New Woman. The woman student became a well-worn trope representing fears that women might abandon family and reproductive duties. The perceived disjunction between "woman" and "student" produced argumentative, literary, visual, and personal attempts to explain, resolve, or solidify the differences between the two.[23] The intensity of stereotyping reactions was far out of proportion to the number of women who actually became university students before World War I. No more than one hundred German women earned doctorates in these years.[24] As the students moved differently in the material world, their options were limited from the outside by the stereotype stigmatizing them as gender deviant. Through novels and memoirs, students responded to mainstream, often satirical, representations that pathologized, marginalized, or explained away their intellectual aspirations.

As Duc's novel had suggested, many doctors were involved in woman student debates. They argued that women's brains were simply not capable of concentrated study. But opposition to women's higher education was not solely, or even mainly, based on the assumption of women's intellectual inferiority.[25] The German reaction to the idea of the woman student reflected anxieties about racial and cultural degeneration. Loss of sharply defined gender difference was widely considered a symptom of decline. Intellectual labor, the doctors were sure, would damage women's reproductive organs and their ability to bear healthy children. The deepest anxiety was not based on predicted biological consequences though; rather the *desire* to study was seen as proof that women were unfeminine and perverse. An 1888 article in the liberal *Kölner Zeitung* concluded, "All vivacity of feeling, all womanly emotions, and physical health as well have left [women students]. Truly educated and cultured men avoid them, uneducated ones flee them, and the healthy, natural women shun their society. Thus these girls stand like hermaphrodites between the two sexes."[26] "Hermaphrodite" has much the same effect as "third sex," placing women students outside the realm of the biologically normal.

Beyond the biological argumentations, novels such as *The Third Sex*, by Ernst von Wolzogen, picked up the stereotype, ridiculing a student character as an asexual, pedantic feminist who declares her passion for scholarship as an alternative to marriage. Although this minor character is inseparable from her female partner, Wolzogen's portrayal of the relationship lacks any hint of erotic or emotional connection between the two women. It simply placed them together outside the heterosexual binary.

A few years later, an article in the popular magazine *Die Woche* asked, "Is the woman student regarded as a degenerate member of the female sex even today? Do the relatives of a woman at the university hesitate to talk about her openly as was the case not so long ago?"[27] The underlying question posed by the discursive figure of the woman student, left submerged by the

Die Woche writer, was whether a female who was not primarily defined by her attraction to and for men could be considered a woman at all.

Another stereotype that women students needed to confront was the scandalous reputation of Russian students in Switzerland.[28] Many Russian students were political radicals and enjoyed flouting bourgeois norms and manners. Tibertius's memoir recounted her contradictory impressions when she first encountered a Russian woman student in Zurich. "Behind the table sat a puzzling being whose natural gender category was at first completely unclear to me," she remembered. "A round boy's head, hair cut short and crookedly parted, huge blue eyeglasses, a very young pale face, thick dark jacket, a cigarette burning in the mouth, everything outward thoroughly boyish—and yet a certain something did not harmonize with the desired masculinity." Tiburtius discreetly glanced at the lower half of the person and, discovering a skirt, had her suspicion confirmed. The casual manners and sociability of the Russians made a lasting impression. In contradiction to Tibertius's expectations of decorum at table, "the dishes were not passed, instead everyone leaned across the table and grabbed what they wanted, the gentlemen without wasting a thought on the ladies." Members of the party "gulped everything down as fast as possible and came and went as they pleased."[29]

For Tibertius, Zurich meant negotiating the cavernous gap between the casual socializing and diminished gender differentiation of the Russian students and the traditional propriety of bourgeois socializing. Despite exposure to alternatives, most of the German students consciously chose to maintain the standards by which they had been raised. They recognized the student years as an unusual period of freedom that had to be protected by proving themselves as respectable women as well as successful academics. Tibertius made sure to be on her best behavior when invited to tea with society women: "I thought that it probably could not hurt the cause I represented if the fancy part of town got to know a student without blue eyeglasses and a sailor's cap for once, one who looked pretty much like other people."[30] The students accepted the burden of monitoring and disciplining their own and each other's appearance and behavior in order to maintain both respectability and respect.

Ricarda Huch also described a rule among the female students of the late 1880s not to differentiate themselves from other girls in any way. She had cut her hair short, but let it grow out when she began her studies. "At that time many still thought it was unfeminine to study; any feature of one's appearance or behavior that could be interpreted as masculine was supposed to be avoided."[31] Ella Mensch's autobiographical novel commented directly on the responsibility borne by women students. "Naturally in that early period, when the harbingers of a new ideal of female education were still a catacomb congregation, so to speak," she wrote, "much depended on the appearance and conduct of the individual." The responsible student should not make things difficult for future women students. "Fanny Stantien," the passage continued, "had brought along with her the feeling that one stood 'on the outpost' and had to avoid any extravagance."[32]

Personal discipline was essential to women students' long-term project of social change. Another text by Mensch, written many years after her studies, reported bitterly that the students of a later generation no longer kept up these standards. She argued that the early women students' refusal to engage in "erotic emancipation and radical politics" had secured women's access to higher education.[33] Mensch's chagrin reflects the rapidity of gender change in the years preceding World War I. She recognized that elite ideologies and aspirations were no longer able to direct its progress.

The overly serious ambitious figure feared by doctors, ridiculed by novelists, and defended against by women students themselves was not the only image of women students in the popular media. She existed alongside a contradictory image of groups of women students socializing together. These portrayed informality, physical freedom, and fun to a more ambiguous effect. They seemed to imply that once women discovered fun, they would be spoiled for the duties of wife and mother. These anxieties were conventionally expressed in representations of all-female student parties. Memoirs of women students reveal that such fears were not unfounded. On these private occasions, women students did enjoy transgressing the norms of bourgeois sociability. Guests drank alcohol, smoked cigarettes, and stretched out on the sofa or the floor.

Fascination with the space of relaxed female socialization provoked visual representation in popular periodicals. A drawing, simply titled "Studentinnen," published in the Munich satire journal *Simplicissimus* in 1899 portrayed four women sitting close together. (Fig. 1.1) The depiction of casual female sociability allowed the artist to highlight two opposing sexual potentials. The three students in the background in masculine clothes or postures embody the unattractive and gender-deviant stereotype. But the figure in the foreground is sitting on the floor, her skirt pushed up to her knees. This woman, cigarette raised to her lips, gazes provocatively out at the viewer. The drawing's combination of satirical mockery and titillation was characteristic of *Simplicissimus's* particular brand of masculine visual pleasure.

It is tempting to read a photograph that accompanied the 1907 article in *Die Woche* as a sly response to the *Simplicissimus* image. Sophia Goudstikker,

Fig. 1.1. "To close our executive committee meeting, I move that we kick Eulalia Müller out of our club and consider her in disgrace. The little pig got engaged!" "Students," drawing by Ernst Heilemann, *Simplicissimus* (Munich), January 2, 1900. Jg. 4, 332.

feminist activist and owner of a photography studio in Munich, where *Simplicissimus* was published, took the photographs illustrating the article. The text interprets the photographs as proof of women students' success at combining hard-working virtue and undiminished femininity. It claims that the photographs of student life would "soothe the consciences of those who prophesied that the loss of femininity would be the unavoidable result of the scholarly activity of women."[34]

While the first four photographs do show serious, yet feminine-appearing students hard at work, the fifth portrays four women students smoking and drinking tea (Fig. 1.2). Goudstikker, posing as one of the students in the photo, composed it to contradict the accompanying text. Two of the women, in masculine postures with disarranged hair and cigarettes in the corners of their mouths, look into the camera as if daring the viewer not to take them seriously. Goudstikker, whose masculine appearance made her a fascinating figure during her lifetime, faces another woman, the tips of their cigarettes meeting.[35] The other participant in this pseudo-kiss radiates pleasure through her flirtatious half-smile. Through the photograph, Goudstikker managed to insert both female masculinity and female same-sex eroticism into the discourse of the female student.

Despite Goudstikker's visual suggestion, homosexuality was not the sexual paradox or fear contained in the figure of the woman student. What was at stake was her presumed refusal of heterosexuality. Had she given up her sexual role in favor of "dry" intellectual pursuits? This was the explicit

Fig. 1.2. Photograph accompanying the article "The German Woman Student" in *Die Woche*, 1907 (13). Sophia Goudstikker second from left.

meaning of the term *third sex* as Ernst von Wolzogen employed it.[36] Or was freedom from domestic roles dangerously fun and appealing? Even more threatening, was part of the freedom she claimed that of sexual activity outside of marriage, perhaps on her own initiative? University attendance placed her in dangerously close unsupervised proximity to male students who were notorious for sowing wild oats.[37] The woman student as a fetish figure contained fears that women would no longer agree to marriage, heterosexuality, and social reproduction in general.

The Third Sex

The problem of the nonheterosexual reproductive woman was taken up in two New Woman novels set in late-nineteenth-century Munich. Both Wolzogen's *The Third Sex* and Helene Stöcker's *Love* used the woman student as one type of New Woman in their attempts to resolve the Heterosexual Question. It was clear to both authors that male-female relations needed to change to accommodate women's emancipation. Yet they worked hard to make philosophical arguments that shored up the "natural" gender binary as constitutive of both social and sexual relations. Wolzogen and Stöcker were progressive intellectuals influenced by Nietzsche and by the application of Darwinian evolution to social and cultural improvement.[38] The invisibility of same-sex erotic potential among their types of New Woman was especially significant given the centrality of love and desire to their engagement with women's emancipation. Both authors were well acquainted with vital women who lived largely in single-sex environments, yet could not represent them as loving each other. In each story, important figures subordinate intellectual and professional pursuits to heterosexual love and coupling, while secondary characters embody the preexisting stereotype of the asexual, pitiable woman student.

Helene Stöcker's novel *Love,* although published in 1926, set its narrative of a love affair between its protagonist, Irene, and a married professor in the 1880s.[39] As an artist, unmarried lover, intellectual, and auditor of university lectures, Irene is clearly a New Woman. Over the course of the novel, Irene, though tortured by doubt, pushes aside her own art and intellectual development in favor of obsessive devotion to her lover. One sequence has Irene visit Switzerland where she encounters young career women who are enjoying life in a sweet, but shallow and naive way, as well as the faded, bitter, schoolmarmish leader of the feminist movement.[40] These encounters with groups of emancipated women confirm for Irene that her love affair, however impossible, is the superior way to live as an independent woman. Although the brief representations of the career women and the feminists contain a hint of homosexuality, emphasis on the shallowness and bitterness of these figures places them outside of heterosexual vitality engendered in the struggle between self-development and devotional love for another. Homosexuality, like casual affairs and asceticism, appears as a solution that is too easy because it avoids the central social and cultural problematic of heterosexuality.

This theme is developed in Irene's conversations with Hermine, a mathematics student in Zurich. Echoing the women students' own focus on the necessity of discipline, Hermine explains that she "did without everything that could be called 'feminine'—even if she got married, she did not want to have a child . . . since an intellectual person, wants at most to live in friendship." Irene, who longs to give her lover a child, is shocked and baffled by Hermine's lack of reproductive instinct. " 'We don't solve the essential problem of our new women's lives—being a personality and a woman at the same time,' thought Irene, 'by ignoring it.' " For Stöcker and others, the goal was not simply emancipating oneself from restrictions and social conventions, but developing "personality" through the struggle between the opposite poles of achievement and devotion to another.

In another conversation with a woman who advocates "free love," Irene declares, "I venture to conclude, that you have not experienced it—otherwise you would know that free love is not a solution either. . . . Love is the strongest bond that there is—the deepest emotional opposite of 'freedom.' " She asks the woman how she resolves the problem of femininity and personality, of having to give up the "blessedness we enjoy as women" to pay for what one "as a creative individual is and wants to accomplish." The woman stuns Irene with her brisk reply that she plans to train a man to satisfy her sexual needs, but otherwise to let her have her own way.[41] Radical "free love" is incompatible with Irene's sacred ideal of agonistic and sacrificial love.[42] The relationship notions Irene encounters form a typology of intellectual friendship, casual sexual connection, comfortable careerism, and virginal respectability. None of these types can satisfy Irene's longing for intense emotion. Her ideological justifications reconcile women's emancipation with her great love by claiming the latter as an ultimate connection with the essence of "life."

Like Stöcker's, Ernst von Wolzogen's novel confronted the changing shapes of love, sex, and gender through a series of encounters and philosophical discussions.[43] The characters who voice these debates were recognizable

caricatures of figures active in Munich feminist and avant-garde circles in
the 1890s. Three of its female characters shuttle back and forth between
Munich and their studies in Zurich. The novel's central figure, Arnulf Rau,
claims the authority to judge whether or not the female characters belong
to the third sex, boasting that he invented the term.[44] Rau explains, "With
the expression 'the third sex,' I categorize all the women's lives, which out
of natural inclination or under the pressure of circumstances have managed
to feel themselves no longer as sexual beings with all the rights and duties
that entails, but rather simply as fellow human beings." The "natural neuters,"
as he calls them, "in earlier times had to fit themselves into the scheme of
women's existences, because law and morality forbid them from participation
in all of the activities requiring mental and physical strength, which were
regarded as the prerogatives of men." Wolzogen's "third sex" describes only
women whose biology causes them to refuse heterosexuality. It contains no
reference to gender-deviant males or to same-sex desire. Although the speech
creates space for exceptional women to share in "the prerogatives of men,"
the novel represents characters that fit Rau's definition not only as failed
heterosexuals, but also as hopelessly incompetent for the male positions to
which they aspire.

　　Rau's speech removes "rights and duties" from their political context
and naturalizes them as inherent in two opposed sexual positions. The danger posed by the third sex, as Rau sees it, is third-sex women's recruitment
of normal women, driving them "with the whip of ambition into competition with men in all areas."[45] Rau's construction of femininity as residing in
"sensual need or motherly instinct" within a sexual gender binary renders
both sexually potent female masculinity and desire between women as
impossibilities.[46] What remains is the asexual woman as the opposite of the
heterosexual woman, the "real" woman, needing a man as complement. In
this conception, sexual desire—and through it vitality—depends on male
response to the female quality of *Reiz* (allure). Since nature is organized
around the reproductive urge of these two figures, the third sex can only
be a barren and marginal aberration.[47]

　　To contrast with his conception of the third sex, Rau analyzes the
character of Claire, one of the women students. In addition to her medical studies in Zurich, Claire lives with her lover Josef in Munich between
semesters. Josef wants to marry and expects Claire to subordinate her life
to his like any other wife. Claire, happy with the current arrangement, faces
the heterosexual New Woman's dilemma of whether to risk the submission
entailed in the legal and cultural institution of marriage. Claire's eventual
consent to the marriage shows Rau that she does not belong to the third sex.

At the wedding celebration, Rau toasts Claire's ability to combine her own career with proper feminine love for her husband. Addressing Claire's emancipated friends, Rau proclaims, "You women who are proud of what your sister has accomplished in a hard struggle for the activation of her free will perhaps will say that she is a superwoman who has already overcome the weaknesses of her nature and the submissive longing for the protection of a man." However, his masculine judgment supersedes their biased self-congratulation. "As a man, however, I tell you," he continues, "and any man who knows her will say the same thing—she is no Amazon and no thing-woman, but rather simply woman, undoubtedly of the second sex. Her being breathes the charm, the perfume of the woman, and it was not destined for her to go through life without love." Claire's compromise serves as an object lesson proving "that one can be completely feminine and still a free person, devoted lover of the man of her choice while still leading her own mental life and practicing her own independent career."[48] Claire's representation of the student variety of New Woman is redeemed through her consent to making heterosexual love primary. Rau, as gender expert, carves out a compromise that allows for real women to pursue careers as long as they perform the sexual role of the second sex.

Newspaper editorials, images, and novels all portrayed asexuality as the danger represented by the woman student. Both male and female observers presented such figures as rejecting contact with men altogether in a way that made them seem silly and superficial. The Stöcker and Wolzogen novels situated and resolved the problematic of the New Woman within a heterosexual framework. Yet there was more at stake than simply marriage. Like the characters Irene and Claire, women students were involved in the struggle to become a "free person." Their writings show that achieving this ideal of subjectivity was equally urgent for them. But they did not accept that the agony of a heterosexual love affair was the necessary path. Neither did they reject relationships with men. Instead, female students adopted behavioral androgyny as a strategic choice in their search for a new, more equalitarian, basis for relations between the sexes.

The Discovery of Collegiality: Exploring Heterosociality

If Wolzogen and Stöcker struggled to make intellectual women sexy for the sake of men and reproduction, women students' texts celebrated comradely relations between the sexes. They wished to escape the enforced and, to them, artificial social formulas that seemed to imprison them in a single subordinate role. Frieda Duensing and Käthe Schirmacher in particular acclaimed heterosocial comradeship as a revolutionary basis for rethinking social relations, gendered subjectivity, and sexual morality. The achievement of equalitarian harmony was a relatively late development in their student careers preceded and accompanied by rejection, hazing, and ridicule on the part of male students. At the beginning of their careers, they were aware of being interlopers, a conspicuous minority with much at stake in the way they performed and interacted with the majority.

Frieda Duensing's description of auditing classes in Munich reflected the isolation felt by pioneers: "I am the only woman, and every class is unpleasant for me, because they all stare at me in these halls and stairways, which have so seldom been desecrated by a profane foot."[49] The atmosphere of male skepticism if not resistance was felt even more strongly at Zurich a generation earlier. Early medical student Franziska Tiburtius described how students policed one another's reactions to defamation. One of her colleagues became aggrieved, "white hot, spewing fire and rage," demanding that the others take up her cause and make an official complaint. Her anger was so dangerous that the other women "formed a security guard . . . to hold her back from such silliness—since the entire upper city [the university district] would be overjoyed if the story got out."[50] The earliest women students felt they had to "take it" when they were teased or jeered to prove that they were neither overly sensitive nor easily intimidated.

Unthinking or deliberate humiliations are vivid in the memories of the women student characters in Shirmacher's novel *Libertad*. One of the professors teaches the latest scientific ideas about gender, defining women's essence as a "preponderance of sensuality and instinct." When the character Lotte tries to argue against this reduction of women to sex, the professor replies scornfully, "My dear girl, you understand nothing of these mysteries." The reexperience of shame as she recounts the memory brings up another memory. A man she met while traveling manipulated her into accepting accommodation in his hotel room with the goal of seducing her. Earlier, on the train, the man had assured her that no woman who lived authentically could be sexually virtuous. Determined to prove him wrong, Lotte called on the double consciousness she had learned in the lab, becoming "as cold and steady as an anatomy student dissecting a body for demonstration." Though overwhelmed with rage and fear, she was also "a cold-blooded observer, who heard herself speak, saw herself move, and watched the 'case' unfold before her with an objective scholarly interest."[51] At the university or away, women students were always on their guard, observing themselves through awareness of the many potential criticisms that might damage their academic success and self-respect. Sexuality, rather than incompetence, was the main and inescapable site of humiliation.

Yet risking humiliation and policing their feelings and behavior were burdens they readily accepted as necessary to inhabit new spaces of physical and intellectual freedom. Lotte's American husband, listening to his wife's memories, wonders whether he would have prevailed in the women students' place. He asks what motivated them to put up with the deprivations and discrimination. Lotte's friend Phil answers, "You see, for us the university . . . was the Promised Land—we had to set out from the wilderness, the desert, in order to reach it. . . . Once we did, we would be willing to bear anything rather than give it up." Phil's biblical image led to a liturgical call and response:

"We were seen as weak—"
"And therefore, you wanted to achieve Herculean tasks."
"As limited in scholarship—"
"And now you had to be the first."
"As fickle—"
"And had to fight until your last breath."
"As the plaything of love and the ornament of life—"
"And had to put the serious men to shame."
"As a cause—"
"And had to create a personality for yourselves."[52]

Looking back, these characters revel in their success in meeting the challenges that the male-dominated university forced on them.

To meet these challenges, women consciously created social personae that steered between masculine and feminine stereotypes. Too much masculinity risked social ostracism, but too much femininity elicited the scorn of male colleagues.[53] Male colleagues, as well as the bourgeois world, reflected back to the women their success at finding the right balance. The end of the litany quoted above is significant: "personality" can be read as synonymous with an autonomous subject position. Creating and inhabiting it was both a strategy and a goal for university women. It encompassed a position from which to express creativity and morality. It located the self in the gender-neutral category of *Person* as opposed to *Weibsperson* (female). Women's reflections on their experiences turned the argument made in *The Third Sex*—that emancipated choices reflected a "neuter" essence—on its head. From an insider's view, women had adopted protective neutrality in order to be taken seriously as students and intellectuals. Too strong an interest in love would only prove their second-class status as scholars.

As they began to inhabit this position, Schirmacher and Duensing celebrated the collegiality that blossomed between the sexes once male students accepted them. As Frieda Duensing expressed it in a letter, "Colleagues! A wonderful obligation, a deep respect, a mutual solicitude, solidarity!" Duensing saw these friendships as fundamental for women's emancipation: "My dear, there is something behind the new idea of freedom for women: it brings the highest morality along with it. In no other social sphere in the world could you find such interaction: so pure, so golden, resounding, unforgettable." She begged the letter's recipient to send her daughter to the university so that she too could experience heterosociability in which both sexes belonged to the same moral community.[54]

Schirmacher's memoir recounts her years in Paris as part of a circle of three men and three women. The group of students enjoyed socializing together in a free and easy way impossible in her hometown of Danzig. From this new sociability she developed a critique of young German women's position as the passive objects of courtship. For her, the modest, yet flirtatious, femininity expected of the girl being courted was artificial and destructive to women's development as moral subjects. When her group socialized in public spaces, the young women were exposed to the gaze of respectable society—a gaze that assumed women socializing so freely with men were their mistresses.[55] This jarring misperception led Schirmacher to imagine the United States as a paradise where all opposite-sex relationships were like those among her school comrades. The American husband in *Libertad* sees marriage as an equalitarian partnership because he grew up with "daily free contact with girls" experienced as "nothing new, horrifying, or amazing." Schirmacher's imagined utopian comradeship carries over to romance. "You could also show them you liked them without fear," he recalls. "Such attractions were returned or they weren't. Neither person died of a broken heart."[56] *Libertad's* characters reveal why women students may have adopted an androgynous, asexual habitus.

In a pamphlet advocating women's higher education, Schirmacher claims students' equalitarian socializing as a key to progressive social change. "Admit it," she wrote, "is it not powerful social progress when young men and women, who naturally enjoy each other, are allowed to meet each other naturally, honestly, and unhindered on neutral ground?" Schirmacher went beyond Duensing in imagining future sexual relations developing on the basis of such socializing. She saw it as "a turn for the better" when a girl no longer has to "squeeze her freshest desires into the corset of 'propriety' " and instead is able to "show her interest in a young man who pleases her without either of them having to think immediately of marriage."[57]

The exhilarating experience of the new heterosociability in the university setting authorized the most extravagant hopes for achieving the "highest morality" and fostering "powerful social progress." Duensing and Schirmacher seized on academic collegiality, however fleeting and illusory it may have been, because it seemed to provide a model in real space for the realization of the utopian genderless subjecthood they strove to inhabit.

However, the optimism in these passages masked the persistent problematic of sex that lay not far beneath the surface. The code of sexual honor internalized by most middle-class young women intensified these submerged conflicts.[58] There was a fine line between a Platonic relationship—one where desire and attraction were sublimated into intellectual exchange—and falling in love, which distracted from one's real work and carried dangerous temptations for women. It was characteristic of Duensing that her heterosocial relationships were not strictly comradely. Her letters to male friends often exhibited a flirtatious erotic energy underlying the intellectual exchange on the surface. Yet Duensing was bitterly critical of women who let Platonic attraction slide into romance. "They are dumb enough to carry on some kind of a love story on the side," she wrote. "Almost all! They succumb to the temptations that are offered to every woman here; the men get the best of it, the women only agitation, fetters, and distraction." Duensing claimed that she firmly rejected romantic overtures; she had "no time for that sort of thing." Women protected their autonomy by keeping men at arm's length while they finished their degrees and established their careers. However, her complaint shows that by the end of the 1890s, women students had already begun shaping student life in the direction of twentieth-century models of emancipation that integrated women into careers while maintaining the division of labor in personal and domestic matters.

Women who wrote enthusiastically about university experiences used their confrontation with questions of love and sex to critique the existing order. Their insights into the harm caused by male domination—clearest and most pressing in the realm of sexuality—gave them a sense of being the harbingers of a new order. The struggle for a universal moral and ethical stance to reform gender relations became the core "truth" on which intellectual women such as Schirmacher and Mensch placed their hopes of renewal.

The most radical insights and goals of the New Women of this period almost inevitably pulled them toward suppression of sexual desire that enabled the flourishing of comradely and equalitarian relations between the sexes in the university setting.

Emancipated Homosociality

While new relations with men were surprising and exhilarating, the university setting also allowed for enhanced intimacy in relationships among women struggling with similar dilemmas and conditions. Since nineteenth-century social life, both within and outside the family, was often gender-segregated, the new homosociality did not carry the same revolutionary import as its mixed counterpart. Beyond their same-sex schooling, bourgeois girls were integrated into social networks through family, church, and local elite social rituals. Involvement in charity work, teas, and balls constructed femininity within existing bonds and hierarchies.[59] Late-nineteenth-century novelists exposed the rigidity, conformity, boredom, and passivity enforced among girls and women within existing modes of elite sociability.[60] At university women had a chance to revise the purpose of female socializing. Tibertius's memoir reflected the jarring gap between student life and bourgeois Zurich. *Die Libertad* also stressed the impossibility of reintegration into existing social structures and manners. Lack of intellectual stimulation and provincial complacency were especially hard to bear: Phil found her former society "narrow-minded and indifferent to the burning questions of the times." Its members were equally put off by her " 'progressive ideas,' critical stance, and coolness towards affairs of love and fashion."[61] Feeling estranged from others' "normal," university women treasured all the more the loving friendship of their female colleagues.

Sharon Marcus's careful analysis of the different meanings of Victorian women's social relationships is helpful in thinking about relationships between women students. Marcus finds that same-sex relations fell into three qualitatively different categories: erotic passion, marriage, and friendship that fit neither of the other categories. She shows that female intimacy in Victorian England was embedded in family and kin relations, including heterosexual marriage.[62] The university setting and later time period clearly put the female intimacies discussed here in a very different atmosphere. Instead of reinforcing women's social roles, the students were engaged in remaking the expectations that accompanied femininity. Marriages, or female couples whose lives were lived largely together, were uncommon at university, although many students entered into female marriages after or outside of their studies. Ricarda Huch's memoir, written from the vantage point of the 1930s, provides an opportunity to gauge the erotic and supportive types of female intimacy.

Huch remembered fondly her friends' strategic construction of social networks that supported their ambitions.[63] She looked back on same-sex solidarity as a valuable creation in its own right: "It is obvious that serious, even sad, things moved us; but the darkness took on a lighter color in the joy of our being together. We felt healthy and strong and the future was ours."[64] Huch recognized that she had transferred her affiliation and intimacy needs from biological family to chosen friendship networks. "In Zurich, I came into possession of myself," she realized. "There I first became conscious of my personality and my own strength, because at home one was always the member of a family, without one's own independent being, integrated into a pre-existing order." Becoming an independent subject was unimaginable without "friends with whom I felt deeply connected, in whose love I could completely relax, in a way that I can hardly hope to find again elsewhere."[65] Huch remembered sending a photograph of herself with her new friends to her grandmother. This symbolic gesture confronted her grandmother, a representative of female power in the traditional family, with a declaration of independence from that female life pattern. Yet it also reassured the earlier generation that female intimacy and support coexisted with career success.[66]

Did eroticism and passion, banned from heterosexual relations, find an outlet between women? In this experimental setting, it is difficult to make such a clear distinction as Marcus does for the earlier British case. Huch's friendships, for example, were not limited to family-like groups; she also entered into dyads with some intensity. In her first years as a student, Huch shared a passionate relationship with Salomé Neunreiter. Huch's description of Neunreiter's jealousy and need to see herself reflected in Huch's feelings revealed that on Neunreiter's side an intimacy deeper than mutual support was at stake.[67] Later, Huch and Marie Baum were so inseparable that friends referred to them as Castor and Pollux, the Gemini twins.[68]

Huch's retrospective openness about couples in the student milieu contrasted with scenarios written by Duensing and Mensch (both of whom remained single, while Huch eventually married). These two authors made female same-sex love visible, but only in spaces far from the university. From Zurich, Duensing wrote to her intimate friend Gretchen speculating on a feeling of strain that had come into their correspondence. She guessed that her new persona, "ambitious Friedrich" wasn't as attractive to Gretchen as "Frieda, who once shone with the bright reddish shimmer of dawn in an outbreak of femininity." Duensing represented assuming student identity as gender change. While in earlier letters, Duensing had imagined the erotic connection between her and Gretchen in fantasies of two carefree male figures, this letter represented it as doubled femininity. From her position at the university her previous same-sex eroticism seemed too feminine, perhaps too unrestrained, to be compatible with the new student persona, the "ambitious, dogged pursuer of goals."[69] Adopting masculinity provided a protective shield against the temptations of love affairs with either sex that might sabotage women students' success.

Ella Mensch's novel also separates carefully controlled university relationships from idealized same-sex love located elsewhere. *On Outpost Watch* demonstrates the dangers that romantic attachment to men meant for women students. The main character Fanny tries in vain to warn a friend of the consequences she would suffer from feminine weakness and sentimentality toward men. Fanny sees men as eager to seduce women by taking advantage of their "modern" ideas and independence. As a contrast to her cynical portrayal of heterosexual love, Mensch includes a subplot about the exalted same-sex crushes of Fanny's sister Hedi. Fanny scorns conventional people's belief that Hedi is going through a phase and that she will eventually " 'fall in love with a man' in every way." Fanny idealizes Hedi's loves as "something that no longer belongs in the realm of the sensual—something de-materialized . . . the intoxication of the born Platonist."[70] Comparing the two love affairs, Fanny declares, "The more insight I gain into the deceitful and cruel love play between the sexes, the more my respect grows for the wonderful tender poetry expressed in Hedi's homages and enthusiasms."[71] Yet the novel cannot find social space for Hedi's same-sex passion. With Hedi's tragic death, Mensch destroys her erotic ideal in favor of the student Fanny's sexual pessimism.

Although memoirs and commentaries published at a later date may have been more reticent about same-sex love due to the stigmatization of mannish women as sexual inverts after the turn of the century, it seems clear that women's relationships with one another prior to that could take many forms without incurring shame or secrecy. At the same time, neither marriage-like coupling nor passionate obsession fit well for women whose attention was focused on the independence of life and mind they sought in becoming students. For them, the key factor was how those relationships fit into their life goals and emancipated self-making.

Frieda Duensing's Struggle for Moral Freedom

Thanks to the publication of her letters and diaries, it is possible to use Frieda Duensing's writing to analyze how her relationships with both sexes fit into a longer life trajectory dedicated to achieving a new kind of female subjectivity. The sources document her emotional and affectional life prior to her decision at around age thirty to study at Zurich. The dominant motif is Duensing's struggle to reconcile her ambitions and quest for moral freedom with her ideology of service and sacrifice. Periods of doubt, depression, and ill health alternated with the excitement of forging a path in the world. Although she was not interested in women's rights as a special cause, her life followed the same general pattern as many in the women's movement. University study followed a long period of experimentation with life and career goals. After accepting that she did not have the talent to become a writer and did not like teaching, she studied law in hopes of solving the social problems of industrial class society.

A diary entry from 1887 expresses the inner struggles girls experienced as they tried to justify their ambitions. The very word suggested selfishness. "The demanding drive is ambition," Duensing wrote. "Can that really be so terrible if it challenges me, drives me on, and makes me capable of work?" "I feel strength and in particular desire and readiness to sacrifice in order to have an impact and to create." She was willing to give up "pleasure, joy, love, everything" in exchange for work that would give her a worthy goal. Duensing's greatest desire was work that used her creativity to contribute to a greater whole. The entry also captures her anxious uncertainty about how to turn her extravagant and "selfless" ambitions into a proper life plan. She considers and rejects becoming a writer, a nurse, or a wife ("I cannot subordinate myself to a man").[72] The choices enumerated in the passage clearly outline the thinkable roles available for a respectable middle-class young woman in the 1880s.

Another diary entry from the same month illustrates the depth of Duensing's desire to achieve selfhood of a very particular kind. "I dare to hope that this inexplicable, boundlessly fierce, tormenting desire in me is not common ambition, but rather striving toward moral freedom," she wrote. Pursuit of ambitions for personal satisfaction could never be the meaning of emancipation for Duensing. The entry continues, "There is something else that could be called moral freedom in an infinitely higher sense: the casting off of the chains of slavery with which our own selves burden us. That is independence from pedantic schoolmasterish caution, from dithering back and forth, from indecisive deliberation."[73] The passage could be valid for a young person of either sex, yet clearly women had far more reason to struggle with indecision.

In German philosophy, the moral subject was defined by an independence of judgment that disqualified women who were assumed to be dependent on their male family members. Although legal and financial independence were in reach, the path to achieving subjecthood in the moral, sociopolitical, and sexual realms was more complicated. Freedom of choice and achievement were secondary to and sublimated in the language of becoming a subject—a person whose opinions and work mattered within the circle of other educated and responsible subjects.[74] Duensing's searching self-criticism over these issues is clear in the passages above. The quest for emancipation entailed constant judgment of whether or not she deserved to be treated as a subject in her own right. For women socialized into Kantian languages of moral freedom and judgment, emancipation was an internal struggle more than a fight to reform injustice or prejudice. The impossible goal for Duensing and other educated women was inhabiting an ideal subject position as proof that the moral subject was a genderless category.

Years later, as a student at Zurich, Duensing expressed the urgency of women becoming subjects in another letter to Gretchen. Both of Gretchen's children should be raised to live to bring "humanity a little bit forward, at least consciously helping in that direction." For boys, it was taken for granted, but girls would have to work hard "to understand and feel that a woman should not only be an object but a subject, a creating, influencing, shaping individual."[75] Here, Duensing succinctly captures the meaning of emancipation.

Duensing's eventual choice of a social work career allowed her to combine moral subjectivity, creative work, and the class-approved goal of bettering industrial social relations. A letter to Gretchen describing her experiences creates a subtle analogy between Duensing's moral liberation and the liberation toward which she hoped to guide "the people." As naive would-be social workers, students romanticized the object of their work as "people hungering and thirsting for justice, people who poured out their sweat in honest work and did not earn what they deserved, people who sighed and looked for comfort for their souls. People whom we could help because they wanted to let themselves be helped."[76] Duensing conceived the purpose of social work as inciting the poor and uneducated to follow her example of struggling and striving toward cultivation and moral freedom. Later, as a practicing social worker, Duensing was disappointed to find that "the people" were not interested in following the path she pioneered. She judged harshly the "people's" childish lack of higher ideals. The intensity of this disappointment mirrored the intensity of her desire to make subjecthood gender-neutral and therefore universal.

The tutelage and appropriation of the right to discipline others reflected in Duensing's attitude toward the "people" have long been identified as characteristic of social work initiatives.[77] As many scholars have established, poor relief was a field within which women could exercise gendered power and authority on the basis of class.[78] This power to discipline was also a channel where social workers' self-emancipation efforts could be acted out in their relationships to their clients. Duensing concludes, "What is true of the child is true of the people, who could be called the nation in a state of childhood." Further, she sees the "people" as "greedy for sweets, easily pacified with sweets, but insatiable, overeating, vomiting, and overeating again."[79] The distress evident in the text is closely linked to bodily desire. Uncertainty about the moral value of her own desire for freedom and achievement is visible in the vehemence of Duensing's reaction to the desires of others for other kinds of social goods. The "people" need to learn renunciation—control of their bodily hungers. In place of sweets, they must learn to desire the sacrifice and struggle that she sees as essential to moral subjectivity.[80]

It is also notable that Duensing evokes notions of adult and child without resorting to the language of motherhood that was so ubiquitous in feminist argumentation. Even though she chooses social work because it is one of the few fields of achievement open to women, she avoids justifying it in gendered terms. Duensing's insistence that social uplift is a task for the morally educated, not specifically for women set her apart from the mainstream women's movement. For Duensing, as for many other German women seeking emancipation, desire was channeled into the desire to be a certain kind of person, one who was hypersensitive to suffering, engaged in moral struggle, and in control of physical drives.

Parallel to wrestling with the moral implications of social work, Duensing struggled to incorporate love, sexuality, and gender into her conception of the ideal moral subject.[81] Her letters and diary entries address these questions obliquely but persistently. On the one hand, the drive toward ideal subjecthood entails denial of bodily desires. But on the other, part of her moral struggle involves transcending rule-based morality. In her reading of Byron, for example, she finds confirmation for the value of "the unbound power of the feelings, the blossoming of the soul against all the laws of society, against the rules of the schoolmasterish moral judge, the drive toward freedom and control over one's own destiny."[82] Before she entered the university, Duensing's sublime feelings were expressed in her letters to Gretchen Herwig, a friend for whom she developed a passionate love. The intense correspondence between the two women continued from at least 1888 until Herwig married and Duensing began her studies at Zurich a decade later. Apparently, the two women were seldom able to spend time together. Separation and unfulfilled desire incited passion that (perhaps) remained safely on the page. The letters, included in the memorial volume by Duensing's friends, give free rein to fantasy.

In these flights of fancy, Duensing imagines both herself and Herwig as masculine. Especially in more personal letters, she addresses Herwig in the masculine as "*Lieber* Herwig." Apparently, feelings between the two had developed in connection with reading Shakespeare together. "Herwig, because I got to know you reading Falstaff," she muses, "I noticed that you were right for me, you could jump out the window, knock down Frau Oberamtmann's lace with a walking stick, march into the Grunewald on the Kaiser's birthday with a piece of sausage and a bottle of schnapps." Further reflecting on these robust fantasy scenes, she continues, "Like me you would gladly have been a boy. Like me you loathed crocheted lace, then I knew you would always be [*der*] 'Herwig' for me."[83] This vigorous affirmation of female masculinity contrasts sharply with Duensing's distressed efforts elsewhere to appropriate the respectable version of masculine subjecthood as gender neutral. The masculine prerogatives of escape from social responsibility, carefree comrade-ship, and bodily freedom in imaginative passages like this one could not be farther from the rigidity and stress of her struggle to inhabit the persona of the moral subject. The disjunction perhaps reveals Duensing's instinctive understanding that moral subjectivity for men did not have to constrain desire and physical freedom. Her romantic adventurous persona in these fantasies forms a contained other to the avowed identity based on genderless and controlled emancipated subjectivity.

The image of the free love of two masculine figures persists in the following letter. Duensing continues, "When I think of you, why do I always have the same crazy idea: oh, if you were a boy and I a man. If we had been granted to live, to storm through a wild youth. You would have been right for me, you alone of everyone. . . . Oh, to drink through the night with you, to carouse through the silent streets, to irritate the philistines. . . . But if your eyes shone for another, if you lost your heart's strength to females, then I would have killed you—"[84] The queerness of female homosexual passionate fantasy acted out by male figures is only intensified by the reference to the potential appeal of (presumably normal feminine) women for the cross-gender lover. Making the relationship parallel to heterosexual infatuations reveals an erotic element that is not just latent but crucial and passionate ("I would have killed you"). Both male homoeroticism and the equalitarian element of gender sameness were required for this staging of desire. It was equally crucial that Duensing not compete for Herwig's love as a woman. In Duensing's view, as we saw above, love relationships automatically meant a crippling dependency for women. The letters contained no hint that others might consider these passions evidence of perversion or degeneracy. No doubts or fears about gender or sexual abnormality intruded on her robust fantasies.

Yet the letter refers obliquely to the two women's desires as transgressive: "If the pastors are right and on that day the sheep are sent to the right and the goats to the left, and we go to the left because we are certainly not sheep—amidst the wailing and gnashing of Hell, I will say, 'Don't be afraid, we have each other.' . . . Love is stronger than the horrors of Hell, eternally and without end!" The Last Judgment scene lent the stamp of the eternal to the bond that was named love. Yet it was left unclear whether same-sex love or simply the insistence on thinking and living outside of convention put Duensing and Herwig on the side of the condemned.

The publication of these and other passages expressing sensuality and desire in the memorial volume indicates that Duensing's friends wished to commemorate her wild and fanciful side along with her achievements and qualities as a friend. Their documentation of Duensing's contradictions makes the source especially useful for thinking about emancipatory ambitions and achievements alongside the role of love and desire in her relationships. In the social realm, Duensing suffered from the perception that she had failed at self-possession and moral subjectivity. She hoped to overcome gender and prove that the ideal subject was genderless by denying desire and embracing suffering. Yet in the realm of fantasy, she exuberantly constructed transgendered personas in which she and her beloved experienced desire and freedom simultaneously.

One of the volume's editors, Marie Baum, interpreted Duensing's years of study as a "daily martyrdom that she took on to meet the enemy on its own ground."[85] Duensing's explanation of her decision to study law at the time reveals the secret of its appeal. "I like to give advice and have an effect in public and worry over things, and also I like scandal and contention—but the goal! If I can help the underclass!"[86] The parallel structure quickly replaced an admission of desire for power, influence, and gender transgression with an assertion of a selfless purpose compatible with her vision of respectable subjecthood. The study of law was Duensing's vehicle for resolving the conflict between ambitions and desires and the ideology of disinterested service.

Disappointment and Morality

With the completion of their doctorates, women students faced the inevitability of returning to "normal" social relations, where once again they were saturated with gender and its sexual imperative. Shirmacher's *Die Libertad* dramatizes the more practical problems of reintegration. Phil, her "hopes of becoming a professor fallen through, independent position given up, financial independence lost, . . . snubbed in 'literary pursuits,' in society a nothing, standing completely alone with [her] ideas and interests," wonders if her degree has been worth it after all. She has had to "crawl back into the parents' nest like a sick chicken."[87] The illness that ends her independence is a voice disability that symbolizes the failure to make her critique heard and heeded. After working so hard to be able to change the world, all she had to offer was "that little desired commodity of critique of the existing order and suggestions for renewal."[88]

At the beginning of the 1890s, when *Die Libertad* was published, Schirmacher's criticism was still directed at German backwardness in comparison with France, Britain, and the United States. Very suddenly in the late 1890s, during her second stay in Paris, Schirmacher turned from admiration of the liberal democracies and progressive ideas about women's emancipation to nationalist conservatism. An intense love affair with a Frenchman—an anti-Semite and bitter critic of the French Republic—and encounters with anti-German Eastern European émigrés influenced the complete transformation. Soon after, she moved back to Germany and began a lifelong partnership with Klara Schleker.[89] Although in a nonnormative position as half of a female couple, she was a founding figure in the post–World War right-wing nationalist German National People's Party (DNVP) in Danzig. She theorized nationalist feminism, emphasizing female influence within the Germanic family as keystone of a strong Germany able to defend itself against threats from West and East.[90]

Although Schirmacher's own work was always oriented to present and future, her ideas were compatible with those of the Romantic or *volkisch* strand of virulent German nationalism that traced German superiority to its origins in an ancient warrior civilization. These ideologues imagined that women held a sacred position within the family defending the purity of culture as the men defended its political autonomy. After the war, they found a political home in the DNVP; many likely migrated to Nazism as it gained a presence on the national political scene. Schirmacher became embittered when party leadership denied her wish to serve in the Reichstag in order to support male candidates and failed to embrace the cause of female leadership.

However, she continued to support the DNVP as the only uncompromising political party. She maintained her active role in nationalist groups focused on recovering and Germanizing the *Ostmark,* or eastern borderlands, seeing her purpose in "saving" Germany from its weak Weimar condition.[91]

Schirmacher's political turnabout was extreme, but she was not the only feminist to support a strong German state that disciplined the working classes. The turn to or appeal of political conservatism for some of the most active feminist critics among this group traces back at least partially to their initial intense commitment to moral regeneration as the defining cause of the New Woman—and as motivation for their pursuit of higher degrees. Duensing, Mensch, and Schirmacher shared the critical view that freedom for women was the basis of a new moral order, but only so long as freedom was anchored in the feminine role of leading the way away from the "lower" instincts and toward "higher" spiritual goals. Their many disappointments when their degrees failed to result in influence and effectiveness reinforced a strange alliance between feminism and the authority of the state. Mensch and Schirmacher chose political conservatism and alliances with the late-nineteenth-century morality movements that fought pornography, prostitution, and venereal disease.[92] Women's critiques became most effective where they were linked through these movements to conservative measures, carried out by the state, to remoralize the "people."[93]

Mensch's student novel highlights Fanny's lonely and ineffective position as a conservative seeking emancipation in a liberal and radical milieu. To her conservative friends, she is the alien "emancipated one" whose pursuit of education is a "whim to be tolerated." At the university, most "counted her among the 'reactionaries.' "[94] Fanny's arguments with her antagonist, the Social Democratic male student Stümke, provide a forum for her ideas on conservative feminist reform. When Stümke points out that conservative military Germany is an uncongenial environment for women's emancipation, Fanny points "to the lessons of history." She hopes that "the protectors of tradition will recognize soon enough that they must be revitalized with the ideas from the women's camp." Women, she claims, do not "want to be drawn into the easy, transient goals that the Red International offers in such a friendly and alluring way. We want to win our portion and place in the solid construction created by the work of a Lessing, a Fichte, and a Bismarck." For her, emancipation—becoming a force for moral reform—can only be accomplished in a state with "force at its disposal."[95]

Ironically, Mensch and Schirmacher became students to protest against the conventional limitations on women within heterosexual relations, yet later glorified marriage and women's domestic roles as the cornerstone of national strength and order. Both women's origins in the Eastern Baltic region no doubt had a lasting influence on their German nationalism. The feeling that their German prestige could be swamped by the opposing nationalist claims of Poles trumped any opening to cross-national connections based on gender. Mensch, like Schirmacher, was unable to convert her literature degree into a solid position among the intellectual elite, though she continued to publish as a cultural critic.[96] The importance of sexual morality in their utopian visions of the future remained, while the content of their feminism changed as they experienced personal disappointments, male antifeminism, and activism on concrete issues.

Although German women university students formed a small, unusual, and privileged group before 1900, their simultaneous intellectual and existential confrontation with gender makes their texts a particularly revealing site for picking apart the connections between emancipation, subjectivity, and desire. In this moment of serious fracture in nineteenth-century gendered social organization, certain individual women found cracks through which they reached for a goal of ethical selfhood and autonomy. They had derived their model of the subject from the German literary and philosophical classics. The diverse national and political cultures in the university milieu offered challenging new alternatives for enacting gender and sexuality. Women students perceived their student years as offering unprecedented freedom for exploring new modes of life and social relations. Yet their renegotiation of gender style and sexual practice navigated the precarious space between judgmental gazes and their own cultural assumptions. There was more than a passing congruence between the stereotype of the asexual student and the strategic performance of gender adopted by women students.

The radical content of the students' feminism lay in its imagining of genderless subject positions and nonsexualized sociability as a basis for social reconstruction. The perception of a kind of comradeship, available among students, in which gender and sexual difference were diminished, gave them a concrete alternative to reductive nineteenth-century ideologies of gender. These were relationships of intersubjectivity rather than pursuit and conquest. They supported and advanced students' ambitions rather than competing with or hindering them. Schirmacher and Duensing saw the outlines of a new moral order in heterosocial relationships of mutual respect and honest communication. Huch chose to give priority to her relationships with women precisely because their supportive and mutual quality allowed her to pursue her work. What was so fresh and promising for them, however, was threatening for modernist cultural critics such as Wolzogen who feared companionate sexual relations as symptoms of feminization of culture, threatening to sexual vitality and male dominance.

The women students used bodily gender performance strategically. The one thing they most wanted to avoid was being reduced to sexual beings. Ruling assumptions about femininity made attention to men's desires compulsory. Scientifically grounded theories "proved" female intellectual incapacity. Sometimes appropriating masculine signs was useful to signal to men that they were not sexually available. If more could be gained from conforming to conventional femininity, they were not averse to adapting their personal styles. Duensing and Schirmacher seem to have enjoyed the mental freedom to imagine themselves as gender changelings. The double consciousness that came along with emancipation created the possibility of imagining oneself as a man in a way that did not threaten feminine identity.

University women's commitments to moral reform were initially closely related to defending themselves against being reduced to a sexualized female stereotype. But moral reform also promised an outlet for making real change with their new credentials. The stronger their commitment to this agenda, the more likely they would eventually connect emancipation to conservative moralizing projects. To avoid the dissolution of subjecthood into sex, ironically many of the women students themselves eventually were drawn into professional and political positions saturated with sex in a negative relation.

The novels by Wolzogen and Stöcker demonstrate the anxieties generated by women students. They symbolized women's ambitions and withdrawal from subordination within the family. For these novels' emancipated heroines, motherhood and love worked as a kind of "natural magic" guaranteeing that women could and would carry out intellectual activity on the side. They provided a model of emancipation that would not damage feminine allure or commitment to fulfilling male desire. The women students, on the other hand, faced with the everyday process of proving their intellectual ability and judgment, distanced themselves from both. Some viewed or experienced passionate love as a dangerous loss of self-possession. In Duensing's and Mensch's varied scenarios, same-sex eroticism was not completely repressed but contained in a fantasy realm disconnected from achievement at the university.

Although concepts of homosexuality had entered the public sphere by this time, neither the public imagination nor the sources linked women students with homosexuality or inversion. Outside critics were much more likely to see the students as sexless and overly rational than to suspect them of abnormal sexual desires. Women students' self-representations consistently subordinated sexual desire. The asceticism of their textual personas was certainly strategic, yet it seems clear that they did not conceive of themselves as having a "sexuality" that defined them in relation to other people.

Women seeking emancipation had to manage all forms of desire carefully. Control of sensuality was subsumed into rigorous self-examination for the signs of selfishness, frivolousness, or weakness. Liberal, Christian, and gender discourses all reinforced the subordination of personal desire to a higher purpose. Restrained and diffuse eroticism experienced with special friends, through extravagant fantasies, or in an exalted Eros of admiration and sacrifice were acceptable outlets for women's erotic energies. For women such as Tibertius, Augspurg, and Schirmacher, the committed female couple eventually may have provided a respectable structure for sexual activity.

The women students sought emancipation in fashioning themselves according to classical liberal models of the subject. Their critique of contemporary gender roles and their joyful discovery of the possibility of relations of mutuality and respect between the sexes anticipated one of the most fundamental changes of the twentieth century. On the other hand, recognizing the liberal subject within themselves reinforced the class hegemony and displacement of desire that defined that subject.

Experiments in Female Masculinity

Sophia Goudstikker's Masculine Mimicry in Turn-of-the-Century Munich

Munich, May 1897. Two women friends, both authors of New Woman fiction, arrive in town for an extended stay, highlighted by visits to theatrical productions and intellectual salons. Through a talented *Jugendstil* architect active in that milieu, they meet a particularly fascinating woman—a feminist activist and owner of a photography studio. Both authors become a bit infatuated with this unusual woman. One of them spends many evenings with her. The photographer in turn travels out from Munich to visit the writers after they move to a vacation cottage in the countryside. Each of the authors subsequently produces a story featuring a character similar to the photographer. These fictions depict her as cross-dressed and transgressing all the rules of feminine decorum. In each fictional portrait, the character practices a form of same-sex eroticism, charming and flattering women and girls with her attentions.

The story related above is a slightly dramatized version of events recorded by one of the writers, Lou Andreas-Salomé, and her biographers.[1] Salomé's diary describes one of the evenings in Munich: "Later with Endell to the premiere . . . where we met Puck and others; went with them and Rilke to Schleich's, dined very merrily until 1:30 A.M."[2] "Puck" was the nickname of Sophia Goudstikker, the feminist photographer. Later entries for May 1897 record Salomé's daily socializing with "Puck," in cafes, in the English garden, and at the theater. On some occasions Salomé spent the night at Goudstikker's, where they entertained each other through the night.[3]

Goudstikker's life is remarkable for her professional independence and her emotional and ideological commitment to women. These elements can be documented through her feminist work in Munich, her couple relationships with two powerful feminist leaders, and in connection with her photography and studio building, the Hofatelier Elvira. The stories written by Salomé and Frieda von Bülow, Salomé's companion on her visit to Munich, add the dimension of female masculinity. The "Puck" characters dress and act in a male style, preach feminism, and court other women. Given the combination of all of these markers, it is surprising that Goudstikker has been largely omitted from German histories of female homosexuality.

American scholars, on the other hand, have been quick to pick up on the signs of lesbianism embodied by Goudstikker. Some have confidently represented her as a self-conscious lesbian. Goudstikker's "liberated" consciousness has been used as a foil for other intellectual and artistic women, including Salomé, Bülow, and painter Gabriele Münter. These better-known artists, who struggled to define their autonomy in the shadow of famous men, appear weak when contrasted with Goudstikker's bold independence. Biddy Martin's study of Salomé identifies Goudstikker as a "self-declared lesbian photographer" and her studio as "a gathering place for gay men and lesbians."[4] In a meditation on her scholarly embarrassment over Münter's passivity, Irit Rogoff argues, "In the world of Munich cultural, artistic, and gender politics, it is the Hof Atelier Elvira which stands out as . . . the site of convergences." Rogoff describes Elvira's founders, Goudstikker and Anita Augspurg as "a couple who wished to live out their lesbian sexual identity openly, and feminists who needed a financial and social base for their political activities."[5] In a chapter on Bülow, historian Lora Wildenthal likewise describes the Atelier as "a hub of gay and lesbian social life and intellectual and artistic life in Munich."[6] These confident descriptions of social circles based on affirmative notions of nonnormative sexual identity would seem to point to a conjuncture of fundamental importance to the history of homosexuality and therefore a fruitful site of research into early lesbian consciousness and community.

But using these sources, as in those describing university students, the search for origins falters. There is no direct evidence that Augspurg and Goudstikker thought of their partnership as founded in sexual identity. Yet, while it is doubtful that Goudstikker fashioned herself in the late nineteenth century out of a self-conscious "lesbian" identity, it is clear that she was juggling and experimenting with elements that would shortly come together in that configuration (as they already had in the sexological imagination). Bracketing the idea of "lesbian self-consciousness" allows a more open-ended examination of the links historical subjects were making between emancipation, emotional ties between women, and female masculinity. As new women engaged in redefining femininity, female performance of masculinity called the whole gendered binary structure into question without yet invoking a pathological diagnosis for observers. Unlike the sexologists, literary observers saw these signs as strategies for gender change and used them to extend the debate about the parameters of women's emancipation.

Goudstikker and her new women friends created their own social spaces in Berlin and Munich. Elsewhere in Germany, such spaces did not yet exist. Journalism and fiction, however, were open to women's imaginative explorations of the potential pleasures, consequences, and limits of reforming gendered social proscriptions. Kerstin Barndt has argued that novels depicting New Woman characters served a "crucial function as a mediator between reading women and the politics of the women's movement around 1900."[7] Even if many women could not change their lives, they became part of an imagined community of women whose aspirations diverged from those of earlier generations.[8] Like the women students, authors, including Bülow and Salomé, and their readers asked questions about how biological and social reproduction could be maintained separately from malleable cultural and social conventions. They realized that rearranging one piece of the social structure would create fault lines all through it. The figure of the masculine woman was one expression of anxieties and possibilities suggested by these cracks in the existing sex-gender system.[9]

The unique strategy captured by the characters identified with Goudstikker is particularly fascinating when posed next to those of the university women of Zurich. While women in intellectually stimulating but provincial Zurich sought to elide the restrictions and assumptions imposed by the sex-gender system, in Munich, the site of a very theatrical avant-garde culture, they found a stage on which a bold woman might explore the implications of emancipation by appropriating male styles and privileges.

Still, any attempt to fix Goudstikker, the historical woman, as an iconic masculine woman is bound to fail. Neither photographs nor written descriptions in memoirs and historical essays depict the woman in anything like the fictional character's striking appearance. Most of the time, she appears as one of a group of new women who affected certain bodily styles as an announcement of their emancipation: simpler clothing, short hair, a more relaxed and direct style of bodily habitus and gesture. Solutions to this discrepancy can be only speculative. The fictional portraits strongly suggest a single source in Goudstikker. While this chapter sketches Goudstikker's biography, its main concern is a careful examination of the significance of female masculinity in the imaginations of historical subjects experiencing rapid gender change.

Their portrayal of characters and milieus provides material for following the significance of female masculinity in the interaction between a performance and its observers, between writers and readers, and between characters that represented contemporary subjectivities. The stories ask how female masculinity, emancipation of women, and erotic and emotional ties to women interrelate without the shorthand of "lesbian" or "homosexual" to explain the connection. If the historical Goudstikker meant to use this temporary performance to provoke, she clearly succeeded, having spurred three authors to recreate and interpret her experiments.

Besides Salomé and Bülow, Ernst von Wolzogen included a version of Goudstikker's masculinity in his novel *The Third Sex*, analyzed in chapter 1 for its depiction of women students. In her first appearance in *The Third Sex*, Box jumps off her bicycle and bursts into a drawing room, suddenly disrupting its heterosexual domesticity. Box is "a hardy medium-tall, stocky figure, whose sturdy legs were stuck into black stockings and blue short pants, while the upper body was encased in a baggy blouse with a sailor collar." On her short hair, Box wears "a velvet cap with a visor, which harmonized perfectly with the bold boy's face."[10] Throughout the novel, Box livens up social scenes with somersaults and blunt assertions of her controversial opinions. She whistles, uses slangy interjections, and favors terms with violent connotations. (Fig. 2.1) Bülow's and Salomé's characters appear with the same short hair, caps, bicycles, and short pants.

Each of the three stories interprets the character's masculine style as an affected, and mistaken, expression of feminism. The characters' embodied

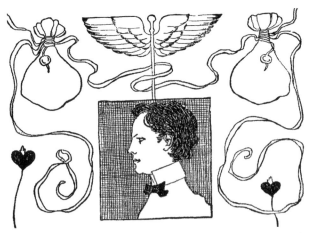

Fig. 2.1. Illustration depicting the character Box from Ernst von Wolzogen's novel *Das dritte Geschlect* (1899), Walter Caspari.

emancipation makes claims on male privilege and simultaneously parodies male style. As with other forms of politicized mimicry, the gender mimic risks ridicule in order to act out questions and contradictions of access to power and respect. The effect of the characters' strategic mimicry is ambivalent. It exposes the artificiality and injustice of gender roles through the woman's visible difference, yet reaffirms the superiority of the masculine through imitation. Masculine mimicry appropriates power by inhabiting male-identified signs, yet it risks reinscribing the gender binary in its dependence on conventional gender difference.[11] Mimetic performances are sites of the pleasure of transgression, yet they risk the pain of being caught in the middle, unable to fit into either category of the "real."[12]

The stories by Bülow and Salomé further represent erotic spectacle as an integral feature of masculine mimicry. The figure has a double appeal, attracting both men and women, though she explicitly and exaggeratedly flirts with other women. As theorists of female masculinity have shown, the masculine woman's sexual appeal for women and claims to sexual subjectivity denied to respectable women made homosexual erotic attraction visible.[13] Yet, as in the case of the women students, none of these representations draws on a concept of a homosexual identity to explain, sympathize with, or stigmatize the masculine woman. The absence of self-consciousness about representing masculinity and homoeroticism in the same character suggests that neither the authors nor the historical Sophia Goudstikker and her friends recognized a hetero/homo binary as determining sexual identity. Nevertheless, in each of the narratives the authors more or less subtly work out the relationship between sex and gender and the implications of changing gender norms for the heterosexual social order.

Each author achieved resolution by forcing the masculine character to recognize the gender binary as necessary for heterosexual love or motherhood as woman's true calling. Her feminism had to be revised in line with the primacy of heterosexuality. Yet, the stories by the two women powerfully make present the charm and eroticism of cross-dressing. In addition, they capture the possibilities for an erotic and pleasurable interaction among women. Although the sexual is elided, this opening to a new dimension of women's love cannot be completely erased by narrative closure.

Erotic Munich

The city of Munich was an appropriate stage for Goudstikker's performance of masculinity. At the end of the nineteenth century, Munich was Germany's avant-garde center. Its connection to Zurich and surroundings was particularly strong. Women students such as Anita Augspurg, Frieda Duensing, and Ricarda Huch lived in Munich between semesters. Munich radicals who fell afoul of Bismarck's Anti-Socialist Laws (1878–1890), which prohibited political writing or meetings promoting socialism, or of Bavaria's strict political censorship fled to Zurich, returning to Munich when the political climate opened up after Bismarck's resignation in 1890. The city benefited from cosmopolitan influences because of its location at the nexus of an east-west axis linking Paris and Vienna and a north-south route between Berlin and Rome. Its crossroads geography nurtured cultural ferment in mingling influences from these larger and more significant metropoles.[14] The Paris-Vienna axis is particular significant because of these cities' intense engagement with issues of sexuality. Salomé's thought and literary work were strongly influenced by her love affairs and encounters in the two capitals.

In contrast, life in Munich was slower paced and less industrialized. Its picturesque Early Modern city center and pleasant surroundings made it an attractive destination for tourists, whose patronage provided a source of income for artists. Although the Bavarian monarchy had been made politically obsolete by German unification, it continued to promote Munich as a center of the arts.[15] A confident and politically liberal bourgeoisie set a tone of tolerance that made life relatively comfortable for the unconventional, who gathered in the Schwabing district. The intellectual and artistic avant-garde ran the gamut from starving artists and penniless émigrés to bourgeois bohemians. Its numerous art schools attracted adventurous young women. Theatrical performances, cafes and salons, and literary and satirical journals flourished as sites of cultural and political cross-fertilization.[16] Manifestoes and debates reached a broader public audience through evenings of speeches and performances.

Female emancipation and its implications were hot topics of debate and activism in the countercultural milieu. Independent young women, especially writers and artists, experimented with freer sexual relations with their peers.[17] The "Woman Question" resonated in bohemian Munich as part of a general rethinking of social norms and relations. The "modern" thinking of Darwin and Nietzsche put sexuality and the erotic in "civilized" life at the center of this social reinvention.[18] For a brief period, new women explored these questions together with bohemians of both sexes.

Reevaluating sexuality was central to intellectual bohemians' savage criticism of complacent bourgeois culture and to their practice of utopian alternatives. Frank Wedekind and Oskar Panizza, prominent theatrical innovators, used sexuality to attack state, church, and bourgeois society.[19] A primarily male group around poet Stefan George dedicated themselves to theorizing and living out the erotic. Influenced by J. J. Bachofen's ideas about matriarchal antiquity, the *Enormen* (great), as they called themselves, planned a pagan colony and "saw in the Munich festivals and their private parties the reappearance of the age of Dionysis."[20] The outstanding female among the *Enormen* was Franziska zu Reventlow, a lifelong bohemian refugee from her strict aristocratic upbringing. Although Reventlow's novels and diary supply uniquely detailed observations on the Munich scene, she was and is more notorious as the "pagan Madonna" who combined bohemian promiscuity with single motherhood.[21] Like Wedekind and Reventlow, Goudstikker's eccentric persona evoked outrage and delight among observers of the colorful Munich scene.

As young women, Sophia Goudstikker (1865–1924) and Anita Augspurg chose Munich as the city most open to a business enterprise run by two women and moved there in 1888. They planned to open a photography studio to support the independent life they wanted to live together.[22] The women were drawn together by their inability to bear the constraints of heterosexual domesticity each had experienced in her family home. For Goudstikker, this involved difficult family circumstances, while Augspurg felt stifled by the narrowness and lack of stimulation in provincial life.[23] In 1886, Augspurg was temporarily living with her sister in Dresden. There she encountered Goudstikker, who was a student at the art school operated by Augspurg's sister.

Once settled in Munich, the couple won notoriety in the Munich scene, where Wolzogen observed them prior to refashioning them as characters for *The Third Sex*. "I stood apart in [the feminist meetings in which Augspurg spoke] as always as a smiling observer and captured these magnificent examples of women's rights campaigners for my collection of models," he recalled, "in order to present them all—idealized, touched up, or caricatured as it suited me—humorously and satirically decked out in masquerade for my readers in my farewell to Munich, *The Third Sex*."[24]

As their photography business grew, Augspurg and Goudstikker became active feminists. Augspurg had connections to two organizations that came into being in 1889 and 1890: German Women for Reform, which agitated for the opening of university study to women, and the Modern Life Society, founded by writers and intellectuals who sought to advance modern trends in the arts and social life. Although its key figures were men, police reports confirm that a handful of women also attended its meetings.[25] Gabriele Reuter remembered the Modern Life Society's inaugural event in her memoirs. As a young writer, Reuter wanted to be at the cutting edge of cultural life, although her companion was nervous about being seen in such a disreputable place. Reuter remembered identifying the local celebrities who were on hand, including "a couple of female figures with beautiful expressive boyish heads whose clothing had a masculine cut: the feminist Anita Augspurg and Sophia Goudstikker, the high-spirited owner of the Atelier Elvira for artistic photography." As the evening progressed, the atmosphere became more and more raucous, the speeches more militant, until they reached a climax in satirical verses attacking the Munich establishment. Amidst the chaos in the hall, "both of the handsome female boyish heads . . . hissed like rattlesnakes."[26]

Because the police suspected the Modern Life Society of atheism, immorality, and socialism and German Women for Reform of violating the ban on women's political meetings, they kept both organizations under surveillance. Augspurg was scheduled to speak at the fourth meeting of the Modern Life Society, but the police report notes that her speech was cancelled due to "indisposition."[27] When Augspurg speeches headlined evenings devoted to feminist agitation, Goudstikker had to convince the police that these were not political or local in character but merely gatherings of the Munich members of a national organization. At one, Augspurg read aloud from John Stuart Mill to an audience that included members of the Modern Life Society. After Augspurg founded a branch of the feminist Reform organization, Rainer Maria Rilke, Wolzogen, Reuter, and other influential writers attended their public events. These were notable because "Ilka [sic] Freudenberg and Anita Augspurg gave fiery speeches against the tyranny of men."[28] The Munich crossover between the avant-garde and feminism was unique; most middle-class feminists met in an atmosphere of respectability and political moderation.

The feverish activity of the public feminist milieu in Munich is reproduced and satirized in Bülow's story, "Just Let Me Forget," and in The Third Sex. As Carol Diethe has noted, the intellectual climate in Munich was particularly open to consideration of the New Woman, despite the ubiquitous ridicule the figure received in the work of male authors and publications. Unlike Germans in general, "hardly anyone who belonged to the vanguard of Munich's artistic life at the turn of the century could avoid taking a position on [women's emancipation]."[29]

For both Augspurg and Goudstikker, the end of the relationship to each other and the beginning of new partnerships in the course of the 1890s seem to have meant a certain mellowing and settling down in their private and political lives. While Augspurg's demands for absolute legal equality kept her within the radical wing of the movement, she was quite conventional in her views on sexual matters. Goudstikker and her new partner Ika Freudenberg turned their feminist activism from political agitation toward practical support for individual women. The Reform group had been reorganized as the Society for Women's Interests, a name under which it still operates in Munich. In 1898, the organization opened a Legal Protection Office. Goudstikker became the first woman in Germany to win permission to represent cases in the youth courts, where a law degree was not required, and led the Society's Legal Office until shortly before her death. Gertrud Bäumer, the leading moderate German feminist and an intimate friend of Freudenberg, described Goudstikker's legal work in her memoir. "Sophia Goudstikker handled hundreds of cases, completely self-taught, but with as much natural talent for defense as for the popular touch," she wrote. "In this capacity, she was a popular figure among the populace of Munich, feared by fathers of children born out of wedlock . . . and a protective figure for abandoned girls and tormented wives."[30]

Augspurg's and Goudstikker's activism focused on liberal emancipation—equality before the law, access to education, professions, and public influence. But in the movement as a whole, these formal concerns were being eclipsed by the growing importance of sexual issues—prostitution, venereal disease, and contraception. What was most at stake for German feminists was women's position within heterosexuality—the relationship between husband and wife, security of children, preventing sexual abuse, and the fate of women who had no opportunity to marry. In the nineteenth century, these issues brought feminists together; in the period before World War I they caused factionalization.[31] Housewives and religious organizations insisted on women's purity and family roles as central to women's interests. A split occurred between these groups and the "abolitionists" who wanted to end state regulation of prostitution. The abolitionist wing split again, as a small group around Helene Stöcker began to affirm women's sexual desire as a fundamental aspect of the female personality, focusing on support for unmarried mothers. The majority held to bourgeois notions of sexual purity and innocence and believed that male sexuality had to be reformed. During the 1890s, disagreements about sexual reform had not yet crystallized into these angrily opposed camps.[32] As sexual issues became more central to feminist identities, the abolitionists' rhetorical equation of men with destructive sexual desire and the radicals' focus on heterosexuality and motherhood made it increasingly hard for feminists to accept masculine mimicry as a critical strategy.

It is telling that the few written sources directly describing the historical Goudstikker—mainly women's movement periodicals and obituaries—make no mention of her masculine persona. One obituary however, characterized the force of her personality, suggesting masculine dominance: "Magic emanated from her, which, with and without her wishing it, subjugated people. She possessed a power of attraction, which created unconditional followers out of weaker natures; the self-willed [acquiesced] with more difficulty." The palpable charisma evoked by this tribute resonates with the power of attraction portrayed in the characters in Salomé's and Bülow's novels. The obituary continued, "All of her friends know of her ardent capacity to love, to lose herself in a beloved person, and seldom has a person possessed so many [friends] connected by such close ties."[33] This passage balances dominance with feminine loss of self in love of another. Even though it appears that Goudstikker no longer performed masculinity later in life, the reference to ardent love suggests an unusual degree of intimacy and eroticism in her friendships. The neutral term *Mensch* for Goudstikker's beloved friends obscures the fact that, as far as we know, these relationships were exclusively with other women.

Salomé and Bülow were clearly among those under the spell of Goudstikker's enchantment. Their visit to Munich in 1897 was typical of their peripatetic lives. Extended visits and retreats, such as the one to Munich, enhanced multiple relationships, independence, and intellectual stimulation for both. Though active in debating social and psychological implications of women's emancipation, neither was involved in the organized women's movement. Following colonial novels that had won Bülow a popular following, she wrote fiction in the 1890s that reflected growing interest in the dilemmas of the New Woman.[34] Salomé's biographers gender Bülow as masculine in contrast to Salomé's girlishness (Fig. 2.2).[35] This polarity in gender style is the mirror image of a perceived asymmetry in their friendship, in which Bülow was the more dependent.[36]

Lou Andreas-Salomé was famous for her close relationships with Nietzsche and Freud and her love affair with Rilke, but she was also a formidable intellectual in her own right.[37] Biddy Martin identified Salomé's major theme in the exploration of "femininity and feminine subjectivity as the fluid interaction of conflictual drives—the impulse toward self-assertion or individuation on the one hand and toward erotic submission and dissolution on the other."[38] For Salomé, an individual's confrontation with the demands and dangers of self-development was situated in interaction between the sexes, in the negotiation of autonomy and desire in heterosexual relationships. Women, more able to experience both autonomy and submission, were thus the more complete and complicated of the two sexes.[39] Male characters fascinated by women unable to fit into conventional social roles often served as narrator figures in her fiction. Her stories' unresolved endings reflected her philosophy that "the relationship of feminine and masculine was a conflict at the heart of culture and subjectivity, not a problem to be solved."[40]

Fig. 2.2. Photograph of Frieda von Bülow and Lou Andreas-Salomé. Reproduced with permission of Lou Andreas-Salomé Archiv, Göttingen.

Since biographers have speculated on the relationship between Salomé's writing and her personal sexual history, her biography is yet another narrative of a new woman's confrontation with sexuality in the 1890s. Salomé's marriage was platonic; she spent time with her many lovers, sexual or not, during her travels. Rudolph Binion reconstructed Salomé's sexual history from her diaries and notebooks. He concluded that, for a long time, she maintained her autonomy by rebuffing sexual pressures from men with whom she carried on love affairs. Binion claimed she finally entered into a physical relationship with Friedrich Pineles in the winter of 1896 in Vienna. Her choice of significantly younger lovers perhaps protected her independence.[41] If Binion was correct, Salomé's active sexual life had begun just more than a year before her encounter with Goudstikker. Whether or not Binion's sexual speculations were accurate, Salomé's apparent equation of sexual relationships with dependency reveals the careful compromises and considerations sexual activity entailed even for very independent women of her generation.

In reading the fictionalized versions of Goudstikker, it is important to keep in mind that these impressions stem from a particular period in the political, literary, and philosophical discussions about the new possibilities for women. In 1897, Goudstikker was thirty-two years old, the veteran of ten years of running a successful business, no longer living with Augspurg, her first partner, and not yet living together with Ika Freudenberg. Goudstikker was conferring with August Endell on plans for the *Jugendstil* atelier building (Fig. 2.3). Personal observation of her new style of living out the vision of the New Woman likely inspired Bülow and Salomé's fictions, created soon after this encounter.

Female Masculinity, c. 1897

The claim that Goudstikker performed a stylized masculinity and was subsequently represented as masculine requires some specification of the signs and gestures that constituted masculinity in a woman at the turn of the century.

Fig. 2.3. Hof-Atelier Elvira building, Munich. From *Die dekorative Kunst,* Jg. 2, 1900.

Unfortunately, there exists no photograph or detailed description of Gouds-tikker that matches the portrayals in the novels. If historical evidence shows no sign of the singular and irritating masculinity of the literary characters, what is the basis for supposing that the characters are based on or inspired by Goudstikker? Correspondences among the texts suggest a single model, fictionalized for different purposes. Sabine Streiter, presumably on the strength of her reading of the letters and diaries of Bülow and Salomé, explicitly connected all three fictional characters to Goudstikker, especially the "temperament, appearance, and behavior."[42] The intensity of the encounter for Salomé is mentioned by all of her biographers.[43] My analysis assumes that the three stories base at least some of the characteristics exhibited by the masculine female character on observations of Goudstikker either in or around 1897. The similarity of the three descriptions suggests that Goudstikker appeared in public in this guise, because Wolzogen would only have encountered her outside domestic space. However, Goudstikker's absence from retrospective descriptions of the Munich scene—and lack of attention to her masculinity where she is remembered—suggests that the exaggerated masculinity was perhaps a short-term experiment in self-presentation.

A sense of Goudstikker's physical presence can be taken from photographs made at Elvira. Two, dating from around 1894, that picture five leading feminists of the radical wing: Anita Augspurg, Marie Stritt, Lily von Gizycki, Minna Cauer, and Sophia Goudstikker.[44] The photographs are posed to capture moments of playful conspiracy. In one, all five women hold pencils to their chins in the pose of intrepid journalists (Fig. 2.4). The pose enacts a masculine professional identity as it simultaneously foregrounds their identities as writing women.[45] Their facial expressions range from mock seriousness to open amusement. Only Augspurg wears a jacket and tie that can be coded as masculine. Goudstikker's and Augspurg's short haircuts do clearly stand out and read as masculine in comparison to the other three with their long upswept hair and decorative hats and veils. The gender contrast is even stronger in the second, less staged photo. In it, Goudstikker smirks puckishly at the camera. Her boldness creates a masculine impression, although her long dress prevents gender confusion.[46] In other photographs, Goudstikker's short hair is the consistent "boyish" feature, while she wears simple but conventional women's clothing. Photos commemorating Elvira's twentieth anniversary are a notable exception. Here, Goudstikker wears a ruffled white dress and poses regally as she receives homage from her admiring staff (Fig. 2.5).[47] The delicate tracery of the studio's *Jugendstil* interior echoes the femininity of Goudstikker's attire.

Fig. 2.4. Photograph of five feminists: (left to right) Anita Augspurg, Marie Stritt, Lily von Gizycki, Minna Cauer, and Sophia Goudstikker. Photograph by Sophia Goudstikker, 1896. Reproduced with permission of ullstein bild/The Granger Collection, New York.

Fig. 2.5. Sophia Goudstikker on the staircase of Hof-Atelier Elvira, twentieth anniversary, 1908. Reproduced with permission of Münchner Stadtmuseum, Sammlung Fotographie, Munich.

Elvira's curves contrast severely with descriptions of the characters' intimate living spaces in Salomé's and Bülow's stories. Repetition of detail here too suggests a model in Goudstikker's actual living quarters. The character Hans in Salomé's "Mädchenreigen" is introduced through overdetermined signs of masculinity glimpsed through the door of the space she inhabits: an animal-skin rug, smoking paraphernalia and a riding whip, a single comb for daily grooming, and photographs of beautiful young women. Hans's entrance, seen through the eyes of a workman, generates surprise through incongruous female possession of masculine space.

The workman easily recognizes Hans as a girl despite her masculine attire consisting of a "bicycling outfit with its short pants," "small cap," and "hair cut short."[48] In a later scene, the figure of Hans gradually emerges from the evening shadows. The narrator first observes only a glowing cigarette end, then "girl's legs" in long black stockings, finally the whole figure: "a slim, dark girl in a boyish costume."[49] In both scenes, Salomé plays with gendered expectations. The room and the cigarette metonymically suggest a male presence. The lone figure sitting in the shadows smoking and exchanging glances with a girl must as surely be as masculine as the inhabitant of the room. Delayed revelation of the figure's sex produces delight, confusion, and dismay, artfully challenging the reader's gender expectations.

Bülow's version of the character, Senta, is one of two main characters in the story "Just Let Me Forget," discussed in the Introduction. Readers first see Bülow's masculine character through men's perceptions in a social setting that throws the masculine woman into relief against the normal performance of gender. The reader encounters Senta as she bursts into a cozy domestic scene wearing "Russian kneepants, leggings, and a Russian blouse," carrying a riding whip, and wearing a "workman's cap" on "hair cut short." Seen through the disapproving eyes of her friend's cousin Edmund, Senta "greets the guests *in corpore* by touching her whip to her cap."[50] Later, Edmund describes a second similar occasion of Senta's disordering of domestic space: "She made noise and smoked and sat straddling her chair and finally performed some gymnastic stunts for us."[51]

When Senta becomes aware of her heterosexual interest in Edmund, her masculine style begins to disintegrate. The love between Senta and Edmund is introduced in conjunction with a story of a drowning. This tragedy has no other significance to the plot and thus works as a displaced image of the violence of Senta's accommodation to the heterosexual order.[52] The death is equivalent to the death of Senta's masculinity. A comment on how quickly the body has been made invisible is an accurate prefiguring of the disappearance of Senta's masculine body.[53] A few weeks later, Senta's altered appearance matches her inner transformation: "Senta's short hair had grown out a little bit and fell in soft, dark ringlets over her forehead. The pale yellow woolen dress she wore brought out beautifully the ivory tone in her skin."[54] Senta's room—like Hans's decorated with "photographs of attractive women," "animal skins, antlers, and weapons," "a bearskin rug, and a table outfitted for smoking"—now serves as ironic contrast to her appearance, almost as an outer skin she is shedding.[55]

At first Salomé's and Bülow's stories incorporate both the political and critical aspects of female masculinity. The feminist woman acts out her claim on male privilege. She also captures the pleasurable aspect—the viewer's enjoyment of surprise and spectacle in contemplating the cross-dressed body. When the characters relinquish their masculinity, the process is accompanied by images of death, pain, illness, and embarrassment.[56] Even though, as the analysis below demonstrates, both women authors redeemed their odd characters for heterosexual love, on some level they registered the loss of the richness and playfulness that was part of New Women's masculine styles.

Female Masculinity in the Heterosexual Plot

As we meet Box, Hans, and Senta, each is professionally successful and proud of her independence. Each interprets submission to love as a loss of self. In the course of each story though, these perspectives are transformed by an improbable romance. European middle-class lives in the nineteenth century had largely been regulated in conformity with a heterosexual plot reiterated in novels. The meaning and purpose of life derived from the awakening to love and the founding of a new household and a new generation.[57] Genre tradition compelled writers to follow this pattern in order to create coherent narratives. The expected melodramatic happy ending shaped the novels' portrayals of the masculine woman's emotional life and potential for social integration.

Frieda von Bülow's "Just Let Me Forget" complicates and intensifies the significance of its heterosexual plot by subordinating the story of Senta to a main narrative told from the perspective of her friend Gunhild.[58] Although Gundhild's happiness has been ruined by an unsuccessful love, she is determined to awaken Senta to the power of romance. This project is nearly hopeless because Senta's masculine characteristics so irritate the men in the story. Senta, in turn, uses her outspoken feminism to challenge Gunhild's hopeless heterosexual passion. She chides Gunhild, reminding her of how heterosexual relationships restrict women. Gunhild, stung by the criticism, replies, "You know that I don't share your infatuation with the bizarre.

Since I am a woman, I want to be a proper normal woman. Abnormalities belong in formaldehyde." In response to the accusations of being bizarre and abnormal, Senta compares women's love obsession to the over-fattened livers of "Strasbourg geese." The aim of attracting men has blinded them to "what they might have been able to be." Women must "look for the center of [their] being in [them]selves."[59] Senta rejects heterosexual love because it holds back women's full emancipation. The novel's love stories test Senta's and Gunhild's philosophical positions. Ironically, Gunhild's choice preserves her independence, while Senta tones down her separatism and masculine mimicry in order to reenter heterosexual normality.

Gunhild tries to set up a match between Senta and her cousin Edmund, a doctor. Each time Edmund expresses his irritation over what he diagnoses as Senta's hysteria, Gunhild counters with her privileged insight into Senta's hidden erotic character. Gunhild uses figures from courtly love to explain that Senta "needs to be conquered." Men "no longer drive themselves to ride up icy mountainsides to win a coy lady," she complained, begging Edmund to take on the "mission" of saving "this poor soul from herself."[60] Gunhild's focus on Senta's love life is a displacement of a repressed wish that her lost love had persisted in his pursuit of her. Gunhild's fairy tale mode inadvertently reveals its fantastical and anachronistic mismatch as a solution to the dilemmas of the new woman.[61]

When Senta and Edmund fall in love near the end of the story, Senta is put into a new domestic configuration. Injured while rescuing an old man, she becomes Edmund's patient. Suddenly, she begins to defer to his expertise. More surprisingly, she now takes Edmund's professional diagnoses of the female psyche seriously, apparently seeing her previous masculine behavior as hysterical. She alters her demeanor to fit feminine norms as they were then naturalized in medical discourse. Although Edmund has come across earlier in the novel as a buffoon and blowhard, in this scene he heals Senta psychologically as well as physically. Senta's earlier reversal of the gendered hierarchy of authority is undone through her sudden experience of heterosexual love for Edmund. Her previous flirtations with women friends give way to looking "dreamily up at the doctor . . . as if to say, 'I'm suffering from myself and no one can help me. Just keep on caring for me a little bit. I will love you too, since I can love well.'"[62]

Gunhild's matchmaking has mediated the incompatibility between the New Woman and the traditional man by excising female masculinity. Senta retains her professional competence, her passionate nature, and her personal sparkle and flair at the price of compromising her absolute autonomy, her critical feminism, and her masculine mimicry. The budding romance between

Edmund and Senta reassures readers that a happy heterosexual outcome is possible for the New Woman.

However, the very improbability of the outcome suggests a second reading by altering the meaning of the love triangle between the three characters.[63] Gunhild uses the matchmaking to engineer for herself a secure social space as an intimate of the couple. In the final scene Gunhild imagines Senta's feelings. In them, she puts second-person verbs and pronouns in the plural. The plea, "just hold on to a little love for me—I want to love you (both) too," seems ambiguously addressed to both cousins. The tie between Edmund and Senta guarantees that Gunhild will continue her intimacy with Senta.

Falling in love with a male suitor also transforms Hans in Salomé's "Mädchenreigen." The story is told from the point of view of the suitor, multiplying the possibilities for identification and desire.[64] Alex, the suitor/narrator also functions as a reality principle, ensuring that Hans will be interpreted through perceptions coded as "really" male. The story's subtle evocation of both male and female same-sex desire suggests that the story is a vehicle for trying out many differently gendered and configured erotic attractions.

Alex gradually realizes that he is attracted to the strange masculine girl he meets at a Munich hotel. When he finally kisses her near the end of the story, she is shaken to the core by the sudden revelation of the intensity and sweetness of passion for a man. As Alex kneels next to her chair, Hans reverses the ideas about women's independence she had forcefully argued, bursting out, "Stand up! You must not kneel. Never to me. I want to serve you in everything. I love you! . . . It seems to me now as if I had always been waiting just for you. To follow you alone, to look up to you alone." The very excessiveness of Hans's ecstasy in submission begins to disturb even Alex.

Forgetting that her androgyny was the source of his original attraction, Alex has not altered his conceptions of the femininity he expects of his future wife. Hans dreams of becoming Alex's devoted assistant in common work, subordinate but with an intellectual purpose. But Alex imagines himself as Pygmalion releasing her true femininity. He enthuses, "Like a beautiful butterfly you will slip out of your cocoon for me. We will also let your hair grow long again. Right? Oh look, what a pity that you've got such a boy's haircut and now I can't play with it." "Shall I tell you what is so beautiful about you?" he continues. "In all your apparent boyishness? That you don't know anything yet about feminine coquetry, but first receive and develop everything through love."[65] Gradually it dawns on both of them that they are talking past each other, that their conceptions of blissful sexual love are incompatible with their social and intellectual needs. Hans's discovery of the joy of submission in heterosexual passion has not completely transformed her. Instead of resolving her dilemma, the awakening has made her conscious of it. Her outsider status retains its critical edge, even as her essential drama becomes a psychological one, a necessary step toward mature selfhood.

The fictional masculine woman serves as an irritant in these narratives. The plots maintain universal sexual love between man and woman as gender destiny. Gender performance, on the other hand, is represented as ephemeral and fungible. Female masculinity is an easily corrected mistake, a misguided attempt to emancipate the self through mimicry of the other. The medicalization of gender, represented by Alex and Edmund as doctors who diagnose the masculine woman, supports the discovery of essential femininity beneath the masculine exterior. The parallel implication is that female masculinity as a reflection of inner essence would indeed be pathological. As in contemporary sexological theories, gender essence determines sexual desire. Feminist female masculinity is figured as something different: a delusion from which characters and elements in the story rescue the otherwise sympathetic figure. Feminist theorizing of the oppression embedded in heterosexual love is shown as unequal to the powerful emotions only possible within such love.[66] Each masculine woman character in the end recognizes the primacy of the gender binary even, as in Hans's case, at the cost of accepting loneliness or a marginal position in relationship to the heterosexual order.

Masculine Feminism?

In each of the three stories, characters point out to the masculine woman the contradiction of working toward women's emancipation by embodying masculine traits. Each author dissects and rejects dogmatic feminism by satirizing feminist organizations and same-sex socializing. At the same time, the stories probe the potentials of social relations between the masculine character and her feminist friends in semiprivate spaces of single-sex relaxation and enjoyment. In addition to the expected negative contrast between single-sex spaces and those encompassing mixed sociability, an edge of danger remains in the portrayal of spaces where female masculinity, feminist critique, and women's socializing come together outside male surveillance.

Ernst von Wolzogen's comic *The Third Sex* accomplishes this through ridicule from a normative masculine point of view. The novel is a full-blown roman à clef—a genre that implies collusion between author and readers in the reinterpretation of known historical figures.[67] Philosophical debates about the implications of changes in the sex-gender order take place in juxtaposition with comic action. Three female characters, sexually emancipated Lilly (based on Reventlow), medical student Claire, and masculine independent Box, form a typology of the third sex of the novel's title. The clumsy, masculine Box bears a nickname encoding a sly sexual reference. In German, "Box" might evoke the sport of boxing, a connection consistent with the character's brusque masculinity. But since Wolzogen was also fluent in English, "Box" might be read as an English translation of *"Büchse,"* a slang term for vagina.[68] The reduction of the masculine character to female anatomy is characteristic of the novel's jokes and tricks.

The novel's portrayal of feminists as mannish and unattractive sets the tone for subsequent similar comic representations.[69] One scene depicts the members of the Agitation Committee for the Evolution of the Feminine Psyche, a parody of Munich's Society for Women's Interests. In comparison with the lively debates and flirtations carried on in parallel scenes of mixed-sex dinner parties, the conversation among the women is dull; the guests seem a bit bored. The two leaders of the Agitation Committee, Babette Girl and Meta Echdeler, are described in terms that identify them as Anita Augspurg and Ika Freudenberg. Girl, "in a smooth black velvet dress that harmonized exactly with her fine, intelligent head and its bold aquiline nose," has a law degree and has "already achieved a meaningful reputation as one of the most eloquent and shrewd defenders of the modern emancipation efforts of her sex."[70] Meta Echdeler, president of the Committee, is "a stately slim figure, probably late thirties, poised, with a highly intelligent, yet pleasant facial expression. In contrast to the pert Hildegard Haider [Box] her being was thoroughly ladylike."[71] The dinner party scene brings the Goudstikker character together with characters representing her two intimate partners, yet it omits any hint of the couple relationships between them.

The party becomes more lively when Girl moderates a debate on the question of whether an independent woman should marry. As long as legal marriage entails the husband's guardianship, is it a betrayal of feminist principles to marry? The masculine feminists are the loudest opponents of marriage and heterosexual love. Frau Stummer declares, "Men can bring us down through free love just as well as through marriage if they want to . . . for the free woman even the freest love is not free enough, since love for us means oppression. But I don't see why a woman must always love a man." Since Stummer and her friend are represented as inseparable, they might be expected to suggest feminist same-sex love. Instead, Stummer continues, "Just love science, Fräulein de Fries, to serve it is an honor!" Stummer's companion, a student at Zurich, cries out, "Bravo! . . . I also love only science and flourish marvelously."[72] Just when women loving each other seems the logical alternative to oppression, the third-sex women, figured as unattractive, unsuccessful in marriage, and insensitive to love and desire, comically present scholarship as an object of desire.

Toward the end of the marriage debate, Box weighs in. "This silly sympathy for men is really the most damaging of the famous weaknesses of our sex," she argues. "Why do so many, even the finest and most intelligent women, let themselves be so miserably taken in?" She answers herself with a critique of courtship dynamics: "Precisely because men know so well how to arouse their sympathy. They all know remarkably well how to pour out such a sob story—they can't live without them, or they will go crazy or be morally depraved if women don't reach out to them as saving angels. Sickening comedy!" Here Box is the critical masculine woman; outside the gendered system of courtship, she critiques heterosexual masculinity from a disinterested position.

However, the rest of Box's speech neutralizes her critique. She concludes, "One of them should just try to talk to me that way. I'll give him a quick right and left."[73] Everyone laughs at the idea of a man courting Box. The comic image robs Box of her authority to expose the artificiality of the heterosexual courtship game because she is oblivious to her marginality in these matters. The plot later demonstrates her incompetence for the feminine role in romance through her clueless infatuation with a swindler. The threatening potential of the masculine woman—that she might play the masculine role more successfully than a man—is made invisible; Box's challenge is unmasked as ineffectual.

In the final scene of the novel, Box bypasses heterosexual love and secures her essential femininity by proclaiming her wish for a child. Her transformation is completed by betrayal of her former friends. "These terrible mannish women who dabble in academics and the arts and make a lot of noise about equality," the mannish woman now argues. "They actually ruin the business of true progress. Those are not at all new women, but rather abnormalities such as exist in all times." The authority of biology erases solidarity between the independent women characters.

Even though Box speaks the words, she is simply parroting the sexual philosophy of the character of Johannes Rau. He defines the "third sex" as women who refuse their heterosexual roles. Linking passion, sex, and heterosexuality, he assumes such women are naturally asexual. His view separates female masculinity from its erotic power and excises homoeroticism from single-sex spaces where the male object of female love and desire might be irrelevant. It is impossible to specify whether Wolzogen was aware—through applying sexological ideas, through gossip and rumor, or intuitively through observation—of the intimate relationships among some of the women in the feminist movement who were models for his characters. Assuming that his knowledge was sufficient to think in terms of sexual inversion, we must surmise that he either could not apply it to the respectable middle-class women of the Munich feminist movement or suppressed this interpretation, consciously or unconsciously, to solidify his philosophy of heterosexuality as the exclusive organizing principle of human society.

The absence of love, desire, and sensuality in Wolzogen's notion of the "third sex" might be read as a strategic denial meant to preserve men's erotic centrality, repressing the potential competition represented by a sexual masculine woman. The novel's intense focus on motherhood as an unlikely solution to the problem of restrictive Victorian morality guarantees that same-sex relationships cannot fulfill women's true desire. Although the novel satirizes feminists as members of the sterile third sex, the characters in the novel are not smeared through the suggestion of "homosexuality."[74]

It was not only Box whose masculinity was transformed in the course of the developing plot, though. As presented above, the masculine characters in the stories by Salomé and Bülow were awakened to the artificiality of their feminist detachment through falling in love with men. This striking similarity in the plots, clearly not taken from the life of the historical Goudstikker, has been read as a disavowal or displacement of the homosexuality present in the situation on which it was based.[75] These texts do dismiss the potentials of female same-sex eroticism. However, this was not censorship of what the authors understood as homosexuality. Instead, close reading of the complete stories shows them experimenting with the interrelationships between gender, sexuality, the erotic, and social relations. These were problems or questions that came up as the authors observed Goudstikker's self-presentation and relationships. Each of the novels could have discounted female masculinity by making the character's same-sex desire pathological or pitiable, as Frank Wedekind did with his character Gräfin Geschwitz, from roughly the same period.[76] Yet, perhaps motivated by their admiration and affection for the character's model, they instead redeem her for the eternal mysterious struggle between man and woman. Each story prefers to read female masculinity as a failed feminist strategy of claiming male privilege and power.

The Homoerotics of Female Masculinity

Despite their rhetorical dismissal of same-sex eroticism, all three novels do include scenes of intimacy and desire among the female characters. Wolzogen's female characters who are otherwise attached to male partners share moments of sensuality and intimacy with each other. Salomé's and Bülow's stories portray the masculine figure as an object of desire for a group of women or girls attracted to her unique blending of gender characteristics.

The sections of Salomé's story prior to Hans's transformation openly represent and address the erotic charge in same-sex attractions. The story's title, "Mädchenreigen," alludes to Arthur Schnitzler's 1896 play *Reigen*.[77] It attacked bourgeois sexual hypocrisy by linking characters from all levels of Viennese society in a continuous chain of sexual relationships and encounters. For readers familiar with the Schnitzler play, Salomé's title might evoke sexual relationships among girls in ironic contrast to the manifest innocence of the image of girls performing a folk dance, the literal meaning of the term.[78] The tension between these two types of female intimacy runs throughout the story.

Conversations between Alex and his friends establish the hotel setting as a market for potential romantic and sexual connections. The currency of this market—gazes, glances, gestures, and conversations—traces the beginnings of a *La Ronde*-like circuit among the groups of guests. Alex, flattered by his sycophantic friend Ferdinand, turns his gaze to a teenage "Madonna." She in turn exchanges glances and gestures with a mysterious figure in the shadows. When Alex discovers that this is the boyishly dressed girl from the room across the hall, he is fascinated, perhaps titillated, by the surprising short-circuit. The flirtation between the teenager and Hans "retained for him something peculiar and coquettish. Even now, as his little Madonna cast a farewell glance toward the glowing cigarette, she exuded feminine shyness and at the same time cunning."[79]

The following day, Alex observes Hans sitting in the hotel's courtyard "surrounded by several young girls." In addition to flirting with individuals Hans uses the erotic appeal of her masculine persona to attract girls as a group. "And now he . . . held court ceremoniously—or more accurately: He courted, since the young girls treated him just like a courtier."[80] By the next time Alex observes a covert meeting between Hans and the "Madonna," the dynamics have shifted; the teenager is no longer the fulcrum of the romantic triangle. Alex and the girl begin to vie for Hans's affections.

Alex questions Hans about her peculiar behavior. The two discuss the erotic problem for the New Woman in heterosexual couples. When Hans explains her goal as giving girls an alternative to men, Alex asks how love is different between two girls. Hans explains, "They live for each other. Specifically, one woman can become for another exactly the same ideal support and protection that she expects of the ostensibly superior man." Alex objects that if one woman plays the male role, then only the other can experience the feminine satisfaction of love. Hans is undeterred. Her "completely coherent theory" defines love as "the mystery of the full co-experience of whatever goes on in the other." Hans does not propose androgynous equality, arguing that one "woman must develop masculine strength for the sake of the other," enjoying the happiness of the other who "is allowed to feel soft, feminine and clinging." The masculine woman experiences feminine love "as if it happened to her, as if it *were* she." The absence of a male in the configuration allows both women to "see how much [they] can do."[81]

Hans's remarkable theory of homosexuality deals with sex obliquely through romantic love. The gender polarity of the female couple preserves the feminine pleasure in submission. The asymmetry of the emotional satisfaction she describes mirrors the butch-femme rules about sexual practice in some postwar American lesbian communities.[82] While this model in both cases enforces strict role delineation, it also relies on the assumption of basic similarity in the two partners. The commonality between the partners allows the active woman to know how to satisfy her beloved and how to co-experience her physical and emotional pleasure. For Hans this goes one step further and allows two women to bond so deeply that they almost become identical.

Romantic love and the sacrifice it demands remain hegemonic in Hans's conception. Same-sex romance undoes the de-eroticized subordination of the wife in nineteenth-century gender ideology. Because of men's need to treat women as ornaments and sex objects, Hans sees the same-sex option as more satisfying for both women. The feminine partner's experience becomes central; she is allowed to compel her partner to fulfill her deepest desires. As a fantasy, Hans's model balances social and erotic power to achieve a kind of equality in the relationship. Hans's theory assumes the essential femininity of biological women. The masculine role is a choice, and has social and erotic benefits that could be enjoyed by any woman. Although subordinating sexual acts to exalted romantic love, Hans's ideas demonstrate the intertwining of gender roles, erotic love, social partnership, and emancipation in the 1890s rethinking of sexuality.

Hans does not practice her theory in a couple, but rather in her multiple relationships with younger women, where the power valences are quite different. In another conversation with Alex, she explains this aspect of her theory. Alex, jealous of the attraction between Hans and the girl, asks, "Isn't it a kind of seduction you are carrying on? A seduction to secrecy?" Hans replies, "Well, yes. A seduction to everything good. Too bad that it has to be secret." "If you only knew how happy it made this little thing," she continues, "she literally looks up to me as to an ideal." When Alex accuses Hans of egotism, she explains that attention from a beloved and idealized figure is "just what we all long for so tremendously!" Acknowledging that

it would be "vain and childish" to attract young people for her own amusement and ego satisfaction, Hans claims to use a young person's infatuation
by guiding it in "a direction that newly encourages and stimulates such a
poor existence, perhaps even gives it a lasting greater foundation. A person
can do no more for another."[83]

This speech associates female emancipation with classical pedagogical
Eros. The theory of the erotic bond between a student and a charismatic
teacher was widely circulated among contemporary educational reformers.
Love for a teacher or leader of the same sex was thought to help the student
achieve gendered maturity. Pedagogical Eros was then closely connected with
instilling masculine strength and social authority in male youth, in reaction
to the perceived feminization of culture.[84] Despite the antifeminism of the
dominant form of the theory, echoes of it could be found among feminist
advocates for female teachers and leaders in female organizations.[85] The
pedagogical model makes Hans's masculine self-fashioning heroic rather
than humorously idiosyncratic or dangerously degenerate. The nobility of
Hans's goals enhances Alex's desire. He feels "that she stood far above him.
But also that he would gladly have taken her in his arms and kissed her,
this extraordinary child with the almost priestly thoughts."[86]

Nevertheless, Alex draws an ugly caricature of how an older Hans
might look. To prevent such a fate, he prescribes heterosexual desire as a
cure for the masculine woman: "She would have to acquire a taste. Acquire
a taste for us. Doesn't really matter how or who: purely as a cure."[87] Alex, a
doctor, doubles as the physician and the cure, reestablishing his priority as
a male in both registers.

At the end of the story, Alex's gendered vision has been altered and
enriched by Hans's ideas. In a fantasy, Alex "saw for the first time today the
alert eyes in such [girls'] faces with all the unclear and extraordinary thoughts
that might be in motion behind the white foreheads. And he thought about
Hans among them, he thought he could hear and understand what they
naively and optimistically dreamed of and longed for." The title image of
a "sweet and tender circle dance of girls" enchanted his imagination. They
formed a circle, "which in truth a man had never broken into. Then came
the man, real life, struggle, and resignation."[88] These mental images of Alex's
expressed Salomé's philosophy that amorphous, playful same-sex eroticism
does not allow for the full development of the person as does the necessary
struggle for adult sexuality that takes place between the genders.

But there was a marked elision in Alex's vision. The girls-in-a-circle
image removes the charismatic, masculine figure at the center of Hans's
court. The circle dance image places her as one like the others, erasing her

masculine difference. All of the girls in the dance are "sweet and tender." Hans's newly revealed feminine qualities are thus written back into the social circle that her masculinity had created. The heterosexual transformation in the story enforces a developmental hierarchy on women's sexuality and removes the threat of fascinating attractiveness exerted by the masculine woman. Female exclusivity and even innocent erotic play are contained within the male image of them. The metaphorical all-female circle superimposed on the heterosocial circle in the courtyard displaces the threatening triangles of the first half of the story.

Alex's attraction to Hans further contains the queer uncertainty about the gender of the object of desire. His desire for Hans grows as they interact with each other as two men. But for Hans's instantaneous gender transformation, their passionate kiss might seem to be an all-masculine affair. This alternative reading of Alex's desires suggests the broad erotic appeal of the masculine woman. Through gender ambiguity she appeals in a heterosexual guise to her own sex and in homosexual guise to the opposite sex. Or is it the reverse? The thrill of uncertainty about the effect of gender on desire adds to her fascination. Alex's contradictory insistence that Hans become a conventional woman is an unconvincing defense against the queer possibilities contained in the original erotic attraction between Hans and Alex.

Bülow's character Senta also "exerted a peculiar enchantment over women" in "Just Let Me Forget."[89] The women's club where her feminist friends gather is the setting for Senta's "ladies' man" persona. Making the rounds of the small groups, she "straddled a chair and paid court to the sportswomen in her role of page," then watched the billiard players, favoring the weaker player with her advice. Finally, she approached Gunhild's table, toasting her as "the best saved for last." Yet the erotic effect of these flirtations is dampened by Gunhild's disapproval. Watching Senta flatter the women, Gunhild thinks, "Senta loved women and was an enemy of men. At the same time, she wished passionately to be a man herself." In Gunhild's view, Senta modeled her behavior according to an idealized image of a young man. Like the sexologists, Gunhild made same-sex attraction part of gender inversion. Gunhild objected to the courting because it appealed to "all the feminine weaknesses" in the objects of her "flirting and flattering." Therefore, Senta's courtship of her friends was inconsistent with her hope for their emancipation.[90] To Gunhild, the underlying sex of the masculine figure made no difference in the dynamic it created. Even as readers of the story are led to imagine Senta as a figure of fascination and attraction, Gunhild's critique disenchants their desire.

A second Frieda von Bülow story inspired by Goudstikker interrogates the social consequences of women's emancipation. When it was written in 1899, Goudstikker and Freudenberg lived together in the new Atelier Elvira building. "She and He" is set in this new building; "she" is presumably another take on Goudstikker.[91] The story's theme is exposing conventional gender roles as socially constructed rather than biologically ordained.[92] The unnamed characters discuss how "she" as an emancipated woman could live in a relationship with "him." At the end of the story "she" asserts that a heterosexual relationship could work if the man would accept a subordinate household role. In light of the analysis above, this appears as another attempt by Bülow to imagine a heterosexual outcome for Goudstikker.

More significant is the discussion between the two characters about the potentials of women's same-sex relationships, perhaps based on Bülow's observations of Goudstikker's same-sex relationships. In response to his suggestion that she hire a housekeeper as a companion, she explains her fear of "too great an intimacy." She fears the stifling burden of doubled femininity in the expectation that she would "devote my brief hours of relaxation to her," while the companion would be constantly preoccupied with her comfort. This solicitousness would only be bearable if the couple loved each other. But in that case, "there would be such an exaggerated pampering of each other, such inseparability as one finds all too commonly among women. I consider that mental suffocation and protect myself against it."[93] Perhaps this doubling of emotion constitutes both the attraction and the danger in a female same-sex relationship for Bülow.

All of the female masculine characters combine features that were also conflated in sexological discourse: appropriation of masculine dress and behavior, feminism, and same-sex attraction. But the interpretation of those features within the stories is very different. They present gender nonconformity not as a consequence of congenital factors, but rather as a wrong-headed strategy for achieving emancipation. Plots and characters' commentary displace the erotic implications of the cross-dressing onto ideology, which the characters easily abandon in favor of "real" heterosexual love.

Female eroticism cannot motivate the plots of narratives that do not represent the subjectivity of the masculine woman. Same-sex desire is depicted as diffuse and secondary, then separated from the masculine woman, and finally overcome by the heterosexual resolution. These narrative devices are strategies for coping with an unconscious or incoherently perceived threat. What was so threatening about sexual love between women? For these writers, I do not believe the answer lies in fear of censorship, loss of sales, or damage to their personal reputations.[94] Although self-censorship cannot be discounted, a sensitively and artfully written treatment of the theme would be unlikely to qualify for official censorship. Other novels published in the same time period did depict women's or girls' love relationships in relatively open terms.[95] Rather, same-sex love was simply unthinkable as a parallel to heterosexual love. On the one hand, the term *homosexual* as a category of person was not yet in wide circulation. On the other hand, "sex" was thought through intercourse and reproduction. Even the Munich "pagans" used the "naturalness" of reproduction to justify freer expression of sexuality. Contemporary discourses overwhelmingly celebrated eroticism based on gender difference as nature's way of ensuring continued reproduction, interpreting women's sexual desire as motivated by the ultimate feminine desire for a child.

The Absent Presence of Sex

One conundrum of reading the stories in the context of Goudstikker's life is the striking absence of her coupled relationships. The literary characters combine female masculinity with diffuse eroticism; that is, same-sex erotic performances were directed at a group rather than occurring between a couple in love. What diffuse eroticism elides is exactly what Goudstikker's life suggests: the committed erotic intimacy (and likelihood of a sexual relationship) between women in a couple. To assume that Goudstikker's coupled relationships were sexual goes beyond what we can learn from the available sources. Yet surely what sets Goudstikker apart from other feminists is her (as the fictional texts portray it) performance of the male prerogatives that signal erotic interest in women. Assuming a masculine subject position entails an assumption of sexual subjectivity. The question to consider in this connection is not what happened between Goudstikker and other women but why the literary imagination could not represent same-sex lovers even in a discreet or veiled way. Perhaps it is female masculinity's very claim to an active sexual subjectivity that made representation impossible.

Judith Halberstam's discussion of the early-nineteenth-century British woman Anne Lister concludes that, during that earlier period at least, "sexual activity between women flourished in spaces where the masculine woman trespassed on male sexual privilege and created not a 'female world of love and ritual' but an exciting sexual landscape."[96] Halberstam's analysis of the erotic effect of female masculinity is useful in reading the erotic aspect of the Goudstikker characters. But this passage recreates the tendency in lesbian history to interpret the sexual practices of historical women either as romantic (probably sexless) friendship or as sparked by the sexual potency of the mannish invert. The overt masculinity of the fictional characters and their courtier performances suggests that Goudstikker could be an example that exposes the limitations of such a strict binary. Goudstikker's masculine mimicry suggests a more overt erotic and sexual component to her intimate relationships with women than might be expected of the many other female couples of the era. Yet this does not map easily onto complementary gender styles within a couple. Augspurg and Goudstikker were partners, though both were gendered masculine—the two women constantly represented in terms of sameness. But Freudenberg and Goudstikker were clearly coded as feminine and masculine respectively. In addition, as we will see, Freudenberg's shared erotic intimacy with Gertrud Bäumer seemed based on a shared femininity.

The performance of gallantry toward women depicted by Salomé and Bülow—and it is likely that Goudstikker acted in the same flirtatious manner in her relations with them—suggests yet another mode of same-sex eroticism practiced in the Goudstikker social circle. The multiple relationships of some feminists also suggest that romantic friendships and gender-differentiated couples existed in different registers at the same time for the same people. The different styles of eroticism—with the lovers similar or different, eroticism sublimated or consummated, coupled or diffuse—should not necessarily be associated with radically different social groups and historical moments. Here, different people within the same group or the same person at different times and with different objects of desire seem able to draw on a number of erotic styles which were in flux at particularly this moment. A more subtle reading of female masculinity in the stories calls for putting erotic relations between women into more specific historical contexts of the 1890s: couples within the German women's movement, discourses and performances of the erotic in Munich, and women's sexual socialization in general.

This diffuse erotic excitement portrayed by Salomé and Bülow captures an important dynamic in the women's movement. Margit Göttert has very convincingly demonstrated and interpreted a pattern of erotically inflected leader/follower dynamics that characterized the women's movement in Germany from the 1860s to the 1930s.[97] Eroticism diffused across friendships also enabled the students in Zurich to achieve a measure of emancipation and independence in shaping their own life trajectories.

Additional dimensions of Goudstikker's relationship with Freudenberg can be recovered from the letters of Gertrud Bäumer. Freudenberg apparently was involved in intimate partnerships with Bäumer and Goudstikker simultaneously, while Bäumer's partnership with Helene Lange, the leader of the bourgeois women's movement, was very public. Bäumer's correspondence documents a network of intense intimacy that paralleled the practical work of the women's movement.[98] After becoming acquainted at a feminist gathering in 1905, Freudenberg and Bäumer spent several weeks of each year together, either in Munich or traveling. Margit Göttert has argued that, for Bäumer the precious fun and relaxation in this relationship was a relief from the strain of a life regulated by the demands of the movement.[99] Bäumer also enjoyed the freer atmosphere and connections to bohemian life that Munich offered in contrast to the constant discipline demanded by her position and relationship to Lange in Berlin.

Bäumer's letters reveal the emotional dynamics among the four women. She was critical of the way Goudstikker treated Freudenberg, feeling that Goudstikker lacked "love that from its depth is able to turn into 'charity.' " Instead of the generosity Bäumer felt Freudenberg needed, Goudstikker exaggerated emotions and was jealous of Freudenberg's other supportive friends. As a result, "Ika is always more given over to taking care of her than being sheltered by her."[100] By 1910 the tension made it difficult for Bäumer to visit Munich at all: "I didn't go to Munich partly because of the falling out with Puck [Goudstikker]. . . . But perhaps the Eternal Feminine will triumph here too over the 'situation,' and I'll still go despite all the good intentions so emphatically approved of by H. L."[101] Another letter described Lange's irritation over the "Munich insanity," as she called Bäumer's visits to Munich.[102] Clearly, both Goudstikker and Lange were jealous of the intimacy between their partners.

Göttert also provides evidence that some friends recognized Bäumer and Freudenberg as a couple, despite their preexisting living-together partnerships with other women known for their strong personalities. The letters quoted by Göttert suggest that Bäumer and Freudenberg enjoyed a kind of playfulness expressed through a same-sex eroticism based on their shared femininity, in contrast to what they perceived as the demands that their more masculine partners made of them. After Freudenberg's death, Bäumer received a letter from the prominent politician and leader of the liberal Protestant movement Friedrich Naumann. Naumann asked, "Was Ika the man, so to speak, in your union? . . . Apparently she was strongly feminine in her inner life, feminine in the good old eternal sense."[103] That Naumann could unselfconsciously ask about the gender roles in a female partnership and that Bäumer, a conservative on sexual issues, could publish the letter as late as 1933 indicates that, whatever their erotic content, educated people did not consider female partnerships between respectable women sexually suspect.

The sexually notorious Franziska von Reventlow presents the radical opposite of the discreet eroticism that protected feminists' respectability.

Reventlow lived out her self-achieved emancipation as publicly visible sexual freedom. Unlike Bülow, Salomé, or Stöcker, she did not confine her sex life to great loves, but had many casual and serious affairs going simultaneously. Sometimes her diary recorded two or three trysts per day. She also practiced prostitution when in need of ready cash.[104] Her scandalous fame—and the enmity between her and the feminist movement—continued past her death. Marianne Weber classified her as degenerate: "When free love ends in indiscriminately seized sensual-erotic adventures and the resulting cash payment is described as a respectable solution, it means that the unbridled lust for life has destroyed . . . the true power of love and the soul of the woman along with it."[105]

Reventlow was the one female writer to link feminists to "lesbian love." She was likely familiar with English Hellenism and the French decadent art movement from her association with the George circle and its neo-paganism. Her sarcastic 1899 report that a feminist conference had voted on the question of whether men should be allowed to enjoy sex insinuated that feminists' lesbianism motivated the vote. "My God, it doesn't occur to us to 'condemn' lesbian love. The condemnatory standpoint is really antiquated to us modern pagans," she claimed. Referring to the contemporary decadent works of Pierre Louÿs, she called same-sex female eroticism "charming" and an "elegant vice." In contrast, "the Viragines [respectable feminists] of our day with their men's vests and loden skirts" give no aesthetic or erotic pleasure. Citing Darwin, Reventlow declared feminist asceticism to be old-fashioned. "The Viragines . . . are mostly hermaphroditic spirits, which the healthy erotic spirit of the new paganism, whose victory we expect in the next century, will soon do away with."

Reventlow's essay illustrates the ways that romantic neo-paganism and the latest scientific knowledge could come together as a basis for opposing another modern phenomenon in turn-of-the-century discourses. But Renventlow's mobilization of homoeroticism in French literature as a counterpoint to the feminists subtly suggested that feminists embrace homoeroticism if they did not want to have sex with men. Elsewhere in the article she calls the feminist movement the "outspoken enemy of erotic culture, because it wants to masculinize women."[106] The masculinization she opposes clearly refers more to plainness in appearance and rationalization of behavior and social relations rather than the stylized masculine mimicry of the Goudstikker figure.

Reventlow was a star of Munich's Fasching costume parties and appears to have enjoyed the erotic thrill of impersonation. A 1907 letter describes an adventure in an Italian homosexual bar, when, dressed as a boy of that milieu, she accumulated three appointments, fifty francs, and an Englishman who possessively called her his boy.[107] Although this openness to homoeroticism and Reventlow's insistence on sexual freedom can be taken as signs of the beginnings of a broader trend toward sexual liberalization, it should be also noted that she did not argue on the liberal basis of personal choice. Along with other turn-of-the-century theorists of the erotic, she affirmed sexual desire as central to life by reinscribing gender essentialism and dismissing the value of women's formal emancipation. Though she later rejected the racialist and cultic elements of neo-paganism, Reventlow initially needed the ideological support of their theory of the erotic in order to complete her extreme break with bourgeois feminine sexual norms.

In judging women's and the feminist movement's difficulties in embracing sexual liberation, it is important not to forget or minimize the overdetermined burden of constraints they faced in rethinking the meaning of sex in their lives. In most young middle-class women's upbringing, church, school, and family combined to emphasize the shamefulness and danger of sexual pleasure. A strong binary of innocence and shamelessness, with the prostitute as the shameless figure, structured their mental maps of sexuality.[108] The costs of emotional shame and social vulnerability convinced most women to accept the wisdom of remaining virgins until marriage, or at least a solid love affair. They made sure their outward behavior betrayed no trace of the sensuality allocated to racial and class others, especially prostitutes.

Women in the Munich environment thoughtfully recognized that coming to terms with sexuality was a difficult and prolonged process for most young women. Ika Freudenberg expressed the insight that long-standing structures of thought and social organization would be difficult to overcome. After centuries of asceticism, "we see sin and wrong in the most vital foundations of our emotional lives, distancing them from the realm of everything we count as good and beautiful."[109] Lou Andreas-Salomé's essay *Erotik* argued that, for women, "in whom the sexual discipline of all the Christian centuries was enforced, at least for many social classes, independence from the naked necessity of the instinctual has become natural." In other words, contemporary women in Christian societies found abstinence more natural than the instinctual sex drive. Such repressed beings "must think it over three times—no, ten thousand times—before they grasp for themselves the fruit that has fallen almost effortlessly into their laps. . . . Many fewer generations are needed for deprivation than for acquisition."[110]

There is strong evidence that Bülow's, Salomé's, and Wolzogen's ideas about sexuality were greatly influenced by personal sexual awakening. For the women, sexual satisfaction was linked to a difficult and fraught decision to seek erotic experience outside bourgeois norms. Wolzogen, in contrast, witnessed a woman's orgasm during a sexual encounter (probably with a woman other than his wife) for the first time at the age of thirty-eight, thus acquiring a new view of women's sexual pleasure.[111] Their revelatory experiences of heterosexuality seem to have suggested to the authors that the lovable and sexy masculine woman they encountered needed rescuing from the dead end of romancing women so that she too could experience the transforming power of intercourse.[112] No matter what the realities of practice, the conceptual certainty of women's receptive erotic character made it inconceivable that sex between women could follow from the same erotic and physical need as intercourse.

The masculine woman had to be dealt with precisely because she performed dissonant elements that were not yet combined in a single legible stereotype. For contemporaries who observed her, Goudstikker fell between the stereotype of the perversely sexual mannish invert who seduced innocent women and the recognizable type of the respectable feminist (assumed asexual) female couple. The characters could not be represented as sexually desiring women because that particular cluster of markers, later legible as homosexual desire, was not yet readable in those terms, particularly to authors who were intensively focused on rethinking the terms of heterosexuality.

Sophia Goudstikker's independence, success in the business world, and social standing coincided fortuitously with a period of artistic and intellectual ferment that took sexuality as its central cause. In the dialectic between changes in the gender system and critical thought that interpreted and responded to different gender potentialities, new spaces opened up. But these were not coherent spaces with widely shared meanings. Intensive leaps out of traditional arrangements coexisted with longstanding assumptions and gaps in logic and consistency. This unevenness of gender change and gender theory shaped the emergence of both women's sexual subjectivity and lesbian identities. Men's greater freedom from family duty, financial dependence, sexual shame, and strict notions of socially acceptable behavior allowed them to engage the sexual dialectic and form (relatively) coherent identities and social groups, whether these were homosexual or freely active heterosexual, earlier in the nineteenth century. Men's encouragement often allowed the women involved with them to make the break with respectability in the course of a love affair; the women who acted this out publicly, such as Franziska von Reventlow, Lou Andreas-Salomé, and Helene Stöcker, were exceptionally strong-willed women. But the terms of this dialectic for a broader segment of middle-class women, at least in Germany, were just beginning to appear in the 1890s. Many, probably most, women had difficulty thinking of the erotic or sexual as a factor that could constitute personal identity. After the turn of the century the assertion of female homosexuality separate from "dirty obsessive habits" began to form along the models of both heterosexual free love and male homosexuality.

The establishment of women as desiring subjects and women's ability to occupy that position were long-term developments of Germany's twentieth century.[113] The diffusion of such ideas throughout the population proceeded slowly and fitfully along with the varying sexual politics of many state regimes and intellectual movements. It is not surprising that middle-class feminism developed on the whole in reaction to women's sexual liberation and that this question split the feminist movement at several points. For those women who chose to contest the conservative sexual positions of the bourgeois women's movement, the choices seemed to have been occupying a marginalized "radical" position within the movement or a disavowal of organized feminism in favor of acting out erotic liberation. This step of asserting female sexual subjectivity was also a necessary precursor to the emergence of homosexual identity in the following decade.

In addition to drawing conclusions about the significance of female masculinity for the development of homosexual and emancipated identities, this chapter puts forward a chronology of change in women's (homo)sexual subjectivity. Increasing emancipation from the family in the 1880s and 1890s, radical sexual theorizing by avant-garde writers, and a more demanding and active young feminist movement in the 1890s supplied the conditions that encouraged a few elite women to experiment with possibilities of women's sexuality. Homosexuality as a discourse and an identity could come into being subsequently in connection with new lives and bodily styles created by the cracks and splits in the sex-gender ideology. Only after 1900 is solid evidence of the theoretical category of the female homosexual and of women who adopted and shaped their lives according to the category available. Within this framework, Sophia Goudstikker's masculine mimicry in the second half of the 1890s was an early and isolated instance of a particular form of "feminism of the deed." Her performance was confusing and challenging for many who witnessed it. After the turn of the century, the discourse of homosexuality supplied coherence to feminist masculine mimicry that was simultaneously a semiotic claim to sexual subjectivity.

3

Asserting Sexual Subjectivity in Berlin

The Proliferation of a Public Discourse of Female Homosexuality, 1900–1912

"So you can't sleep either," she said. "I'm lying here and longing for you, as I have been longing for weeks—don't you feel it, you beautiful, sweet, marvelous woman?

And she laid her arms heavily around my neck—

Then she fell to her knees in front of me, kissed my feet, embraced my knees—

"Be mine, completely mine in unbounded tenderness—that's how I want to enjoy you."

And before I could recover from my astonishment, she lifted me with her strong arms and carried me over the threshold into my room.

She fell on me now with an urgent and ravenous tenderness. I couldn't defend myself against this right away, since I was completely unprepared for it.

Finally however, I succeeded in freeing myself from her.

Firmly but carefully, since I felt sorry for her, I took her in my arms—and led her back to her room and closed the door between us.

Then she understood me and knew that it wasn't Sapphic love that I wanted, that my feminine instincts were too complete and too healthy for that.

And we parted ways.

Because the New Woman wants purity at any price.[1]

This passage from Elisabeth Dauthendey's 1900 novel *The New Woman and Her Love* marks a radical departure from the veiled eroticism and absence of stigma characterizing descriptions of same-sex intimacy in the sources from the 1890s. This same-sex erotic scene drew a strict boundary between the figure of the New Woman and sexual activity between women. Dauthendey's recognition of the homosexual woman as a threat to the sexual innocence and normality of the New Woman is symptomatic of a significant shift in public discourse about sexuality in relation to "masculine" independent women who enjoy intimacy with other women. This turning point came right at the turn of the century.

All of a sudden, German publications explaining homosexuality to a general audience proliferated. In the 1890s the term *the third sex* referred to the New Woman. After the turn of the century, its use as a synonym for homosexual began to predominate. In both meanings the term provoked with its sense that the rigid binary of nineteenth-century gender roles could be complicated by a third term—a third that threatened the stability of male-female opposition. However much the existence of intimacy between people of the same sex might have aroused fear or disgust, its more significant role was to add new force to interpretations and critiques of the existing binary—an opening that was threatening to some and liberating to others. As the slippage from gender to sex indicates, writers and readers were becoming more aware of discourses about homosexuality and were beginning to think about their implications beyond psychiatry, where they had been developing since the 1860s. Although the debates of the next decade were rooted in nineteenth-century issues such as urbanization, women's emancipation, law reform, and criminology, a discursive figure called the homosexual woman now became clearly visible.

A crucial factor in changing public perceptions was the increasing activity of Magnus Hirschfeld's Scientific Humanitarian Committee (Wissenschaftliches humanitär-Komitee [WhK]).[2] In order to achieve their goal of repealing Paragraph 175 of the Criminal Code, which criminalized certain sexual acts between males, leaders of the WhK published several pamphlets meant to enlighten the public with the "scientific truth" about homosexuality. For example, in 1901 Hirschfeld published a pamphlet about homosexuality titled *What Should the People Know about the Third Sex?*[3] As might be expected, male homosexuality was central to the WHK propaganda campaign. Yet a tone of objective authority and claims that homosexuality was biologically natural and distributed equally across human populations meant that women were implicitly subsumed in these explanations.

The emerging problematic of female homosexuality was debated in four public sphere arenas between 1900 and World War I. Women, including some with a personal stake in the debates, made their voices heard in responses to sexological information, feminist sexual politics, scandal-mongering newspaper articles, and law reform proposals. These early debates bridge what has often been taken for granted as a caesura separating the female couples of the prewar era from the postwar mass movements.[4] The formation of semipublic female homosexual communities prior to the war was of crucial significance for the more visible movements of the 1920s.

The underlying issue in each of these public forums was the nature of female desire. European culture was built on female binaries—Madonna/whore, Christian wife/witch, republican mother/aristocratic wanton—that separated the evil desiring woman from the obedient and modest wife and mother. During the nineteenth century, biological theories of gender incorporated new variations on this theme—shameful/shameless, respectable/criminal—that attributed female desire to heredity and/or corruption. A woman could be a wife and mother without sexual desire, but to be a homosexual meant acknowledging one's essential sexual nature. As women began to place themselves gingerly on one side or the other of the homo/hetero divide, they contended uneasily with the cultural assumption that the sexual woman had to be immoral, selfish, uncontrolled, fickle, vain, degenerate, and possibly evil. As women broached the possibility of female homosexuality, they developed several different strategies for managing or disavowing the implications of desire.

Psychiatry had diagnosed homosexuality as a pathology characteristic of isolated perverts who required treatment. In the nineteenth century, this monstrous image was incompatible with the actual lives of middle-class women, even those who challenged gender norms. Twentieth-century discourse began to consider whether many of these apparently normal individuals might be living secret sex lives. It was not easy to merge all of the disparate stereotypes associated with female homosexuality into a single identity; experts and observers alike attributed contradictory characteristics to the figure. Lack of coherence in discourses allowed women who lived in same-sex environments to defend their close relationships as harmless.

"What the People Should Know": The New Common Sense of Homosexuality

Hirschfeld's 1896 publication *Sappho and Socrates* was followed by a steady stream of books and pamphlets meant to educate the public about the existence of homosexuality.[5] The Max Spohr Verlag, working closely with Hirschfeld and the WhK, published most of them.[6] These texts repeated a common set of messages: homosexuality was a natural variation; it could be understood best as a third sex between male and female; homosexuals were no more immoral or criminal than heterosexuals; prejudice against homosexuality ruined the lives of many otherwise valuable citizens. The texts effaced sexual subjectivity even as they claimed it. They conceptualized homosexuality as an inner drive that ruled both gender characteristics and object choice. Prominent claims that Socrates, Sappho, Plato, Michelangelo, and other historical figures were homosexual aimed to persuade readers that homosexuals tended to be intellectually and culturally gifted. Hirschfeld minimized the importance of physical sexual acts in homosexuals' lives and relationships in his emphasis on the social and cultural role they played outside the everyday reproductive order. He appealed to readers' pity by emphasizing the loneliness and despair, often leading to suicide, suffered by these victims of society. The quintessential Hirschfeldian homosexual devoted his time and energy to creative work, while his sexual desires, overemphasized by society, were a secondary (and harmless) aspect of his being.

As the title of *Sappho and Socrates* indicates, expert authors theorized that male and female homosexuality were mirror images of each other. In claiming that homosexuals were morally no different from heterosexuals, they implied that morality was also equivalent for both sexes. In 1901, the Spohr Verlag's scholarly journal *Yearbook for Sexual Intermediates* published two autobiographical pieces by women who discussed their same-sex loves and desires.[7] Anecdotal lay testimonies such as these often appeared alongside doctors' articles in the *Yearbook*. Neither author used terms such as *homosexual* or *invert* to describe themselves; instead, they referred to their "condition" or "the way I am." Sexological terms had yet to become common usage among those who identified with the "condition." Both authors emphasized the relief and self-insight they gained through reading about their condition in popular literature or in the works of sexologists. The biographies fit Hirschfeld's "third sex" notion very closely. Each author felt she had a masculine inner character consistent with her sexual feelings toward other women. For readers of the journal, these sketches provided a unique instance of women narrating their own lives and experiences, albeit in ways that confirmed the notions of the doctors and theorists with whom they shared the journal's pages.

A few years later, Hirschfeld published *Berlin's Third Sex* as part of the series *Big City Documents*.[8] The popular series engaged experts to explain aspects of the urban underworld for a lay audience.[9] Hirschfeld gave readers a lively tour of homosexuals' lives as he observed them in the city. As with most of Hirschfeld's work, *Berlin's Third Sex* was mainly about homosexual men, yet it also reported on a few female subcultures. Hirschfeld described a group of sophisticated female inverts that met afternoons in cafes and an annual women-only costume ball.[10] Readers also learned that about 20 percent of the prostitutes in Berlin were homosexual. He explained their elaborate system of gender-differentiated couples made up of a "father" and a "mother." The father enjoyed sexual freedom while the mother was expected to remain faithful. According to Hirschfeld, some of these prostitutes had wealthy women among their clients.[11] These piquant sociological observations often contradicted Hirschfeld's sober claims about homosexuals' cultural significance.

A second volume in the *Big City Document* series, *Tribadism in Berlin*, took up the subject of female homosexuality in more detail.[12] Wilhelm Hammer, its author, was a doctor in a facility for the incarceration of prostitutes infected with venereal disease. In the course of his work there, he had plenty of opportunity to examine and interview women in sexual relationships with other women. Having acquired this knowledge, he fashioned himself as an expert on the subject, observing and interviewing homosexual women in other situations.

Hammer treated his subjects as "cases" in need of the analysis and diagnosis of an authority. While Hirschfeld lumped all homosexuals into one "third sex" category, Hammer investigated the question, raised by earlier sexologists, of whether perversions were congenital or acquired. His categorization followed Krafft-Ebing's division of people into those with a lasting and seemingly congenital condition (perversion) and those who had sex with others of their sex in specific conditions (perversity). These were well-accepted and lasting categories among experts well aware of the situational homosexuality of sailors and prisoners. Many doctors also included a subcategory of the oversexed, individuals who engaged in same-sex relations along with other perversions for variety or an additional erotic charge. Doctors' anxieties focused especially on "normals" who had been seduced into homosexual habits.

Hammer applied these possibilities to his case studies, examining the women's genitals, collecting information on their family backgrounds and childhoods, and interviewing them about their attractions and sexual experiences, in order to sort them into the proper categories. The most striking recurring incidents shaping sexual subjectivities related in the case histories are social rather than biological, including abuse at home, very early first sexual experience, often linked to prostitution or adult seduction, and lack of alternatives for an independent life. Yet Hammer judged almost all of his cases as congenital homosexuals. He used specific Latinate terms, such as *"paradoxia homosexualis feminina monogamia uranica"* in his diagnoses.[13] While Hirschfeld tended to use "third sex," "uranian," and "homosexual" interchangeably, Hammer used "homosexual" for congenital cases, "uranism" for those who had sex exclusively with women, and "lesbian" for those who had sex with both sexes.[14]

Many of Hammer's subjects came from working-class or artisan families. The few life narratives of middle-class or wealthy women primarily recall their crushes on teachers. One of these was celibate, sublimating her sexual drive into art. The other was a professional editor with a strong sex drive and many lovers. Hammer diagnosed her as having a "deviant character" in addition to congenital homosexuality. Another woman, a factory worker, lived in a happy monogamous relationship with her lover. The remaining seven cases involved women working in the sex and entertainment industries. Their stories revealed the existence of networks of women who participated in a particular culture of same-sex attraction and partnership.

Hammer's case studies show that the father/mother roles Hirschfeld observed among prostitutes were fixed within a given relationship rather than defining an individual. At least some women described learning the roles while incarcerated. Women played one role in one relationship and another with a different partner. Most commonly, women were "mothers" in their first relationship, and then later became "fathers." There was little to suggest that roles were tied to physical appearance or style, although sometimes the "fathers" adopted a more masculine look. What made a partner the "father" was that she initiated the relationship. The "mother" could then accept or decline. In addition to the double standard mirroring heterosexual society, it was the "father's" privilege to use violence against "his mother" if she were suspected of infidelity. According to Hammer and at least one of the interviews, "mothers" also commonly worked as prostitutes for their "fathers."[15] These relationships expressed the reality of poor women's lives and resembled heterosexual relationships in the same milieu. But in the same-sex culture, women could aspire to gain power and privilege once they acquired the experience and confidence to act in the "father" role.[16] The masculine "father" offered protection, belonging, and desire to his "mother," while the feminine partner enhanced the status and self-esteem of her masculine lover. Power was understood as asymmetrical, but the couple together could survive and support one another in an uncertain existence.

Those in the mother-and-father culture usually found lovers among other women in similar circumstances—often waitresses or taxi dancers. Some had had sexual encounters with women or passionate nonsexual friendships with a friend beforehand. About an equal number of cases describe first relationships with women while institutionalized. The women lived their lives alternately between the street and the care home or hospital; both milieus offered fertile ground for forming same-sex love partnerships. Hammer's informants, not surprisingly, describe passionate love much differently from the middle-class women otherwise quoted in this chapter. A diary of one self-described father, remembering her first love affair, spoke of "indescribable delight . . . when two women, breast to breast, body to body, give themselves up to passionate lust."[17] Another part-time prostitute told Hammer about going to visit a friend after their shifts at the café where both worked. They had a "respectable dinner" together. Then the interviewee exclaimed, "I stayed there the whole night. Fourteen days I lived there. That was love, Dr. Hammer!"[18] Sexual love appears as the sole pleasure for women without skills or family support who could only afford an independent life by working the streets. Most of them told Hammer their goal was to get back to enjoying freedom together with their lovers.

Though Hammer's cases were heavily shaped by his role as diagnostician, they also contained excerpts from autobiographical essays, letters, and diaries given to him by inmates. Letters from both "mothers" and "fathers" contained extravagant expressions of love and devotion, often expressed in poetry. A "mother" wrote to her "father," "I am glad that you are at least honest enough to tell me right away that you are not able to break up with . . . [sic]. It's all the same to me; the main thing is that you don't flirt with someone else here inside. . . ." Addressing the "father" as "beloved boy," she continued, "It is my only wish that we will see each other again in golden freedom." She hoped her "sweet boy" would be able to do without the rival on the outside, since the writer was willing to "go out on the street" for her. She assured "him" that she would "never get involved with another woman in the queer way, except for you."[19] Letters like this suggest that incarcerated women were particularly keen to "belong" to someone who saw them as desirable and offered them security. Their life circumstances made achieving the idealized monogamous love partnership unlikely, adding to the intense jealously and possessiveness expressed in the letters.

Hammer found his subjects' homosexuality regrettable, but since most of them, in his judgment, were congenital inverts, he accepted their orientation as unchangeable. Judgmental as he was, Hammer also expressed affection and sympathy for the incarcerated sex workers. He recognized that their relationships had the same mix of "coarse sensual and refined feelings" and the same "scale of joy and pain" found in heterosexual relationships.[20]

The tendency he observed among female homosexuals that particularly bothered him was their attitude of superiority vis-à-vis heterosexuals. They often expressed disgust toward women and girls who "wasted their lives" on men.[21] These convictions led them to try to convince other women to join them in the culture of same-sex love. To Hammer, this was the great danger of female homosexuality. He advocated segregation in institutions to prevent it. He attributed these beliefs among educated middle-class women to "man-hating."[22] Hammer was one of the few who saw a threat in female homosexuality. He feared that feminist homosexuals "pressur[ed] weaker non-homosexual women into life positions they cannot lastingly fulfill." It was necessary above all to prevent such women from interfering with orderly middle-class marriages.[23]

Hammer's particular nemesis was Johanna Elberskirchen, whom he claimed was one of the dangerous feminist homosexuals. Elberskirchen was attuned to emancipation in her hometown of Bonn and became self-supporting at the age of twenty, working as a bookkeeper. By the time she was twenty-seven, she moved to Switzerland to begin medical studies. She did not have the funds to complete this degree or the legal studies she began later. She became a prolific writer on topics such as children's health, education, and violence against women, in addition to theorizing on sex and gender. At the time she wrote the books discussed here, she was back in Bonn living with a female partner. During World War I she moved to Berlin and worked in infant care, was active in Social Democratic causes, and opened a homeopathic practice. She supported feminist causes throughout her life, though her particular views meant that she was never a leader in any organization. Her views aligned best with those of the outspokenly antimale abolitionist group. She joined Hirschfeld's WhK and the World League for Sexual Reform, which sponsored her speaking engagements in the 1920s.[24]

Even thought Elberskirchen did not have a degree, she published several pamphlets on women and sexuality between 1896 and 1907, including *The Love of the Third Sex: Homosexuality, a Bisexual Variety, Not Degeneration, Not Sin*.[25] In these she argued from a scientific perspective, drawing heavily on Darwin and other evolutionary scientists. Although Elberskirchen did not explicitly identify herself as homosexual, she belonged to the WhK and explained and dignified homosexuality as a natural variation in human sexuality in her publications. Elberskirchen and Hammer attacked one another viciously in their works on the subject.

Elberskirchen differentiated between emancipation, a socially significant process, and homosexuality, a congenital condition of the individual. Homosexuality was simply irrelevant to the real problems with social life, which she believed urgently needed reform. She confronted Hammer's use of the word *homosexual* as a weapon to intimidate women who dared to challenge men's interpretations of sex and gender. "We won't be silent. We won't retreat," she declared. "For the woman . . . power and strength are characteristic without homosexuality, independent of sex, whether normal or abnormal."[26] Her polemics sidestepped the issue of her own sexual orientation, calling on gendered experience to lend authority to her critique.

Scholars interpreting lesbian history have long seen sexology as a source of antifeminist stigmatization of emancipated women.[27] In the case of Hammer's response to Elberskirchen's arguments, we have a clear instance of something that looks very like that. Yet to see this as a straightforward tactic of homosexual repression misses the larger issues in which homosexuality debates were embedded. Instead of concentrating on women as victims of powerful masculine authority, the discussion here focuses on the forms and methods with which a number of feminists advanced idiosyncratic theories of male sexual degeneration as a strategy for asserting female authority over sexuality.[28]

Like many feminists of the era, Elberskirchen was outraged by the apparent increase in prostitution and syphilis in the late nineteenth century. She criticized men and male sexuality as the source of these social evils in all her works, but especially in *What Has Man Made of Woman, Child, and Himself?* Hammer quoted some of her raging accusations against heterosexual men as proof of man hating within the women's movement, which he attributed to its invert element. Countering Elberskirchen's claim that the sex-gender system of the time was itself degenerate, Hammer declared, "The thriving women's movement, the fall in the number of marriages, declining fertility could all be causes, or simply symptoms of the decline of a people."[29] For Hammer, prostitutes and perverts were not threatening—they could be safely diagnosed and contained. But feminists who combined attraction to women with seductive theories obsessed with male abuse were the real threat.[30]

Hammer went beyond argument to bring Elberskirchen as an individual under his diagnostic gaze. He claimed that the "sexual hate" expressed in her book was the "discharge from same-sex dissatisfaction." Since the word translated as "discharge" is most commonly used in medical references to vaginal discharge, the metaphor of radical feminism as the disgusting symptom of a medical condition was clear.[31] The claim that feminists were insulted and bullied by doctors using the concept of homosexuality rings true in the hostility of the Hammer-Elberskirchen exchange. Hammer did explicitly use allegations of homosexuality to discredit a feminist's critique of men.[32] But such a direct personal attack was rare, at least in print sources.

Elberskirchen, one of the few women to join in the theoretical analysis of homosexuality, drew an extreme binary separating heterosexual love, with its brutal mistreatment of women, from homosexual love, which she described as "full of refinement and beauty and naturalness." Like other feminists of the era, she extolled the ideal, spiritual side of love in opposition to bodily sex and lust, which she coded as male and bestial. She theorized that homosexuals operated outside of the degraded dynamic of heterosexual sex. Therefore, as she saw it, "[the homosexual person] desires the soul, the 'human', the person. Where would be space and sense and longing for the subhuman, the bestial, the lusts and vices . . . ? The strong wings of his strong soul-love lift him high above all that and carry him with strong wingbeats far from the realm of darkness."[33] Using her expressive rhetoric to portray homosexual love as so spiritual, so eager to renounce everything common and mean in bodily love, that one kiss satisfied the homosexual's sensual longing, Elberskirchen was one of homosexuality's most enthusiastic female apologists. Her rejection of the physical replayed in especially florid language the stance taken by many women who found it very difficult to claim pleasure and desire as normal aspects of sexuality. In order to assert authority as a female she had to deny sensuality and desire for all homosexuals. As a result, she created a fantasy of homosexuality as the mirror opposite of her perception of heterosexuality.

The *Big City Documents* series included a volume by Ella Mensch, one of the writers discussed in the chapter on university students, that took a similar stand on women's sexuality. However, while Elberskirchen contrasted high-flown visions of feminist love with degraded sexuality, Mensch bitterly denounced feminists who had betrayed her vision of iron-willed conservative feminism. Her venom was directed toward authors who wrote frank novels and spoke out in favor of free love and women's right to sexual satisfaction. She also made a point of regretting the new genre of informational texts on homosexuality. She was dismayed that the topic had become a subject of fashionable debate, so that "to be able to participate in a conversation in Berlin, you have to know about 'the third sex.'"[34] Her disgust evaded direct judgment of erotic relationships between women, but it expressed a perception that talk about homosexuality was ubiquitous in educated circles shortly after the turn of the century.

Mensch strictly differentiated ideal love from sexual desire, whatever the object.[35] Some women, including Helene Stöcker and Ruth Bré, were beginning to extend gender emancipation to include a woman's right to sexuality, bringing the entire enterprise of feminism into dangerously selfish territory.[36] For Mensch, "unbounded love partnerships" were simply a demand of "tortured, love-starved females" who wanted to evade the responsibility of disciplined social reproduction.[37] Like other conservative feminists, she idealized marriage and motherhood even though she lived in a single-sex environment.

Mensch also disputed the idea, spread by popular science, that female homosexuals were prominent in the women's movement. "Only completely normal women could be the bearers of the women's movement—its top leaders—because urnings tend to solitude and are unlikely to dedicate themselves to the general struggle," she argued. Referring to the biographies in Hammer's volume, she judged it impossible that such "less worthy types could play a role in the women's movement."[38] Like Hammer, but for different reasons, Mensch found the idea of feminist homosexual middle-class women alarming and dismissed it categorically.

As the figure of the homosexual woman became more visible in popular sexology, titillating exposés of urban sexual practices, and feminist critiques, one woman publicly argued for positive recognition of female homosexuality. Anna Rühling spoke at a 1904 meeting of the WhK on the topic "What Interest Does the Women's Movement Have in the Solution of the Homosexual Problem?" Subsequently published in Hirschfeld's *Yearbook*, the speech has become influential in late-twentieth-century accounts of lesbianism in German history. It has been hailed in hindsight for combining feminism and lesbianism in a way that was congenial to many lesbian scholars working in the last third of the century.[39] Rühling accused the mainstream feminist movement of shying away from homosexual rights, despite the fact that its hardest workers and leaders were homosexual. In contrast to Mensch, she argued strongly for more open discussion of sexuality and claimed "the free development of the individual's personality" as the common goal of both movements.

Rühling built her argument on Hirschfeld's third-sex concept, linking discrimination against women to discrimination against homosexuals. She declared that all three sexes were of equal value and ought to be allowed to take up suitable careers. The notion of the third sex was useful for Rühling's conception of homosexuality as gender inversion. As she explained it, feminine women were in fact best suited to be wives and mothers, while only masculine men could be soldiers and physical laborers. Since inverts had a mixture of masculine and feminine, each would be suited for different types of jobs. She departed from most feminists in arguing that an active sex life was healthy. She asked her audience to "observe an unmarried homosexual woman between 30 and 50 years old," promising that they would find nothing of the hysteria and pettiness attributed to celibate old maids. The comparison proved "that a sensible and moderate satisfaction of the sex drive keeps women, too, happy, fresh, and energetic."[40] Rühling called on all women to assert sexual subjectivity and criticized the social norms that hindered women's sexual development.

Rühling's assertiveness about sex may have stemmed from her strong reliance on the inversion component of homosexualiy. Rühling emphasized that the sex drive came out of the personality. "The homosexual woman possesses many qualities, preferences, and capabilities that we usually see as the rightful possessions of men," she argued. "She is, like the average normal man, more objective, more energetic, and more determined than the feminine woman, her thoughts and feelings are those of the man." She also criticized ridicule of masculine women as failed mimicry: "She doesn't imitate men, she has the same tendencies as they do, this is the decisive and essential point."[41] Rühling cited Otto Weininger's claim in his *Sex and Character* that all famous or important women were homosexual.[42] He had argued that homosexual women's larger proportion of masculine characteristics allowed them to become great. In assimilating homosexual women to masculinity, Rühling's argument was directly opposed to that of feminists such as Elberskirchen, who emphasized the feminine in both same-sex attraction and emancipation. Insistence upon masculinity allowed Rühling to claim sexual subjectivity along with new gender roles. This view became the leading philosophy of the organized homosexual movement in the 1920s. This standpoint allowed homosexual women to assert their suitability for careers, freedom of judgment, and other privileges that they did not advocate for other, "normal" women. Despite Rühling's attempt to create a bridge between homosexuals and the women's movement, her conceptualization did not favor gender solidarity.

Elberskirchen, Mensch, and Rühling made their arguments heard in the male-dominated sphere of debates about sexuality. Women's same-sex sexual subjectivity became visible in the biographies included in sexological discourse. Intellectuals such as Rühling and Elberskirchen connected same-sex sexuality with women's striving for independence. From this insight came two opposed theories of female homosexuality and two different strategies of justifying women's assertion of a sexual self. One claimed masculinity, while the other rejected male-dominated heterosexual norms. The working-class women Hammer examined found his ideas superfluous to their culture and practice. They found his interest more amusing than threatening. They looked to each other in shaping sexual subjectivity that fit their circumstances. For them, same-sex love and attraction were obvious and extensive; their feelings and actions were not those of alienated outsiders, but part of a social world.[43]

The figure of the female homosexual had begun to appear, largely because of sexologists' interest in creating a standard diagnosis. As the idea of such a being circulated, readers responded with their own ideas and concerns. Should this figure be imagined as a psychopath, an oversexed prostitute, a sexual rebel, a gifted idealist, a mannish feminist, or a spinster with a devoted friend? Did all of these figures have something in common? Was the deviance caused by sex drive or gender? The figure was still more of a cipher or a possibility than a concrete stereotype. Feminist women clearly had the most investment in situating themselves with respect to sexual subjectivity. The strategies they chose split feminists into contending factions.

"Repulsive and Pathological"— Rejecting Male Sexual Subjectivity as a Model

From the 1890s on, the organized women's movement began to focus its attention on social problems its leaders attributed to male sexuality: venereal disease, prostitution, and loss of control over adolescent girls. For younger women thinking about or in fact living their lives more autonomously, coping with sexual questions required a more fundamental confrontation with gender ideology and practice. They were or had been entangled in the rituals of courtship and the assumption that an attractive healthy girl lived in expectation of marriage. As they rejected that outcome, many intellectual young women began to question and rethink the entire existing sex-gender system.[44] Theorizing correlated intimately with examining how they might become sexual subjects. The personal process usually could not be expressed publicly. Reception of the new sexological category of the homosexual woman took place within this broad reimagining. Most of the women who wrote theoretically about sex and gender were less interested in diagnostic categories than in social reform. Utopian theorizing about women's desires began by confronting women's position in sexual life as object of male desire. Writers explained how that deplorable situation had come about and imagined how it might change. They created visions of the future that imagined women's sexual subjectivity as a factor in human progress.

Since Elberskirchen lived her life in long-term same-sex partnerships, it is possible to speculate that many of her "findings" did in fact represent her personal experience of same-sex love and sexuality, despite her use of scientific evidence in defending her positions.[45] In her view, the evils of prostitution and venereal disease could only be explained by masculine cultural norms that valued physical weakness and docility in women. Elberskirchen argued that men thwarted evolution by choosing their mates for weakness rather than strength.[46] In her model, nature had placed women at the center of evolutionary reproduction, while patriarchal culture had harmfully overturned nature's rules. Men's sex lives had become "bestial," "dehumanizing," and "unnatural." "Sexual life in its most repulsive and pathological form became the first and deepest sense of life for the men," she claimed. "[Men's] own miserable selection and training of women" would inexorably lead to the "downfall of civilized humanity." She described men as "nothing but weak-willed, hysterical lechers, incapable of self-control, incapable of energetic, liberating action and work."[47] Addicted to sexual lust and pleasure, they could only see women as sex objects. Male culture thus deprived women of their active role in human evolutionary progress. Society was caught, according to Elberskirchen, in a vicious cycle of mutually reinforcing male lust and female oppression.

A similar vision of gender relations animated the plot and ideas in Elisabeth Dauthendey's 1901 novel *On the New Woman and Her Love: A Book for Mature Minds,* the source of the scene that began the chapter. The novel's protagonist, Lenora, is a self-proclaimed New Woman who suffers from the existing gender system and looks forward to a future where women have been restored to their proper position in society. Lenora's experiences bring to life Dauthendey's argument that men need to develop in a new direction that matches the progress made by New Women. The New Woman no longer accepted her position as sex object and refused to play the coy games of courtship. When men develop the same spiritual depth, mutual respect, and purity of love that characterize New Women, Lenora argues, society will have reached a new level of harmony and happiness for both sexes. Women's boycott of marriage will force men to adopt a new attitude toward women. In the meantime, New Women should focus on each other and depend on each other for support and love.[48]

Vivid scenes in the novel portray Lenora's rage and shame when she is treated as a sex object. One admirer flirtatiously observes, "A woman with such a splendid figure should get married." The novel evokes Lenora's outrage as his "eyes pass over [her] body sharply and penetratingly." Her fury is compounded when she learns he is married. Confronted about his inappropriate seductiveness, he openly proclaims the pleasure and desire that her beauty evoke in him. While he sees seduction as a healthy expression of masculinity, she is forced to recognize that she is "just a plaything." Looking back on her humiliation, she concludes that he has a soul like most other men—"hard and small" and lacking "understanding for her holy beauty."[49]

As a medical doctor, the admirer plays a second role as the voice of male-dominated scientific authority. When he discovers Lenora's nonsexual affair with a paraplegic scholar, he is enraged that she is betraying her feminine desire for sexual fulfillment and a child. "Don't you feel that my blood demands yours, demands that I force my man's will on your proud neck."[50] The doctor/admirer justifies domination as being "in his blood" and "knows" that a woman's desire and sexuality is essentially masochistic. While he sees sex as a biological imperative that melds male dominance with evolutionary reproduction, she imagines sex as mediated by a culture of spiritual love that brings together ideal partners. This spiritual ideal of love is found in her affair with the paraplegic scholar. As her ideal "New Man," he understands what nondisabled men do not: that love unfolds "person to person in full mutual freedom and in the wonder of a new love becoming higher."[51] Dauthendey's portrayal of the clash between male lust and women's idealized emancipation is more intimate than Elberskirchen's, yet both assert a New Women's critique of male sexuality.

A third and very different take on women's sexual subjectivity in the light of male norms of the era was elaborated in Austrian writer Elsa Asenijeff's 1898 manifesto *Uprising of Women and the Third Sex*.[52] That same year she met and became the lover and model of the painter Max Klinger in Leipzig. Asenijeff's book was scathingly critical of emancipated women, whom she saw as imitating the worst features of men. However, its critique of male sexuality was strikingly similar to Elberskirchen's and Dauthendey's. Asenijeff also disdained men's failure to understand the purpose of love and sex. Men focused on conquest, seeking women they could shape to their ideal.[53] Asenijeff, however, found a place for women's sexual desire by mystifying reproduction. Sexual bliss led women to communion with the infinite and cosmic; the presence of the male partner, satisfied with physical release, "befouled" her sacred moment.[54] She too believed that women were naturally more spiritual and responsible, but linked it to their nurturing reproductive role. Men, she claimed, subordinated reproduction to pleasure in conquest; therefore, they viewed women as sex objects rather than mothers. Men saw women who rejected their advances as cold and antisexual; they didn't realize that women were evaluating them as fathers for their children.[55]

One of Asenijeff's characteristically arch suggestions was that emancipated women who wanted to invent things could best help other women by inventing a coin-operated automat that could "satisfy the ten-minute love of man." If emancipated women wanted to combat prostitution, they would need to provide a physical outlet for male sexual energy. Asenijeff concluded that men were naturally incapable of experiencing sex as a spiritual merging of two souls rather than as an individual conquest.[56] Although Asenijeff did not hope that men could be reformed, she shared the feminists' view of current sexual norms: women longed for a union of souls; men saw women as sources of stimulation and release.

Educated women were responding to a gradual cultural shift away from family strategies toward the couple's mutual love as the foundation for marriage partner choice. Far from feeling liberated by choice, many women were alarmed that men's judgment of their sexual attractiveness was driving the process. A few vehemently rejected the expectation that they accept their role as object of men's desires. Eagerly seeking a basis for their demand that sexual partnerships allow them dignity and agency, women looked to biological evolution and human historical progress to prove that the contemporary sex/gender system was anything but natural and progressive. Elberskirchen and Asenijeff engaged in radical reinterpretations of history placing present conditions in a sweeping narrative of past and future.

Elberskirchen's views on early human history were strongly influenced by Friedrich Engels's and J. J. Bachofen's theories about preliterate matriarchal societies. Combining this historical framework with the evolutionary theories of Darwin and Ernst Haeckel, Elberskirchen developed what she claimed was clear proof of women's biological superiority. She argued that during the matriarchal era, women had been able to live in harmony with their biology. Childbirth and protection of the young were tasks that engaged women in the competition for survival, keeping them strong and healthy. Even more important, women played the decisive role in sexual selection by observing men and choosing the best providers for mates.[57] In this period of Mother Right, women brought about a "world historical triumph" and "created a culture of innocence and chastity," directing their sexuality to its biological purpose rather than enjoying pleasure for its own sake.[58] In the next stage of human history, the accumulation of private property gave men an advantage that allowed them to suppress women's power and autonomy.[59] Elberskirchen also used the new science of embryology to claim that every human had the same essential biological characteristics inherited from both mother and father. If women appeared weaker than men, it could not be attributed to biology.[60] Elberskirchen argued that society, and in particular men, needed to be reformed in order to restore evolution to its natural course.

Asenijeff's view of human history was clearly influenced by Hegelian and Nietzschean concepts rather than evolutionary biology. Yet Asenijeff made women's motherhood as central to her gendered interpretation of history as Elberskirchen did. Turning Elberskirchen's view of women as increasingly marginalized from power on its head, Asenijeff claimed that over the course of human development, women had assigned men the troublesome tasks of subsistence and labor, freeing women to play a purely spiritual role in guiding human progress and development. She saw the contemporary women's movement as a male plot. Luring women out into public to take over some of their work, men had tricked emancipated women into betraying the true source of their power—their spiritual depth and their ability to generate and nurture new life.[61] Women's role and glory was to suffer so that geniuses could be born to, and then supported and inspired by, women who under-stood them.[62] In this supportive role women were the hidden drivers of the cultural progress of humanity.

Across divergent ideologies, educated New Women at the turn of the century agreed that their male contemporaries were brutal and lustful. The similarity of these denunciations opens a window on their own struggles to define themselves as sexual subjects. Trained to guard purity and ideal-ize love, they were shocked to find that even young men of the same class, apparently intelligent and sensitive to other issues, looked at them and saw only a potential sexual conquest. They experienced men's pursuit of sexual pleasure as a brutal attack on their honor and sensibilities.

Once Asenijeff, Elberskirchen, and Dauthendey established a theoretical basis for their claims to women's central role in human advancement, they experimented with possibilities for women's assertion of sexual subjectivity. They all saw women's spiritualized love as the master value against which everything else was measured. Effacing sex in favor of love was one of new women's strongest discursive defenses against negative cultural meanings attributed to female desire and sexual subjectivity. This reaction was not universal; other young women advocated and practiced "free love." But most could not condone pleasure for its own sake, even though they read about and discussed sexuality, debating its role in erotic love and in reproduction.

Asenijeff imagined erotic love as a battle of the sexes. Men's desire to conquer women for ego and pleasure made it easy for women to manipulate them, turning the tables to make men simply "foreplay" or a "necessary evil" in their pursuit of spiritualized reproduction. She tied a woman's experience of orgasm to conception, describing it as "the last terrible fit" and "the separation in which the best of her blood enters existence as something new."[63] Asenijeff justified women's enjoyment of sex because they were always conscious of its purpose: "Each time she gives herself, it is a new agonizing heaven and hell of being robbed from which she emerges pure, chaste, and fearful—an eternal virgin."[64] Women's sacrifices for the sake of their children enable them to achieve a nobility of spirit possible for very few men.

When Asenijeff referred to the "third sex" in her title, she was evoking its 1890s meaning of sexless New Woman. She did not imagine any potential for same-sex desire in her erotic scheme. Since same-sex love would not produce a child, she would likely have included homosexuals among other childless women she saw as sterile, "contemptible, impotent beings," useful only for completion of routine tasks in the workplace.[65] Asenjieff invented a philosophy of the world centered on women's sexuality. But justification of sexual subjectivity and activity meant angrily distancing women from men and from other women seeking emancipation, along with an exalted view of women's sacrifices and suffering as holy.

In contrast, Elberskirchen's *Revolution* portrayed women's sexuality as restrained, responsible, and subordinate to other life achievements. She constructed it as an opposite to men's degraded desire rather than as a positive claim to sexual subjectivity. Although her pamphlet *Sexual Life and Sexual Abstinence for Women* argued that sex was a physical necessity required by most healthy mature women, it spent most of its energy proving that abstinence was not harmful.[66] She decried the unhealthy effects of "a burden of erotic fantasies" in women and girls.[67] "The strongly sexual person will never be able to develop into a great, a real personality," she claimed.[68] New Women strove for personality and intellect; therefore, she claimed they were not very interested in sex. Elberskirchen's disgust at the outcomes she associated with men's desire prevented her from endorsing autonomous sexual subjectivity for women. Although she did not address it directly, her model did leave space for restrained sexual expression as part of the love of female couples.

Dauthendey's novel systematically explored the implications of the New Woman's sexual desire. The first kiss Lenora shared with her paralyzed lover awakened her to bodily pleasure and the frustration she would feel at its absence: "With this kiss, I lost myself in a stream of bliss—but at the same time something froze into a terrible, cruel pain within me."[69] At night this pain returned and her "wound" bled with her "glowing woman's wanting."[70] This passage is notable for Dauthendey's portrayal of women's experience of sexual desire. The male object of her desire is simultaneously an enlightened "new man" and unable to consummate a sexual relationship due to his disability. The disability, besides representing the "normal" man's inability to appreciate the meaning of women's desire, also allows Lenora to explore sexual feelings without having to make a decision about whether to enter into a sexual relationship. Lenora is allowed desire because she is protected from its consequences by her lover's incapacity.

After the scholar's death, Lenora thinks back on the love that lacked the "last complete unification." It gives her a vision of what sex could be if based on a relationship of mutual respect. With new confidence she expresses herself as a sexual subject. "She [the New Woman] wants to feel herself swept away by the eternal beauty, which any strong and pure person can nurture," she enthused. "In the ecstasy of intoxication of love," the soul is lifted "into a glowing flight through the heavens of joy to land on the heights of completion over the weight of the world and the bodily." The flight takes its subject "to the completion of the new, the future, the coming, more worthy, so that it creates a new ring, and climbing stair to the eternity of becoming." The obscurity, the piled-on language, and the vague transit from earthly sensation to abstract bliss indicate the writer's difficulty in finding concrete expression for pleasure and desire. Nevertheless, she is struggling to place sexual love in her future utopia. As with Elberskirchen, the sexual makes a brief appearance, but then becomes a mere steppingstone to the "higher" and "stronger" in the ideals of the New Woman.[71]

Having disqualified men as lovers in present conditions, Lenora dreams up a plan to share love with another New Woman. She seeks a partner who "understands my refusal [of heterosexuality] and comes to meet my loneliness with her warmth, so that we can bind ourselves in a new union, in which the holy richness of goodness and love remains fruitful in women's hearts." The passage is open to the potential of same-sex love, yet it is qualified as a stopgap measure, filling the gap until men and women are reconciled.[72] As promising as the "holy richness of love" between women was, Dauthendey insists that women must eventually return to their true destiny as mothers.

As the scene quoted at the start of the chapter indicates, Dauthendey puts Lenora into a situation that tests the limits of same sex love. The scene portrays Lenora's reactions to the advances of Nasti, a woman with whom she has developed an intimate friendship. Lenora enjoys Nasti's beauty, figure, thoughts, and mannerisms. Nasti's "Spanish blood" made her the attractive Southerner, a common trope in German narratives signifying freer sensuality than was characteristic of Nordics. The exotic other is a figure of displacement, enticing desire and serving as an object of moralizing judgment. As Nasti embraces Lenora and declares her desire, Lenora lets herself be swept away for a moment. Then she gently disentangles herself, with the explanations that "her feminine instincts were too complete and too healthy." Lenora rejects physical homosexual love "because the New Woman wants purity at any price."[73]

New Woman novels from before the turn of the century represented aspects and signs associated later with female homosexuality without invoking a particular sexual identity; now same-sex sexuality becomes explicit. What remains less clear is exactly how and why Lenora differentiates between heterosexual and homosexual when it comes to love and sex. If a bond of love was the precondition for sexual intimacy, why was sex between women in love "impure"? The sequence with Nasti seems to offer an alternative, only to reject it firmly. What troubles Dauthendey is the contradiction between love that exists for itself and love that is tied to women's maternal destiny of responsibility for social cohesion and reproduction. At the end of the novel, Lenora finally finds her perfect solution in a mother-like mentoring relationship with a younger woman. Sexual subjectivity, claimed but left unfulfilled, made way for love that stayed safely in the realm of the non-sexual maternal.

Dauthendey's panicked rejection of sexual love between women as "impure" seems to have been modified over time in light of the emerging information on homosexuality. In an article she wrote a few years later, Dauthendey cited research proving that inversion was a congenital condition that was natural and deserving of sympathy. She described inverts here as gender deviants—men who dressed like women and women who would be hard to recognize as female. Despite this strangeness, they were "harmless people who wanted nothing more than to be left alone."[74] The article was addressed to "normal" women, urging them to understand the condition in order to respond with sympathy if one of her children or her husband should exhibit signs of inversion. In the novel, same-sex desire appeared as an erotic alternative that was open to all, yet "impure," while the article recognized inverts as a safely separate category of person deserving of sympathy. The figure of same-sex love also changed from the seductive Spaniard to the pronouncedly mannish woman.

Logically and historically, the dilemma of the woman who wanted both emancipation and a sex life would seem to create an opening to consider the alternative of same-sex sexuality. Yet none of the authors openly embraced this possibility. Although Dauthendey and Elberskirchen did acknowledge the alternative as they developed their theories, they continued to restrict its practice to the twin contexts of biological causality and pure spiritual love.

The clear binary between sensuality, on the one hand, and intellectual and spiritual development, on the other, likely reflected young middle- and upper-class women's socialization as well as the particular historical moment. If their training had been successful, an admission of sensual feelings and desires triggered automatic shame. Clearly this mental and emotional framework would not allow them to seek the kind of sexual freedom they observed in young men. The need of these writers to elaborate grand theories of human development testifies to the difficulty such young women encountered when they began to assert sexual subjectivity. Each writer fell back on motherhood and purity in her justifications.

The turn of the century was an extraordinarily fertile and febrile moment for women feeling their way toward feminine sexuality that was not defined through reference to men's needs and desires. Their struggles belong within a broader framework of the transition in marriage from family formation to individual satisfaction. Industrial society provided wage-earning opportunities supporting autonomous marriages chosen by the partners based on love and sexual attraction. The collective wisdom of society and culture was not yet comfortable with women being able to claim the rights and desires that men had acquired. Therefore, many feminists struggled in small groups and isolated texts to reconcile new notions of sexual love as central to life with women's continuing acceptance of parts of gender ideology that denied or stigmatized women's sexuality.

"Sickening Orgies":
Debating the Dangers of Female Homosexuality

Political activism against immorality was yet another consequence of this late-nineteenth-century conjuncture. The main targets of the proliferating morality-promoting organizations were pornography and prostitution. The morality lobby sometimes denounced male prostitution, but female homosexuality remained invisible and unremarked.[75] Then in the first decade of the new century, male homosexuality became more apparent and threatening to the general public due to scandalous revelations about homosexual activity and cross-dressing among the Kaiser's closest associates. The allegations, published by prominent political journalist Maximilian Harden, led to a series of trials that kept the so-called Eulenburg Affair in the public eye between 1907 and 1909.[76] Although female homosexuality could not invoke the same practical and symbolic state security implications, the trials created an appetite for scandal that could also be fed by reports of women's transgressive behavior. The minor Berlin weekly *Große Glocke* (*Great Bell*) attempted to exploit this potential. In a series of articles, it exposed groups of women asserting alternative sexual subjectivities in Berlin. Not all women were as distressed about claiming sexuality as the writers discussed above. Some claimed to be and defended themselves as homosexuals, even as they objected to *Große Glocke*'s salacious characterization of their activities. Others were bold enough to sue its publisher, Felix Wolff, for defamation.

Published from 1906 to 1922, *Große Glocke* navigated the line between tabloid titillation and preaching moral purity. The timing of its founding and its focus on sexual misconduct among the upper classes suggests a close connection to the Eulenburg exposé in Harden's weekly in the same month. Wolff did not limit his editorializing to high politics like the well-connected Harden. Instead, he reported on the seamy underworld of Berlin's decadent elite. *Große Glocke*'s combination of moralizing and sensationalism reflected more than just an attempt to cash in on celebrity scandal.[77] Wolff's editorials on some sexual issues, including abortion and "free love," took a permissive position. He carefully countered conservative anti-Semitic discourses claiming that pimps and pornographers were greedy Jews with a defense of Jewish respectability. Wolff aimed to demonstrate that German Jews were equally committed to sexual morality, respectability, and national strength.

In 1908, *Große Glocke* first alerted Berliners to the scandal of the female homosexuals among them when it printed a story about a landlady's shocked discovery of "a sickening orgy" in one of her apartments. Her tenant, the nineteen-year-old orphan S., had invited six women to her apartment, where they drank alcohol and smoked cigarettes. The article described two of the guests as a Frl. T. and a dentist G., both "notorious 'lovers'" of S.[78] Frl. T wrote a detailed denial of *Große Glocke's* representation of the gathering. Although some of those present were homosexual, she insisted, "[a]ny one of the six women can tell you under oath that no such activities took place. There were not even any exaggerated caresses in a distasteful form." She denied that she and Frl. G. had ever been "lovers" of S. The editor's commentary appended to the letter recognized Frl. T's statement as "an important document from the pen of a homosexual woman" since "urnings so seldom express themselves publicly about their Vita sexualis."[79]

Frl. T. used the word *homosexual,* indicating that middle-class women by this time categorized themselves as such and that some were not afraid to defend their essential respectability in a public forum. The newspaper writer and Frl. T. agreed that the important issue was not whether one had homosexual desires or adopted a homosexual identity, but that one behaved respectably.

A 1909 article, "The Homosexual Club 'New Women's Community,'" informed the public that networks of such self-described homosexual women were beginning to organize and reach out to potential members. The club met Wednesdays at the Nollendorfkasino, a café open to the public. The president, an "Amazon," wore a tuxedo on special occasions. Another member, who lived together with a woman "who dresses in a thoroughly masculine style," had been the third party in a divorce case and had testified in court about her affair with the wife. After the public was excused from the court, she allegedly told the judge "intimate and thoroughly shady facts and episodes" about the relationship. Yet another member was a married woman who brought her sixteen-year-old daughter to club meetings, where she was "forced to witness the ladies' effusive caresses" and "given the opportunity to carry on an intimate friendship" with another of the married club members. The daily *Berliner Tageblatt* later reported that the club had placed classified advertisements seeking "like-minded" women. The passwords "Sappho" and "Aphrodite" and a red rose would identify the group for newcomers.[80]

At the subsequent libel trial, several hostile witnesses testified that the club president encouraged members to recruit as many couples as possible. They also claimed that she had made immoral advances to women who "were unsuspectingly attracted to the club because of the outwardly advertised ideal goals." The unsuspecting "normal" women accused her of treating them rudely after they rejected her advances. Other witnesses confirmed that they had sought out the club because they were homosexual.[81]

Wolff tied his criticism of the club's immorality to the lack of legal prohibition on women's sexuality. His detailed description of the club's members and activities touched on every controversial aspect of female homosexuality: performance of masculinity, lack of sexual shame, interference in marriage, and endangerment of youth. These issues surfaced wherever female homosexuality was seen as dangerous. Most significant was Wolff's accusation that the members "allowed the woman what is only appropriate for the man."[82] The sexual assertiveness of the New Women's Community members burst the boundary that separated middle-class women from sexual desire.

Like Frl. T., five members of the New Women's Community thought it possible to contest Wolff's characterization of homosexual sociability. They asked the state to defend their honor by bringing a defamation complaint against Wolff. Although the readership of Große Glocke was undoubtedly small, coverage of the suit in Berlin's major newspapers allowed discourses about female homosexuality to circulate in mainstream print media. Wolff's attorney argued that the newspaper objected only to the women's deviant behavior, not to the fact of their being homosexual. Große Glocke had no objection to homosexuals meeting to discuss their common problems or to socialize among themselves, as long as they "sail under their own flag and strictly avoid any offense against the generally prevailing morality."[83]

That homosexuality had been a factor in one divorce case and the breakdown of a second marriage seemed to have made a decisive impression on the judge, who decided in favor of Wolff.[84] The judge regarded the witnesses' statements as having proven that immoral activities took place at club meetings and that the innocent bylaws of the organization were simply a cover for the real purpose of attracting potential sex partners. Wolff's subsequent articles exposing the presence of unashamed homosexual women in Berlin were no doubt encouraged by what he saw as complete vindication.

The conservative Berliner Lokal-Anzeiger's extensive report on the libel case called on the morality lobby to "turn against the spread of similar attempts [to promote immorality] among women." The Lokal-Anzeiger explained the sudden increase in female immorality as the effect of "a certain literature, those shameless books that seldom have a man as an author." The conservative response to proliferating reports of same-sex sexual behavior was to deny sexual subjectivity to all but a malicious few intent on seducing the others. In their eyes, the activities of the "tribades" made the "German woman, the entire female sex [feel] degraded, shaken to the core, and insulted." The *Lokal-Anzeiger* writer was aware of the literature that described homosexuality as a congenital variation in human biology. He or she emphatically rejected its claims of biological determinism: "Don't tell us that these tribades are not women, that they are only wretched pathologically inclined females. . . . That might apply to a few—into the sanatorium with them."[85] Here was a more fully developed negative stereotype of the female homosexual as a psychologically disturbed obsessive seducer of innocent women and girls. Seduction to satisfy compulsive of desire required incarceration to protect society. But the *Lokal-Anzeiger* still maintained that most women engaged in such behavior were simply immoral, oversexed women.

Over the next two years *Große Glocke* regularly printed exposés of sinister public behavior by groups of women. "Homosexual Neighborhood in the Bavarian Quarter" announced the "disgrace of a whole neighborhood . . . gradually becoming a ghetto for homosexual women."[86] These shameless women were alleged to have bothered "normal" women and girls, talked about themselves openly in streetcars, and confused children with their cross-dressing. Because the Bavarian Quarter was also a Jewish neighborhood, Wolff may have become aware of the women there through observation or conversations with friends.[87] A shop in the Lutherstraße was really a front for clubrooms where homosexual women met.[88] Women wearing knee pants belonged to a homosexual bowling club.[89] Elegant women and prostitutes met in clubrooms in the Zimmerstraße, where "two waiters, Charlie and Ernst, both young women without a trace of femininity" served as pimps for the homosexual prostitutes. Recently the regulars had been seen at a ball at a bar in the Möckernstraße that turned into the "most depraved orgy."[90]

Taken together, these revelations provide an index for the possibilities of performing homosexual desire, female masculinity, and same-sex sociability semi-publicly in the immediate pre–World War I period. By this time observers were making definite connections between those signs and homosexual orientation. While the range of behaviors and social patterns behind the titillating descriptions was wide, from social circles of middle-class girls to wealthy living-together couples to sophisticated married women seeking a sexual connection, the "signs" were collapsed in Wolff's titillating descriptions into a single phenomenon of dangerous inner desire acted out in public. Wolff's furious denunciations were exacerbated by the women's apparent enjoyment of urban leisure. The more fun they seemed to have and the less concern for social disapprobation they exhibited, the more Wolff felt required to shame them. The articles increasingly resembled a vice crusade.

Yet Wolff protested that he was in complete sympathy with the suffering of those who were crippled by nature and ostracized from society. He imagined respectable homosexuals "suffer[ing] under the existing law and [happy to] hide their orientation from the world's gaze like a cripple striv[ing] to keep his defect a secret, shameful and hidden." Such shameful homosexuals were, Wolff claimed, critical of the public displays of confident sexual identity his newspaper exposed.[91] Wolff's argumentation in this passage is one key to understanding why conservative conceptions of sexuality were more appealing to some homosexual women than liberal ones. Though Wolff spoke out in favor of striking Paragraph 175 from the criminal code, he expected a *quid pro quo*—homosexuals had to accept their condition as an embarrassment to be hidden from public view. Perfect conformity to middle-class morality and gender normativity was the price to be paid for legal inclusion in the nation. Conservative viewpoints, on the other hand, defined homosexuality as depravity connected with a general coarseness in the public sphere, leaving conceptual space for middle-class women's ideal love and friendship.

Gender played a pivotal role in *Große Glocke*'s politics of shame. Wolff's strongest critiques were, with a few exceptions, leveled against female homosexuality rather than male. His attacks on the shamelessness of "ostentatiously" homosexual women always combined the masculine appearance of some with physical contact and flirtation between women. Two Wolff editorials on feminism made clear that he grounded his moral politics in the maintenance of bourgeois norms of sexual difference and particularly in male authority. "Tradition has directed the woman not unjustly to a position that should make her life easy and pleasant under the protection of a man," Wolff declared. In his opinion, women's work in the commercial economy entailed disastrous consequences for the culture and the nation. Competition from women weakened men and made their "struggle for existence" more difficult. He concluded that women's employment gave nonemployed wives the confidence to "convince men of their importance and superiority, and so the condition gradually forms that the common people refer to as 'henpecked,' a condition that cannot simply be dismissed as a joke."[92] Although Wolff's articles did not make explicit connections between feminism and female homosexuality, his ultimate goal of maintaining male privilege tied them together. The underlying problem presented by both homosexual women and working women was that both influenced "normal" women to want more than they had. Wolff's reaction to changes in the gender order demonstrates how emancipation and homosexuality posed a critique of the status of wife.

Wolff tried to shame and intimidate women whose appearance in public gave evidence of their sexual subjectivity. Yet, when he focused his criticism on particular women, they refused to efface their presence or their claims; writing back to him or pressing charges of libel against him, they objected to his salacious implications rather than his characterization of their sexual orientation. Though Wolff clearly maintained his privileged position, the actions he publicized provide evidence of the emergence of homosexual assertiveness and identity among women in Berlin, for contemporary readers as well as later scholars. His exposés perhaps gave interested women points of contact and strengthened the growing network of sociability based on sexual identity.

Gender Equity: Criminalizing Female Homosexuality

Wolff's exposure of the evils of female homosexuality coincided with the publication of the Preliminary Draft of a new criminal code that proposed to extend the criminality of "unnatural indecency" to both sexes.[93] In his editorial function, Wolff joined discussion of the Preliminary Draft of the criminal code while the Justice Department's Criminal Law Reform Commission debated it in 1911. He used typical liberal reasoning to advocate decriminalization, but limited it to "true homosexuals" who should be certified by experts. Severe punishment was needed for the rest, those "who in disgusting perversity and violation of normal shame feelings assault others homosexually or pursue these behaviors although they are not homosexual." Of course such punishment required a law similar to Paragraph 175. The new law, he believed, should apply equally to both sexes. "The homosexual excesses of women," he argued, "so harshly castigated so often here, are only possible as long as tribadism does not carry a legal penalty. . . . They endanger family life, motherhood, sexual ethics, and not least the full vigor of coming generations."[94] From a starting point opposing Paragraph 175, Wolff came full circle to a demand that sexual activity—and here he seemed to imply suspicious touching, flirting, or open talk about homosexuality—be criminalized. Like Elberskirchen and Dauthendey, he had difficulty accepting that women's sexual subjectivity was compatible with the essential roles of wife and mother. Female homosexuality was, for Wolff, an especially egregious example of the way "modern" women were threatening men's exclusive privileges.

The 1909 Preliminary Draft was the product of a process of thorough revision of the criminal law code begun in 1902. Lobbying by the WhK and the active constituency it represented ensured that the provisions of the law related to homosexual behavior would generate public controversy. It hoped that the Justice Department would remove Paragraph 175 from its proposal. Instead the draft retained the prohibition while removing the specification "between men." Yet the judicial experts had difficulties in conceptualizing how the law might work in the case of women. The debate over the proposed changes in 175 elicited feminist comment on contemporary practical implications of female homosexuality.

A justification explaining the committee's thinking accompanied each section of the new draft law. Wolfgang Mittermaier's justification for the section on sexual crimes showed the same ambivalence toward homosexuality expressed by other liberals and progressives.[95] Mittermaier had earlier signed the WhK petition, and he acknowledged that the trend was toward decriminalization. He saw no objective difference between male and female homosexuality and was critical of the existing law for its single-sex application.[96] Yet in the few paragraphs he devoted to the extension of the law to women, Mittermaier argued, "The danger for family life and youth is the same. Such cases are on the increase in modern times. Therefore, it is in the interest of morality and the general welfare that the law be extended to women."[97] His thinking revealed that for some lawmakers anxiety about the perceived spread of homosexuality motivated extending the law to women. The Eulenburg and Krupp scandals generated a moral panic that seemed to demand increased state action in the form of stricter laws.

In addition to Mittermaier's anxiety about modern family life, Felix Wolff's argumentation in *Große Glocke* confirms feminist scholars' claims that another context for extension was the growing political visibility of the feminist movement and women's claims to a place in formerly all-male spheres. The work of these scholars claimed that the proposed criminalization was a strategy of intimidation meant to stigmatize and intimidate single career women, especially those in intimate same-sex relationships.[98] It is likely that a general notion of the dangers of emancipation played a role in the call for extension. Yet I do not think it likely, as has been argued, that the lawyers on the commission or the doctors who advised them were particularly concerned with the private lives of teachers and social workers living in couples.[99] Consideration of just such respectable women was one reason the commission dropped the extension following its deliberations.

The zigzag pattern in arguments on extension to women reflects the ambivalence of the moderate middle, which fell between the moral condemnation of the conservatives and the decriminalization demands of supporters of the WhK. The moderates' conflicting goals can be seen in the vacillating positions held by Wilhelm Kahl, the law professor charged with steering the criminal law revision process. As referent on the morality sections at the time of the 1911 commission discussion, Kahl wrote a long explanation of his preferences. Like Mittermaier, Kahl here retreated from his earlier readiness to accept a new law code without Paragraph 175, instead making a strong case for keeping the law specific to "persons of the male sex." He vehemently argued, "Such activity is perceived by German lawmakers as a revolting and disgusting filthy mess [*Schweinerei*]. . . . I am an unconditional opponent of the movement to abolish Paragraph175 of the existing law, the continued existence of which I regard as a basic component of our German moral and legal order."

His change in perspective must have been a response to the scandal trials and publicity that had occurred in the meantime. But women, less relevant to the "German moral and legal order" apparently, did not require criminalization. "I am an equally unconditional opponent of its extension to the female sex," Kahl continued, "which I have to recognize as a disastrous source of [illegible] and many other evils."[100] Although the condition of the archival records makes Kahl's reasoning unclear, other commentators cited blackmail and stigmatization of innocent women. He declared that he would rather abolish the law altogether than extend it to women. Moderates such as Kahl reserved the right to make a strong moral judgment about the kinds of homosexual behavior that deserved judicial punishment. Yet, from their liberal conception of law and from practical experience, they had to admit that the law caused more problems than it solved. Opposed to regulation of private behavior, they still wished for legal barriers to young people's experimenting with homosexual sex. Moderates invariably opposed extending the law to women, although their reasons remained quite vague because it was embarrassing to speak publicly about the details.

The existing law did not describe specific acts, referring only to "unnatural indecency." Judges commonly required allegations of penetration before prosecuting a case. Mittermaier's rationale defended this legal standard, but did not specify which acts between women would be prosecutable. Lawyers felt uncomfortable making explicit how the legal precedent for men with its focus on penetration would apply to women's sexual practices. It also seems that they preferred to remain ignorant of these practices, which would have to be discussed if they were to be criminalized. Friedrich Bechly addressed this problem in the journal *Sex and Society*. He cited the sexologist Hermann Rohleder's list of the forms of sexual practice between women: mutual masturbation, cunnilingus, and tribadism (rubbing the clitoris against another's body). He forthrightly considered whether each of these acts might be considered "similar to intercourse." In Bechly's opinion, the potential for insertion of a finger or tongue into the vagina, as well as the rubbing movements that stimulated orgasm could all be reasonably interpreted as "similar to intercourse." Ambivalence among "experts" became visible in the long series of nervous notes the journal's editor ran alongside the text of Bechly's article. The editor disagreed with Bechly, taking the position that the position of the penis was decisive and therefore only use of an artificial penis would make female acts punishable in line with current legal usage.

Bechly focused on three problems for judicial practice in extending the law to women. First, the acts he saw as least objectionable, tribadism and manual stimulation, were most likely to be punished, since they were most similar to heterosexual intercourse. Second, the same acts practiced by a man were not legally punishable. Finally, lacking a witness statement by a third party, a judge would be hard-pressed to find evidence of acts having taken place. He concluded by arguing for gender-neutral laws that explicitly described the illegal acts. Bechly hoped that his article would lead to detailed study among "Reichstag representatives, members of the Bundesrat, Justice Departments officials, medical expert witnesses and so on."[101] But open discussion that specified what sex between women entailed was distressing for most of these men.

In a second article, Bechly quoted Magnus Hirschfeld's rationale for abolition: "Acts practiced in the stillness of the bed chamber do not cause public offense. The most embarrassing situations occur first because fact-finding in the courtroom requires discussion of all the details, which is much worse than the homosexual acts themselves."[102] Hirschfeld specifically appealed to mainstream embarrassment, seeming to agree that the harm of talking about it was greater than the harm of doing it. The same embarrassment and avoidance of detail influenced the commission's work on turning the draft into a proposal for the legislative bodies.

As in the other arenas where female homosexuality entered into the print public sphere at the beginning of the century, women responded, defining the ways their lives might be affected by the proposed changes. The mainstream women's movement did not take a position on the new Paragraph 175, but several women associated with its "radical" wing engaged in vigorous public discussion in 1911 and 1912.[103] Helene Stöcker, leader of the League for the Protection of Mothers, wrote a long editorial urging the members to oppose the proposal. For their organization, "normal love, the love between man and woman, and parenthood seems the highest and most desirable goal." However, current conditions of sexual morality kept so many women single that some were bound to seek satisfaction of their "tenderness drive" in relations with other women. Using the editorial to advocate for her usual causes of easing the social stigma and legal prohibitions on sexual love outside marriage, single motherhood, and children born out of wedlock, she urged the "favored and happy" not to worsen the situation of the "less normal, less happily predisposed" whose private sexual affairs made their lives bearable and harmed no one else.[104]

Like many other groups and individuals, Elsbeth Krukenberg sent material directly to the commission.[105] She opposed extension because "women's lives would suffer so much more" than men's from what she called the "ban on tenderness." Relying on the power of gender stereotypes, she explained that women were capable of a "close and lasting life together," while "tenderness toward another man and a lasting life together is so much more seldom and so much less compatible with nature."[106] This argumentation implied that women's intimacy was innocent of sexual content. Yet in her defense of the female couple, Krukenberg allowed some of the erotic potential of female relations to lurk just below the surface. "Words like my love and darling, etc. flow easily from their lips," she claimed. "Are women supposed to do without all that in order to avoid being falsely accused? The world would be a colder place." She was bold enough to address women's sharing the same bed: "When a writer describes for us how a troubled female creature looking for protection, in order to become calmer, yes just to warm herself against the cold, flees at night into the arms of a sister, a friend, I would like to see the man who takes offense at that."[107] Avoiding the word *homosexual* to describe either sex drive or choice of intimate partner of their hypothetical female couples, Krukenberg used "natural" female difference to detach the meaning of what women did from the implications of similar behavior among men.

Anna Pappritz, a doctor active in the abolitionist and anti–venereal disease movements, opposed extension because penetration was impossible between women. Like Elberskirchen, she denounced the depravity of lust for both sexes, with a focus on the relatively greater evils, such as child abuse, pimping, seduction, and egotistic demands of husbands, resulting from male sexuality.[108] Pappritz used her medical and moral authority to reinforce conventional ideas about women's sexual innocence.

The apparent taboo against feminist women's claiming sexual subjectivity makes Käte Schirmacher's frank discussion of the possibility of sex in women's relationships, all the more surprising. Schirmacher made the strongest case for a radical difference between male and female same-sex behavior, but attributed that difference to social norms. She argued that sexual relationships between women usually should be understood as different from sexual intercourse between men. "The man has the whole realm of natural sexual intercourse open to him," she reasoned. "The woman is usually unacquainted with the possibilities for natural sexual intercourse that are freely available for men. She is kept on a much tighter leash . . . and hindered to a much greater degree than the man from natural sexual intercourse."[109] Schirmacher's logic depended on the assumption of essential gender parity in sexual needs and desires. Further, she implied that women deserved the satisfactions of sexual relations as much as men. Where gender was important for Schirmacher was in the social restrictions that limited women's choices. Schirmacher also engaged with sexological knowledge, arguing that she was not talking about cases of inborn homosexuality. Here she accepted the conservative view that congenital cases of compulsive homosexual behavior were few and something other than the more common forms of women's same-sex relationships. The latter, she implied, were chosen, and chosen specifically as a strategy of achieving sexual satisfaction. Perhaps she hoped that readers would accept feminist couples as a necessary *faute de mieux* with fewer social consequences than heterosexual affairs. But Schirmacher's assertion of female sexual subjectivity is unmistakable.

Shirmacher, Pappritz, and Krukenberg each lived with a woman. The evasiveness in their positions is partially attributable to their personal vulnerability to prosecution or suspicion. Yet, there were subtle differences in the way the three defined and positioned female same-sex relations. Krukenberg made women's feelings the dividing line. As long as what women did in bed was motivated by love and comfort, acts and labels were unimportant. Pappritz put correspondingly greater emphasis on perverse acts as signs of inner perversion, as disgusting for women as for men.[110] Schirmacher, on the other hand seemed to make a stronger division between the congenital invert and the woman who chose a marriage-like relationship with another woman. These differences reflected continuing fluidity in thinking about how concepts and relationships evolved in connection with the homosexual category. For these writers, love and sex between women were still perhaps defined by acts, perhaps an accident of life circumstances, perhaps a medical condition, perhaps an innocent pleasure, but not yet an identity, as it had become for the women responding to Wolff's salacious reports in *Große Glocke*.

The Law Reform Commission, in its first vote on September 30, 1912, unanimously rejected the new gender-neutral form of the law and returned the previous language to the draft. The reasons were very close to the arguments made by the women essayists. The minutes of the commission summarized the consensus: "No need for the extension could be recognized. Instead serious harm would have to be taken care of: it would lead to unfounded accusations and be a source of blackmail. The damage to public morals from court trials for these kinds of offenses would be greater . . . than the preventative effect.

Besides, the acts to be placed under punishment would be very difficult to delimit."[111] Law reformers justified unequal treatment largely because male homosexuality was already present in the public sphere. Female homosexuality had only a vague public face. The best way to keep it that way would be to avoid scandal trials by leaving female homosexuality out of the law.

The publication of popular sexology texts in the first years of the twentieth century undoubtedly supplied a new category for interpreting women's lives, relationships, and statements about sexuality. It did not create the growing urban networks of women defining their erotic and affectional life through their choice of female objects and partners. Rather, these two phenomena were mutually interdependent. A convenient label and accessible defining literature surely made it easier for women to find others with whom they felt they shared a centrally important facet of their lives. Urban communities and individual women entered into dialogue with experts and commentators to influence the meanings associated with the term *homosexual*.[112] Though this shared understanding included a set of terms, including *invert* and *contrary-sexual*, by the end of the decade, the term *homosexual* had become common across all of the spheres of discussion considered here. They left few traces, yet women who identified with the figure made themselves visible in responding to others' efforts to stigmatize or reform them.

The meanings of the term fluctuated from writer to writer. The assertion of sexologists that there was one phenomenon called homosexuality that was a congenital property of the entire person was largely rejected by the mainstream as accounting for the broader phenomena they heard about. Sexual depravity resonated better with their assumptions. Important sections of the anti-175 and "men's" movements, along with radical feminists, preferred not to use the term in reference to themselves.[113] The precise relationship between emancipation, female masculinity, and homosexuality remained an uncertain and contested area of debate.

There is no clear way to untangle these phenomena. They are present together everywhere, except among those feminists who radically rejected everything male (and, even then, masculinity remained as a disavowed figure of shame). Yet female masculinity can be closely connected to the claim of sexual subjectivity. Nineteenth-century separate-spheres ideologies made women the shame-filled and passive objects of sex. Male privilege authorized men to act on their supposedly natural desires. Desiring women's assertion of sexual subjectivity was consistently stigmatized as evil or unnatural or both. Women experimenting with ridding themselves of this ideology used the signs of masculinity as a way of acting out sexually active personae. In this sense, the link Wolff drew in *Große Glocke* between women's adoption of masculine clothing and suspicious sexual activity was well placed.

Although the criminal code process had symbolically re-suppressed female homosexuality from the national agenda, women continued to adopt it as an identity term. The rapid appearance of bars, publications, and organizations after the war is evidence enough to demonstrate continuity in community formation and solidification of a female homosexual identity across the difficult period of the war. Despite its lack of clarity, the dissemination of the term and category throughout the educated public sphere made it less easy for new women to experiment freely with personae, relationships, and erotic attachments than it had been before 1900. The emergence of the figure of the homosexual woman created a conceptual break between homosexual women and emancipated women, two groups who increasingly adopted different strategies to justify their pursuit of individual autonomy and independent lives.

4

Denying Desire

Professional Women Facing
Accusations of Homosexuality

The chaos following defeat in World War I brought Germans both hope and mourning. Groups of individuals who had been loosely affiliated as homosexuals before the war began organizing and publicizing as never before when restraints ceased to operate after the collapse of the monarchy in November 1918. Magnus Hirschfeld pioneered spreading his enlightening messages about homosexuality through the relatively new medium of film. He appeared as himself in the film *Different from the Others,* part dramatization of blackmail, part platform for Hirschfeld's arguments in favor of repealing Criminal Code Paragraph 175. One person who saw the film following its release in 1919, allowed under the relaxed censorship of the new Weimar Constitution, was Anna Philipps, a teacher in an elite girls' secondary school near Bremen. "[The film] interested me," Philipps wrote in a later autobiographical account, "so I ordered Hirschfeld's book about homosexuality and studied the questionnaire. Through conscientiously answering the questions, I wanted to clarify whether or not I was homosexual."[1] Philipps's statements imply that the concept of homosexuality struck her as a plausible explanation of her feelings and relationships. Philipps's story is significant evidence of how some women became aware of sexological labels and adopted them as personal identities.

But Philipps's story is much more complicated. She included the vignette of her curiosity about homosexuality in the autobiography (and wrote down her life story in the first place) because she had come to reject the label for herself and apply it to a shadowy conspiracy of "real homosexuals." "Whoever has read my account, will notice that all my efforts to bring clarity to the affair are thwarted," she wrote. "It is perfectly clear who has an interest in keeping things in the dark—the homosexuals."[2] By 1932, she believed that these secretive and corrupt people were to blame for her having been fired from her teaching job. As one of their victims, it was her duty to expose their pernicious influence on the state. Other evidence included in the book she published suggests that she pushed some of her colleagues to consider whether their relationships and feelings might mean they were also homosexual. Her persistent questions blew up into an investigation of the relationships between teachers, of relationships between teachers and students, and of Philipps's mental state and professionalism. The investigating officials tried to steer the case away from the teachers' sex lives, but suspicions and charges of homosexuality were central to conflicts among the teachers. In their circle, same-sex intimacy was unremarkable until Philipps insisted on classifying it with a term widely understood as synonymous with perversion, and thus as a threat to their professional standing.

Philipps's case was not unique. This chapter analyzes Philipps's documents along with archival files from two similar cases of workplace discipline involving charges of homosexuality to address three important questions in the history of women's same-sex sexual relationships.[3] This evidence allows us to investigate the texture of daily life among emancipated women to assess the role that intense friendships, feelings of attraction, and couples played in their social and professional worlds. Secondly, testimony from these cases gives us a window into the ways that people in general understood and used the concept of homosexuality in the 1920s. Finally, by the 1920s many doctors were trained in the basics of sexology. Their expertise was called upon in each case, demonstrating medicine's effects on emancipated women's sexuality.

In historical accounts of the interwar period, the most visible kind of New Woman is the sexually active, matter-of-fact consumer employed in the white-collar economy.[4] Yet contemporaries were also aware of a very different type of New Woman: the educated professional. Professional women—teachers, social workers, and government inspectors—cultivated scrupulously respectable reputations. Most of them were single and worked in human service bureaucracies with other women. Like the university students of the previous generation, the career women conformed to expectations of asexuality in order to be taken seriously in the workplace.[5]

Josefine Erkens, another of the women involved in a disciplinary case, was head of the Women's Section in the Hamburg Police Department and a tireless advocate for the expansion of women's professions.[6] Her writings expressed the shared hope of professional women—to experience "the clear consciousness of their own worth, and . . . the feeling of joy in work and capacity for sacrifice in the service of the whole."[7] The key phrases "joy in work" and "sacrifice in the service of the whole" captured a spirit of purpose and commitment out of tune with the stereotype of the sexually experienced, somewhat cold and calculating Weimar New Woman.[8]

Homosexuality appears somewhat differently in each case, yet the deployment of accusations of homosexuality by women against other women is common to all. The accusations were weapons in their conflicts with one another. The cases collectively provide vivid evidence of the pressures and contradictions that fostered hostility within all-female work groups. None of the three women charged was dismissed due to suspected homosexuality, but all were terminated for a combination of insubordination and inability to perform the duties of a civil servant. The workplace was a tense space where women's emancipation, women's careers, and women's relationships intersected with discourses of homosexuality.

In most previous accounts of women's expanding employment, pioneering women and male authorities face off in a battle of the sexes. Men, whether doctors or employers, fight women's advancement openly or covertly through sabotage, or use antifeminist discourses to demean women. The "master" narrative of women's struggle for liberation against male repression casts the spotlight on women's achievements and men's resistance to change.[9] A strong early argument claimed that male sexologists used discourses of homosexual perversion to intimidate and pathologize single emancipated women.[10] This is a valid line of analysis as a reading of the discourses themselves, but we know relatively little about the reception and effects of these discourses for female historical subjects. These three cases show how sexological knowledge was circulated, understood, and appropriated in the context of the professional single-sex workgroup. Evidence does not confirm the assumption that male authorities used scientific knowledge to damage and intimidate their feminist subordinates (thereby stigmatizing and repressing women's intimate relationships in general). Instead, it reveals women making use of their knowledge of sexology eagerly and effectively against one another. When doctors did pathologize women's sexuality, their judgments had ambiguous effects on professional women's lives. Further, the stereotype of the mannish feminist lesbian, so prominent in the history of female homosexuality, had little resonance in the discussion of professional women's homosexuality in interwar Germany.[11]

Conflicts among women were more damaging to women's careers than homosexual panic. Deployment of the category took place within a particular culture that idealized women's work by rooting it in dominant gender stereotypes. Professional women's claims to emancipation required a parallel rhetorical allegiance to sexual asceticism.[12] The reality of same-sex intimacy and attraction within some women's work groups clashed with these ideals, creating a fertile environment for escalating tensions. When hostility replaced intimacy, the discourse of homosexuality became a weapon more effective within the group than with male authorities. Their commitment to emancipation as female professionals enabled categorical rejection of "homosexual" as a label applying to them or their relationships. Regardless of their actual intimate relationships, they robustly denied desires incompatible with their identities as professionals, making common cause with their employers in protecting their reputations.

The Three Cases

This first section of the chapter outlines what happened in each of the cases. These condensed reconstructions of the events from collected testimony will give readers an introduction to the historical subjects, their relationships, and the primary conflicts and issues that shaped each case. The following sections discuss analytical questions in a thematic arrangement to allow maximum opportunity for comparison between the cases. The thematic sections discuss one, two, or all three cases as they provide material useful to thinking through the problems at stake in each.

The Philipps Case

In 1914 many male teachers went off to war, allowing women such as Anna Philipps (1881–unknown) to find positions at girls' academic secondary schools. Teaching was not a new female profession, but the expansion of higher-level schooling for girls since the turn of the century had opened more prestigious positions in these schools. Teachers worked within a school bureaucracy under the direction of a male principal. Although teaching did not entail the intense idealism of the new social work professions, pedagogy was invested with considerable national import. Teachers shaped the character and worldviews of the next generation and imparted the knowledge expected of a political subject.[13] The death of Philipps's father, also a teacher, made it necessary for Philipps to support herself. One of her grandmothers paid for her basic teacher-training course. Philipps financed with her own savings the university degree she needed to move from elementary teaching to the academic high school in Geestemünde (near Bremerhaven), the site of her conflicts.

Philipps and her colleagues were more than just co-workers. They socialized with one another, vacationed together, and accompanied each other on visits to relatives. At least some of them shared living quarters. In Philipps's account, triangles of "special friends" often characterized intimacy among the teachers. The intense rejection and jealousy Philipps experienced when intimacy formed between two other teachers can be felt near the surface of her narrative. When she became fascinated with the idea of homosexuality through Hirschfeld's work, Philipps attempted to use it define relationships between teachers. Her co-teachers recalled Philipps's frequent mention of the subject of homosexuality and her urging them to read books about it. They reported that they always felt and expressed embarrassment on these occasions. One remembered Philipps repeatedly asking other teachers whether they thought she was homosexual. The others testified that they responded to this question by laughingly assuring her that she was not (despite their additional testimony about Philipps's unwelcome advances).[14]

In addition, teachers were on friendly terms with some of their students. The pedagogical ideals of the time emphasized the emotional bond between an older student and his or her same-sex teacher. Proponents of erotic pedagogy left unspecified the potential that such a close bond could have sexual consequences.[15] School authorities eventually disciplined Philipps because of her relationship with one of her students, Anni Sültrup. The charges and countercharges between teachers reflected the growing tensions resulting from uncomfortably ambiguous personal relationships.

Philipps's relationship with Sültrup had aroused anxiety among the teachers because of the latter's daily visits to Philipps's apartment. Just before Easter 1922, Philipps asked fellow teacher Fräulelin Fricke for advice on the relationship with Sültrup. Fricke became alarmed at Philipps's implication that Fricke had enjoyed similar improperly intimate relationships with her students. Apparently in something of a panic, she "strongly advised Fräulein Ph. not to go to some of our colleagues as she intended and not to get herself into trouble by spreading it around."[16] Using the vocabulary of homosexuality while talking about special relationships with students set off alarm bells for several other colleagues, who discussed Philipps's indiscreet assertions among themselves. One of them confronted her directly and demanded that she take back her slanderous implications about teacher-student relationships. Philipps threatened to bring the matter to the school's director. The next morning, "all these people were running back and forth," giving Philipps the feeling "of having stirred up a wasp's nest."[17] Indeed she had; the allegations of impropriety involving a student required that the school's director launch an investigation. As it proceeded, hostility toward Philipps escalated, leaving her feeling like the victim of a conspiracy of her closest friends.

The Atteln Case

Betrayal and isolation also marked the troubled story of nurse Hedwig Atteln (1888–unknown).[18] Atteln was an older daughter in her parents' household until she was twenty-eight. Shortly after the outbreak of the war, she began nurses' training. Nurses, called "sisters," reflecting the origins of the profession in religious orders, lived together in dormitory-like homes where their lives were closely entwined. While working in Düsseldorf, Atteln met Erna Westheider, a colleague from Cologne (Fig. 4.1). The two became an inseparable pair, going on vacation together and visiting each other's families. In 1922, Atteln applied for positions for both of them at the city hospital in Frankfurt, where they became roommates in the nurses' residence.[19]

Around 1930 Atteln's record began to reflect regular complaints from both co-workers and patients about her moodiness, rudeness, and lackadaisical work habits. The meager circumstances of nurses' lives during the depression were perhaps reflected in suspicions that Atteln stole butter from patients and coffee from communal supplies.[20] In late 1932 Westheider separated from Atteln and moved in with another sister. Atteln expressed her rage in letters to Westheider, accusing her of homosexuality and general sexual depravity. Westheider claimed she was afraid of Atteln and turned the harassing letters over to the head sister, perhaps hoping that Atteln would be fired, sparing her the unpleasantness of Atteln's anger. Thus exposed, Atteln attempted suicide, leaving another letter venting her grievances against both Westheider and the head sister.

The Erkens Case

Allegations of unwanted advances also emerged in the conflicts encountered by Josefine Erkens (1889–1974) in her position as head of the Hamburg Women's Police (Fig. 4.2). Erkens had lived at home with her parents in Düsseldorf until the wartime absence of men gave her her first opportunity to earn money as a bookkeeper. When she was laid off after the war, she took social work training at the Women's Academy in Düsseldorf and was hired as a social worker for the local Police Department. She headed the first women's police service in occupied Cologne and then worked in Frankfurt before being hired to develop the Hamburg Women's Police in 1927.[21] The Hamburg department agreed to hire two of her subordinates from Frankfurt, Theresa Dopfer (1897–1931) and Maria Fischer (1896?–1931). Dopfer and Fischer had met and become a couple in the early 1920s, when both held rural social work jobs.[22]

Fig. 4.1. Sisters (nurses) Hedwig Atteln and Erna Westheider. The photo was sent with their job application to Frankfurt. From Atteln's personnel file, Institut für Stadtgeschichte Frankfurt am Main, Bestand Personalakten Nr. 52.667 (Hedwig Atteln).

In Hamburg, Erkens succeeded in assembling a substantial team of women police officers and social workers under her direction. Erkens promoted her founding role with the Hamburg Women's Police as a model for other cities in Germany and Europe. As with the teachers and nurses, the policewomen formed a social circle, enjoying informal gatherings and joint

Fig. 4.2. Josefine Erkens, soon to become head of the Hamburg Women's Police. From Lothar Barck, *Ziele und Aufgaben der weiblichen Polizei in Deutschland,* 1928.

vacations. Here too, strong emotions of resentment, betrayal, disillusionment, and rage festered below the surface appearance of feminist comradeship. Erkens increasingly felt threatened by what she perceived as Dopfer's ambition and attempts to subvert her leadership. Hostile factions threatened to undercut feminist claims for women's leadership and solidarity. The tensions in the Women's Police disrupted day-to-day work and made working hours unbearable. Erkens blamed the discord on Dopfer, her closest subordinate. "I have asked for a thorough investigation of Frau Dopfer, who fights me so openly with my boss that I declared myself unable to continue working under these circumstances," she wrote to a friend in Berlin. "Such a betrayal of women is an outrage for the entire work of the Women's Police."[23]

On the other side, Dopfer's partner Maria Fischer confided her disillusionment in a letter to her sister, "We've had so much ugliness and meanness from Frau Erkens that I often thought I couldn't go on. . . . One struggles to the end not to give in to these ugly female moods. Never before have I felt how mean and worthless life is, how selfish people are, how much everything is politics, politics of the lowest sort."[24] A newspaper quoted Theresa Dopfer as having said she'd rather work as a cleaning lady than continue under Erkens.[25] Earlier that spring she had begun a letter to her sister, "Sometimes I curse my position as an official. . . . It's a disgrace for women's work that so many fail, especially when they get into leadership positions."[26] The vehemence of these statements reflects the depth of the women's commitment to professional ideals of purity and selflessness—ideals apparently betrayed by others they had trusted to share them.

The conflict was fundamentally a power struggle between rivals, but another statement in Erkens's letter revealed that it also involved intimate feelings between the women. She confided, "Since [Dopfer] couldn't force me into the friendship she wanted, her hate fuels all the flames."[27] When tensions led police authorities to examine Dopfer's and Erkens's complaints about one another, co-workers faced questions about inappropriate intimacy between the two. Rumors about Dopfer and Fischer's relationship spread beyond their immediate police colleagues. In shame and despair, Dopfer and Fischer traveled to an island in the North Sea and committed suicide together. By then, Dopfer and Fischer had lived together as a couple for almost a decade. After their deaths, speculation about the Dopfer-Fischer relationship as well as that between Erkens and Dopfer became fodder for city hall gossip and newspaper coverage. In Hamburg women's relationships with their colleagues became the subject of a politicized scandal that threatened to tarnish the whole of women's professional work.

Career Women's Precarious Worlds I:
Emancipation, Sex, and Power

The interwar period was an extended adjustment phase in the history of women's emancipation. The major feminist demands had been formulated by the end of the nineteenth century. Postwar conditions allowed several types of New Women to become more visible, consolidating and broadening participation in social change that only a few could afford a generation earlier. Media images promoted consumption by matter-of-fact young secretaries and pleasure-seeking glamour girls.[28] But women who supported their independence through their work in professional careers also became much more numerous.

The professional women involved in the cases of homosexual accusation belonged to a particular generation in the middle of this transition.[29] Born in the 1880s, they were younger than the pioneering university and feminist women described in the first two chapters, yet older than women who came of age during and after World War I—the "modern girls" of the 1920s. The key figures in these cases began living as independent adults when they were nearing forty. Their attempts to negotiate workplace politics and to forge social communities often seem impossibly clumsy and naive. Socialized to fulfill domestic roles, they were ill-equipped to manage the contradictions between their idealistic ambitions and the postwar struggle for survival. They experienced themselves simultaneously as pioneers in their work lives and as already old-fashioned in the eyes of younger and more fashionable urban consumers.

World War I and the economic instability of the early Weimar Republic shaped the careers of working women in this cohort. Before the war, families had reabsorbed their daughters who had finished school. Marriage was the only exit from the parental or sibling household. Respectable independent space for young women, except those few with funds at their disposal, was limited. The war opened work in the wartime welfare bureaucracy or as replacements for men, lending patriotic validation to women's efforts. Once the war was over, a number of them held onto their careers. Although the market for educated women's labor was depressed after the war, some of these older, now experienced women were able to gain a career foothold and build independent lives.[30]

The chronic Weimar financial crises resulted in unusual mobility in women's careers. By the 1930s, many had held three or more positions, often widely spread across Germany. Therefore, work groups functioned for many as a source of social connection and ersatz family. Some female couples that had formed during the war or in the first job posting survived frequent moves and job changes. The depression of the 1930s intensified workplace conflicts as options for leaving to take another job evaporated.

Some professional women worked for private or religious charities, but many, including those in these three cases, worked in public employment. Women's opportunities were enhanced with the adoption of the Weimar Constitution (1919), which guaranteed women's legal equality and opened the door to appointment of women to civil service titles. In Germany, educated state employees (*Beamten*) enjoyed considerable prestige and shared an unwritten code of rights and duties, consistent with their ideals of professionalism, loyalty to the nonpartisan state, and the rule of law.

Women hired for these desirable positions justified their inclusion by emphasizing the specifically feminine and motherly contribution they would make to state administration. They hypothesized that socially problematic individuals would respond positively to the understanding and caring approach of a female official.[31] Women's organizations in Germany had long made similar arguments in advocating the creation of state positions for women as upper-level teachers, social workers, and police officers.[32] Gertrud Bäumer, spokesperson for the moderate bourgeois women's movement during the Weimar Republic, responded to the Erkens disciplinary case in the *Vossische Zeitung*. To refute doubts about women's ability to serve as police officers, she passionately reasserted the women's movement's conception of the ideal working environment for professional women. She demanded that women work "with their own female leadership—something like the sisterhood of a hospital under the head nurse." The implied administrative positions for women had "nothing at all to do with ambition and power-seeking." Women's essential qualities were needed at higher levels of government to create "new functions of understanding, treatment, and protection of women and children."[33] Bäumer's editorial restated the basic assumptions supporting the new women's professions and of the women's movement itself.[34] Its advocacy of female employment was grounded in belief that female presence itself would lead to reform.

Service and sexual purity were the two feminine ideals particularly powerful in shaping women's work communities. The group ethos expressed their feminist critique of masculine desire for power and sexual indulgence, particularly as represented in the policing of prostitution.[35] Women's gender-difference-based claims on public roles required them to deny desire—both career and sexual. The archival records in each case show that the desire for a secure livelihood, official recognition and rank, and competition with one another motivated career women's choices. Yet these "selfish" motivations could not be acknowledged. Their culture associated ambition with masculine characteristics their careers were intended to counteract.

Although official rhetoric disavowed power, the positions of social worker, police officer, teacher, and nurse all involved giving women the power to regulate the behavior of the patient, client, suspect, or student. Professional women used their power to enforce their own middle-class values on working-class or resistant women.[36] Acknowledgment of the exercise of power fundamental to their work was smothered by excessive repetition of bromides about the female roles of caring, helping, and protecting.[37] Women civil servants associated uncaring and corrupt male bureaucracies with personal ambition and political scheming. However, the desires constantly denied returned as rivalry, jealousy, and foiled ambition permeating both professional and personal spaces and relations. When these emotions combined with equally denied attractions and erotically tinged friendships, the results were toxic. Eventually, the discord became so intense that institutions were called in to intervene.

In all three cases, interpersonal conflicts with roots in women's intimate relationships and women's exercise of power, the exact issues at the heart of professional ideals, precipitated into investigations and scandals. The resort to suicide following accusations of homosexuality in two of the cases demonstrates just how deeply sexual suspicions violated the professional women's sense of self, identity, and professional belonging. Their independence from family rested on a fragile conjuncture of wartime and postwar reorganization of state, economy, and society. Yet what touched them most deeply was the ethos and ideal of professional service that justified their claims to emancipation. Because women police were still a contested novelty, the documents of the Erkens case show most clearly how advocates of expanded professional opportunities for women constructed their identities to support their claims.

Both policemen and feminists hoped women police officers could reduce what they saw as an increase in prostitution and disorderly family life after the war. Feminists pointed to the same feminine qualities that suited women for social work.[38] Erkens specified the object of women's police work as girls and young women "already on the dangerous path without being seen as regular or conscious prostitutes." Policewomen referred to the young women they aimed to correct as "*Gefährdete*" (those in danger). Erkens explained, "The young and inexperienced, who go out into the world passionately with sails unfurled, full of longing for adventure and life, or those who are stamped by lack of willpower, weak character, or suggestibility, and therefore are open to all the influences and attractions of the street" were in danger of "falling victim to seduction and exploitation due to their inability to resist."[39] When "the endangered" was interpreted broadly as "vulnerable," it encompassed the policewomen's task of assisting those in public places who appeared to need help, often with a focus on girls and young women who might be threatened with male harassment. But insider discussions emphasized the specific goal of rescuing women in moral danger. Although social workers did not always impose a moral judgment on those in trouble, most feminists and social workers could not escape the conditioning of middle-class girls that divided women sharply into the respectable and the fallen. Feminist advocates imagined that policewomen would prevent prostitution by reforming girls' behavior before they were entrenched in the fallen category.[40]

Thus, for professional women working with girls and young women, sexual purity was not only an ideal and an expectation, but also the source of professional authority. Weimar's endangered girls, who had grown up too fast during the war and were tempted by the pleasures of entertainment and consumer culture, needed the positive model of restraint provided by teachers, social workers, and policewomen. The task of the policewoman in particular was to recognize women and girls in danger of losing their sexual shame.[41] The nineteenth-century idea that sex represented the lower, bestial nature of the human being remained integral to women's professional identities. Their benevolent influence, they believed, would restore respectability and domesticity to endangered young lives. Their ability to tame sexuality made policewomen's careers essential to society and the nation. Therefore, suggesting that a colleague experienced sexual desire implied that she had crossed the boundary between respectable and fallen. If professional women felt inner conflicts over pleasure or desire, they did not express them publicly. No one asked whether women who were officially inexperienced in and possibly ignorant about sexual matters would be the most credible advisors for young sexually active women. This question was left to male skeptics after the suicides.[42]

Erkens served on a committee organized by the Federation of German Women's Organizations in the mid-1920s to promote women's police forces.[43] The committee hoped to move the focus of police work from punishment to prevention, rehabilitation, and support.[44] In line with the ideals of professional women in general, feminist advocates of women police exploited the image of women as caregivers, sympathetic listeners, and loving disciplinarians. As Erkens put it, "The power and order principle therefore is pushing developmentally towards its complement through the 'motherly' principle of the intention to protect and help."[45] Some Weimar police reformers were willing to accept a certain level of feminization in order to give the police a softer image. They agreed that feminine attributes justified the existence of women's police units; however, for them this meant limiting the women's sphere of activity to "preventing, helping, protecting, in a word, representing the more feminine moment."[46]

The committee hoped for feminine enclaves under female leadership within the overwhelmingly masculine police departments.[47] But they feared that women would be seen simply as helpers, who had no role in reforming public service in general. Their ultimate goal was a new model of bureaucracy and state power based on female values and humane solutions to social problems.[48] The committee's guidelines explicitly denied that their advocacy of women's leadership was motivated by a desire to "create a new women's career."[49] Police chiefs, however, disagreed with feminist advocates about the autonomy of the planned women's units, which they argued had to be firmly subordinated to police department administrators.[50]

In this atmosphere of contention over the autonomy of women's work, women advocates felt compelled to defend ideas that both asserted and denied female power and authority. Erkens, in particular, sought to secure a "protective wall" against the influence of the existing all-male police force with its overwhelming numbers and long-standing traditions. Erkens argued that women who had to work side by side with men would be conscious of male "mistrust and resistance." They would be tempted to give up their "own special ways of working" in order to fit in and live up to male expectations. "The most creative women, full of passion and the capacity for devotion to an ideal" might give up on the profession or "break down emotionally" because of the exposure to "strong personal misunderstandings, enmity, and slander."[51] As it turned out, Erkens's words were prescient. However, the "personal misunderstandings, enmity, and slander" that made working in the Hamburg women's police unbearable for many of its officers emerged among its women officers rather than between the sexes.

Sexuality and power, then, triggered and exacerbated tensions and conflicts in the single-sex work environment in these cases. Erkens, for example, tried to discredit Dopfer, her perceived rival, by accusing her of violating both sexual purity and the workplace ideals of selflessness and solidarity. Women's work faltered in realizing its ideal of positive social change for multiple and complex reasons.[52] In these instances, women's inability to adapt to conflicts and power struggles in the everyday workplace was a significant factor. Since co-workers were also friends and substitute family, disappointment and betrayal had the potential to rip apart the whole of a woman's world.

Career Women's Precarious Worlds II: Ideal Friendships

The sources for these cases document the texture of the same-sex intimate relationships that were so central to the lives of many professional women. Witnesses—professional women, as well as those who observed them—interpreted relationships, feelings, and meanings of the term *homosexual*. Their statements reveal the fluid and multiple knowledges about homosexuality circulating among different groups of observers. In the background, we can also tease out some of the details of daily life for the female couples among groups of professional women. The ethos of service and desirelessness that guided their professional careers shaped their intimate bonds as well. While the emergence of homosexual accusations clearly reveals that at least some had begun to question whether their feelings fit into the parameters of that category, for the most part, they continued the pattern of "romantic friends."[53]

By the twentieth century, the effusive emotionalism and flexibility of earlier patterns of women's intimacy had diminished. For professional women, claiming sexual subjectivity was officially taboo. Professions of love among co-workers were seldom articulated, perhaps because popular culture now tied "love" more closely to heterosexual romance. Instead, collegial friendships supported professional self-esteem and solidarity. Emancipated women needed each other. Intimacy was expressed through codes and symbols, which can be partially recovered from testimony in the cases. These markers of a special friendship became vulnerabilities when exposed and reinterpreted by an accuser. Usually the accuser was a colleague feeling pain over rejection by a beloved individual and the loneliness of being left outside the circle of protective intimacy.

The investigations that accompanied workplace conflicts necessarily threw a spotlight on the couple relationships that had formed in each of the workgroups. The women's friends referred to these obvious pairings as "ideal friendships." "Ideal" should be understood as an opposite to "material." It meant that friendships entailed harmony of minds and souls, explicitly excluding physical relationships. Ideal friendships were a clear successor to romantic friendships. However, in the 1920s, use of the "ideal" descriptor did not completely dispel suspicions of homosexuality. Given the importance of denying desire, even the suggestion of abnormal attraction could be damaging. Women in couple relationships had to monitor expression of their feelings for one another carefully. By maintaining a strategic ambiguity, supported by their public avowal of respectability, professional women created space for intimate pair relationships between colleagues. The intensity of camouflaged love and desire was nearly obscured by the hostile investigations. But accusations were not smears concocted from nothing. Feelings and observations of feelings were the raw materials that allowed participants to use discourse about homosexuality to disgrace those they perhaps had once desired.

The rich testimony about everyday life contained in the Erkens and Philipps case files allows a glimpse of how professional women lived and construed their intimate relationships with each other. The atmosphere of accusation and denial that produced the testimony inevitably shaped these descriptions. The accused women and their colleagues were keen to protect themselves from public and judicial scrutiny. Yet their statements reveal the tacit rules governing how passion between women might be acknowledged and communicated within professional women's common culture of respectability.

Professional women used the familiar form of address—*Du*—as a metaphor for intimacy in relationships.[54] Among members of the upper and middle classes, the use of *Du* implied a degree of intimacy beyond that of casual acquaintances or colleagues. A woman testifying about her relationships to individuals being investigated invariably insisted that she was very selective about whom she offered the *Du* status. Although the use of *Du* did not automatically signal a sexual relationship, it transgressed the respectful distance proper in collegial relations and might be seen as the first step toward other advances. An embarrassed admission that a woman had used *Du* with another required her to add that she agreed to it reluctantly when the other insisted.

The teachers who worked with Anna Philipps emphasized Philipps's transgression of the *Du* boundary in their testimony against her. Philipps's apartment mate Frl. Sickermann insisted, "Fräulein Ph. asked to be addressed as *Du* in the fall of 1917 and received my assent only after long resistance." Then, at the end of 1921, Sickermann "found out for the first time that [Philipps and a third teacher, Hardrat] used *Du* with each other. Although I controlled myself and bit back a remark, Fräulein Ph. made it sound as if Fräulein Hardrat had offered a *Du* relationship."[55] Surrounding testimony makes it apparent that at one point the two apartment mates were an intimate couple. Sickermann was dismayed by the suggestion of infidelity represented by the second *Du* relationship.

Anxiety over the use of *Du* was also central in the Hamburg police investigation. There, Josefine Erkens claimed that Theresa Dopfer had requested a *Du* relationship with her, which she had rejected because she didn't "approve of it among women."[56] Dopfer likewise complained that Erkens used *Du* without being invited to do so.[57] Dopfer's partner, Maria Fischer confirmed Dopfer's statement: "Frau Dopfer was constantly called by her first name Tesi and addressed with *Du* by Frau Erkens. . . . Frau Dopfer, on her side, had never invited the use of *Du* much less used it with her."[58] As the investigation unfolded, Erkens used the *Du* claim to deflect blame for the conflicts in the police department on to her subordinate. In this context, the *Du* suggested insubordination as well as inappropriate intimacy. Erkens connected the two connotations to suggest that Dopfer suffered from a biologically pathological personality that caused her to transgress ideal social and professional boundaries integral to professional identity.

Hostility between Dopfer and Erkens seems to have dated from 1928, four years before the disciplinary investigation. Erkens's associates testified that she had begun confiding in them about Dopfer's "demands" for a closer relationship around that time.[59] Dopfer and Fischer had also complained to friends about Erkens's unwanted intrusions into their home life soon after their relocation to Hamburg.[60] Several policewomen testified about events that took place during lunch breaks in the same period. The nine policewomen gathered around a common table for lunch. Erkens teased Dopfer during these breaks in an ambiguously sexual way. One colleague said that "certain signs" convinced her that Erkens was the aggressor. "Frau Erkens constantly used the familiar '*Du*' toward Frau Dopfer at work," she testified, "and also called her '*Goldschatz*' (Golden Treasure), although these familiarities were visibly unpleasant for Frau Dopfer." She "never in the least noticed any advances from Frau Dopfer toward Frau Erkens."[61] A co-worker added that Dopfer "did not want to let herself be latched onto by Frau Erkens." This witness interpreted Erkens's behavior as "a joke" rather than "advances." "It must have occurred to Frau Erkens that this contact was unpleasant for Frau Dopfer," she continued. "But instead of stopping it, Frau Erkens repeated this supposed joke more and more often and more and more embarrassingly, until Frau Dopfer had no more peace."[62]

Questioned about the accuracy of these accounts, Dopfer described Erkens's behavior as "teasing" and emphasized that Erkens continued to address her as *Du* even after she had expressly forbidden it.[63] Since this questioning took place following the spread of sexual rumors, Dopfer clearly wanted to deemphasize sexual connotations. She focused instead on the breach of workplace etiquette, a claim likely to be more persuasive to the investigating bureaucrats.

Six of the twenty-four pages of the protocol of Erkens's testimony before the disciplinary hearing judge dealt with the sexual innuendo, which had by then become an unavoidable part of the case. Erkens's statements reversed those of Dopfer and Fischer, claiming that Dopfer "became a pest after our move to Hamburg through her almost constant wanting to be together." "She also tried to show signs of her affection," she continued, "for example, putting her head in my lap. I found all this unpleasant, I think it is unhealthy, after trying to put her off for a long time I also tried to say it in a kind, but direct, way." "Frau Dopfer's unconscious sexual feelings were not completely normal," Erkens judged. She saw Dopfer's alleged "attempts to win [her] affection" as "erotically tinged, although not overtly sexual." She claimed that Fischer had once said, "Now it's you, before Frau Noack, then Fräulein Schoepke; I'm only there in between."[64] Whether or not Dopfer had had feelings for any of these women, Erkens implied that Dopfer's advances toward women were consistent, promiscuous, and therefore pathological.

When other policewomen were asked about their perceptions of the Dopfer/Fischer relationship, the sameness in their testimony indicates a strategy of answering overtly sexual questions as briefly as possible. Virtually all repeated that they regarded Dopfer and Fischer's relationship as purely a friendship; they had never noticed any caresses or suspected them of anything sexually abnormal. In a letter to the court, the couple's friends strenuously objected to the "ugliest defamations" that Erkens had spread about Dopfer and Fischer, accusing Erkens of dragging "their friendship through the mud" outside the workplace. "It can only be repeatedly emphasized that this friendship was an ideal and pure one and that it would have been impossible for these human beings to live in an atmosphere of the kind implied by Frau Erkens," they wrote. "Both of them have doubtless suffered much and gradually drawn back from all their acquaintances."[65]

The specifics of Erkens's accusations, along with other testimony, suggest that when two women had declared their love for one another, they called each other *Du* and other pet names, gave one another flowers, spent their free time together, and exchanged physical intimacies in private. Statements consistently brought up and then denied these signs. It was important to women that their attachments to each other be treated with extreme discretion in public. Formality at work was necessary to maintaining the ambiguity that was required by their group norms and by potentially prying outsiders. Testimonies always included a denial of any conspicuous "tendernesses," suggesting that the investigating judge considered it the most compelling evidence of whether a homosexual relationship existed. As is also clear in the family testimonies given below, the meaning of *Zärtlichkeiten* (tendernesses or caresses) hinged on who was performing the acts. For friends and colleagues, everyday physical contact, love, living together, and so on did not and could not indicate homosexuality, which was conceptually associated with sexual contact for pleasure or the satisfaction of an inner compulsion. Whatever went on between their idealistic, hard-working friends in private to express affection could not be lumped together with the open sensuality of "shameless" women.

The extensive depositions in the Erkens case provide documentation of what witnesses were willing to tell the judge about their perceptions of female couples. The families of both Dopfer and Fischer, like their colleagues, defended the respectability of the relationship. The couple had visited and sometimes lived with the witnesses' families. Their testimony explicitly drew on the authority of close observation. Male witnesses apparently felt comfortable drawing on their knowledge of sexuality and of the signs that might indicate homosexuality. Their comments on the sexual and gender character of the two women were more extensive than those of female witnesses. Dopfer's male cousin called the relationship "purely friendly"; it was "out of the question that there was a more intimate, especially a sexual relationship, between the two." He considered his cousin "too sensible and sexually cold" for a romantic involvement.[66]

Dopfer's and Fischer's eldest brothers acted as spokesmen for the families after the suicides. Fischer's brother was glad that his somewhat sickly and sensitive sister had found someone to watch out for her. He found "the way Thesy Dopfer sacrificed herself for [his] sister . . . touching." Like the other witnesses he affirmed his opinion that this was a "pure friendship relationship." After the suicides, he had found a letter from Fischer to Dopfer, which he described as "excessively gushing." Even after reading this letter though, he did not see any "kind of an abnormal sexual relationship between the two women." "After the death of my sister," his statement continued, "I naturally thought about this question and asked about it in Hamburg among the colleagues of my sister." None of them admitted to seeing anything but a "pure friendship relationship." Probably responding to the judge's questions, he added that he had "no knowledge of [his] sister ever having any kind of a serious crush on a man." He further described Dopfer's interactions with men as "normal, cheery, and open."[67]

The brother casually reported that he had destroyed the letter, a bit of concrete evidence that might have been harder to force into the ideal realm. His repetition of the phrase "pure friendship relationship" helped create an unbridgeable conceptual boundary between it and its opposite, a "abnormal sexual relationship." Sympathetic witnesses could only place Dopfer and Fischer on one or the other side of this divide. It would take direct evidence of sexual behavior to change their perspective on the prim and proper women they knew. The juxtaposition of Fischer's gushing and Dopfer's protective, sensible character did not suggest to them a gender-differentiated sexual attraction.

Dopfer's brother, questioned about the "love letter," explained its tone as stemming from Fischer's penchant for "exalted" expression. He too had found written evidence of the couple's emotional connection. Packed away with their Christmas crèche was a note in Fischer's handwriting. The brother paraphrased the note's content: "Dear, good little Thesy, you are already asleep in your little bed and I am still putting away the manger. I will take good care, so that it will be a great joy to us again next year." He was convinced that his sister would never write something so sentimental and speculated that Fischer was attracted to the contrastingly "robust" Dopfer. He saw the relationship as based in complementary needs—Fischer's for someone to rely on and Dopfer's to express sympathy for someone "rather weak." He acknowledged the likelihood that the emotional bond between the two might have led to "mental and emotional dependency on each other." But he too found a "sexual relationship between them completely impossible." As evidence, he cited his close observation of the relationship during three summer vacations spent together. He had seen none of the "caresses between them, such as are to be observed among sexually abnormal women."[68] The head of the family claimed the authority to differentiate between "sexually abnormal women" and friends who were "mentally and emotionally dependent on each other." Many of the signs that meant innocence for Dopfer's brother—the complementary active-passive relationship or the "we" assumed in the fanciful New Year note—could easily have been taken as evidence of a hidden sexual attachment by a doctor or unsympathetic observer.

Similar testimony given by the Spiras, an older couple who had been substitute parental figures for Fischer, found the relationship innocent because of both women's devotion to their "priestly" calling. They thought Fischer "had found a congenial friend and companion in Frau Dopfer." Theodor Spira wrote to the judge, "I still remember clearly my strong first impression of the inner purity of both women. . . . It never entered our minds that in the personal closeness of the friendship of the women, so strongly rooted in their common professional tasks, that this factor, even unconsciously, played a role." The Spiras described Fischer as "motherly-feminine," while Dopfer, "even with her unbending will and strong temperament, had a pronounced feminine nature."[69] Unlike the other witnesses, Spira brought up gender stereotypes. At first pointing to Fischer's femininity as evidence against homosexuality, he seems to have realized that the contrast between Fischer and Dopfer might throw suspicion on Dopfer. He then suppressed the notion that Dopfer's temperament might be construed as masculine.

Erkens's relatives had also observed Dopfer and Fischer during a group vacation trip in 1926. Erkens's brother-in-law had quite a different impression from that of Dopfer's and Fischer's brothers. The remarkable testimonies about his statements given by Erkens's sister and another woman present were the only ones to characterize Dopfer and Fischer as a lesbian couple. Erkens's sister Berta recalled that her husband was visibly uncomfortable with the situation in the cabin. He told her that she ought to warn her sister about her sick and perverse friends. Subsequently Berta began to pay closer attention to how Dopfer and Fischer interacted. "I saw for myself then the physical contact between Frl. Topfer [sic] and Fischer," she reported. "I observed for myself, several times, that Frl. Topfer touched Frl. Fischer high up on the thigh as we sat together around the table and that they stroked each other." When Berta asked Dopfer if she ever wanted to get married, Dopfer was alleged to have replied, "Why should I get married anyway, I am the man, and Fischer the woman." It was obvious that her husband believed the two were living in "lesbian love" (lesbische Liebe).[70]

The other witness, Maria Korr, claimed not to have noticed anything out of the ordinary, but she gave a more colorful version of the conversation between Dopfer and Erkens's sister. She recalled Dopfer saying "she would never get married," because she had a "completely modern marriage." Dopfer referred to Fischer as "the good housewife." Because Dopfer was laughing, Korr didn't think much then about the implications. But later, she "found out that Herr Lagarie, a friend of the Erkens family, got especially irritated because his wife spoke rather enthusiastically about the friendship between Frl. Topfer and Fischer." Lagarie told his wife to be quiet about the "unnatural friendship," adding "that sort of thing didn't go over well with him at all."[71]

In these observations of disinterested parties, the very signs denied by Dopfer and Fischer's friends and relatives become visible, especially through the eyes of men who apparently were reacting to Dopfer's and Fischer's lack of interest in them. Even though these were housewives rather than professional women defending their purity, the women did not notice physical closeness or gendered roles until men made them aware of these signs of homosexuality. Frau Lagarie's enthusiasm over the qualities of the female relationship further indicates that observers did respond to the closeness between the two, perhaps even comparing it to their marriages.

Erkens's sister also reported that after the trip she had told Erkens what her husband had said. She described Erkens as being very upset about the revelation and saying she didn't believe it.[72] Erkens's knowledge of others' interpretation of the Dopfer-Fischer relationship is significant for her subsequent fascination with and apparent interference in it. About two years after this vacation trip Erkens began to suggest that Dopfer had made inappropriate advances toward her. Did Erkens use her new perspective on the relationship to nurture an attraction of her own toward Dopfer and try to break up Dopfer and Fischer? Or did she simply see an opportunity to smear and intimidate her professional rival? The answer is impossible to determine from the sources. Yet the Philipps case too suggests that romantically tinged jealousy contributed to accusations.

The teachers also thought of their intimate friendships in ideal terms. Fräulein Hardrat said that she and Philipps were "related by choice, people who wanted to mutually help each other improve themselves."[73] Kissing became an issue when Philipps referred to it in her telling of events. Sickermann described Philipps's attempts to kiss and caress her while they were living together as "thoroughly against my nature." Sickermann claimed, "Philipps forced herself into my bedroom when I was already in bed, and sat down on the my bed in such a way that I instinctively jumped away."[74] Their colleague Hardrat also connected Phillips with ambiguous kissing. Hardrat admitted to giving Philipps "a light goodbye kiss once, which she took as permission to be tender toward me." Hardrat recalled that Philipps had repeatedly asked whether she "kissed [her] friends or the young girls who were [her] former students." Hardrat claimed to have answered "no" without thinking much of it. Later, on returning to school after holidays, Hardrat gave Philipps "a quick kiss in the happiness of seeing each other again." She was alarmed when

Philipps remarked, "I have read that every kiss releases a sexual effect." She claimed that she vowed then never again to give Philipps a friendly kiss.[75] Defensive testimonies such as Hardrat's explained intimacies as friends' misinterpretation of innocent affection. Though Sickermann and Hardrat positioned themselves in their testimony as the targets unwelcome advances, both remained emotionally involved with Philipps until the scandal emerged.

Another teacher, Frl. Fricke, reported that just before the issue of Philipps's alleged inappropriate relationship with her student Anni Sültrup came under investigation, Philipps had come to her in a state of agitated excitement over kissing Sültrup. Fricke quoted Philipps as saying, "I am terribly in love with Anni Sültrup. Anni Sültrup came to me and blurted out, 'I want to have a friendship with you like Anneliese Burgdorf has with Fräulein Fricke.' Anni Sültrup and I kissed each other senseless." Philipps gushed further, "I can no longer leave it alone and neither can Anni Sültrup. I have a right to do it. I don't know what will come of it. But I can't go back. Once she slept with me (or was with me the whole night . . .)." The talk of sexual kissing, especially a student, clearly broke a taboo. Fricke responded to Philipps's suggestion that she had a similar relationship with a student by proclaiming "complete incomprehension."[76]

The Philipps case strongly suggests that intense friendships and jealous triangles were frequent occurrences among the teachers, who managed their feelings by not naming what was going on. They trusted each other to be discreet about what happened between two women in private since both would naturally be implicated if the physical aspects of the relationships were openly discussed. After the war, Philipps tried to get the other teachers to talk openly about what was happening and to acknowledge that their attractions were part of a homosexual identity that they shared. When Philipps threatened to extend this to relations with students, the other teachers panicked and reported Philipps to the school's director. They were afraid that Philipps would share her "modern" ideas beyond the confines of the teachers' own circle.

The testimonies of women who felt exposed and those of sympathetic witnesses display some important similarities in their refusal to identify themselves or people they knew with the concept of homosexuality. With the exception of Philipps, all of them knew that homosexuality or same-sex sexual desire made explicit would entail serious stigma and ostracism. All witnesses clearly differentiated "pure friendships" from "abnormal sexual relationships." These categorizations relied on stereotypes of the sexually active, pleasure-seeking woman. For many witnesses, being convinced of a friend's or relative's idealism and belief in sexual restraint allowed them confidently to reject the homosexual label. At the same time most acknowledged behavioral signs that others might interpret as indications of homosexuality. Once the issue became explicit, signs of affection became sites of anxiety. Friends could interpret caresses, kisses, and use of *Du* as evidence of deep nonsexual caring. But outsiders looking for evidence might well interpret these same signs as evidence of abnormal desire. The ambiguity and discreet silence about what happened in a couple's private life was threatened.

Deploying Accusations of Homosexuality

Closing ranks against a threat did not silence colleagues who felt betrayed. Rage and jealousy found an outlet in escalating accusations of perversion and corruption. The pattern of the accusations reveals a submerged story of love triangles and emotional manipulation made possible by ambiguity in couples' public presentation. The three stories could be read as tales of spurned lovers' revenge: Erkens shut out by the Dopfer-Fischer partnership, Atteln rejected in favor of another nurse, Sickermann and Hardrat coming together to shun Philipps. When the pain of losing love could not be expressed directly, the rejected party turned to the language of medicalized perversion to express hurt and rage. Once allegations circulated, ambiguity was no longer effective. Instead, campaigns of counteraccusation, gossip, and ostracism aimed to expose the real "abnormal" in hopes that she would be removed from the work group. The investigating authorities found themselves in the position of adjudicating competing claims of sexual perversion and innocence. Although male authorities tried to brush the embarrassing sexual revelations aside, some professional women clung to the discourse of homosexuality to hurt and smear their colleagues.

Philipps, for example, brought the principal a written statement of her counteraccusations against two other teachers.[77] When these were not investigated, she speculated that those teachers, in order to entrap her, had conspired in a plan to have Sültrup seduce her and then write incriminating letters.[78] Philipps was transferred to another school because "her behavior toward the student Sültrup lack[ed] the necessary pedagogical tact."[79] She interpreted this as a tacit finding that she was guilty of homosexual acts. Her campaign to be reinstated and vindicated involved repeated charges of similar behavior among her colleagues.

In 1926, Philipps filed charges with the local prosecutor accusing one of the other teachers of "crimes against morality." She accused her former friends, the secret homosexuals, of protecting themselves by accusing and ostracizing her. The prosecuting attorney refused to bring charges because the accusations were too "general" and the alleged incident had happened too long ago.[80] When life went on and both the educational bureaucracy and law enforcement dismissed her accusations, she came to be convinced of an even broader conspiracy against her.

Hirschfeld's works enabled Philipps to consider and discuss homosexuality as a scientifically validated word that described the teachers' feelings for each other. The more she insisted on using it, the more she violated sexual and relationship ideals the teachers shared. Philipps's testimony claims that she saw herself as honestly believing in Hirschfeld's benign theory and helpfully enlightening her friends. The panicked reactions of her principal and fellow teachers shocked her, leading her to interpret their denial of desire as dishonesty. Feeling betrayed and mistreated, Philipps constructed a narrative of good versus evil to explain the betrayal and the disinterest of authorities in her escalating grievances. With each telling, she escalated her new belief that homosexuals were evil and powerful rather than the harmless outcasts depicted by Hirschfeld. Since she knew that the teachers were homosexuals, she attributed their duplicity to homosexuality. Consequently, she saw it as her duty to expose the perverts' corruption of the state. When the minister of education and her Reichstag representative dismissed her claims, she concluded that the conspiracy reached all the way to the highest levels of government: "Teachers who are prostitutes and homosexuals can do what they like—they are protected."[81] Her superiors were fed up with the unending string of accusations against public officials and ordered her to stop appealing or be fired. The order only confirmed her perception of herself as the lone voice of civic virtue. She persisted and was terminated in 1931.[82] Rebuffed by the Nationalist Party (DNVP), which, she insinuated, "played a certain role in homosexual circles," she declared that the "National Socialists had taken an interest in the affair."[83] In short, anyone who refused to validate her innocence had to be in league with the powerful cabal of homosexuals, who protected the secrets of their own.[84] There is no evidence that the Nazis ever responded to her effort to bring them into the controversy.[85] Having painted herself into this kind of a corner, Philipps must have led a lonely and bitter life after the publication of her book.

The accusations in the case of the Frankfurt nurse, Hedwig Atteln, are particularly tragic examples of the effects of denied desire turned to hatred. Atteln's desperate need to hurt Erna Westheider, her former partner, are clear in threatening letters to Westheider and in a suicide letter discovered next to her comatose body. The letters were prompted by Westheider's move from the room shared with Atteln to the room of another nurse, Regina. Attlen accused Westheider of being "pathological" because of her "homosexual inclination." In Atteln's reconstruction of the history of their relationship she was the victim of Westheider's "masculine" aggressiveness. The suicide letter described Westheider's sexual aggression and open expressions of desire. "She lured me into her room, locked the door, turned out the lights, threw me on the bed, and smothered me with kisses," Attlen claimed. Later on an outing to Cologne, where Westheider's parents lived, Atteln alleged that Westheider "dragged me into a car and took me to her house. Her parents were not home and we were alone there. I was terribly afraid of her character and did not want to get undressed. Then she ripped off my clothes and raped me with all her strength." Atteln could not clearly explain why she had subsequently initiated a move to Frankfurt with a woman who had raped her. She wrote that she was "paralyzed" and "ashamed," and claimed that Westheider convinced her that "it wasn't so serious, a lot of people do it." Then she "no longer had a will of her own" and allowed Westheider to "cool her passion on me every evening."[86] She justified her participation by framing it as a sacrifice that protected other women from Westheider's seduction.[87]

Despite the allegations of victimization, "over time [Atteln] had attached [herself] firmly to Westheider and [they] were satisfied with each other in every way." Atteln wrote bitterly to Westheider, "Like a sheep, I thought I had a true friend in you, but really I was nothing but a cover for your affairs with the younger sisters." Here Atteln suggested that she had tried to maintain the relationship as an ideal friendship, despite the sex, while Westheider had betrayed that model of bonded connection. To underscore Westheider's failure to conform to the pattern of denial of desire and affirmation of purity expected of professional women, Atteln catalogued Westheider's "depravity," "debauchery," and "dissipation." Westheider had introduced Atteln to "erotic jokes, books, and pictures," and had told her about "all kinds of things that she did with two girls" and with "a man, a former lover of hers." In these affairs, "there [could] be no talk of love, since she went from one to the next." Atteln, writing in rage and despair, differentiated between her pure, self-sacrificing same-sex love ("true friend") and the depraved attributes of a homosexual orientation, which she attributed to Westheider. This strategy allowed her to interpret her own feelings as "not homosexual."

Unlike Erkens or Philipps, Atteln attributed desire, abuse, and betrayal to Westheider's "masculine character." Writing to Westheider, Atteln claimed, "Everyone else knows you are 'gay' and is amazed that your masculine character and appearance—and especially the masculine emphasis in civilian clothes—did not make it obvious to me."[88] Atteln's use of peer gossip to shame suggests that homosexuality was more openly acknowledged among the nurses. Citing masculinity completed the list of homosexual indications from medical discourses that also included seduction of younger women and uncontrolled desire as evidence of the female homosexual's masculinity.

Atteln's suicide attempt followed a meeting with the head sister about the threatening letters. Her hopes of having Westheider's guilt and her own innocence recognized were destroyed when the head sister reprimanded her. Despite the clearly self-serving purpose of the letters, the accusations reveal the power of the shared ideal of the women's utopian community. When illusions of innocence, solidarity, and feminine caring were shattered, only accusations of the most extreme forms of sexual depravity and abuse of power were sufficient to express the rage released. Atteln's claims that sex had been forced on her allowed her to deny desire and refuse sexual subjectivity—qualities that she demonized and displaced onto Westheider.

After Atteln's suicide attempt, it was not difficult for the hospital administration to terminate her employment. Unlike Erkens and Philipps, she did not have the standing or self-confidence to pursue a robust campaign for vindication. Nevertheless, her suicide letter asserted that she was a National Socialist and asked that the Party be informed about the situation in the hospital.[89]

Atteln's suicide attempt was meant to reclaim an innocent reputation, resembling the suicides of Dopfer and Fischer in Hamburg. Though they hoped to end gossip, the investigation into the suicides only made the sexual innuendo in Erkens's criticisms of her subordinate Dopfer more public. Increasingly, in conversation with outsiders, Erkens made carefully worded speculations that Dopfer's hostility was caused by "original attraction [that] later turned into burning hatred," extending her insinuations to the relationship between Dopfer and Fischer.[90] However, Erkens chose her words carefully so that she could deny that her assessments meant to imply homosexuality.

Testimony from Dr. and Frau Lohse, a prominent couple in the Hamburg social welfare establishment, described a party conversation they had with Erkens. Erkens's account of it claimed she had called the Dopfer/Fischer relationship "*schwül*" (sultry or overheated).[91] Frau Lohse, however, remembered Erkens saying that it would be a good thing for Dopfer and Fischer to spend some time apart, using the word *schwul*, slang for homosexual. Frau Lohse continued, "Frau Erkens spoke of a 'queer relationship' between Fräulein Dopfer and Fischer; it could also be that she said they lived in a 'queer atmosphere.' According the context however, there can be no doubt that the statement about the Dopfer-Fischer relationship was meant in a sexual sense."[92]

Her husband recalled that Erkens made remarks attributing Dopfer's mental and emotional state to a tainted hereditary condition. He concluded,

"It can definitely not be said that I mistakenly interpreted that kind of statement by Frau Erkens in a sexual direction. . . . In the same context, [she]
also talked about how Fräulein Dopfer was exaggeratedly sweet [*zärtlich*]
toward her during the time when they still got along."[93] Although Dopfer's
existing relationship might have cast doubt on Erkens's claim that Dopfer
wanted a relationship with her, Erkens seems to have hoped that gossip
about the Dopfer-Fischer relationship would reinforce the idea that Dopfer
specifically was homosexual or at least abnormal. Whether truthfully or not,
Erkens drew a direct connection between same-sexual attraction and disorder
in the workplace. This suggestion struck at the heart of the policewomen's
ideals and professional justification.

As the investigations went on, the sexual element of her accusations
against Dopfer came back to haunt Erkens. As supervisor, she was responsible
for creating an efficient work team. When it began to seem likely that she had
spread sexual innuendo, her image as a leader fostering harmonious work
was undermined. Like Atteln and Philipps, Erkens found that accusations
against others brought more intense scrutiny of her own behavior. As Erkens's
authority and sexual purity were called into question, she demanded that her
superiors restore her good reputation. Although the court investigated all
three women's sexuality in case abuse might be discovered, it tried to address
the issues discreetly and make every allowance for misunderstandings. On
the other hand, Erkens's exposés and demands kept the sexual dimension
in the public eye.

The Erkens case became tangled up in the deteriorating political
environment of the 1930s. By 1933, it seemed that not only the Women's
Police, but also the entire city was divided into pro- and anti-Erkens camps.
The disciplinary court eventually found her guilty of five charges, including
insubordination. The charge of improper treatment of her subordinates was
not sustained. The judge's final report of over two hundred pages gave scant
attention to the "ambiguous and legally moot" sexual issues of the case.[94]
The Nazi Party, which had recently gained control of the city, had once supported Erkens in order to discredit the former Socialist (SPD) administration.
Now it turned on her. Since she had been on paid leave, they ridiculed the
former administration for paying an employee who was not working, while
hard-working Germans were being laid off.[95] She was officially fired without
pension in May on the basis of the April Civil Service Law.[96]

In all three cases, once historical subjects expressed interpersonal
conflicts in sexual terms, they violated group norms. Professional women
closed ranks against accusers, leaving them dangerously isolated. They then
informed authority figures as a way of smearing their former close friends.
On the one hand, Erkens, Atteln, and Philipps must have seen homosexual

accusations as a credible and practical vehicle for attack or revenge. Given the importance of sexual purity in the professional women's ethos, sexual suspicions could be damaging to both a career and a social network. Since most of the women socialized and lived with women, accusations of homosexuality might be more believable than rumors of affairs with men. Yet the vociferousness with which accusations were insisted upon also likely reflected uncertainty about the meaning of relationships, as well as unspoken group rules about protecting that ambiguity. The uneasy solution of modernizing romantic friendships by maintaining ambiguity was vulnerable in a time when knowledge about homosexuality had become widespread.

In a very literal sense, the accusations traced in this chapter are examples of the circuits of capillary power Michel Foucault theorized in *The History of Sexuality*.[97] The cases are points of resistance where sexual allegations became a channel for power that disrupted the functioning of bureaucratic systems. Accusation and denial of homosexuality circulated and proliferated through networks of unequal relations. Through innuendo and scandal, interpretation and investigation, repressed knowledge became the site of "spirals of power and pleasure" that not incidentally also generated considerable shame and psychic pain. The effects of the circulation were not neutral. In each case, authorities succeeded in removing the person who claimed knowledge of homosexuality among professional women. But to interpret this outcome as the story of male dominance and female victimization would be to miss ways that women who were supposed to be officially "pure" seized the power to talk publicly about sex. Authorities preferred to smother charges of homosexuality—allegations that threatened to bring their agencies into disrepute—as quickly and effectively as possible. They were not eager to consider and investigate whether their employees were sexually involved with one another. In two of the cases denials were accepted at face value without further investigation. Each instigator was fired largely because she would not let the matter drop, demanding that the authorities correct their error in disciplining her by officially and publicly certifying her sexual innocence.

Medical Diagnosis

It was not only professional women that applied expert knowledge about homosexuality to the lives of their colleagues. Administrators also invited medical professionals to validate suspicions or certify innocence. But women under suspicion also actively sought out such opinions, unafraid that doctors would find their relationships or desires pathological. On the contrary, they were confident that they would be found "normal." While the witnesses tended to make binary judgments that labeled women as "perverse" or "pure," medical experts gave assessments that were more complicated, yet contradictory. Authorities called upon experts and their knowledge in order to justify disciplining subordinates, but they rarely gave the findings decisive importance. Experts' reports demonstrate the prominence of eugenic thought in diagnosing conflicts and behavior. Rumors of relatives' mental illness, drinking, or questionable sexuality were investigated and used as evidence just as readily as observing or questioning the object of diagnosis.

Superiors did not initially seek doctors' opinions on employees' sex lives. Perhaps calling on notions of female hysteria, they believed that psychological disturbances caused the workplace conflicts they were forced to resolve. Mention of sexuality only seemed to reinforce this perspective. Authorities were pleased to have their beliefs about troublesome subordinates' disturbed mental states and pathological personalities confirmed. But in the absence of solid evidence of sexually unacceptable behavior in public, they had no legal or bureaucratic reason to act against an employee on the basis of a doctor's diagnosis of homosexuality. They clearly did not officially disadvantage employees merely based on suggestions of improper sexual desire, even when the suggestions came from medical professionals.

Police authorities in Hamburg called on Dr. Peter, a medical consultant for the Hamburg Women's Police, to diagnose Erkens, Dopfer, and Fischer based on his workplace observation of them. His statement made it clear that he was far from a disinterested observer, having already decided that Erkens was psychologically disturbed. He thought that this basic "psychopathic condition" had affected "the sexual life of Frau Erkens, in which direction—especially whether in a homosexual sense—is, of course, difficult to determine and prove." In his opinion, a "woman's on-going intensive occupation with sex crimes and perversities alone has something unnatural about it." He thought it most likely that Erkens had initiated a flirtation with Dopfer. He found the Dopfer-Fischer relationship "emotionally doubtless somewhat overwrought, but . . . not based on abnormal sexual character." He praised Dopfer and Fischer for their reliability and idealism, declaring the suicides a loss of the more "valuable people."[98]

When Erkens obtained the transcript of Peter's testimony, she was outraged and demanded that the court request a report from a more competent and objective doctor.[99] The court complied, but the second report, from Dr. Rautenberg, was not the ringing endorsement Erkens sought. Rautenberg described Erkens as "ambitious not just for her own fame but also intent on the priority position of criminal psychological welfare work for the state; in many ways, however a sensitive and unstable woman, not able to handle resistance."[100] These assessments only added to her supervisors' suspicions about Erkens's mental state. Rautenberg also expressed admiration for Dopfer and Fischer. He testified that he had not noticed or suspected any abnormal relationships among the three. Both doctors' views matched up with gendered expectations of professional women. They did not associate abnormal sexuality with dedicated and respectable women who conformed well to professional norms.

Erkens and her attorneys intended to use expert opinion from Albert Moll in Erkens's defense. Erkens petitioned the court to ask for the preeminent sexologist's expert opinion. She claimed that he would confirm her sound-ness and Dopfer and Fischer's sexual and psychological problems, including their homosexuality. Although Moll, active in Berlin since the turn of the century, subscribed to the then-progressive congenital theory of the etiology of homosexuality, he did consider it an abnormality. Although he supported decriminalization of male homosexuality, he was unwilling to consider it a natural and unproblematic variation. This stance caused a rift with Magnus Hirschfeld as well as the organized homosexual movement in the 1920s.[101] Moll was famous for his claim that homosexual women compulsively mas-turbated while thinking about young girls. His diagnosis of homosexuality would therefore be especially damaging when directed at women charged with protecting and reforming "endangered" girls.[102]

The petition to admit Moll's testimony summarized its expected con-tent. He would interpret the double suicide as "unequivocally indicat[ing] a pathological predisposition." Using existing witness testimony, Moll would show that Dopfer and Fischer each experienced the other's problems as her own, that Dopfer was pathologically jealous of any third person disturbing their close relationship, and that both Dopfer and Fischer had mentioned previous suicide attempts. He would cite the romantic letters mentioned by their families as proof of an "unhealthy—or at the least deviant—friendship of the two deceased officers."[103] In the end, the court decided that the suicide question was outside of its jurisdiction and declined to call Moll.[104]

Hedwig Atteln's suicide attempt also prompted her head sister to ask the Frankfurt Health Department's neurologist to supply an assessment of Atteln and her former friend Westheider. Dr. Fünfgeld, who had previously treated Westheider for nervous problems, based his report on his observa-tions of both nurses then. He saw the evident attachment between the two women as evidence of homosexuality. "I was sure after the first conversation with her that a homosexual relationship existed between Hedwig Atteln and Erna Westheider, although we never discussed this point. Sister Atteln's behavior left no doubt that, at least on her side, the closest of bonds existed." Using typical sexological binaries, he concluded that Westheider was the passive partner. "She showed herself to me as a reserved, prim, very tense personality," he wrote. "On her side a connection with Hedwig Atteln was also apparent, but Erna Westheider appeared essentially more reserved and objective than Hedwig Atteln." Fünfgeld dismissed Atteln's accusations in the suicide letter out of hand, because they contradicted his assessment of their complementary personalities. "This 'rape' is absolutely improbable," he reported. "A strong person like Hedwig Atteln can defend herself *if she wants to*. . . . If [she] fails to, that means the 'dragging' was not so unpleasant for [her]." For the same reasons, he discounted Atteln's concerns about Westheider's relationships with other sisters. He didn't believe she posed a "danger to other sisters in reference to homosexual seduction due to her much more passive tendency."[105]

Fünfgeld's complete reversal of the relationship dynamic claimed by Atteln is striking. Atteln had characterized Westheider as a masculine aggressor, but Fünfgeld found her "prim" and "passive." The available evidence is insufficient to speculate on whether Atteln's version might have been a guilty projection of her own behavior or whether Westheider simply modulated her behavior to fit the situation. Fünfgold apparently did not find the couple's homosexuality, of which he was convinced, a reason to alert their supervisor or disqualify them from their professional positions.

A doctor was also called in to rule on whether Anna Philipps was fit to resume teaching. The resulting eugenic diagnosis made reference to her brother's homosexuality as proof of a "pathological sexual predisposition," manifesting in "a completely indifferent attitude toward the opposite sex and an inclination to their own sex," shared by the siblings. Perusing Anna's file, he cited "numerous indications of a homosexual orientation."[106] To defend herself against the local doctor's eugenically derived diagnosis of homosexuality, Philipps sought out medical opinion she knew would absolutely not connect homosexuality and degeneracy. Familiar with Magnus Hirschfeld's view of homosexuality as a valuable variant type, Philipps spent three weeks at Hirschfeld's Institute for Sexual Science in Berlin so that he could evaluate her. Hirschfeld's report explained her behavior as a normal stress reaction to false accusations of homosexuality and supported her demand for a disciplinary hearing to clear her of these suspicions.[107] However, the conflicting doctors' opinions on Philipps's homosexuality were peripheral to her dismissal. Officials took action because of annoyance and embarrassing publicity related to her pursuit of grievances rather than because of fears about her sexuality.

The evidence of reception and application of knowledge about the category of homosexuality shows that both authorities and subjects of

diagnosis exercised considerable agency and flexibility in using these discourses. Erkens and Philipps realized that doctors' assessments differed
and exploited the uncertainty to their benefit. All parties understood the
discourses in relation to their previous assumptions about gender and sexual
respectability. Certainly, accusations of homosexuality were facilitated by
wider circulation of knowledge about the category. The deployment of this
knowledge probably did have inhibiting and anxiety-producing effects on
women's assertion of emancipation and sexual subjectivity. But in these
cases there was no direct line from doctors' diagnoses to women's abject
acceptance of pathology and stigma. Authorities preferred to act against
the person causing conflict; they did not need a witch hunt to restore the
reputations of their institutions.

The evidence does not support an interpretation of the women's denial
of homosexuality as internalized shame and stigmatization of desire resulting
from the intimidating new expert knowledges. Their commitments to ideals
of female purity and service and their culture of denying desire preceded
concerns about homosexuality. These ideals were far more important to
their self-conceptions and choices than finding a label that helped to make
sense of their relationships. Whatever we may think in retrospect about their
negativity toward sex, this was for them part of a positive life philosophy and
identity that enabled them to pursue independence in their lives.

The policewomen and their colleagues found psychological and sexological diagnoses of "sexual deviance" useful to their mission of steering young
girls away from sensuality and sensation, temptations which they themselves
had presumably overcome. Still, they had no clear theory about the causa-
tion or biological basis of same-sex attraction. Like other sexual transgressions it might be the result of improper upbringing, seduction, unrestrained
adventurousness, or a congenitally weak character. These strongly reinforced
moral judgments precluded most of the women from giving much thought
to the evidence around them of colleagues who chose to arrange parts their
lives according to their same-sex desires, as long as those women were
competent, moral, and in conformity with bourgeois norms. The statements
of these women do not show that the female couples in their midst were
stigmatized or subjected to suspicion. Only when the term was applied to
them in a threatening way did professional women feel fearful of damaging
gossip or accusations. They and most of their male colleagues were secure
in their belief that they could diagnose deviance—and it did not look or act
like the women with whom they worked.

The prominence of homosexual accusations made by professional women
in these workplace conflicts confirms that many were aware of same-sex

attraction and desire among their colleagues. Sex connected to those desires would have contradicted their commitment to a moral female utopia that excluded sensuality and desire. When women experienced painful rejection, denying desire where it was clearly present created a battlefield where women fought one another to claim the ground of desirelessness. Their need to be found innocent meant more than simply being cleared of specific charges—it meant being restored to the circle of professional women. Their ethics and sense of themselves as moral exemplars facilitated strict separation between their feelings and the signs of sexual deviance they associated with "homosexuality." Nevertheless, the structural similarity between the female couple and lesbian love also created a reservoir of potential connections that could be deployed as strategic channels of power.

For laypeople whose connections to the cases forced them to define homosexuality, the significant marker was summed up in the word *Zärtlichkeit*. Both female homosexuals and prostitutes were imagined to display their sexual natures in public with exaggerated feminine caresses and flirtation. The taboo on displaying erotic desire in this way made it the crucial aspect of homosexuality in accusations and denials. Feminine *Zärtlichkeit* replaced turn-of-the-century stereotypes of masculinity as a sign of female homosexuality. Perhaps the masculine fashion styles of the 1920s gave female masculinity other implications.[108] Professional embodiment of the feminine principle already ruled out an exaggerated masculine style. Yet surprisingly, professional women did not point to their normative femininity to defend themselves. For the policewomen especially, femininity may have already been a point of anxiety.

In the 1920s, emancipation was no longer a standard marker of sexual deviance. Professional women's contribution was generally, if grudgingly, accepted. Middle-class women born between 1885 and 1900 lived under conditions radically different from those of their mothers' generation. They could be independent, mobile, employed, and active in public life. But when contrasted to younger women of the same class, their ideals and lifestyles seemed prudish and old-fashioned. The 1920s New Woman's supposed embrace of self-directed production, consumption, and sexuality was precisely the temptation against which professional women constructed their identities. "New Women," like other signs of modernity, were becoming outmoded generation by generation.

The men in power in these situations did use gendered expectations against subordinates they found difficult or nonconforming. They reinforced and exploited the prohibition against female ambition and assertiveness to which the women themselves already subscribed. However, there is little evidence that they were concerned about employees' sexuality or lives outside the workplace. Where doctors made diagnoses of sexual abnormality they did not use them to disqualify women from public service.

Although doctors and many laypeople thought of homosexuality as a congenital perversion, they did not yet use it as a discreet identity the way women who joined the homosexual movement did. "Homosexual" referred to acts, relationships, perhaps tendencies, but not the essence of the person. Yet the word's meaning had begun to approximate the late-twentieth-century sense of "homosexual" as an indication of same-sex desire. Gender inversion was already secondary to sexual implications.

Anna Philipps was a particularly significant transitional figure. Her attempt to make homosexuality a compatible element of her subjectivity ("Am I a homosexual?") was a strange and unique occurrence among her peers. At the beginning of her story, she was clearly seeking a label to legitimate her desires. But boldly asserting the potential of such an identity ran up against the counterflow of power in the form of censorship, ostracism, and repression. When her exploration was stigmatized, she faced a contradiction between her subjectivity as a respectable professional subject and integrity in claiming her desires. In this contest, respectability won out and Philipps extruded her desires onto a conspiracy of sinister power responsible for her mistreatment.

Rejecting sexual identity, of course, prevented solidarity between professional women and their contemporaries who claimed homosexual identities. As the next chapter demonstrates, they also claimed respectability. But respectability had widely divergent meanings in different milieus. In one case, respectability meant denying desire, sexual or other, which might be interpreted as unfeminine assertion of the self. In the other, it meant an appropriately controlled and expressed desire consistent with a biologically determined constitution.

5

Emancipation and Desire in Weimar Berlin's Female Homosexual Public Sphere

The figure of the female homosexual, increasingly visible in the years after 1900, retreated from public view during World War I. Sexual anxieties focused on a more immediate female figure: the soldier's wife.[1] After Germany was defeated, the revolution and the establishment of a democratic republic set new terms for the German public sphere that made homosexuality—along with other nondomesticated forms of sexuality—more visible there than ever before. The founders of the Weimar German state attempted to purge Germany of its imperial paternalism. Law reform, for example, moved from the justice ministry to the Reichstag. Censorship and political surveillance were drastically reduced, at least in the Republic's early years. These openings made the Republic fertile ground for the growth of new movements and identities. Homosexual organization emerged on a greatly expanded scale when activists founded a national mass membership association, the German Friendship Association (DFV).

The organizing and entrepreneurship expanded to an extent that readers in the late 1920s could choose between two periodicals written for an audience of female homosexuals. They could be purchased at most any news kiosk in central Berlin. In the pages of *Die Freundin*, the most widely circulated, interested readers could peruse advertisements for events and meeting places, gawk at nudes on the cover, read fiction with homosexual women as protagonists, or become acquainted with the real women who asserted themselves as leaders of the movement. Lotte Hahm's image frequently appeared in the advertising section and occasionally even on the cover. She was an energetic master of ceremonies at balls, president of the Ladies' Club Violetta, and "captain" of the annual steamboat trip on the Spree River.[2] In the early thirties, Hahm opened a club of her own where she performed a cabaret act. Hahm enthusiastically promoted the events. "Arriving at our destination after a merry boat ride, we'll dance the night away until 5 a. m." she wrote. "We'll be free and easy among ourselves there and each can have a splendid time as she pleases."[3] Young women exploring the fashionable masculine style in the heyday of the "Golden Twenties," might look to Hahm, the public female homosexual, as a figure of identification and emulation (Fig. 5.1).

Another set of women striving for emancipation in a more decorous style might follow the example set by Selli Engler. Like Hahm, Engler embraced visibility as a club leader and public persona. She used her photograph in advertisements for her books and in membership appeals for organizations she headed (Fig. 5.2). Engler dreamed of founding a club where aspiring business and professional women could socialize comfortably with others of their class as well as sexual "type."

The ebullient embrace of homosexual identity embodied by Hahm and Engler contrasted sharply with the defensiveness of the middle-class women "exposed" as belonging to the subcultures of the metropolis before the war. They spoke for themselves rather than through the mediation of doctors and journalists. A new assertiveness about lives and values was not unique to sexual subcultures. At the end of the war, many young people rejected bourgeois conventions and

Fig. 5.1. Lotte Hahm in her role as leader of the Women's Club Violetta. *Die Freundin,* December 11, 1929.

Erâto ruft die Einsamen

Ich sah das große Hungern nach Sonne und
nach Glück: in tausend Frauenaugen sah ich den
wehen Blick.

So viele schmale Lippen, in Einsamkeit ge-
bleicht, die schwellend rot wohl wären, hätt' sie ein
Kuß erreicht.

Oft sah ich Hände zittern in übereiltem Tun;
die Angst, zu spät zu kommen, ließ sie doch nimmer
ruhn.

Und manche wunde Seele hat sich mir an-
vertraut; so tiefverborgene Klagen wurden mir zu
gernd laut.

Das Einsamsein ist traurig, das Finden ist so
schwer, und suchen kann nicht jede und — hoffen
auch nicht mehr.

Es fehlt an schönen Wegen, für Frauen unsrer
Art, wo sie sich finden könnten, wo Lieb' sich offen-
bart.

Dank denen, die geschaffen ein Heim zum
Fröhlichsein, doch das ist keine Stätte für die, die
so allein.

Dort war das große Hungern nach Sonne und
nach Glück; in tausend Frauenaugen sah ich den
wehen Blick.

O, ihr verwand'ten Seelen, euch rufe ich nun zu,
vielleicht, daß eine Heimat uns gibt die inn're Ruh.

So streben wir gemeinsam zu diesem hohen Ziel,
doch, helft mir aufzubauen, ihr seid ja gar so viel.

Wir schaffen eine Stätte, wo Ernst und Fröhlich-
keit, wo Glück und wo auch Sonne und Zuflucht
allezeit.

Selli Engler,
1. Vorsitzende des Damenklub „Erâto"

Damenklub Erâto
Orientalisches Casino, „Zauberflöte", II. Etg.
Kommandantenstraße 72 (Spittelmarkt)
Ab Sonnabend, den 19. Oktober
Täglicher Betrieb (außer Montag) mit **Tanz und Überraschungen**
beginnend mit **4-Uhr-Mokka** Sonntags und **5-Uhr-Tee** wochentags

Bitte brehren Sie meinen Freundinnen Besuch
Selli Engler d. Vorsitzende

Fig. 5.2. Selli Engler, head of the Women's Section of the Bund für Menschenrecht in publicity for Erato, a women's club she tried to establish. The poem is titled "Erato calls the Lonely." *Die Freundin,* October 16, 1929.

the tutelage of their parents. A letter to oral historian Ilse Kokula captured young people's new openness to conceptual spaces and sexual subjectivities: "I personally experienced a feeling of freedom, obsolete Wilhelmine customs had collapsed, the opinions and outlooks of our parents—for me anyway—didn't count anymore. . . . At that time it was chic to oppose the moral pressure of the Empire. It was chic to be gay, or to act as if you were."[4] Another eyewitness, Charlotte Wolff, who frequented Berlin's notorious homosexual bars and engaged enthusiastically in same-sex love affairs, remembered that era as "heaven on earth in the German metropolis."[5] Seizing the enthusiasm for transgression and freedom in the postwar period, young men and women began to create a public sphere of homosexual citizens asserting their legitimate needs and rights. Their citizenship claims, however, clashed with the prominence of meeting spaces where erotic excess and titillation were offered as commercial pleasures.

After the 1918–1919 revolution, police regulation of bars, cafés, and dancehalls was relaxed. Disreputable and titillating districts of the dangerous and naughty metropolis became a hallmark of city life and tourist attraction, especially in Berlin. Public bars specialized in cross-dressing, same-sex dancing, and overt sexual performance. In the economic disruption following the war, sex was also a reliable source of income for some young men and women. Prostitutes of all kinds and both sexes populated the districts where nightlife was concentrated. Later in the decade, bars where female homosexuals met became more widely known through advertising and guidebooks that publicized the commercial infrastructure of sexual transgression.

Popular German books depicting women in the 1920s frequently celebrate the period as an exhilarating time of erotic liberation.[6] However, the evidence supplied by the organized homosexual movement calls into question the degree to which this apparent erotic freedom was experienced as liberating. For many participants, the tension between respectability and sexual fulfillment could not be resolved so easily.

The concept of the public sphere is useful for analysis of the arguments and self-policing practiced by these courageous pioneers of homosexual identity. As they worked to create a homosexual movement that could function as a public sphere they were conscious of their interface with the realm of respectability and power.[7] Many writers positioned themselves as competent actors who could critique the state as representatives of an organized public. Close attention to the process and conditions behind the rhetoric reveals the intensely political nature of the struggle for a place from which to speak and be taken seriously, a process that was far from completed in the ten tumultuous years that ended when public representation was driven underground in 1933 by the Nazi seizure of power.

Building a Public Sphere

Earlier elite advocacy organizations such as Hirschfeld's WhK, which propagated the notions of homosexual identity and homosexual rights, were a crucial precondition for mass organizing. Initially, the German Friendship Association (DFV) was primarily oriented to homosexual men. Organizations specifically for women, formed later in the 1920s, depended on the flourishing male homosexual rights movement for institutional support. In 1920s Germany, associations sponsored events, advertised for members, and published their own newsletters without fear of police harassment or legal consequences, until a limited form of censorship returned with the 1927 Protection of Youth Law.[8]

The existence of the organized and visible movement distinguished Berlin from other European and American cities that also had flourishing homosexual subcultures. A letter from Brooklyn to *Die Freundin* informed Germans that in New York the names and locations of homosexual bars could not be published, because they "would have to close down immediately if it were publicly known that 'fairies' [English] (our derogatory name here . . .) socialized there." "In the 'Land of the Free,'" the correspondent continued, "people are inexpressibly prudish about sexual matters," assuming homosexuals were "degenerate, lascivious, and disreputable." Criticizing American homosexuals for their lack of organization and knowledge, she concluded, "America is fifty years behind Germany."[9] Whether or not Berlin became the "international center of female homosexuality" in the 1920s, it was the site of a new kind of homosexual community—one that claimed its right to be recognized as composed of citizens who were just as moral as other Germans.[10]

The social conditions of the 1920s brought young people together in new ways that facilitated their participation in a homosexual public sphere. The accelerated loosening of family ties and responsibilities after the war and a more mobile labor market created possibilities for young people to live away from their families. Expanding employment in the retail and clerical sectors was particularly significant for women.[11] This employment was suitable for women of almost all classes. Working-class girls "traded up" from domestic service and factory jobs. Middle-class girls without qualifications also found office work congenial for gaining independence.[12] Gender segregation in the white collar sector kept women concentrated in low-skilled and low-paid positions as typists, stenographers, and bookkeepers. About half of the employees in these categories earned less than one hundred *Reichsmark* per month—an income below poverty level.[13] The new economy corroded class boundaries. But tensions related to class intensified. The mixed backgrounds of members of the homosexual clubs led leaders to insist on middle-class standards. Diversity was cause for considerable anxiety, despite sexual identity as a potentially integrating factor across class difference.

In sum, chaotic uneasy territories crisscrossing the erotic underworld, bohemian creativity, scientific knowledge, and middle-class sexual and gender emancipation allowed some people identifying themselves as homosexual to organize local social collectives affiliated with mass organizations. Even so, claiming sexual subjectivity, especially in connection with women's hopes for gender emancipation, continued to be a fraught process. The temptations of the nightlife scene only intensified the urgency of male and female homosexuals' arguments claiming respectability and controlled sexuality. In movement newsletters women debated their conflicting and contradictory ideas about sexual identity, sexual pleasure, morality, and gender style. These struggles were characterized by bitterness and vilification. Anger and intensity of opinion likely indexed acute internal conflicts experienced by the historical subjects.

The divisions associated with Weimar Germany were replicated in axes of self-definition. In addition to class difference, they negotiated between the received figure of the serious emancipated career woman and the new image of a more frivolous, pleasure-seeking Modern Girl of the 1920s. Weimar's political and cultural polarization, barely bridged in the early years of the Republic, returned with intensity during the Depression years of 1929–1933.[14] Homosexual organizations survived in this atmosphere by claiming nonpartisan status and carefully navigating between extremes. Identity tensions produced obsessive explanation and boundary setting in their essays, stories, and debates. For most of the women struggling to stake out an emancipated but respectable middle, the Marlene Dietrich–style femme fatale was at best an ambivalent model.

Two particular themes, masculinity as the essence of the homosexual woman and anxiety about the control of sexual desire, shaped the process of forging a coherent identity. These themes recurred in planning social events, confronting medical discourses, political rhetoric, and discussion of the ideal couple. The experience of discovering identity was not erotic emancipation; the new spaces, physical and conceptual, were sites of struggle. Claiming identity entailed disciplining the self while denouncing and excluding others. Yet the emerging contours of identity demonstrated that an important qualitative change had taken place. "Homosexuals" now saw themselves as a minority defined by congenital difference, a view that is a direct precursor of (middle-class) gay identities and communities of the late twentieth century.

Overlapping Spaces and Spheres: Female Homosexualities in Interwar Germany

Though the identity category implied a sameness of inner character, historical traces reveal a multiplicity of different ways of expressing same-sex attraction uneasily occupying the same conceptual ground. A 1928 guide to Berlin lesbian venues provided an index of the erotic subcultures represented in the gathering places for homosexual women at the height of the Golden Twenties.[15] On the exclusive end of the spectrum, Ruth Roellig, the guide's author, described Club Monbijou West as accessible only by invitation of one of its six hundred members. The hostesses, Mali and Igel, greeted the clientele personally and enforced a "refined yet promiscuous" atmosphere.[16] In her memoirs, Weimar cabaret performer Claire Waldoff recalled another club, Pyramide, as a meeting place of homosexual celebrities—elegant, exotic, fun, slightly bawdy, offering frequent scenes of lovers' quarrels and jealousies as part of the entertainment.[17]

At the Hohenzollern Diele, older patrons could be taken for men "because of their haircuts and ties." In between them sat much younger "delicate-limbed, slim, girlish women, . . . the personification of the wife." The author of *Naughty Berlin* interpreted these couples as the reassertion of "normal" marriage among the abnormal. "In these homespun women," it was hard to recognize "the longings that stir in their blood and determine their anti-bourgeois existence." Moreck's contrast of transgressive same-sex desire and its bland reality suggests that this pattern was now behind the times.[18]

Verona Diele and Toppkeller were Parisian-style cafés for high-end prostitutes, their customers, and bohemian women.[19] Charlotte Wolff and Dora Benjamin frequented the Verona Diele in the early 1920s, fascinated by the women and by the men, "shadowy figures, sitting like wallflowers at small tables," who came to watch the women in action. The women dancing with each other "pursued their pleasure [reaching] an erotic pitch that enthralled the on-lookers as well as the dancers." Dora was drawn to the bar because she admired the women's authenticity.[20] Wolff also used to dance and hang out at the Toppkeller, where she and a friend made a game of chatting up and then evading married couples looking to spice up their sex lives. Retrospectively, Wolff described it as "the real thing, a place where lesbian women of all classes met, danced, and engaged in odd rituals."[21] Wolff and Benjamin's emphasis on the open sexuality among the women in these bars as "authentic" and "real" reveals the extent to which even sophisticated women saw sexual subjectivity as a victory over bourgeois respectability.

Despite Wolff's claims about class mixing at Toppkeller, one of Kokula's informants who had patronized bars for "daughters of workers" in Hamburg emphasized the absolute class boundaries structuring homosexual nightlife there.[22] Few working-class bars were mentioned in the Berlin guidebooks. A prominent exception in Berlin was the Taverne, known for its open displays of sexuality, beery rough atmosphere, and frequent outbreaks of physical violence.[23]

Sexualized metropolitan spaces constituted a semi-public sphere based on pleasure and desire rather than judgment, cultivation, and critique. Their media were looking, performing, and touching. For middle-class women constructing lives and identities around same-sex desires, sexually laden spaces were necessary, yet they clashed violently with the public sphere presence they imagined as emancipation. The private club was a better fit for them. In 1924, *Die Freundin* advertised several private clubs that met one or two nights per week.[24] By renting party rooms, homosexual sociability escaped the voyeuristic scrutiny of the general public. The club Old Money celebrated anniversaries of its 1912 founding. At its seventeenth anniversary party "the blue, white, and red banner of Old Money, decorated with many streamers, led off, followed by the Funny Nine with their white and lavender banner and then the women who were members of both clubs."[25] The solemnity of familiar rituals gave the clubs cohesion and dignity, connecting them to similar mainstream socializing (Fig. 5.3).

Fig. 5.3. A page of advertisements from *Die Freundin,* including the clubs Hand-in-Hand and Altes Geld (Old Money.) *Die Freundin,* August 28, 1929.

A 1923 novel, *Girlfriends,* by Maximiliane Ackers, reflected the discomfort that less bohemian middle-class women felt in the bar atmosphere.[26] The provincial middle-class characters were caught between domestic spaces— untenable due to family pressure—and a bar world that clashed with the morality and decorum that shaped their self-worth. As the protagonist sat in a Berlin bar, she confronted a stark choice between desire and self-respect: "In horror she closed her eyes. She and Ruth somehow belonged here? . . . It was God's will to become so miserable that you felt sheltered here?"[27]

"Branda," an eyewitness interviewed by Kokula in1982, expressed similar discomfort. Asked whether she had gone to lesbian bars, Branda replied, "A friend took me along once. No! To this day I don't go to them!" Branda particularly remembered her embarrassment when the singer, dressed in a tuxedo and top hat, approached her. Middle-class homosexual women such as Branda felt an urgent need for more respectable spaces of sociability. To address this need, middle-class organizations, with their periodicals, lectures, and discussion evenings, attempted to recreate the traditional bourgeois public sphere as an alternative site of self-development and critique. The DFV was the first such national organization. The president of the Berlin group, Friedrich Radszuweit, took over the national leadership in 1923 and renamed the organization the Human Rights League (BfM).[28] Local groups dissatisfied with Radszuweit's leadership seceded and re-formed the DFV. For the rest of the Weimar period, the BfM and the DFV competed with each other.[29] While only a very few women were active on the national level, each of the organizations sponsored a women's division, local women's social clubs in large cities, and a publication especially for women.

These periodicals supply the most extensive view into the lives of women calling themselves homosexual prior to the women's and gay movements of the 1960s. They gave print space to ambitious leaders and writers, tying together a large group of loosely connected individuals that extended far beyond Berlin through shared reading.[30] *Die Freundin,* edited by Aenne Weber, began publication in 1924.[31] Its early issues did not list an address or price, suggesting hand-to-hand distribution rather than newsstand sales. The third issue explained, "*Die Freundin* will advocate the equality of women in social life [and] promote the cultivation of ideal women's friendships. We ask all women who feel called to do so to send us relevant articles and work."[32] At this early stage, the appeal gave as much weight to women's emancipation as to sexual preference. This approach changed after 1928 when men affiliated with the BfM held the editorial position and wrote lead articles addressing issues primarily of interest to men.[33] The DFV began publishing a competitor, *Frauenliebe,* in 1926.[34] A group of regular contributors coalesced around Karen as editor, with Carl Bergmann as publisher.[35]

Bergmann and Radszuweit imitated themes and devices of the popular periodical formula of Weimar media corporations. Content, including lifestyle articles, serialized novels, and cover photographs, was addressed to a market of homosexual women and transvestites. Although this was the era of photojournalism, the periodicals were unable to afford to produce their own photographs, except for occasional portraits such as those of Hahm and Engler.[36] Instead, despite the renewed risks of censorship after 1926, both periodicals used nude cover photographs, acquired in sets from picture agencies. *Die Freundin* claimed that putting nudes on the cover fulfilled the wishes of readers (Fig. 5.4).[37] It is likely that the publishers also hoped that nude cover photographs would attract the attention of male kiosk browsers.

Fig. 5.4. Typical cover of *Die Freundin,* January 15, 1930.

Whatever their success in this secondary market, evidence shows that the periodicals did provide a print public sphere for women readers. Kokula's source Branda remembered buying *Die Freundin* "where I was not known, at a kiosk where nobody knew me." Walking around Berlin, she "felt as if [she] had a bomb in [her] pocket." She read it secretly "on the toilet! Where no one could disturb you."[38] Correspondence from readers documented the periodicals' international reach and importance. A Swiss reader emphasized the necessity of such a sphere for the "victorious breakthrough of our movement." She enthused, "*Garçonne* [a later title of *Frauenliebe*] makes the blind see, gives the despairing courage through the palpable bonds of community." She also confirmed that it gave some readers "an opportunity to create a blissful twosome."[39] As these reactions show, the print public sphere facilitated secrecy and solitary identity work while also fostering imagined social connection and a presence in public.

Although the two publications were similar in form and content, they differed significantly in the extent to which women found a voice in them. Carl Bergmann and the DFV seldom appeared in *Frauenliebe*; decisions on content seem to have been left up to the editor, Karen, and her staff (Fig. 5.5). Controversial reader submissions often led the front page. Public readings of contributors' work gave it an embodied presence in the community.[40] Although *Die Freundin* occasionally included exchanges of ideas and opinions sent in by readers, Friedrich Radszuweit or his male successor wrote most of its lead articles. Radszuweit ran the BfM as his own personal empire.

There were probably some demographic differences in the readerships of the two periodicals. Critics at a 1928 DFV meeting wanted "good intellectual contributors recruited in order to be able to raise [*Frauenliebe*] to a higher level."[41] The concern about cultural level indicates that *Frauenliebe*'s readers were probably the more highly educated.[42] However, *Die Freundin*'s popular tone and Radszuweit's tight control allowed it to become the more widely recognized and stable of the two.[43]

Besides the print public sphere, the clubs attempted to foster intellectual and political solidarity through their women's divisions, sponsoring discussions, meetings, and lectures. The BfM's efforts were more politically oriented, but less successful. The DFV women created belonging through attendance at its authors' reading nights and theatrical productions. Both organizations also sponsored hikes, sports, and parlor game nights. *Frauenliebe* listed DFV-affiliated clubs in Eastern cities such as Dresden, Chemnitz, and Königsberg, while *Die Freundin* reported on organizing a club in Hamburg. But news from the Berlin clubs dominated the newsletter content.

Fig. 5.5. *Frauenliebe* cover, September, 1929. The conflict between the two clubs is seen in the text at the bottom: "The merger with 'Violetta' is a brazen lie!"

The group of writers that supplied *Frauenliebe,* and later *Garçonne,* with stories, poems, and opinion pieces created an alternative women's culture. Their public readings fostered development of a celebrity culture of desire. V. R., author of a poem titled "An Ilse Schwarze," had read Schwarze's stories avidly and identified with the feelings they evoked. Of Schwarze, she wrote, "Whoever feels like this, feels like I do . . . since that moment, I love you!"[44] Encountering Schwarze in person, she longed to comfort her, reading sadness and longing in her expression. However, she decided to be content with admiring her from afar, indulging in the satisfying fantasy of a shared emotional world.

A Sappho memorial created an opportunity to give homosexual desire culturally solid roots. *Garçonne*'s editor Karen led this solemn, almost religious, event. Karen spoke surrounded by "flaming white candles in antique lanterns" creating a space "resembling an altar." When a drapery was removed from the bust of Sappho, the reporter enthused, "The dead world came alive. It lives in us and we are the ones who live in it." She encouraged Karen to take this priestly role more often: "As movement leader, as intellectually dazzling disciplined human being, she is followed with full commitment by her willing congregation."[45] The classical connection as a founding basis for same-sex love recalls the experiments of men such as the Enormen in Munich and Adolf Brand, who attempted to reenact Greek homosocial bonding.[46] At least a few women strove to create a public sphere that was intellectually and spiritually nourishing.

Despite the wide range of activities, the clubs realized that success depended on providing space for dancing and meeting potential partners. In 1926, Ladies Club Violetta, affiliated with the DVF, advertised a New Year's Eve Ball, hosted by Hahm. Violetta became a permanent feature of the Berlin scene and specialized in balls with themes like "Bad Boys Ball" and "Carnival in Cologne." A promotional article enthused, "The good jazz band will create the atmosphere as usual and Lotte will do her utmost to add to it. She is now the soul of Violetta"[47] (see Fig. 5.1). Performances by singers and comedians alternated with dancing.[48] One of Kokula's interviewees remembered going to dances at a ballroom called Zauberflöte: "Sometimes we didn't know each other, but we were all glad to be there. . . . They were only for lesbians and always led by a woman. . . . The places we went were created by us on our own initiative. We rented the space for such and such a day. It never looked from the outside like a bar at all." She recalled that these dances were attended by "at least a couple of hundred women." Prompted by Kokula, she confirmed that elite women patronized expensive bars, while "ordinary" women attended the cheaper balls. This informant also made clear that what is perceived in historical hindsight as unprecedented visibility and openness was sometimes quite secretive. Homosexual spaces were "a little bit hidden," with doors locked and windows closed so that no one outside would know what was going on.[49]

Occasionally a writer evoked the visual pleasure and eroticism that made these spaces such a tempting alternative to more staid club meetings. A sketch narrator "sacrificed a whole Reichsmark and fifty pfennig to make myself beautiful and please all the sweet women! I bought a cap and a bright red tie, got a suit on a huge credit advance (Hear! Hear!), and ended up at the Zauberflöte." Enjoying the sights of the ball, she continued, "Boys, that's where it was happening! I was in the mood, I had money, and I had women, lovely enticing women! . . . There was no one who didn't want to dance, dance tirelessly, eye to eye with a beautiful woman or a bad boy!"[50] This expression of high-spirited anticipation of pleasure was rare in the periodicals; more typical was assurance that club events offered a restrained and dignified alternative to the sexual atmosphere of commercial bars. A description of the café Dorian Gray emphasized that it was not "a nightclub of ill repute: just the opposite." "A note of quiet refinement" allowed "Berlin's lesbian women to cultivate their social life like the women of ancient Greece on the island of Lesbos."[51] The tension between refined symposium and "lovely enticing women" was central to power and politics within the membership organizations (Fig. 5.6).

These themes were central to Selli Engler's appeal for readers of *Die Freundin* to join the BfM. She guaranteed the movement's respectability as if she were speaking personally to readers. "I know why you have thus far not affiliated yourselves with any organization," she confided. "In the existing circles and associations for women, one always encounters questionable elements." She understood that her imagined reader would avoid such places "because of the danger to your good reputation." "You respectable and impeccable women," she urged, "come to our events confidently; then certain women will no longer feel welcome and will leave on their own."[52] Engler promised that her influence would strip the "questionable elements" of their power to set the tone, restoring bourgeois norms to their proper hegemonic status.

But dancing and flirting attracted the crowds and the cash needed to support the organization. The two potential publics—a rowdy one where bourgeois norms were flouted and an organized and sober one capable of claims and critiques taken seriously by other bourgeois publics—overlapped in uncomfortable ways. The tension between them shaped each organization as well as the conflicts between them.

The goal of constructing respectable homosexuality was mobilized in bitter conflicts that erupted between the two organizations at the height of their success. In 1928, the DFV adopted a second women's club, Monbijou, headed by singer Kati Reinhard.[53] Soon after, Violetta switched its affiliation to the BfM and the two rival women's groups displayed the bitter rivalry of the two men's organizations (see Fig. 5.5). In the ensuing feud, each club claimed to represent the moral and respectable space of the homosexual movement. A writer in *Frauenliebe* accused the new Violetta of allowing "the

Fig. 5.6. A page of advertisements from *Die Freundin*. Small ad for Dorian Gray, top right. *Die Freundin*, March 23, 1932.

entry of voyeuristic men in ever-greater numbers." She attacked Lotte Hahm personally as "arrogant" and eager to find "ways to fill her own pockets." She predicted a boycott of Violetta and Hahm because of their "complete betrayal of the women's movement: joining the B. f. M., the men's movement!" Former members of Violetta apparently valued their autonomy within the movement. Their club was separate space where women were in charge. The financial precariousness of public spaces of sociability was evident in the accusation that Hahm's move was "the end result of evil Mammon."[54] The allegation that Hahm hoped to make more money in the BfM probably had some basis in reality. Between 1929 and 1931, she was very visible, organizing and using her personal image to promote the BfM and *Die Freundin*.[55]

Hahm also used gender politics in telling her side of the story: "The homosexual women who socialize in Damenklub Monbijou have always found it grotesque that . . . a heterosexual man, of all people, should be the leader of homosexual women." Hahm was referring to *Frauenliebe*'s publisher, Bergmann, whom she claimed had embezzled club funds. She also contended that former Violetta members would be horrified if they knew what she knew.[56] Hahm's vague indictment must have been strengthened when Selli Engler left to join the BfM a week later, citing "many deplorable circumstances." Declaring her new loyalty to the BfM, Engler placed herself "exclusively at the disposal of Herr Radszuweit, in whose reliable hands the entire homosexual movement has been for years."[57] Radszuweit and Engler focused on homosexual solidarity, while *Frauenliebe*'s defensive rhetoric of greed indicated its relatively weak financial position.

Hahm and Engler both left the BfM in 1931. While Engler suddenly disappeared completely, Hahm opened a bar, Manuela. Its advertisements represented Hahm as a fun-loving "improv comic with accordion"[58] (Fig. 5.7). Although Hahm's departure and personal ambitions could be read as a turn away from the political, Hahm, more than any other visible figure in the movement, anticipates late-twentieth-century queer activism. She shared the political rhetoric of respectability while active in the BfM, yet refused to moderate her own queer persona as an object of transgressive visual desire. Michael Warner's and Lauren Berlant's concept of the counterpublic predicated on spectacle, play, and acting up allows us to see political significance, perhaps even acuity, in Hahm's move.[59] While Radszuweit was still trying to persuade Hitler to support the repeal of Paragraph 175, Hahm staked her claim in the carnivalesque queerness of her cabaret act.

Women's economic vulnerability complicated middle-class women's formation of publics of their own. The mediation of men's organizations enabled women to establish a public presence, but providing social space had proved extremely tricky. As consumers, members demanded space for dancing and socializing. Drinking and dancing, though, attracted "questionable elements" that interfered with the movement's politics of respectability and integration. The dance floor was unstable ground for a political movement. Ironically, defending spaces for dancing became political in 1932. Following the Papen coup against the liberal Prussian administration in July, the new government instituted measures to clean up the streets of Berlin.[60] An "exceptional clause"

Fig. 5.7. Lotte Hahm in an advertisement for her bar Manuela. *Die Freundin,* May 1932.

prohibited the police from licensing bars in which "the only persons who participate in their dances belong to homosexual circles."[61] A complete ban on same-sex dancing in public places was to become effective in 1933. The dancing ban made clear that a turn to the right meant new repression for the homosexual organizations.

This overview of the landscapes of female homosexuality in Berlin demonstrates that the conditions of Weimar created common ground for previously separate cultures. Out of this mixing a sexual identity emerged that suggested linkage across class, gender, and culture.[62] Homosexual cultures of independent working- and lower-middle-class women had likely emerged with urbanization and industrialization in the course of the nineteenth century. Already outside the family, traveling performers and prostitutes inhabited spaces where homosexual relations could be practiced and acknowledged. Whether or how either of these groups fostered classification of the self according to sexual desires still needs investigation. The networks and couples formed between upper-middle-class emancipated women developed in isolation from and perhaps ignorance of the other, more frankly sexual, patterns of same-sex relating. Berlin, as a place of in-migration, international influence, and rapid infrastructural development, brought women from previously segregated social strata into close proximity in new contexts. Wealthy or socially secure women such as Charlotte Wolff and Claire Waldoff found this mixing stimulating and freeing. But less secure middle-class women experienced the collision as a confusing process requiring them to rework self-concepts, behavioral codes and norms, and the boundaries and definitions of community.

"To Be Taken Seriously":
Science and Politics in the Public Sphere

The clash between emancipation and desire also shaped serious discussion of homosexuality as a minority group identity. Since the German unification era, scientific explanations of homosexuality had been closely tied to political goals. The claim that homosexuality was a congenital condition implied a scientific certainty that supported political rhetoric. The congenital thesis reclassified acts from unnatural (the law code's term) to natural and justified public openness about one's orientation as honest and honorable. The homosexual movements' use of science was part of the broader trend toward politicizing biology. Since the nineteenth century, eugenicists and social reformers had evaluated citizens' biological value or cost to the state. However, the congenital claim could also support arguments that homosexuality was a degeneration that required medical intervention or permanent incarceration—ideas that became a matter of life and death in the Nazi period.

For Weimar advocates, though, this premise seemed to guarantee that a rational, informed public could not define homosexuals as morally different from other citizens. Their arguments contrasted homosexual self-control and honest friendship with the parlous state of postwar heterosexual marriage and the perceived spread of prostitution, highlighting the ubiquitous issue of exploitation and violence in heterosexual relations. Homosexual movement leaders challenged the assumption that heterosexual males were responsible fathers and household heads. Pushing against the foundational notion of political competence as belonging to heads of households, they drew a new boundary emphasizing judgment, culture, and respectability as the keys to responsible citizenship.

The DFV and the BfM shared a commitment to these central ideas about the etiology and meaning of homosexuality. Both frequently published excerpts by doctors and sexologists, especially in response to threats of censorship and periods of lobbying for repeal of Paragraph 175. Hirschfeld's public appeals portrayed homosexuality as analogous to physical disability and homosexuals as mistreated victims of law and society. The clubs rejected the pitiable victim image, preferring to make claims for justice as equal citizens who were wrongly stereotyped. Advocates made the case that homosexuals were as moral and respectable as their "normal" counterparts. Sexology reinforced respectability claims that separated the organizations from the urban sexual sphere. Even though women writers had less at stake in law code reform, they too defined homosexuality as inherently respectable. Their definition of the term excluded women whose desire was too present and visible.

Movement leaders were pointed in urging readers to act accordingly. Quoting sexologist August Forel, Elspeth Killmer, then editor of *Die Freundin,* argued that all individuals of whatever sexual inclination had responsibility for their sex acts.[63] Political action could only make sense if those engaged in it policed their sexual behavior. "Don't make the struggle more diffi-cult . . . through unlovely conspicuous behavior in public," she pleaded. She exhorted, "Show that you can fight, not just dance and amuse yourselves."[64] Claiming equality involved subordinating desire: "Only that person is free who is master of his lower drives."[65]

Lou Steffen and Edith Weymer's call for political mobilization shamed German women, claiming that Austrian women "take the fight for equal rights much more seriously than the Germans." They added, "What do our same-sex loving women in Germany do? They dance, dance, dance." Steffan and Weymer doubted the homosexuality of many present at the dances: "[Our members] think that the women present at these events do not have a homosexual orientation at all, rather are more likely to be counted among those 'ladies' who populate the so-called popular streets of Berlin in mass quantities."[66] Steffen and Weymer appealed to middle-class women's fear of contact with prostitutes, not only as distasteful, but also as an occasion where they might be mistaken for prostitutes themselves. Fear of being associated with prostitution motivated even Lotte Hahm to speak out against a book claiming her events were "sex parties."[67] The code word *einwandfrei* (impec-cable) began to be ubiquitous in BfM advertisements and prose appeals. In other words, "prostitutes not welcome." Leaders in the movement had seized the authority to define homosexuality, resisting sexological discourses that made prostitutes an important type of homosexual woman. At the same time, they categorically excluded certain individuals and ways of expressing desire.

Karen, editor of *Frauenliebe,* used sexological concepts of congenital and acquired homosexuality to draw a strict boundary between the two. She argued that anyone seeking same-sex love out of enjoyment of transgression [acquired homosexuality] damaged society and should be "separated from the public." On the other hand, Karen continued, "Same-sex behavior, entered into voluntarily and clearly by both partners [congenital homosexuality], belongs, like every intimate heterosexual behavior, to the realm of things one accepts but does not talk about."[68] Karen also warned aspiring writers to avoid writing explicitly about sexual experience in their stories and essays.[69]

Categorical exclusion shaped a debate in *Frauenliebe* about bisexuality. Like prostitutes, bisexuals were excluded from homosexual community. *Frauenliebe* printed fifteen responses to a letter asking readers to express their view on women who had relationships with both sexes.[70] They saw homosexuality as moral and bisexuality as immoral. It was not only movement leaders who wanted to discipline sexual desire in their followers. Letters from readers grouped bisexual women with prostitutes and "sensual" heterosexual women, accusing all of seeking homosexual experiences out of curiosity or sensual desire rather than as an expression of their inner character.[71]

Many letters expressed antimale sentiments. Hanni Schulz wanted to protect herself "against loving where a man desires at the same time."[72] Her gender binary was clear: women love, men desire. Many responses found the idea of making love with a woman who had just come from a man disgusting. Bisexuality seemed indicative of promiscuity. As G. B. put it, "Pure and upright love demands unconditional exclusive possession!"[73] Bisexual women, to these writers, gave free rein to undifferentiated, therefore male, desire.

Scientific categories enabled the "true" homosexuals to disassociate themselves radically from others who openly flaunted their desire for other women.[74] Marie Rudolf agreed that bisexuals had "nothing in common with our orientation."[75] Cläre summed up the majority view: "Each of us must insist that the type of 'ladies' I described disappear from our ranks, that is, our clubs, associations, and so on. I call on you to have courage; out with them; we lose nothing without them!" Homosexual love was purified through exclusion of those who pursued perverse pleasure. Cläre continued, "These people shall not drag what is holy to us through the mud by their opportunism. We can only use people of value, character and ideals, for whom the girlfriend and women's love is holy."[76] Construction of an acceptable homosexual self required the figure of an other upon whom to project the threatening realities of sexual desire.

Writers also accused bisexual women of greed. Tropes of the prostitute and the pornographer circulated by morality campaigners around the turn of the century had fused sensuality and greed. Denigration of bisexual women along these lines expressed the reality of women's financial vulnerability. When Karen claimed that bisexuals would "inevitably return to a man at some point," she brought into the open the material stakes of the wish to exclude.[77] Women struggling to "make it" independently were hostile to those who seemed want women's love and financial security too.

Vilification of bisexual women allowed women the opportunity to enter into the classification and definition work of sexology and to create a purified figure of the female homosexual suitable for political citizenship. The "sexual" in homosexual was tamed through strict denial that irresistible desire defined the category. Rejection of prostitutes and bisexuals allowed women to construct "female homosexuality" as materially and sexually pure. As a type, they argued, "true" homosexuals kept desire under the control of the individual will.

In addition to the work of political identity construction, women engaged with sexology to work out the gender implications of same-sex female love and desire. The term *invert,* commonly used by sexologists, conflated gender nonconformity with sexual difference. According to the dominant theory, women desired other women because of their essential masculinity. For the men of the movement, being labeled feminine was a threat to their masculine prestige. For women, though, the masculinity diagnosis offered a more complicated field of options. Early in the history of the clubs, when German women had only recently begun to exercise their right to vote and hold office, women wanted their organizations to work for women's equal rights. Some writers who continued in this tradition challenged sexologists' conceptions when they rejected masculine identification even as they called into question the whole idea of a unitary congenital homosexuality.

Hortense Hohensee was one of several *Frauenliebe* writers who explained homosexuality without reference to the congenital view, suggesting that same-sex love was a choice available to any woman. Hohensee used the term *Neigung* (inclination), but her argument put shared enjoyment of the feminine at the center of "lesbian love." Women's love began in pursuit of "common goals out of pure zest and optimism toward life." Desire was generated by mutual appreciation that "women's bodies are beautiful—women's souls tender." For Hohensee, the intense mutuality of same-sex love satisfied every need, leaving "no more space for the man." Her same-sex-loving woman experienced a purely feminine erotic intensity rather than a congenital condition.[78]

Annette Eick used negative stereotypes of masculinity to revalue women's love for each other. She also rejected biological determinism in favor of choice. As Eick described it, when a woman discovers the possibility of same sex-love she struggles to decide whether to be with women or with men. Finally, she decides: "Woman, since she recognizes the egoism in men's love, his irresponsibility, his emotional crudeness."[79] Eick echoed the earlier feminists Elberskirchen and Dauthendey, rejecting masculine desire as she saw it manifested in men. Yet she asserted same-sex relations as a desirable option in a way they could not, reflecting the increased social acceptance of sexuality and new gender roles. Dauthendey and Elberskirchen were obsessed with purity and reproduction, while women in the Weimar era were more likely to claim sexual subjectivity, as long as their desires were managed by responsibility and selflessness.

Other writers gave more weight to gender ideas in sexological knowledge, using science enthusiastically, but not uncritically, to justify complete emancipation from traditional feminine roles. Elspeth Killmer explained that the "so-called masculine woman" suffered most in a society that had "subordinated women's brains to sex." But Killmer departed from the invert concept by implying that female "masculinity" was in the eye of the beholder—and beholders often stigmatized intelligent and ambitious women as masculine. Her articles drew on early women sexual theorists, such as Johanna Elberskirchen, linking but clearly separating feminism and homosexuality.[80]

The sexological theorist who was the most visible in women's attempts to revise the claims of sexology was not the liberal Magnus Hirschfeld, but rather Otto Weininger. Weininger's turn-of-the-century book *Sex and Character* was enormously influential throughout the Weimar period.[81] Weininger's theories were useful to homosexual women because they anchored masculinity in the body without making it exclusive to men. Weininger proposed that each individual contained a combination of masculinity and femininity expressible in an M/W ratio. An individual with an M/W ratio of 25/75 would be very feminine no matter what the external organs. The corollary of this premise was that people with complementary M/W ratios were attracted to each other—a 60/40 would be most compatible with a 40/60. Weininger's numerical reduction of gender accounted for "normal" heterosexual attraction, but might also explain attraction between similar androgynous individuals. Weininger sorted masculine and feminine traits using nineteenth-century gender assumptions. His gender continuum was in essence a hierarchy using science to justify masculine social predominance and moral superiority. Its suggestion that masculinity was not the exclusive property of men appealed to women who emphasizing their "masculine" intellect and competence for public roles.[82]

Die Freundin published an excerpt from *Sex and Character* titled "The Emancipated Woman," which explained homosexuality as an effect of the gender ratio. According to Weininger, "homosexual love honors the woman more than a heterosexual relationship," because "the inclination to lesbian love in a woman is the result of her masculinity." Weininger believed that "the real woman, the W, has nothing to do with the emancipation of women. Historical research confirms the result that folk wisdom had long anticipated:

'The longer the hair, the shorter on brains.' It is only the man in them that wants to emancipate itself."[83] The article's enhancement of women's status through masculinity entailed denigration and denial of femininity, ruling out gender solidarity. Since men were editors of *Die Freundin,* it is hard to tell whether female readers shared these ideas. The editors also excerpted two texts that used biology to associate femininity with sexual shame and sensuality. These articles explicitly ridiculed the critical claims of feminism.[84] These male-authored texts implied that masculine-identified women did not need to fight for women's rights, because normal women did not need or want them. Homosexual women, assumed masculine, naturally should be allowed to claim rights normally assigned to men. Masculinity also made desire respectable; according to this ideology, the masculine individual was able to control it through his superior will.

Frauenliebe authors used Weininger's ideas as a jumping-off point for asserting their own interpretations of the relationship between gender and sexuality. Herta Laser rejected Weininger's idea that masculinity was the only source of women's "development." Laser historicized gender conditions and norms in order to counter Weininger's biological determinism, recognizing that his theories would be used to oppose women's emancipation. For Laser, neither emancipation nor homosexuality could be reduced to female masculinity. "That the same-sex loving woman dedicates herself to [emancipation] with all her energy is not surprising," she argued. "For her it means radical liberation."[85] Laser implicitly created space for feminine or androgynous homosexual women who were just as committed to women's rights. Annette Eick also drew on Weininger to think through the mystery of same-sex desire. She raised questions about Weininger's binary assumptions: "Is an opposition required before being attracted to something beautiful? Everything feminine . . . attracts; why shouldn't it attract a woman with a sense for art and beauty in the same way?"[86] Eick's thinking here made a link between intellect and same-sex attraction without the intermediary of masculinity.

The debates and discourses in the periodicals demonstrate that women who conceived of themselves as part of an organized collectivity did not simply receive sexology passively. They vigorously rejected the notion that same-sex love was pathological, even if they sometimes did so by attributing pathology to others. Through exchanges of opinion, the print public sphere allowed authors to apply abstract theory to their experiences and observations. The term *orientation* allowed women to appropriate sexology as the scientifically accurate interpretation of nature without forcing them to abandon their own perceptions of same-sex pleasure and desire. Sexology supported their highest aspiration: claiming a cultivated, responsible subject position.

Women's engagement in politics was not limited to the internal debates of the homosexual movement, which were so often exclusionary. Although it was rare, writers in the periodicals addressed national politics and the actions of the state in various ways. Scholars of male homosexuality have long dismissed the DFV and the BfM, suggesting that they failed to be political.[87] In the BfM, movement and national politics were closely connected with Radszuweit's vision of masculine respectability and lobbying. He saw himself as the primary political actor with the women playing a supportive role through their membership and dues.[88] The DFV did not have a clear political goal; its vision of social change called for enlightenment and cultural renewal rather than legal reform, yet its periodicals for women were not apolitical.

Many of the women who wrote politically charged articles in the periodicals did so from a feminist standpoint, yet they clearly rejected the politics of motherhood that has been central to analyses of women's political mobilization in Weimar.[89] Neither homosexual men's parliamentary lobbying nor the orthodox politics of the contemporary women's movement offered a satisfactory conceptual place of political engagement for homosexual women. The issues pursued by those groups simply were not directly relevant to their lives. Their grievances were more amorphous. Being taken seriously was not amenable to legal reform. Nevertheless, in 1927, before Radszuweit intensified his control, some BfM women attempted to organize a politically active Association for Women's Rights.[90] A leader of the short-lived association, Irene von Behlau, assessed the 1928 elections for *Die Freundin*, urging readers, "Our votes for Social Democracy."[91]

After the reimposition of limited censorship in 1927, Karen, editor of *Frauenliebe*, testified before a review board deciding whether the publication could be openly displayed. Humiliated by the experience, she published an open letter describing the demeaning confrontation. It demanded that society recognize women's contributions in the public sphere. Political rhetoric in Germany, she charged, valued women for their reproductive capacity rather than for their work. Karen argued that homosexual women deserved recognition and protection precisely because of their contribution to the nation: "The great possibilities (be it outward success, or ethical and artistic possibilities) in us Germans are still oppressed and misunderstood by our own people."[92] Her claim that homosexual women were an honorable and productive subset of all Germans was a rhetorical move typical of Weimar interest group politics.[93] Germany would be stronger if it granted "freedom of difference" to its homosexual minority.

Inspired by Karen's arguments about the movement in relation to the nation, Rita Volker composed a polemical "Sapphic Pamphlet." Volker refused to define the movement as solely for the repeal of Paragraph 175, which she argued would not change what mattered. "The state might make concessions worthy of recognition through the changing of paragraphs," she wrote, "but what benefit is that to us when its citizens continue to do everything they can to denounce us." Volker spoke as if she represented the entire movement, "We want to be taken seriously, because love is just as serious and holy to us and as much a factor in our human fulfillment as it is for anyone else. . . . Whoever is denied the proper respect . . . must therefore take those things and himself all the more seriously in order to prevail."[94] Volker's impassioned demand to be taken seriously asserts the core of women's emancipatory aspirations going back to the 1890s.

Despite her emphasis on same-sex love as serious and holy, Volker used vivid scenes of same-sex attraction to claim that the same-sex erotic potential of all women was a cultural good in itself. Her vignettes of ideal love and erotic contemplation of the beautiful female body reworked the concepts of "masculinist" male homosexual writers, while at the same time calling their equation of love and masculinity into question. In one vignette, the "I" figure "glowed with a pure worshipping ecstasy of beauty" as she watched "a Russian woman in red silk" dance. The narrator's obvious embodiment of desire embarrassed the other spectators, who shunned her in disgust. Like Karen, the narrator turned humiliation and ostracism into politicized anger. Instead of demanding political inclusion, she called for recognition of the aesthetic and ethical value of erotic love. Rejecting minority politics and sexological categories, Volker imagined a radically new culture where women's same-sex eroticism guaranteed cultivation and judgment.

The gendered politics of the movement was also obvious in calls for women to become more active. Helene Stock, writing in *Die Freundin,* demanded ascetic renunciation as a sign of political seriousness, encouraging members to prove that they were as political as the men. Selli Engler became a visible political leader for BfM women. She appealed to their action-orientation and independence as masculine women, while she obsequiously praised Radszuweit for his leadership and political work on behalf of the homosexual cause.[95] These calls for action were constantly repeated, however reports on results were conspicuously absent. Most readers apparently chose not to rally to what they saw as a men's movement focused on men's issues.

Despite the subdued presence of women in the political work of the organizations, there is no doubt that many conceived of themselves as activists for change. One *Frauenliebe* writer called out to her sisters, "We are here and will fight for our rights, fight down to our last breath."[96] Herta Laser recognized that women's anger represented a political potential that had not yet found an outlet. She asked rhetorically why the movement had "no real woman leader." Her call to action, like many others, created a dichotomy between serious political dedication and frivolous dancing: "[Individuals] do not want to be bothered in daily life; they dance and wear a tie and believe they have done their duty."[97] Hanna Blumenthal demanded, "Freedom for love across the entire front!" Blumenthal cited masculinist writers like Friedländer, Wynecken, Blüher, and Brand, suggesting that politics involved living and thinking differently rather than legal reform.[98] As long as Paragraph 175 did not apply to women, even those who saw themselves as political actors found it difficult to move beyond rhetoric.

Even though most women were not active in lobbying or working for specific reforms, the internalization of the model of the bourgeois public sphere was itself an indication of a stance toward the state and a form of elite politics associated with an earlier period. Their newly won educations had prepared them for a critical position in relation to the state, but not for the politics of compromise and mass action that were required in the republican context of Weimar.[99] What appear in hindsight as contradictions and blind alleys were signs of active formation of political subjectivity in a context that was politicized to an unprecedented degree. Their experiments in political assertion mobilized a wide range of cultural materials as they felt their way toward a means of waging politics that would fit their inherited images of the political subject.

The writers quoted above were local intellectuals who attempted to define and police a public sphere within which they could realize political subjectivity. Their relationship to the mass of members who attended social events cannot be specified with precision. Leaders' constant admonitions about public respectability indicate that class differences were at work and suggest that many casual members may have been resistant to bourgeois discipline. The defensive and exclusionary aspects of the middle-class homosexual public sphere were a response to ostracism and shame. Bourgeois socialization had constructed emancipation as cultivation of a self worthy of being taken seriously by other political actors. Squeezed between spaces of emancipated desire and a men's movement accommodating itself to mass identity politics, the women intellectuals struggled to create viable organizational forms for the sphere they were constructing.

Those who combined radical feminism with affinity for the antifeminist masculinist thinkers drew on a structural similarity in their conceptions. Both used the universal potential for same-sex desire as a basis for gender solidarity. Both connected elite cultural capital to claims that same-sex lovers were politically competent. Just as the male writers emphasized the necessity of unconstrained masculinity in building culture and society, women saw a particular social and cultural value in women's love for each other. Unlike later cultural feminists, they were less concerned with combating patriarchy than with creating a usable space for developing both sexual and political subjectivity. The image of culturally potent same-sex spheres provided useful grounding for them. The strategies of both sexes were reactionary in constructing positions in opposition to mass politics and ideas of equality. Still, women's attempts to combine sexological, political, and cultural ideas about sexuality were highly eclectic and modern. The process of working toward a serviceable identity, social sphere, and political agenda was dynamically evolving when it was overtaken by the Nazi seizure of power.

Love, Sex, and Masculinity in the Homosexual Private Sphere

Like the classical public sphere, the homosexual public sphere of Weimar Berlin was guaranteed and supported conceptually by relations of power and emotion in a coordinated private sphere. While the homosexual public sphere operated outwardly in relation to public spaces, society, and the state, the private sphere created the individuals capable of responsible action in enclosed spaces for the practice of self-cultivation, love relations, and mastery of self and others.[100] Intense idealization of the private love relationship was inseparable from women's desire to be taken seriously in the public sphere. Although historical actors did argue for protection of their privacy from state regulation, the complexity of their emancipation strategies cannot be reduced to liberation from oppression.[101] Homosexual private lives, like any others, were predicated on complicated social and economic ties and functions. Demands for liberation required private behavior demonstrating sober judgment, independence, and responsibility.

The periodicals' fiction reinforced these standards.[102] Stories as well as essays depicted dancing in bars as unhealthy for the individual and the loving couple. The implications of dancing space were as crucial for private life as for constructing a public sphere. Selli Engler's serialized novella "Bianca Torsten's Women" is one among many narratives that contained sexual desire within respectable domestic space.[103] The title character Bianca is distinguished by her "sacrificial dedication," "the purity of her good heart," and her pursuit of "fairytale passionate courtship." She steadfastly upholds the high moral standards expected of the masculine homosexual woman. At first she competed with men for the love of women. However, her quest for ideal love was frustrated when her beloveds could not resist heterosexual social norms. An affair originating in erotic desire produces a different set of conflicts. The painful trials of these unhappy relationships temper her passion and improve her judgment. Her persevering progress through them is rewarded with an ideal love relationship.[104]

The climactic obstacle to this paradise is Bianca's relationship with Johanna. At first encounter, Bianca experiences overflowing sexual desire. Erotic expression she had previously denied "forced itself out like a volcano." Embracing Johanna, she "shook and cried." The story evokes passionate desire only to call it into question. Johanna is irresistibly drawn to erotic adventures. Bianca eventually has to renounce the openly desiring Johanna in order to maintain self-respect. As the narration puts it, "a Bianca Torsten laid her heart only on an altar, not a heap of dirt."[105] Bianca sets out to reform Johanna. She tutors her in appreciation of fine art, hoping to replace Johanna's plebian preference for drinking, dancing, and sexual conquest with more refined pleasures. She employs Johanna as her secretary, hoping to teach her to fill her time with work and art. Bianca's ultimate goal is to coax Johanna into conformity with middle-class values.

Much later, after the couple's breakup and Johanna's return to erotic freedom, Johanna attempts suicide. Nursing Johanna back to health teaches Bianca humility, responsibility, and caring, softening her rigid ideals. At Johanna's sickbed, the two characters debate the role of sexual pleasure in love. Even as she argues for love, Bianca is tempted by the pleasure and erotic satisfaction Johanna embodies. Bianca breaks Johanna's erotic power once strengthened by her partnership with Marry. Marry is everything Johanna is not—serious, spiritual, and disciplined. Marry gives Bianca a love that, unlike Johanna's, deserves to be enshrined on an altar. Instead of the explosive passion of her first kiss with Johanna, Marry's kiss inspires "deep, honest joy and tender, growing love."[106] The pun in Marry's English name is only too obvious: as an inspirational Madonna figure, Marry allows Bianca to form a lasting marriage-like union based on ideals rather than erotic desire.[107] The encounter with Johanna's desire and love of pleasure teaches her to appreciate the moderate spiritual love of her final partner.

The stories often evoke shame in conjunction with the experience of sexual desire. In the "Bianca" story, Bianca tutors Johanna in the proper shame reaction: the "unpleasant feeling of having the exquisite fineness of [their] love . . . exposed in broad daylight."[108] Many other stories banished desire through a similar optics of shame in scenes where the narrator becomes aware of the judgmental witnesses to her feelings of arousal. Reading melodramatic novels shaped teenage girls' ideas about sex by inciting love but reinforcing virtue.[109] Impure desires, sensual pleasure, and bodily enactment of either were subject to interpenetrating social surveillance and self-consciousness.

Given the powerful force of this socialization, the intensity of shame triggered by desire makes the proportional vehemence of the discourse of love in the periodicals comprehensible.

The ideology of love was hegemonic, but women had few models for imagining how love might organize the practicalities of 1920s life. Homosexual women's distance from heterosexually structured society invested love with the entire burden of social support and stability. Heterosexual women exploring freer relationships at the same time faced similar dilemmas. However, the possibility of eventual marriage lent greater stability to their partnerships.[110] The practical concerns that might restrain their sexual choices—avoiding pregnancy and attracting a husband—did not apply to homosexual women. Lacking the "traditional" options and consequences, "modern" homosexual women reactivated ideologies of sentimental love borrowed from medieval Courtly Love and nineteenth-century Romanticism as mechanisms for controlling sexual desire. As in Bianca's story, they conceived of love in a religious idiom using the adjective "holy."

The essays of Ikarus fused emancipation, denial of desire, and the ideological master concept of "holy love" in a particularly fierce manifesto. "One grows and becomes a personality when one sees his longing as holy," she proclaimed.[111] Holy love placed emotional fervor and transcendence within the couple relationship. The ever-present shadow of lust was sublimated into "longing," a spiritual and emotional substitute with a long pedigree in German thought. Romantic ideas entwined love with the process of education and self-actualization.[112] The figure of love worked as a fetish containing the contradictions of desire and emancipation and acting as a defense against persistent sexual shame. Stories and essays embedded sexual desire in stereotypical scenarios that used pure love and devotion to a beloved to contain its disruptive potential. With its heavy social, spiritual, and ethical burdens, love became integral to emancipation.

Ikarus, writing in *Frauenliebe*, mapped a terrain strictly divided between the space of honor—connected with love, modesty, history—and the space of shame—linked to erotic display, frivolousness, and desire. Occupying the latter meant exile from moral community. For Ikarus, homosexual emancipation's claims to freedom, happiness, and justice depended on homosexuals' remaining within the space of honor. As she put it, "nothing is denied to a high, fervent longing, but sensuality turns everything to dust." Given the near consensus about the necessity of renouncing desire, its obsessive reiteration suggests that the texts themselves were spaces for resisting temptation and avoiding shame. Ikarus predicted, "When people say that erotic episodes bless you, you can be sure that a semantic error is in play. It should be depress you, not bless you. The apparent freedom or satisfaction is absolutely no happiness, but rather a deep breath of new anguish."[113] In a second essay, Ikarus, like many of the writers who addressed sexological and political themes, predicated homosexual emancipation on excluding the "bacteria represented so hugely among us." The right to "be who we are" could never include the right to "carelessness or carnality." Holy love, and its denial of sexual desire, was not simply a private ideal; it underwrote standing to claim rights.[114] Asserting sexual subjectivity paradoxically meant renouncing the right to desire.

Other writers went a step farther, eroticizing renunciation itself. Quasi-religious exaltation stood in for arousal and sexual satisfaction. Eroticized renunciation, taken to a masochistic extreme, was the central element in a story titled "The Sacrifice." In the love triangle involving Lilo, Margot, and Friedel, all three women accept sacrifice as the proof of love. Margot had sacrificed to take care of her partner Lilo during a serious lung illness. Now, for Lilo's sake and to conform to the demands of holy love, she and Friedel are prepared to give up the attraction between them. But Lilo cannot bear to accept their sacrifice. In this orgy of selflessness, she is driven to make the greatest sacrifice of all. The story describes Lilo's sacrificial act in erotic detail. She smokes cigarettes while lying naked on her balcony during a snowstorm until she is certain she will die.[115] As she braved the cold, "the fever rose in her, licked her body with greedy tongues." Excitement mounted as she plunged toward melodramatic suicide. Imaginative embodiment of the Camille-like sacrificial heroine had become in itself a source of erotic arousal wrapped inside the code of holy love.

While opinion and commentary strictly disavowed sexual desire, many narratives found convenient niches for eroticism before containing it. Courtly Love frequently supplied a model for the proper function of love with its tropes of the knight serving his lady or the page his knight. Emulating these tropes confirmed the masculinity of homosexual women, distancing it from degraded modern masculinity and making it compatible with the nineteenth-century feminine ideals of self-sacrifice, service, and devotion. Outdated love imagery reflected deeper group and individual struggles to master the contradictions between emancipation and desire. The complex renunciation of desire indicates the persistence of sexual shame in a time of supposed sexual liberation.

Very occasionally, letters to *Die Freundin* expressed the tensions of everyday experience elided by the fantasies of holy love. These brief texts provide a rare glimpse into women's perceptions of their relationships in the interwar period. One writer, using the language of holy love described new love as a "holy time," "golden days," and "a paradise." But the couple's shared goal of being able to live together crumbled once it was achieved and "the trifles of daily life estranged [them] emotionally." Even though their love survived, "the constant battle [had] an effect of unnerving permanence." Along with several other writers, she hypothesized that ideal love could be maintained only if the partners lived separately, in order "to keep the hours that we give each other as a holy experience." "Keep love for yourselves as something holy," she advised.[116] The editors' note that they had received a "flood of mail" on the topic suggests the urgency of disappointment when daily intimacy could not live up to the promises of holy love.[117]

"A former *garçonne*" responded to the letter with a critique of holy love: "Here we have summarized the entire great marriage problem in a short concise question, and if we could answer it here in 'our' newspaper, we would have truly made ourselves worthy of the Nobel Peace Prize." Reviewing her own relationship history, she wrote, "Now I'm in my middle thirties. I was very often unofficially 'married' to women whom I honestly and sincerely loved—but again and again it was impossible to bear daily life together." She urged readers not to give up, because eventually she found a partner, much younger than herself, with whom she could live. Despite the new lover's youth, the writer claimed, "she forced me to dare the impossible. I, old sinner that I was, was forced to forget all—and I mean all—of my selfish demands."[118] One interpretation of the apparent success of this relationship might be that the age difference between the partners allowed for some relaxation in expectations. One of the attractions of same-sex relationships was their apparent equality and mutuality, a quality that allowed women to live out their emancipation. Yet without a preordained hierarchy, self-assertion and the ideology of holy love came into conflict, perhaps expressed in covert power struggles.

Power struggles when love ideals conflicted with individual desires in the *Die Freundin* letters might also be explained by the particular gender pattern of *Die Freundin*'s readers. According to Ruth Roellig, Violetta, associated with *Die Freundin,* was composed of "young business women, sales clerks, hand workers, and lower-level clerical workers." Hahm, "the dashing young leader," demanded that everyone participate in mixers, giving "each of the women the opportunity to become known to these others," making it "easy for compatible women to find each other."[119] This portrait of undifferentiated masculinity and mutual erotic interest may have correlated with their difficulties in reconciling love and emancipation.

Ruth Roellig's description of the differences between Violetta and Monbijou linked difference in gendered erotic cultures to class and intellectual ambitions. The members of Monbijou came from the "better circles of young girls." Their socializing was "very officially" divided into two separate types: *Bubis* and *Mädis*. Mixer dances paired up the two types, as in "the popular Bell Dance, in which only the *Bubis* get bells so they can ring for their *Mädis*." The atmosphere in Monbijou also offered ersatz elegance in contrast to Violetta's rambunctious quality. Colored lights, moonlight effects, and Kati's passionate love ballads set a romantic tone.[120] A heated discussion about relationships also erupted in *Garçonne*, connected to Monbijou. Here, participants bitterly fought out power relations within the couple in explicitly gendered terms.

In addition, the exchange of opinions among the *Garçonne* writers drew attention to generational differences between the contributors socialized before the war and those who knew only wartime and postwar conditions. Actual birth dates for the women are unknown, so my conclusion that these tensions were partly generational rests more on their arguments and attitudes toward each other than on chronological ages. What appears to be a generational difference may have more to do with the point in time when the woman began identifying as homosexual.

Käthe Wundram, who seemed to enjoy acting as a provocateur, kicked off the debate with an article arguing that the feminine woman in a relationship should understand and tolerate her partner's need to engage in outside affairs, even though the masculine partner could not grant her feminine lover the same privilege. In Wundram's nineteenth-century conceptions of gender difference, masculinity meant superior intellect, independence, leadership, responsibility, and the psychological need to conquer a lover. Feminine women were jealous and "petty by nature." Since love was their singular purpose in life, they needed a masculine partner to admire and protect them.[121]

Though Wundram's age is hard to specify, it seems likely that she was part of the older generation. Her conceptions reflected the subculture of bars and clubs where the ideology of binary desire required participants to specify and stick with a particular gender role. She understood erotic attraction as based on gender opposition. Love required mystery and tension between the partners, while friendship, only possible between masculine women, offered relaxation. Wundram's boldest claim was her celebration of the erotic as necessary for individual and relationship satisfaction. Her description of masculinity as polygamous transgressed the ideology of holy love.[122]

Karen accepted Wundram's gender binary for "normal" men and women, but argued that all homosexual women had a "masculine streak." The central meaning of homosexuality to Karen was gender nonconformity. In her view, homosexual women were all more intellectual and less sensual than "normal" women.[123] Karen's concept of the masculine kernel in all homosexual women supported a minoritizing model of homosexuality, where inner masculinity made all homosexual women essentially the same, and gave them special claims to emancipation and sexual subjectivity.

Karen further implied that common masculinity was the secret to attraction between homosexual women. Confident of the masculinity in their nature, both lovers could play with gender roles and styles, experiencing a unique erotic charge from the novelty and transgression inherent in female masculinity. Karen's long tenure in the movement, the fact that she had been married previously, and her feminist critique of heterosexuality suggest that she was older than the average and came to the homosexual movement by way of the prewar women's movement. Her feminism via masculinity was representative of emancipation strategies dating back to Anna Rühling's 1904 speech demanding emancipation for homosexual women on the basis of inner masculinity.

Ilse Schwarze also represented a somewhat older generation. She admitted that her first love experience had been so far in the past that she could hardly recall it. Her sharp criticism of masculine arrogance and dismay that the evils of heterosexuality were being reproduced in homosexual relationships reveal the influence of prewar feminism. For women like Schwarze and Karen, a single-sex world represented liberation from confining gender stereotypes and limitations. Schwarze's conceptions of love were compatible with the nineteenth-century model of romantic friends. Along with several others, Schwarze rejected Wundram's gender stereotypes as outdated antifeminist views that oppressed women. She decried Wundram's hierarchy of power, morality, and esteem in which masculinity was taken as license for freedom for oneself and oppression of others.[124] These writers felt that their intellect, freedom, morality, and right to respect had been insulted by Wundram's sweeping generalizations. Schwarze was adamant that love meant mutuality rather than the attraction of opposites. Feeling differently gendered still did not justify the more masculine lover's claiming to be superior.[125]

The debate was unusual because women who identified as feminine participated, completely rejecting Wundram's characterization. They cited the unenviable position of the feminine woman betrayed by her lover: feelings hurt, love poisoned by jealousy, knowledge that she was not her partner's first choice. Lo Hilmar attacked Wundram's claim that masculine women were loyal. She had experienced just as much fickleness with "masculine-feeling comrades." Hilmar argued, "We different ones should take our love relationships more seriously than any other woman her marriage or love relationship . . . because our relationships must replace so much that every petty bourgeois housewife takes for granted and that will always remain denied to us."[126] Hilmar's wish for the security and social integration of marriage was unlikely to persuade Wundram.

The security of marriage Hilmar longed for was in tension with the promise of emancipation. Hilmar asked, "Haven't you ever had the thought that many women might flee to your kind because they simply cannot bear the masculine need to dominate, the outrageous injustice of the opposition of the sexes?"[127] Wundram's version of masculinity threatened to reproduce gendered oppression inside the same-sex couple. Karen's, Schwarze's, and Hilmar's resistance to gender polarization connected them with the feminism of the previous generation and stigmatized them as old-fashioned and provincial.

Thea Neumann insightfully pointed out that they clung to love as a fetish that could contain and resolve the contradictions of their position. She ridiculed the naivety of their love-conquers-all ideology. "Well now, even if all the many angels get together in couples in order to chase after happiness together, in the course of time it almost always seems that one of these tender beings—scratches." For Neumann, the masculine woman was attracted to the feminine lover's purity, motherliness, and power to forgive the her transgressions. A feminine partner's unfaithfulness destroyed this illusion and the relationship.[128] Neumann's Marian image of femininity clashed with her sarcastic tone.

Neumann's and Karla Mayburg's matter-of-fact attitudes toward relationships seem to mark them as typical of young women later in Weimar. Although their standpoints were very different, they understood each other. Mayburg resisted any grand utopian scheme in favor of practical accommodations that might ameliorate vulnerability. For her, eroticism was not so much wrong as exhausting. Between occasional moments of intense feeling, "one always returns to the somewhat prosaic everyday, for which an atmosphere of warm sincerity is much more pleasant and necessary." Mayburg's short story "Notice of a Visit" was a very literal translation of her philosophy. In it, two very similar young businesswomen meet, fall in love, and save each other from a life of loneliness and struggle.[129] Each has a partner ideal that is androgynous and similar. The protagonist hopes for a partner who is "clever, energetic—like a comrade—understanding, cheerful, yet serious," someone who plays sports and works in a laboratory.[130] For Mayburg, the couple was the simple solution to isolation.

Mayburg's reduced expectations of both love and desire reflected the survival mentality of the 1930s. Her essay mediated between viewpoints. Her conciliatory tone could not have been more different from Schwarze's and Hilmar's bitterness, Wundram's provocation, and Neumann's sarcasm.

Mayburg warned against constructing stark gender binaries, refusing to oppose intelligence and attractiveness. She found gender opposition equally absurd for the biological sexes and for homosexual women.[131]

Shortly after the debate, *Garçonne* published a sketch by Wundram that could be read as her last word. "Definition of Love" emphasizes the inequality of the couple, in the story differentiated by age rather than by gender identification. The younger character expresses the idealism and rejection of the erotic characteristic of the advocates of "holy love" and Wundram's antagonists in the debate. " 'Brrr, sensuality,' said Kitty theatrically . . . 'How bestial, disgusting!' " Ruth, older and experienced, wants "to destroy the lively young thing's . . . naive and innocent, if also confused, conception of love, but not clumsily or unwisely." Kitty is angered by Ruth's argument that love is just a polite form of sensuality. Although "Ruth senses with a finely-tuned instinct that Kitty is ready to surrender," she waits, arousing the younger woman's desire as proof against Kitty's prim rejection of sensuality. Finally, Kitty feels "the gradual slipping down of the narrow strap of her dress, without doing anything to stop it. Hotter than any words, the bared young breast cried out to Ruth. Then the red-blonde woman finally took her corrected stubborn child into her quaking arms."[132] In Kitty's seduction desire confronts holy love, emerging victorious. Wundram's story cleverly invited partisans of comradely love to enjoy vicariously the erotic thrills they were missing. The story also did without gender labels, substituting the erotic dynamic of seduction and surrender.

Some historians of Weimar female homosexuality have emphasized the gender role division into *Bubis* and *Mädis* as the normative form of homosexual self-definition and couple formation. My reading of the periodicals suggests that the butch/femme model was more limited, tentative, and contested than earlier analyses have acknowledged. In their debates about relationships, as well in reinterpreting sexology and asserting political visions, the women constituting the middle-class homosexual public sphere were still rethinking and arguing the precise nature of all of the elements that constituted homosexual identity, including female masculinity. Rather than reading established subcultural norms from these sources, I see them as an indication of provisional and fluid combinations of conceptions, experiences, and identifications being considered and worked through.[133] Careful reading of multiple genres from the sources shows that there was no single pattern of sexual and relationship practice in the interwar period. It is even hard to claim with certainty that there were multiple stable subcultures. Rather, middle-class women who began to identify themselves as homosexual experimented with many gendered self-concepts and relationship ideologies.

The pattern of the two clubs sketched above contradicts the usual association of masculine/feminine pairing with working-class women and feminism,
rejection of gender roles, and androgyny with middle-class women.[134] In this
case, the club characterized by stronger feminism and higher education was
also associated with gender-differentiated desire and coupling. In addition,
disagreements about this pattern that emerged in the debate are surprising
since the contributors were regular writers for *Garçonne* and presumably
came from similar class and educational backgrounds and subscribed to the
same notions about love and sexual attraction.[135]

The public discussion of relationship ideologies reflects various kinds
of disappointment in the Weimar homosexual community. The feminists
felt that the majority of the women in the movement discounted their most
important victories and social criticisms. Their imagined utopia of women's
freedom and love had seemingly reincorporated all the worst elements of
masculinity in the form of masculine women. One could be abused and
betrayed by a female lover just as by a man. Wundram, on the other hand,
seemed disappointed that masculine privileges were no longer respected by
young women who felt justified in complaining or having affairs of their
own in response to a partner's infidelity. For Karen, denigration of the more
feminine women broke down the solidarity of the movement and called their
claims to inner masculinity into question.

Intertextual reading of the stories and the opinion pieces demonstrates
that the codes of love were contested and confused in the interwar period.
The *amour passion* model of resistance and surrender persisted in shaping
erotic fantasies of seducing and being seduced. But discourses of shared love
between similar partners also mobilized heightened intensity through recourse
to images of courtly love and heroic sacrifice. At the same time, awareness
of the practical role of the couple in multiple dimensions of modern life was
never far from the narrative screen. The need for sickbed compassion and
financial security was as great as the need for erotic intensity, and it was far
from clear how these needs could be secured in a single love relationship.

Sweetness, tenderness, womanly intuition, and extravagant, romantic
gestures all mark sexual desire within many stories as explicitly feminine.
Yet their hopes for emancipation were underwritten with female masculinity. The homosexual woman's gender ambiguity allowed this struggle to be
played out along multiple axes. The disparate threads are difficult to pull
into one coherent picture of love and desire in the Weimar women's homosexual community. Women asserted sexual subjectivity but differed in their
conceptions of how to live out that subjectivity in an unstable era. Ideas,
discourses, and experiences were still in a dynamic state of flux that wrote

old scenarios into new conditions, shaped new senses of self using inherited values, and asserted new privileges within symbolic systems that had already lost their relevance.

Epilogue

The radical rupture of 1933 serves as the endpoint for the Weimar homosexual movement. The publication of *Die Freundin* survived Hitler's appointment as chancellor on January 30. But immediately after the elections of March 5, 1933, in the aftermath of the Reichstag fire and emergency decrees, the state moved to end the conditions that allowed homosexuals to construct a public sphere of their own. The last issue of *Die Freundin* was dated March 8, 1933. In one of the Nazi regime's first official moves calculated to win the approval of respectable society, authorities in Berlin "cleaned up the streets" that same week by shutting down homosexual bars, organizations, and meeting places as well as publications. Some of the more visible leaders were arrested. Throughout the Nazi period, homosexual men were sporadically purged or rounded up and sent to concentration camps. Repression of female homosexuality was less evident; most homosexually identified women in the camps were sent there as Jews, leftist activists, or prostitutes. Nevertheless, fear of denunciation drove many women to police their own public profiles.

Claudia Schoppmann has documented the afterlife of the Weimar community. Lotte Hahm was arrested and sent to a concentration camp for a time. Rumor had it that the father of a lover denounced her on a trumped-up charge of corrupting a minor. After her release, she continued to be active in homosexual gathering places and tried to open another bar. She and Kati Reinhard opened a club for women in the 1950s. Selli Engler turned up in the archives because of a play entitled "Heil Hitler!" that she sent directly to Hitler in 1933. There is no way to tell whether she was a convinced Nazi at that point or whether she was trying to cover up for her questionable past. She continued to live in Berlin with her mother and applied to join the writers' guild in 1938, as did Ruth Roellig. Elspeth Killmer apparently accommodated her feminism to the new regime and was active in the Nazi women's organization. Annette Eick and Charlotte Wolff, in danger as Jews, emigrated to England where they remained after the war.[136]

Although Nazi punishments were extraordinarily harsh for those subjected to them, repression of public homosexuality did not destroy social contact. The "gay life" retreated to its more discreet subcultural forms and spaces. Some women even found a congenial site for finding lovers in the single-sex work places of the Labor Service. One of Schoppmann's informants remembered that a woman she knew from Violetta later became a district leader of the Women's Labor Service.[137] The Nazi state may have created space for a covert homosexual sphere in their *Arbeitsgemeinschaft*.

Conclusion

Desiring Emancipation has used a microhistorical and marginal approach to reveal the underlying dynamics of broad historical questions concerning women's emancipation and sexuality.[1] Focusing on the late nineteenth and early twentieth centuries in particular, it has traced the coincidence of popular discourses about the New Woman and the formation of scientific discourses describing what came to be known as female homosexuality. Elements common to both meant that scholars have found considerable overlap in debates about the two phenomena.[2] In German sources these overlaps make possible analysis of a multitude of dense sites for negotiating frictions in the articulations of gender and sexuality, emancipation and affiliation, politics and identity. Reading these sources through the lens of theories of subjectivity and subject formation explains and clarifies the desires and aspirations of middle-class women who claimed aspects of gender emancipation. These assertive sources reveal affective and ideological reactions in fantasies and narratives that interpreted interrelations between self, society, nation, and state.

The case studies in this volume enable an interpretation of a long transition in German women's claiming of emancipation and sexuality. They also document a part of the history of homosexuality, including the transition from category to identity, formation of community, and the effects of medical discourse. Neither of these realms supports a story of women realizing inner truth and confronting repression in favor of liberation. By embedding the emergence of homosexual identity within a broader and deeper historical context, it can be more closely and more complexly connected to changes in gender and sexuality that were affecting most of Western society in the period.

Emancipation

The four case studies constitute a grid of middle-class women engaged in gender emancipation struggles over a half-century. The Zurich students and the Munich feminist avant-garde represented a privileged elite and a very narrow slice of the women of their generation. They constructed new gender ideals in opposition to a strictly enforced nineteenth-century social norm of female domesticity. Frieda Duensing, Sophia Goudstikker, Frieda von Bülow, and Käthe Schirmacher asserted personal independence and made strong claims for emancipation from family tutelage and duty. The question of what a woman could be outside the structure of family and reproduction was central. Their solutions were highly individual. As activists, some turned to conservative nationalism, others participated in mainstream liberalism or apolitical intellectual life, a few remained campaigners for radical gender change. Regardless of political affiliation, organized feminists, urban avant-gardes, and university women maintained their relationships with one another. Anita Augspurg participated in all of the groups.

By the Weimar era, female emancipation affected much broader levels of society. As a result, most of the historical subjects in these case studies left few historical traces. Despite Weimar's reputation for modernity and rupture with the past, many Weimar women's experiences of emancipation were heavily influenced by socialization in the earlier era. Higher girls' schools successfully inculcated the nineteenth-century nationalist bourgeois values of cultivation of the self and service to the whole. Emancipation in the name of personal liberation was subordinated to these inherited values. This way of legitimating individual desire resonated with feminist rhetoric of social motherhood, but these unmarried women muted or refused motherhood as a discursive strategy. Homosexual movement women embraced inner masculinity as a positive qualification for contributing to society and culture.

The central social question in both eras was whether women's emancipation would interfere with the robust reproduction needed by the modern nation.[3] The Wilhelmine generation created an uproar that helped trigger a reexamination of the entire structure of heterosexual desire. Male and female authors of the era produced literary experiments that refastened the knot between femininity and heterosexuality. "Modern" reassertions of gender polarity and heterosexual desire often required mystification of reproduction and/or love. Anxieties about feminine roles fed stigmatization of female masculinity and feminist assertion as asexual and asocial.

While Anita Augspurg and Sophia Goudstikker reveled in challenging and transgressing old and new heterosexual normativity, others including Frieda von Bülow, Frieda Duensing, Käthe Schirmacher, and Ella Mensch experienced frustration and despair when their aspirations were blocked or ridiculed. Though their more conservative colleagues were usually anti-feminist, each of them continued to identify with the women's movement in one way or another and wrestled with the problem of how to incorporate a "healthy" feminism into a strong state. Schirmacher and Mensch, supported by their partnerships with women, cobbled together an unstable position for themselves as female intellectuals outside the family. Their rhetorical elevation of domestic femininity served as a kind of psychological counterweight to their personal nondomestic work lives. Adventures, appropriation of masculine gallantry, and enjoyment of comradely relationships with men expressed their rejection of hegemonic femininity. As if to compensate for this transgression, their writing proclaims the sacred national duty of Germanic culture's domestic mother.

Despite the great differences between the two eras, Weimar women's emancipation clearly had deep roots in the earlier feminist movement. The larger Weimar cohorts resulted from wartime circumstances that called upon women's patriotism and labor. An emancipated life, suddenly facilitated by the war, continued into the Weimar period. Women's ambitions concentrated more on personal action and less on rethinking the whole of the social order. Frieda Duensing serves as a telling figure connecting the two generations. The goals and anxieties she worried about as a teacher in the 1880s resonate with the justifications and anxieties of the Weimar groups. Moving from teaching to law and social work, she finally combined these by training the next generation of social workers. In each career, she drew on her personal struggle for moral autonomy as a basis for contributing to society by moralizing others.

The Weimar women civil servants followed Duensing's lead, displacing their personal ambitions and desires into their calling of reclaiming the "people" for the nation by preventing the "endangered" from falling out of respectable moral society. Feminine qualities of love and trust gave them a privileged claim to reforming the existing state.

The visible leaders and writers of the homosexual movement emphasized an unstable combination of love and masculinity as a way of situating their emancipation within an assimilationist national framework. Because homosexuality as an identity was impossible without acknowledging desire, their construction of a usable ideology was convoluted. They followed the masculinity strategy visible in the various personae of Duensing and Sophia Goudstikker, as well as the rhetoric of Anna Rühling. Masculinity as an inner character authorized their independent lives, careers, and participation in culture and public sphere. The masculinity they claimed was not a sexualized rugged modern masculinity; rather, it drew on archaic models of the knight and the courtier—idealized figures from earlier periods of class formation thought to represent cultivation and respect for women. Character after character in the movement's fiction learned that sexual freedom was a false goal and that sexuality had to be subordinated to a responsible inner self that approximated that at the core of the civil servants' identity.

Recognizing the centrality of the aspiration to becoming a responsible moral subject capable of contributing to the social whole helps explain why women's emancipation did not go the way it "should have." This "failure" of feminism was not fundamentally an issue of liberal versus conservative or difference versus equality. Those interpretations are based on a retrospective misrecognition of what emancipation's promise was for most middle-class women. Since they wanted the same kinds of social importance and freedom of action that their fathers and brothers modeled, it is not surprising that they assimilated nationalist and class-bound assumptions and myths even as they tried to revise the gender qualification.

Seen from the perspective of gender emancipation, the entire long period of Wilhelmine and Weimar Germany can be conceptualized as a hinged joint between the nineteenth-century bourgeois era and twentieth-century mass society. The war was the sharpest point in the hinge, but also a connection between the two arms. Both Weimar groups were modern innovations made possible by the new constitution and moderate socialist reform initiatives. Yet new structures and subjectivities could not be conjured from nothing. Weimar gender and sexual emancipation, especially for women who had been socialized before the war, meant looking back to past ideals.

Homosexuality

Late-nineteenth century sources demonstrate decisively that homosexuality was not a conceptual category recognized or used by women encountering each other in the quest for emancipation. The concept of homosexuality, or even perverse desire, was not evident as a diagnosis, identity, or stigma; it did not affect their relationships, fantasies, or self-making. The lack of a specific concept fostered exploration in women's relations with one another, precisely because those relations bore no assumption of marriage commitment or destabilizing grand passion. Women in these circles understood and supported each other's striving toward autonomous subjectivity. Their relationships with one another sometimes generated jealousy, but evidence does not reveal internal conflict or anxiety about the morality or social acceptability of intimacy between two women.

Their ability to enjoy the pleasures of each other's proximity can be situated in its disconnection from the dangerous sexual desire they had been warned would characterize "fallen women." Contemporary stereotypes defined feminine desire as greedy compulsion. They well knew that men were only too willing to categorize a desiring woman as a sex object and nothing else. These assumptions allowed them to see their feelings for one another as something quite different. Since they felt no compulsion to seek sexual satisfaction with anyone, intense mutual attraction was not interpreted as sexual desire. For most women of the Wilhelmine period, becoming an autonomous subject meant at least nominal acceptance of bourgeois sexual norms. As the stories by Bülow and Salomé reveal, sexuality was clearly implicated in emancipation, but it was a puzzle that had yet to emerge into open debate by the turn of the century.

Dissemination of the conceptual category of female homosexual in the print media starting around 1900 coincides with emergence of urban middle-class women's separatist communities. *Große Glocke*'s coverage of the New Women's Community and other urban spaces suspected of harboring the newly visible homosexual woman clearly had a basis in reality since some women explicitly protested the newspaper's characterization of homosexuality. These small new social formations before World War I seem to have thrived on the energy of transgression and innovation. The growing number of commercial spaces associated with same-sex-desiring women indicates an expanding population into the Weimar period.

As the figure of the homosexual woman became more recognizable to the general public, it played a dual role as opportunity and threat. Some women gathered under its sign, creating a new subculture that fulfilled their needs. Others found their relationships smeared as the fulfillment of perverted desire. Most of the time, professional women found it possible to appear authentically respectable to themselves and others despite living in couples. In the Erkens case, an array of friends and relatives denied that the marriage-like relationship between Therese Dopfer and Maria Fischer could be categorized as mutual homosexual desire. But the label, once suggested by an angry, possibly rejected, colleague, made sense to observers who did not know the two women personally. The shame of assumed perversion triggered the women's mutual suicide.

In case after case among the professional civil servants, unmasterable denied desires came to the surface as accusations of homosexuality, accusations used as weapons against colleagues they likely desired. Far from being frightened by the power of doctors to stigmatize or smear them because of their emancipation, professional women were confident that doctors would diagnose them as "normal." Yet the category itself was inescapable once desire escaped the bounds of carefully shaped professional identities. What was extruded as incompatible with professional women's subjectivity returned as suspicions of others, perhaps vast numbers of conspiring others, as in Anna Philipps's fantasy of a homosexual conspiracy as the power behind the Weimar state.

Meanwhile, Weimar cities provided spaces where another group of women could construct subjectivities that embraced the notion of homosexuality as justifying and supporting their emancipation. Willing to experiment with new identities, many experienced inner conflict because these spaces were simultaneously spaces of acting out desire. Individual people moved flexibly between the multiple publics and positions that were made possible by new media and urban space during the Weimar years. Yet, when rivalries between mass membership clubs broke out, each side tried to portray the other as contaminated by desire coded feminine. Using Michael Warner's gloss on Habermas, it is possible to see these contentions as emerging between an alternative or counter public embracing socially unacceptable desire and a public sphere aspiring to respectability.[4] The intellectual leadership of the homosexual organizations felt called to police the porous boundaries between the unruly alternative public and the homosexual public sphere, drawing on the familiar ideological commitments connected with aspiring to become autonomous subjects.

The periodicals of the homosexual organizations provide overwhelming evidence that a significant number of their members also had difficulty reconciling themselves to a subject position defined by desire. Especially as women became more economically vulnerable in the 1930s, their discourses emphasized the idea that "holy love" was necessary to redeem women's relationships from their association with the desiring public of Weimar nightlife. Selli Engler and other leaders exhorted homosexual women to relegate their desire to discreet private spaces in order to behave as respectable masculine ladies.

The discourses of sexology were indispensable to the development of middle-class homosexual identity. No matter how negative the implications, the sanction of scientific recognition provided a solid platform from which to construct subjectivity. Yet women did not passively accept the claims of doctors and experts. They concentrated on the ideas of congenital nature and masculine character that were useful for justifying emancipation, confidently disputing elements of sexological discourse that did not fit their sense of themselves.

Though masculinity was fundamental to self-definition, the gender of desire remained contested. My research complicates the assumption of lesbian studies that butch/femme roles were associated with lower-middle- and working-class cultures, while upper-middle-class women developed more androgynous and feminist models of the lesbian couple. Although both clubs in the homosexual movement were middle-class, one, Violetta, was clearly associated with a more educated, aspiring, and feminist group. This group was described as socializing around *Bubi* and *Madi* gender polarity and as having more affinity with the "masculinists" of the male homosexual movement.[5] The terms of middle-class emancipation, described above, explain the latter paradox. Both men and women mobilized cultural elitism to contrast the noble ideal of their same-sex love against modern heterosexual relations of possession, violence, and mundane material concerns of economics and reproduction. Claiming masculinity for themselves allowed them to disassociate themselves from the "normal" women the masculinists denigrated.

The heated debates in the periodicals show that masculinity was a highly mobile and unstable component of the female homosexual identity and one that interfered with formation of a single culture of desire. Gender roles were imperfectly spread across the couple and highly contested in both groups. Both partners needed to claim masculinity if both had ambitions to fashion themselves as emancipated subjects. Movement ideology stigmatized sensual, irresponsible, fickle femininity, excluding "normal" women from the autonomy homosexual women sought to claim for themselves. The gender politics of female masculinity left "feminine" partners in an uncertain position and rejected bisexual women because of their alleged continuing feminine dependence on men. Many of the stories exploring identity and relationships portrayed the couple as alike and androgynous. While some opinion writers claimed masculine privileges over their feminine partners, this scenario was seldom expressed in fiction. The utopian mode of the stories preserved autonomy and desire for both partners.

But there was second potential to female masculinity. Some women experimented with impersonations of masculinity that took the androgyny of the New Woman image and pushed it to a new level. The women who dared to act it out (or imagined doing so) expanded the gender possibilities of the female body. Clearly, Goudstikker's performance in particular provoked and challenged a wide variety of observers to write scenarios that restored her femininity. The erotic potential of Goudstikker's masculine woman was neither feminine seduction and submission nor masculine conquest and possession. It clearly pointed toward the pleasures of homosexual desire without quite claiming them.

Goudstikker at the turn of the century and Lotte Hahm's entrepreneurial Weimar cabaret persona stand out as figures that boldly refused gender and sexual norms without imposing new forms of discipline. No direct line can be drawn from Goudstikker's Puck persona to later communities of same-sex lovers. Nevertheless, there is clearly a genealogical link in the expansion of urban space and female autonomy that Sophia Goudstikker and Anita Augspurg self-consciously created for themselves. The rhetoric in the *Große Glocke* stories simultaneously suggests that urban spaces of female desire were sites where some women seized opportunities for bodily, erotic, and psychic pleasure.

During Weimar, playful, erotic, and challenging female masculinity was confronted with an official female masculinity that disavowed pleasure and transgression. It seems to me significant that at a certain point Lotte Hahm took her performances of masculine mimicry outside the movement and back into the commercial sphere. Despite a dominant trend in the periodicals' fiction toward reincorporating female homosexuality into the family, the economy, and the public sphere, Lotte Hahm's comic presence was evidence of the survival of the homosexual public as a resistant and alternative public, as a site for fracturing the mechanisms of social discipline. These two representatives of trickster masculinity are also the least implicated in aspirations to national belonging. National claims required a securely gendered standpoint.

Subjectivity

For better or worse, sexual subjectivity was a conscious feature of the emancipated female self by the 1930s. *Desiring Emancipation* has traced some of the emotional and ideological factors that shaped women's emerging consciousness of themselves as sexual beings. Imagining themselves as sexual set off internal struggles for middle-class women heavily socialized to believe that sexual desire was a bestial or even evil force, shameful to recognize in oneself. While sexuality could still be pushed into the background in the nineteenth century, by the twentieth few could avoid its presence in defining femininity.

Throughout the book, the erotic has struggled to break through to the surface of representation. Shame and aspiration combined to ensure that these elements were mostly contained and suppressed even well into the twentieth century. It is striking that even the women of the homosexual movement, who did not have to fear pregnancy, claimed sexual subjectivity almost as gingerly as their turn-of-the-century counterparts. The stereotype of the dangerous sexual woman was too deeply entrenched to be dislodged by the precarious claims of a few marginal women.

The popular media constituted a much more powerful force for cultural change. Films such as *Pandora's Box* and *The Blue Angel* circulated the dangerous seductive woman trope, yet they also portrayed the lead actresses as attractive figures of identification and models of sexual subjectivity. The role of popular culture in making pleasure and desire ever more present in everyday life during Weimar meant that a stance of emancipated national purity became more and more difficult to sustain. This tension suggests that the next collective embodiment of the nation would have to overcome the gulf between pleasure and the nation, offering Germans an erotic patriotism as well as greater scope for sexual subjectivity.[6]

Because some women wanted to become autonomous subjects, they made history. It was not a history of their own choosing, nor was it the history scholars of a later period might wish to choose for them. It involved bitter conflicts, shame, and categorical exclusion or denigration of other women seeking emancipation. Their determination to live independently certainly made them vulnerable on many fronts. But their intervention into discourse did create a change in the potential meanings of the female subject. For them, construction of a usable sexual subjectivity remained incomplete and hedged in by what it could never be, given their core identities. But their claims did challenge the cultural binary between the innocent domestic woman and the dangerous sexual woman. A new path for claiming sexual subjectivity through consumption, fashion, and glamour emerged in the 1920s. The paths taken by the somewhat older subjects of *Desiring Emancipation* rejected this emerging commercial model; they continued to find the pleasure-seeking woman incompatible with service and love.

The friction between gender emancipation and sexual subjectivity that emerged and took shape in this crucial transition period continues to trouble women's status and life choices in society in the twenty-first century. Although popular consensus represents women's emancipation as complete, young women are still awkwardly poised between the constantly reiterated stereotypes of hot babe and nurturing wife and mother. Industrial societies continue to depend on most women's fashioning their social and sexual selves to accommodate caregiving roles. Although the problems captured by the figure of the New Woman have long since ceased to be new, the contradictions she brought into the open still define the possibilities of feminine sexual subjectivity.

Notes

Introduction

1. Frieda von Bülow, "Laß mich nun vergessen!" in *Die schönsten Novellen der Frieda von Bülow über Lou Andreas-Salomé und andere Frauen,* ed. Sabine Streiter (Frankfurt: Ullstein Taschenbuch, 1990), 69–142.

2. Kerstin Barndt, "Frauen-Litteratur um 1900." Paper presented at the annual meeting for the German Studies Association, Atlanta, Georgia, Oct. 4–7, 1999.

3. Joan Scott, "Gender: A Useful Category of Analysis," *American Historical Review* 91 (1986): 1073–74.

4. Bülow, "Laß mich," 83–84.

5. Ibid., 104–105, 76–77.

6. Ibid., 75–77, 92.

7. Ibid., 84.

8. Mary Louise Roberts, *Disruptive Acts: The New Woman in Fin-de-Siècle France* (Chicago: University of Chicago Press, 2002), 3–7; The Modern Girl Around the World Research Group, *The Modern Girl Around the World: Consumption, Modernity, and Globalization* (Durham: Duke University Press, 2008); Elizabeth Otto and Vanessa Rocco, eds., *The New Woman International: Representations in Photography and Film from the 1870s through the 1960s* (Ann Arbor: University of Michigan Press, 2011).

9. Atina Grossmann, *"Girlkultur* or Thoroughly Rationalized Female: A New Woman in Weimar Germany?" in *Women in Culture and Politics: A Century of Change,* ed. Judith Friedlander et al. (Bloomington: Indiana University Press, 1986); Lynne Frame, "Gretchen, Girl, Garçonne? Weimar Science and Popular Culture in Search of the Ideal New Woman," in *Women in the Metropolis: Gender and Modernity in Weimar Culture,* ed. Katharina von Ankum (Berkeley: University of California Press, 1997).

10. This topic has a long historiography including Esther Newton, "The Mythic Mannish Lesbian: Radclyffe Hall and the New Woman," and Carroll Smith-Rosenberg, "Discourses of Sexuality and Subjectivity: The New Woman, 1870–1936," both in *Hidden from History: Reclaiming the Gay and Lesbian Past,* ed. Martin Duberman, George Chauncey Jr., and Martha Vicinus (New York: New American Library, 1989); Sheila Jeffreys, *The Spinster and Her Enemies: Feminism and Sexuality 1880–1930* (London: Pandora Press, 1985); Lillian Faderman, *Surpassing the Love of Men: Romantic Friendship and Love between Women from the Renaissance to the Present* (New York:

William Morrow, 1981); and the essays in Laura Doan and Lucy Bland, eds., *Sexology in Culture: Labelling Bodies and Desires* (Chicago: University of Chicago Press, 1998).

11. Carole Pateman, *The Sexual Contract* (Stanford: Stanford University Press, 1988); Joan Wallach Scott, *Only Paradoxes to Offer: French Feminists and the Rights of Man* (Cambridge: Harvard University Press, 1996); and Isabel Hull, *Sexuality, State, and Civil Society in Germany, 1700–1815* (Ithaca: Cornell University Press, 1996).

12. Geoff Eley, *Reshaping the German Right: Radical Nationalism and Political Change After Bismarck* (Ann Arbor: University of Michigan Press, 1991 orig. 1980), 19–24; Dieter Langewiesche, *Liberalism in Germany*, trans. Christiane Banerji (Princeton: Princeton University Press, 2000 orig.1988), 228–29.

13. Elizabeth Harvey, "The Failure of Feminism? Young Women and the Bourgeois Feminist Movement in Weimar Germany 1918–1933," *Central European History* 28 (1995); Detlef Peukert, *The Weimar Republic: The Crisis of Classical Modernity*, trans. Richard Deveson (New York: Hill and Wang, 1989), 14–18.

14. An example of this mobilization is the Munich Modern Life Society, described in Peter Jelavich, *Munich and Theatrical Modernism: Politics, Playwriting, and Performance, 1890–1914* (Cambridge: Harvard University Press, 1985), 26–44.

15. This seems to contrast with the case of women in the United States and Britain. In these settings, middle-class women lived independently, sought education, and formed couples much earlier in the nineteenth century.

16. Patrice Petro, *Joyless Streets: Women and Melodramatic Representation in Weimar Germany* (Princeton: Princeton University Press, 1989), 103–10; Atina Grossmann, "*Girlkultur*"; Lynne Frame, "Gretchen, Girl, Garçonne?"; Cornelie Usborne, *Politics of the Body in Weimar Germany: Women's Reproductive Rights and Duties* (Ann Arbor: University of Michigan Press, 1992).

17. See Richard W. McCormick, *Gender and Sexuality in Weimar Modernity: Film, Literature, and the "New Objectivity"* (New York: Palgrave, 2001), ch. 5.

18. Cornelie Usborne, "The New Woman and Generational Conflict: Perceptions of Young Women's Sexual Mores in the Weimar Republic," in *Generations in Conflict: Youth Revolt and Generation Formation in Germany 1770–1968*, ed. Mark Roseman (Cambridge: Cambridge University Press, 1995), 157; Dagmar Herzog, *Sex After Fascism: Memory and Morality in Twentieth-Century Germany* (Princeton: Princeton University Press, 2005), 16.

19. Quoted in Roger Perret, " 'Ernst, Würde und Glück des Daseins,' " afterword to *Lyrische Novelle*, by Annemarie Schwarzenbach (Basel: Lenos Verlag, 1999), 130.

20. On the ambiguous sexuality of the androgynous "girl" figure, see Grossmann, "*Girlkultur*"; Frame, "Gretchen, Girl, Garçonne?"; McCormick, *Gender and Sexuality in Weimar Modernity*, ch. 1, and 117–21. On androgynous style in interwar Britain, see Laura Doan, *Fashioning Sapphism: The Origins of a Modern English Lesbian Culture* (New York: Columbia University Press, 2001), ch. 4; for France, see Mary Louise Roberts, *Civilization Without Sexes*, ch. 3.

21. Luther H. Martin, Huck Gutman, and Patrick Hutton, eds., *Technologies of the Self: A Seminar with Michel Foucault* (Amherst: University of Massachusetts Press, 1988).

22. Carl Westphal, "Die conträre Sexualempfindung," *Archiv für Psychiatrie* 2 (1869). Quoted in Manfred Herzer, "Das Jahr 1869," in *Eldorado: Homosexuelle Frauen und Männer in Berlin, 1850-1950: Geschichte, Alltag und Kultur* (Berlin: Edition Hentrich, 1992, orig. 1984), 10.

23. Harry Oosterhuis, *Stepchildren of Nature: Krafft-Ebing, Psychiatry, and the Making of Homosexual Identity* (Chicago: University of Chicago Press, 2000). However, see the work of Johanna Elberskirchen analyzed in chapter 3.

24. Anna Rühling, "Welches Interesse hat die Frauenbewegung an der Lösung des homosexuellen Problems?" *Jahrbuch für sexuelle Zwischenstufen* 7 (1905). Reprinted in Kokula, *Weibliche Homosexualität,* 195-211. English translation available as Anna Rueling [*sic*], "What Interest Does the Women's Movement Have in the Homosexual Question?" in *Lesbians in Germany, 1890's-1920's,* ed. Lillian Fadermann and Brigitte Eriksson, (Tallahassee: Naiad, 1980).

25. Claudia Schoppmann, *Days of Masquerade: Life Stories of Lesbians During the Third Reich* (Columbia: Columbia University Press, 1996); Claudia Schoppmann, "National Socialist Policies Towards Female Homosexuality," trans. Elizabeth Harvey, in *Gender Relations in German History: Power, Agency, and Experience from the Sixteenth to the Twentieth Century,* ed. Lynn Abrams and Elizabeth Harvey (Durham: Duke University Press, 1997).

26. Faderman and Ericksson, eds, *Lesbians in Germany.*

27. Heike Schader, *Virile, Vamps und wilde Veilchen: Sexualität, Begehren und Erotik in den Zeitschriften homosexueller Frauen im Berlin der 1920er Jahre* (Königstein/ Taunus: Ulrike Helmer Verlag, 2004); Kerstin Plötz, *Einsame Freundinnen: Lesbisches Leben während der zwanziger Jahre in der Provinz* (Hamburg: Männerschwarmskript, 1999). See also Katie Sutton, *The Masculine Woman in Weimar Germany* (New York: Berghahn Books, 2011).

28. *Eldorado*; "Fluch, Vergnügen oder . . . ? Facetten weiblicher Homosexualität," special issue of *Ariadne: Almanach des Archivs der deutschen Frauenbewegung* 29 (1996); Ilsa Kokula, *Weibliche Homosexualität um 1900 in zeitgenössischen Dokumenten* (Munich: Frauenoffensive, 1981) and Ilse Kokula, *Jahre des Glücks, Jahre des Leids: Gespräche mit älteren lesbischen Frauen: Dokumente* (Kiel: Frühlings Erwachen, 1986); Plötz, *Einsame Freundinnen.* Most of these publications have been supported by the gay and lesbian movements rather than the academic establishment. I am much indebted to the persistent empirical research of the scholars and researchers working against the limitations and constraints of academic historical research on sexuality in Germany. In my specific field of inquiry, a thoroughly researched monograph reflecting more recent analytic trends is Margit Göttert, *Macht und Eros: Frauenbeziehungen und weibliche Kultur um 1900: Eine neue Perspektive auf Helene Lange und Gertrud Bäumer* (Königstein/Taunus: Ulrike Helmer Verlag, 2000).

29. For a fuller treatment of the comparative state of the research, see Leila Rupp, *Sapphistries: A Global History of Love between Women* (New York: New York University Press, 2009), ch. 6-8.

30. Annemarie Jagose, *Lesbian Utopics* (New York: Routledge, 1994), ch. 1. Jagose notes that acknowledging the uncertainty of the category is "*de rigeur*" in

criticism, 9. For the German field, see Sabine Hark, ed., *Grenzen Lesbischer Identitäten: Aufsätze* (Berlin: Querverlag, 1996).

31. Examples include Terry Castle, *The Apparitional Lesbian: Female Homosexuality and Modern Culture* (New York: Columbia University Press, 1993), 13–17; Nicki Hallett, *Lesbian Lives: Identity and Auto/Biography in the Twentieth Century* (London: Pluto Press, 1999), 10–13, 15–16. On "lesbian-like" see Martha Vicinus, "Lesbian History: All Theory and No Facts or All Facts and No Theory," *Radical History Review* 60 (1994): 66–67; Judith M. Bennett, " 'Lesbian-Like' and the Social History of Lesbianism," *Journal of the History of Sexuality* 9 (2000); "Introduction," Lesbengeschichte, accessed March 13, 2012, http://lesbengeschichte.de/Englisch/seite_e.html.

32. Valerie Traub, *A Renaissance of Lesbianism in Early Modern England* (New York: Cambridge University Press, 2002); Sharon Marcus, *Between Women: Friendship, Desire, and Marriage in Victorian England* (Princeton: Princeton University Press, 2007), esp. 12–14. Other recent studies have picked different entry points. Using cross-dressing, see Alison Oram, *Her Husband Was a Woman! Women's Gender-Crossing in Modern British Popular Culture* (New York: Routledge, 2007); female masculinity, Sutton, *Female Masculinity;* sexual love between women, Rupp, *Sapphistries.*

33. Mel Gordon, *Voluptuous Panic: The Erotic World of Weimar Berlin* (Venice, CA: Feral House, 2000), 104. Gordon lists about twenty different terms, most only in English translation.

34. The equivalents for "lesbian" as a noun, *Lesbe* and *Lesbierin,* were seldom used until the postwar period. As in the United States, feminist lesbians claimed these terms in the 1970s to increase their visibility and to differentiate themselves from homosexual men.

35. Judith Butler, *Bodies That Matter: On the Discursive Limits of "Sex"* (New York: Routledge, 1993); Eve Kosofsky Sedgwick, *Epistomology of the Closet* (Berkeley: University of California Press, 1990).

36. Scott, "Gender: A Useful Category of Analysis," 1063–67.

37. Anna Philipps, *Um Ehre und Recht: Mein Kampf gegen das Provinzial-Schulkollegium Hannover und das Ministerium für Wissenschaft, Kunst und Volksbildung.* Unpublished printed manuscript (Neuminster, 1931[?]).

38. Aimée Duc [Minna Wettstein-Adelt], *Sind es Frauen? Roman über das dritte Geschlecht* (1901; repr. Berlin: Amazonen Frauenverlag, 1976).

Chapter 1. "Are These Women?"

1. Aimée Duc [Minna Wettstein-Adelt], *Sind es Frauen?: Roman über das dritte Geschlecht* (1901; repr. Berlin: Amazonen Verlag, 1976), 16–17.

2. A peculiarity of the faddish term was that some authors used it to mean asexual "mannish" women, while others used it as a synonym for homosexual. Wettstein-Adelt combined these two meanings in her novel. Other titles include Elsa Asenieff, *Aufruhr der Weiber und das dritte Geschlecht* (Leipzig: W. Friedrich, 1898); Johanna Elberskirchen, *Die Liebe des dritten Geschlechts: Homosexualität, eine bisexuelle*

Varietät, keine Entartung, keine Schuld (Leipzig: Max Spohr Verlag, 1904); Magnus Hirschfeld, *Berlins drittes Geschlecht* (Berlin: Hermann Seemann Nachfolger, 1904), all discussed in chapter 3. See also Mark Lehmstedt, *Bücher für das "dritte Geschlecht": Der Max Spohr Verlag in Leipzig: Verlagsgeschichte und Bibliographie (1881–1941)* (Wiesbaden: Harrassowitz Verlag, 2002). The novel *Das dritte Geschlecht*, by Ernst von Wolzogen, is discussed later in this chapter and in chapter 2.

    3. Duc, *Sind es Frauen*, 20.

    4. Ibid., 10.

    5. The novel was republished during the intense period of lesbian-feminist activism in the 1970s, as the reprint date suggests. The Foreword claimed, "This lesbian love achieved its matter-of-fact self-evidence through the mutual experiences and life connections between the two women and a group of lesbians who were, the novel implies, in turn connected to a larger network of lesbians in large European cities." Introductory notes in Aimée Duc, *Sind es Frauen?*, [3]. At that time, the novel was seen as a breakthrough in that the "lesbian" characters were not isolated and suffering because of social ostracism or fear of discovery and that the lovers enjoyed a happy ending. It is unknown whether Wettstein-Adelt knew women who might have served as a model for the characters.

    6. Duc, *Sind es Frauen?*, 89–90.

    7. While the German universities restricted women's access, several of the newer and more liberal institutions in Switzerland, especially Zurich, allowed women to matriculate as regular degree-seeking students.

    8. On the centrality of a certain concept of self-cultivation in German upper-middle-class culture, see Laura Tate, "The Culture of Literary *Bildung* in the Bourgeois Women's Movement in Imperial Germany," *German Studies Review* 24 (2001). Tate emphasized the influence of Weimar Classicism and Wilhelm von Humboldt's institutionalization of a classicist curriculum in Prussia (268). In addition, it is likely that the philosophical positions of Kant and Hegel on the relationship between morality and politics were formative as ambitious intellectual women considered their potential roles in a reformed polity. See Jürgen Habermas, *The Structural Transformation: An Inquiry into a Category of Bourgeois Society*, trans. Thomas Burger (Cambridge: MIT Press, 1989), 102–22.

    9. Universities in Germany remained under provincial governance after unification, so openness to women varied from place to place. An outstanding individual woman might be granted a place or allowed to attend lectures as an auditor if the professor agreed. Organized opposition to women in the university increased in the 1870s and 1880s in response to rising numbers of women's requests to study. Some universities actually strengthened the requirements that made it difficult for women to matriculate. In the example of Leipzig, one of the more accessible universities, the *Landtag* voted against the general admission of women in 1879 after having admitted several individuals in earlier decades. Many professors opposed granting degrees to women because degrees would qualify them to join university faculties. Finally, after the turn of the century (in most cases around 1908), women were allowed to earn degrees. Sonja Brentjes and Karl-Heinz Schlote, "Zum Frauenstudium an der

Universität Leipzig in der Zeit von 1870 bis 1910," *Jahrbuch für Regionalgeschichte und Landeskunde* 19 (1993); James Albisetti, *Schooling German Girls and Women: Secondary and Higher Education in the Nineteenth Century* (Princeton: Princeton University Press, 1988), 128–29. Patricia Mazón puts these halting developments within the context of a late-nineteenth-century "crisis of the universities." Professors and administrators reacted with defensive anxiety to increased numbers of Jews, foreigners, and middle-class students, as well as women, who recognized the German university as a path to upward mobility. Patricia Mazón, *Gender and the Modern Research University: The Admission of Women to German Higher Education, 1865–1914* (Stanford: Stanford University Press, 2003), 4–6. According to Lisa Zwicker, the atmosphere in German universities became more open and diverse as women students became a recognized part of the student body. Lisa Fetheringill Zwicker, *Dueling Students: Conflict, Masculinity, and Politics in German Universities, 1890–1914* (Ann Arbor: University of Michigan Press, 2011).

10. Ute Frevert, *Women in German History: From Bourgeois Emancipation to Sexual Liberation* (Oxford: Berg, 1989), 115–17; Albisetti, *Schooling German Girls and Women*, xx–xxii; Mazón, *Gender and the Modern Research University*, chs. 2 and 3.

11. Foucault, Michel, *The History of Sexuality*, vol. 1 *An Introduction*, trans. Robert Hurley (New York: Vintage, 1990), 77–80; on subjectivity, see also Louis Althusser, "Ideology and Ideological State Apparatuses (Notes towards an Investigation)," in *Lenin and Philosophy and Other Essays*, trans. Ben Brewster (New York: Monthly Review Press, 1971), 172–78. On women's political and economic subjectivity, see Carole Pateman, *The Sexual Contract* (Stanford: Stanford University Press, 1988) and Mary Poovey, *Uneven Developments: The Ideological Work of Gender in Mid-Victorian England* (Chicago: University of Chicago Press, 1988), esp. 10–11, 52. Although he only dealt fleetingly with the gendered nature of the public sphere subject, Habermas's conceptualization of the political public sphere is also important in my thinking on the construction of emancipated subjectivity. Habermas, *The Structural Transformation*, 46–51.

12. Mazón, *Gender and the Modern Research University*, 177–87.

13. On the lasting influence of this "founding generation," see Detlev J. Peukert, *The Weimar Republic: The Crisis of Classical Modernity*, trans. Richard Deveson (New York: Hill and Wang, 1989), 14–18; on generations in the women's movement, see Margit Göttert, *Macht und Eros: Frauenbeziehungen und weibliche Kultur um 1900: Eine neue Perspektive auf Helene Lange und Gertrud Bäumer* (Königstein/Taunus: Ulrike Helmer Verlag, 2000), 44–70. The authors of the novels analyzed below also fit into this generational cohort: Helen Stöcker (1869–1943), Minna Wettstein-Adelt (b. 1869), and Ernst von Wolzogen (1855–1934).

14. Frieda Duensing, *Frieda Duensing: Ein Buch der Erinnerung*, ed. Huch et al. (Berlin: F. A. Herbig, 1926).

15. Ilse Kokula, *Weibliche Homosexualität um 1900 in zeitgenössischen Dokumenten* (Munich: Frauenoffensive, 1981), 40; Mazón, *Gender and the Modern Research University*, 188–89.

16. Ella Mensch, *Auf Vorposten: Roman aus meiner Züricher Studentenzeit* (Leipzig: Verlag der Frauenrundschau, 1903).

17. Ricarda Huch, *Frühling in der Schweiz: Jugenderinnerungen* (Zurich: Atlantis Verlag, 1938).

18. Käthe Schirmacher, *Züricher Studentinnen* (Leipzig and Zurich: Verlag von Th. Schröter, 1896).

19. Käthe Schirmacher, *Flammen: Erinnerungen aus mein Leben* (Leipzig: Dürr u. Weber, 1921); Käthe Schirmacher, *Die Libertad: Novelle* (Zurich: Verlags-Magazin, 1891).

20. The dual biography by Gustava Lida Heymann devoted only a couple of pages to Augspurg's studies. Lida Gustava Heymann with Anita Augspurg, *Erlebtes— Erschautes: Deutsche Frauen kämpfen für Freiheit, Recht und Frieden, 1850-1940,* ed. Margit Twellmann (Meisenheim am Glan: Anton Hain, 1972), 16-20.

21. British advocates of women's intellectual life and careers opened separate women's colleges attached to the existing major universities in the second half of the century. These institutions functioned as supportive dormitories to prepare women for examinations. They enrolled very few students before the turn of the century. The residences cultivated a respectable, even conservative, view of the class conformity expected of women and gave them fewer opportunities for organizing their own lives than the Swiss universities. See Martha Vicinus, *Independent Women: Work and Community for Single Women, 1850-1920* (Chicago, University of Chicago, 1985), ch. 4.

22. On the history of the University of Zurich, see Sigmund Widmer, *Zürich: Eine Kulturgeschichte,* vol. 9 (Zurich: Artemis Verlag, 1982); Robert Leuenberger, "Politik und Wissenschaft in der Anfangzeit der Zürcher Universität," *Schweizer Monatshefte: Zeitschrift für Politik, Wirtschaft und Kultur* 61 (1981). The university was founded in 1833 by the city of Zurich as one outcome of the revolutions of 1830. In the mid-nineteenth century it attracted liberal professors from Germany seeking a better academic atmosphere after the post-1848 repressions.

23. On the contradiction between conceptions of "student" and "woman" within university culture, emphasizing academic study in the formation of masculinity, see Mazón, *Gender and the Modern Research University,* ch. 1.

24. Ibid., 10; Schweizerischen Verband der Akademikerinnen, *Das Frauenstudium an den schweizer Hochschulen* (Zurich: Rascher, 1928), appendix table, unpaged.

25. The most influential works opposing the higher education of women were Hermann Jakoby, *Grenzen der weiblichen Bildung* (Gütersloh: C. Bertelsmann, 1871) and Theodor von Bischoff, *Das Studium und die Ausübung der Medizin durch Frauen* (Munich: T. Riede, 1872). These works are discussed in Albisetti, *Schooling German Girls and Women,* 126; and Mazón, *Gender and the Modern Research University,* ch. 3.

26. This is a much-circulated quotation; Albisetti took it from Helene Lange. The original was published in *Kölner Zeitung,* 14 October 1888. Albisetti, *Schooling German Girls and Women,* 195.

27. Jenny Springer, "Die Deutsche Studentin," *Die Woche,* 1907, 563.

28. During Russia's tumultuous nineteenth century, many radical and intellectual women migrated to Switzerland to study. Their bold styles were used as an example of the deleterious effects of freedom and education on women students in debates in Germany on women's higher education. Campaigners for women's higher education and women students were careful to distance themselves from the unrestrained Russian women. Albisetti, *Schooling German Girls and Women,* 126–31.

29. Franziska Tibertius, *Erinnerungen einer Achtzigjährigen* (Berlin: C. A. Schwetschke und Sohn, 1929), 115–17.

30. Tibertius, *Erinnerungen einer Achtzigjährigen,* 147.

31. Huch, *Frühling in der Schweiz,* 36–37.

32. Mensch, *Auf Vorposten,* 58–59.

33. Ella Mensch, *Bildstürmer in der Berliner Frauenbewegung* (Berlin: Hermann Seemann Nachfolger, 1906), 86.

34. Springer, "Die Deutsche Studentin," 566.

35. Goudstikker's masculine persona is the subject of chapter 3.

36. Ernst von Wolzogen, *Das Dritte Geschlecht* (Berlin: Richard Eckstein Nachf., 1901).

37. Mazón, *Gender and the Modern Research University,* 33.

38. Stöcker audited courses at the University of Berlin and eventually took her degree from the University of Bern. Like Duensing, Schirmacher, and Mensch in this chapter, Stöcker closely connected women's emancipation with a new morality. Stöcker's "New Ethic" justified sexual pleasure and motherhood outside marriage as long as these were authorized by love. On Helene Stöcker's long career as feminist and sex reform activist, see Kristin M. McGuire, "Activism, Intimacy, and the Politics of Selfhood: The Gendered Terms of Citizenship in Poland and Germany, 1890–1918," PhD thesis (Ann Arbor: University of Michigan, 2004); Ann Taylor Allen, "Mothers of the New Generation: Adele Schreiber, Helene Stöcker, and the Evolution of a German Idea of Motherhood, 1900–1914," *Signs* 10 (1985): 418–38; Amy Hackett, "Helene Stöcker: Left-Wing Intellectual and Sex Reformer," in *When Biology Became Destiny: Women in Weimar and Nazi Germany,* ed. Renate Bridenthal, Atina Grossmann, and Marion Kaplan (New York: Monthly Review Press, 1984). On Wolzogen's career, see Peter Jelavich, *Berlin Cabaret* (Cambridge: Harvard University Press, 1993), ch. 2. For more on Wolzogen, see chapter 2.

39. Helene Stöcker, *Liebe: Roman* (Berlin: Verlag der neuen Generation, 1925). The novel is regarded as a semiautobiographical account of Stöcker's affair with a married professor. Stöcker conceived of homosexual relations between women as a substitute for the heterosexual love and parenthood that for her was the highest goal of human life. See chapter 3.

40. Ibid., 305.

41. Ibid., 300–302.

42. A declaration of this with herself as suffering martyr immediately preceded the trip to Switzerland, ibid., 292.

43. A fuller account of Wolzogen's authorship and some of the characters and scenes in the novel is given in Brigitte Bruns, "Das dritte Geschlecht von Ernst von

Wolzogen," in *Hof-Atelier Elvira, 1887–1928: Ästheten, Emanzen, Aristokraten,* ed. Rudolf Herz and Brigitte Bruns (Munich: Münchener Stadtmuseum, 1985).

44. According to Brigitte Bruns, Rau served as the mouthpiece for Wolzogen's opinions. Ibid., 172.

45. Ernst von Wolzogen, *Das dritte Geschlecht,* 92–93.

46. Three of the women, Augspurg, Sophia Goudstikker, and Ika Freudenberg, who were identifiable as models for characters, were involved in a triangular love relationship in Munich in the 1890s. Whether Wolzogen knew of their relationships with each other is unknown. See the discussion in chapter 2.

47. Women students also encountered these ideas in their relationships. Hedwig Bleuler-Waser recalled that she and her future husband argued about her studies indirectly through the symbol of her hair. When she declared herself willing to sacrifice her long hair to her studies, he objected, "Feminine attraction is lost without it." Hedwig Bleuler-Waser, "Aus meiner Universitätzeit," in Schweizerischen Verband der Akademikerinnen, *Das Frauenstudium an den Schweizer Hochschulen,* 66.

48. Wolzogen, *Das dritte Geschlecht,* 152.

49. Letter to Gretchen (Herwig) Schuchhardt, 23 June 1897. Duensing, *Frieda Duensing,* 148.

50. Tiburtius, *Erinnerungen einer Achtzigjährigen,* 135.

51. Schirmacher, *Die Libertad,* 51–52.

52. Ibid., 26–27.

53. Mazón discussed students who appropriated masculinity as a strategy of claiming the right to be students. Mazón, *Gender and the Modern Research University,* ch. 6.

54. Letter to Gretchen (Herwig) Schuchhardt, 12 February 1899. Duensing, *Frieda Duensing,* 172.

55. Anke Walzer, *Käthe Schirmacher: Eine deutsche Frauenrechtlerin auf dem Wege vom Liberalismus zum konservativen Nationalismus* (Pfaffenweiler: Centaurus-Verlagsgesellschaft, 1991), 24–27; Hanna Krüger, *Die unbequeme Frau: Käthe Schirmacher im Kampf für die Freiheit der Frau und die Freiheit der Nation, 1865–1930* (Berlin: Hans Bott Verlag, 1936), 37–45.

56. Schirmacher, *Die Libertad,* 63.

57. Schirmacher, *Züricher Studentinnen,* 33.

58. See Elisabeth Meyer-Renschhausen, "Zur Geschichte der Gefühle: Das Reden von 'Scham' und 'Ehre' innerhalb der Frauenbewegung um die Jahrhundertwende," in *Unter Allen Umständen: Frauengeschichte(N) in Berlin,* ed. Christiane Eifert and Susanne Rouette (Berlin: Rotation Verlag, 1986).

59. Nancy Reagin, *A German Women's Movement: Class and Gender in Hanover, 1880–1933* (Chapel Hill: University of North Carolina Press, 1995) provides a detailed local study of such networks and occasions for sociability.

60. Detailed fictional portraits are found in Gabriele Reuter, *From a Good Family,* trans. Lynne Tatlock (Rochester: Camden House, 1999); and Theodor Fontane, *Effie Briest,* trans. Hugh Rorrison and Helen Chambers, (New York: Penguin, 2000).

61. Schirmacher, *Die Libertad,* 58.

62. Sharon Marcus, *Between Women: Friendship, Desire, and Marriage in Victorian England* (Princeton: Princeton University Press, 2007), 30–32.

63. Huch was a prolific writer of history, fiction, and poetry and an important figure within the intellectual elite, but she was never strongly affiliated with the women's movement or any other movement or circle.

64. Huch, *Frühling in der Schweiz*, 84–85.

65. Ibid., 118–19.

66. Ibid., 42.

67. Ibid., 38–39.

68. Marie Baum's memorialization of Huch after her death testifies to the continuing centrality of this relationship for Baum. Marie Baum, *Leuchtende Spur: Das Leben Ricarda Huchs* (Tübingen: Rainer Wunderlich Verlag Hermann Leins, 1950); Marie Baum, *Ricarda Huch: Briefe an die Freunde* (Tübingen: Rainer Wunderlich Verlag Hermann Leins, 1955). She also contributed to Duensing, *Frieda Duensing*.

69. Letter to Gretchen (Herwig) Schuchhardt, 10 November 1897. Duensing, *Frieda Duensing*, 155.

70. Mensch, *Auf Vorposten*, 30.

71. Ibid., 48–49.

72. Diary entry, 3 October 1887. Duensing, *Frieda Duensing*, 35–36.

73. Diary entry, 4 October 1887. Ibid., 36.

74. On a larger rethinking of moral subjectivity in the period, see Tracy Matysik, *Reforming the Moral Subject: Ethics and Sexuality in Central Europe, 1890–1930* (Ithaca: Cornell University Press, 2008).

75. Letter to Gretchen (Herwig) Schuchhardt, Easter 1900. Duensing, *Frieda Duensing*, 177.

76. Letter to Gretchen Herwig, 14 August 1893. Ibid., 78–80.

77. On the complicated interaction of nineteenth-century gender ideologies and social work, see Poovey, *Uneven Developments*, 184–93.

78. On the social service aspect of the women's movement in the nineteenth century and the language of "social motherhood," see Reagin, *A German Women's Movement*; Christof Sachße, *Mütterlichkeit als Beruf: Sozialarbeit, Sozialreform und Frauenbewegung, 1871–1929* (Opladen: Westdeutscher Verlag, 1994); Dietlinde Peters, *Mütterlichkeit im Kaiserreich: Die Bürgerliche Frauenbewegung und der soziale Beruf der Frau* (Bielefeld: Kleine, 1984); Ann Taylor Allen, *Feminism and Motherhood in Germany, 1800–1914* (New Brunswick: Rutgers University Press, 1991).

79. Letter to Gretchen Herwig, 14 August 1893. Duensing, *Frieda Duensing*, 78–80.

80. See Edward Ross Dickinson, "Dominion of the Spirit over the Flesh: Religion, Gender, and Sexual Morality in the German Women's Movement before World War I," *Gender & History* 17 (2005): 392–94.

81. "Homosexuality" or any other similar concept is absent from the commentaries and Duensing's writings, although the collection was first published in 1923. Nevertheless, the selection of materials to include same-sex attraction suggests

that her friends wanted to make this aspect of Duensing's personality visible without explicitly labeling it.

82. Diary entry, 22 October 1887. Duensing, *Frieda Duensing*, 41.

83. Letter to Gretchen Herwig, 3 February 1889. Ibid., 48.

84. Letter to Gretchen Herwig, 15 April 1890. Ibid., 48–49.

85. I assume that Marie Baum wrote the anonymous biographical sketch, since she assembled that part of the book. Ibid., 299–300.

86. Letter to Gretchen (Herwig) Schuchhardt, July 1897. Ibid., 151.

87. Schirmacher, *Die Libertad*, 58.

88. Ibid., 70.

89. On Schirmacher's love affair with Henri Chastenet, see Anke Walzer, *Käthe Schirmacher*, 57–59; and Amy Hackett, "The Politics of Feminism in Wilhelmine Germany," PhD thesis (New York: Columbia University, 1976), 288–90. Schirmacher's memoir did not mention him by name. She attributed her conservative turn to scandals in the French government and her observations of Eastern Europeans in Paris, prostitution, and anti-German sentiments in France. Schirmacher, *Flammen*, 37–45. She described her new convictions as if scales fell from her eyes: "The strangest thing about this development was that I, originally oriented toward liberalism, made it against my will, so to speak. I did not seek it, but it me. This recognition forced itself on me in complete opposition to my personal advantage, my family background, my inclination, and my obligations of gratitude" (45). Published during the National Socialist period, Krüger's biography pasted together large sections from Schirmacher's own writing to emphasize the nationalist and anti-Semitic turn. Krüger, *Die unbequeme Frau*, 94–95. Schleker and Schirmacher's relationship after the turn of the century, documented in the voluminous correspondence in Schirmacher's papers, has been designated by historians of female homosexuality in Germany as "the only known lesbian couple in the first women's movement." Kokula, *Weibliche Homosexualität*, 31. Kokula and others cited Amy Hackett's dissertation in making this claim. The particular selection of words is ambiguous, but gives the impression that the lesbian nature of the relationship was affirmed by Schirmacher and Schleker and recognized by contemporaries. However Hackett's footnotes show that Hackett made assumptions based on equivalence in the way Schirmacher portrayed relationships with Schleker and with male lovers, and the effusiveness of the style of her letters to Schleker (290–91). Hackett's evidence is suggestive of a sexual relationship, but that would not necessarily imply a lesbian identity, and is not evidence that others recognized Schirmacher and Schleker as such.

90. On women in conservative parties and movements, see Elizabeth Harvey, "Visions of the Volk: German Women and the Far Right from Kaiserreich to Third Reich," *Journal of Women's History* 16 (2004); and Rafael Scheck, *Mothers of the Nation: Right-Wing Women in Weimar Germany* (Oxford: Berg, 2004).

91. Krüger, *Die Unbequeme Frau*, 178.

92. The conservatism of the bourgeois women's movement has been the subject of a historiographical controversy. A recent overview of this debate is found

in Dickinson, "Dominion of the Spirit," 378–79. For a full account of the morality movements, see John C. Fout, "Sexual Politics in Wilhelmine Germany: The Male Gender Crisis, Moral Purity, and Homophobia," *Journal of the History of Sexuality* 2 (1992): 338–421.

93. A British example of the strange connections that feminism attracted, in this case racist eugenics, see Carolyn Burdett, "The Hidden Romance of Sexual Science: Eugenics, the Nation, and the Making of Modern Feminism," in *Sexology in Culture: Labelling Bodies and Desires,* ed. Lucy Bland and Laura Doan (Chicago: University of Chicago Press, 1998). Burdett analyzes Olive Schreiner's parallel adoption of the archaic Teutonic woman as a historic model of women's social and moral influence (55–56). For a fuller account of the diversity of feminist ideas in the Anglo-American realm, see Lucy Delap, *The Feminist Avant-Garde: Transatlantic Encounters of the Early Twentieth Century* (Cambridge: Cambridge University Press, 2007).

94. Mensch, *Auf Vorposten,* 132–33.

95. Ibid., 170–71.

96. Mensch apparently made her living primarily as a journalist and edited the feminist paper *Women's Review (Frauenrundschau).* As an activist she was involved in advocacy for women teachers as well as in the campaigns against prostitution and pornography.

Chapter 2. Experiments in Female Masculinity

1. Biddy Martin, *Woman and Modernity: The (Life)Styles of Lou Andreas-Salomé* (Ithaca: Cornell University Press, 1991); Ursula Welsch and Michaela Wiesner, *Lou Andreas-Salomé: Vom "Lebensgrund" zur Psychoanalyse* (Munich: Internationale Psychoanalyse, 1990); Sabina Streiter, "Nachwort," in *Die Schönste Novellen der Freida von Bülow über Lou Andreas-Salomé und andere Frauen* ((Frankfurt: Verlag Ullstein, 1990).

2. The excerpt was published in the notes to her memoirs because it was the first reference to Salomé's lover, poet Rainer Maria Rilke. Diary entry, 14 May 1897. Quoted in Lou Andreas-Salomé, *Looking Back: Memoirs,* ed. Ernst Pfeiffer, trans. Breon Mitchell (New York: Marlow, 1995), n68, 194.

3. Welsch and Wiesner, *Lou Andreas-Salomé,* 136; Streiter, "Nachwort," 244.

4. Martin, *Woman and Modernity,* 10–11.

5. Irit Rogoff, "Tiny Anguishes: Reflections on Nagging, Scholastic Embarrassment, and Feminist Art History," *differences: A Journal of Feminist Cultural Studies* 4 (1992): 56.

6. Lora Wildenthal, *German Women for Empire, 1884–1945* (Durham: Duke University Press, 2001), 66.

7. Kerstin Barndt, "Frauen-Literatur um 1900" (paper presented at the annual meeting of the German Studies Association, Atlanta, Georgia, 1999, text provided by the author), 2.

8. Benedict Anderson, *Imagined Communities: Reflections on the Origin and Spread of Nationalism* (London: Verso, 1991).

9. See Marjorie Garber's work on cross-dressing and her argument that cross-dressing figures are evidence of a crisis in categories, which was clearly the case at the turn of the century. When the artifice of cross-dressing is visible, it calls the structure of binary differences into question. Marjorie Garber, *Vested Interests: Cross-Dressing and Cultural Anxiety* (HarperPerennial, 1993), 16–17.

10. Ernst von Wolzogen, *Das dritte Geschlecht* (Berlin: Richard Eckstein Nachf., 1901), 15–16.

11. Garber, *Vested Interests*, 158–61. On reinforcing the binary, see Halberstam's critique of Garber. Judith Halberstam, *Female Masculinity* (Durham: Duke University Press, 1998), 25–29.

12. Homi Bhabha, "Of Mimicry and Man: the Ambivalence of Colonial Discourses," in *Tensions of Empire: Colonial Cultures in a Bourgeois World*, ed. Frederick Cooper and Ann Laura Stoler (Berkeley: University of California Press, 1997), 153.

13. Esther Newton, "The Mythic Mannish Lesbian: Radclyffe Hall and the New Woman," in *Hidden from History: Reclaiming the Gay and Lesbian Past*, ed. Martin Duberman, Martha Vicinus, and George Chauncey Jr, (New York: Meridian, 1989); Halberstam, *Female Masculinities*, ch. 2. On Germany in a later period, see Katie Sutton, *The Masculine Woman in Weimar Germany* (New York: Berghahn Books, 2011).

14. Georg Jakob Wolfe, *Die Münchnerin: Kultur und Sittenbilder aus dem alten und neuen München* (Munich: Fran Hanfstaengl, 1924), 5–6.

15. Robin Lenman, "Politics and Culture: The State and the Avant-Garde in Munich, 1886–1914), in *Society and Politics in Wilhelmine Germany*, ed. Richard Evans (London: Croom Helm, 1978); Peter Jelavich, *Munich and Theatrical Modernism: Politics, Playwriting, and Performance, 1890–1914* (Cambridge: Harvard University Press, 1985), 6–10.

16. Jelavich, *Munich and Theatrical Modernism*.

17. Rogoff, "Tiny Anguishes," 48–49; Wolf, *Die Münchnerin*, 218–19, 255–60.

18. Martin, *Woman and Modernity*, 141–49; Carol Diethe, *Nietzsche's Women: Beyond the Whip* (Berlin: Walter de Gruyter, 1996), ch. 5.

19. Jelavich, *Munich and Theatrical Modernism*, esp. ch. 2. Wedekind's Lulu plays featured a prominent character, Gräfin Geschwitz, considered the first lesbian character in modern drama. See Marti Lybeck, "Gender, Sexuality, and Belonging: Female Homosexuality in Germany 1890–1933," PhD thesis (Ann Arbor, University of Michigan, 2007), ch. 4.

20. Helmut Fritz, *Die erotische Rebellion: Das Leben der Franziska Gräfin zu Reventlow* (Frankfurt: Fischer Taschenbuch Verlag, 1980), 60 and 16. Fritz celebrates Reventlow as the true forerunner of modern sexual liberation. For a more critical interpretation, equally problematic, see Elisabeth Kleemann. *Zwischen symbolischer Rebellion und Politischer Revolution: Studien zur deutschen Boheme zwischen Kaiserreich und Weimarer Republik—Else Lasker-Schüler, Franziska Gräfin zu Reventlow, Frank Wedekind, Ludwig Derleth, Arthur Moeller van den Bruck, Hanns Johst, Erich Mühsam*

(Frankfurt: Verlag Peter Lang, 1985) 65–68. Carol Diethe traces this Nietzschean stream of influence on thinking about sexuality among various literary and art groups in Munich. Diethe, *Nietzsche's Women*, 113–27.

21. Fritz, *Die erotische Rebellion*, 10, 61.

22. The only primary source on the early relationship is the joint autobiography of Augspurg and her later partner, Lida Gustava Heymann. Written mainly by Heymann in 1941 in exile in Switzerland (not published until 1972), it clearly situates Heymann and Augspurg as heroines, marginalizing Goudstikker. Lida Gustava Heymann, with Anita Augspurg, *Erlebtes—Erschautes: Deutsche Frauen kämpfen für Freiheit, Recht und Frieden, 1850–1940*, ed. Margit Twellmann (Meisenheim am Glan: Verlag Anton Hain, 1972). My information is taken largely from Rudolf Herz, "Das Fotoatelier Elvira (1887–1928): Seine Fotografinnen, seine Kundschaft, seine Bilder," in *Hof-Atelier Elvira, 1887–1928: Ästheten, Emanzen, Aristokraten*, ed. Rudolf Herz and Brigitte Bruns (Munich: Münchener Stadtmuseum, 1985).

23. Goudstikker's family had moved from Amsterdam to Hamburg to Dresden. Her father, an art dealer, left the family to return to Hamburg in 1886. Augspurg escaped to Berlin to study for the teacher's exam at about age twenty. Lacking interest in teaching, she secretly took acting lessons. She had a moderately successful acting career until she became unsatisfied with the life in 1885.

24. Ernst von Wolzogen, *Wie ich mich ums Leben brachte: Erinnerungen und Erfahrungen* (Braunschweig and Hamburg: Verlag von Georg Westermann, 1922), 188. Neither Wolzogen's memoirs nor Wolf's *Die Münchnerin* mention Goudstikker in connection with Freudenberg or Augspurg (or the photo studio) in their recounting of the revolutionary young women of Munich in the 1890s. Although she was still alive when those texts were written, Goudstikker seems to have been forgotten, perhaps because she, along with the women's movement, became more moderate (and apparently more conventional in appearance) in later years. Wolf, *Die Münchnerin*, 217–19.

25. Police report, 1891. Staatsarchiv München, RA Fasz. 3795 Nr. 57851, Akten der Königlichen Regierung von Oberbayern Kammer des Innern. Gesellschaft für modernes Leben.

26. Gabriele Reuter, *Vom Kinde zum Menschen: Die Geschichte meiner Jugend* (Berlin: Fischer Verlag, 1921), 429–31.

27. Information on the public activities of Augspurg, Goudstikker, and others is taken from Brigitte Bruns, "Weibliche Avantgarde um 1900," in *Hof-Atelier Elvira*, ed. Herz und Bruns, 191–95.

28. Wolzogen, *Wie ich mich ums Leben brachte*, 188.

29. Diethe, *Nietzsche's Women*, 113–14, quote on 125.

30. Gertrud Bäumer, quoted in Renate Lindemann, *100 Jahre Verein für Fraueninteressen* (Munich: Verein für Fraueninteressen, 1994), 37.

31. Irene Stoehr, "Fraueneinfluß oder Geschlechterversöhnung? Zur 'Sexualitäts-debatte' in der deutschen Frauenbewegung um 1900," in *Frauenkörper/Medizin/Sexualität: Auf dem Wege zu einer neuen Sexualmoral*, ed. Johanna Geyer-Kordesch and Annette Kuhn (Düsseldorf: Schwann, 1986); Edward Ross Dickinson, "Dominion

of the Spirit over the Flesh: Religion, Gender, and Sexual Morality in the German Women's Movement before World War I," *Gender & History* 17 (2005).

32. Elisabeth Meyer-Renschhausen, "Die Männerhaß der Polizeimatronen," in *Dokumentation 4. Historikerinnentreffen* (Berlin: Technische Universität Berlin, 1983), 254; Elisabeth Meyer-Renschhausen, "Zur Geschichte der Gefühle: Das Reden von 'Scham' und 'Ehre' innerhalb der Frauenbewegung um die Jahrhundertwende," in *Unter allen Umständen: Frauengeschichte(N) in Berlin,* ed. Christiane Eifert and Susanne Rouette (Berlin: Rotation Verlag, 1986), 116.

33. Obituary, *Münchener-Augsburger Allgemeine,* 6 April 1924. Quoted in Streiter, "Nachwort," 244.

34. Bülow grew up in Turkey in a diplomatic household. She was a strong supporter of German nationalism and imperialism, and twice lived in German colonies in Africa. Like Käthe Schirmacher and Ella Mensch in the previous chapter, Bülow linked freedom for women to the cause of a stronger nation. Her great love was the colonial adventurer Carl Peters. For more on Bülow, see Lora Wildenthal, ch. 2; on the role of the Peters affair in her friendship with Salomé, see Rudolph Binion, *Frau Lou: Neitzsche's Wayward Disciple* (Princeton: Princeton University Press, 1968), 177.

35. Lou Andreas-Salomé's gender performance resonates with Joan Riviere's argument on the femininity of the woman intellectual. Salomé's feminine performance might be compared with Goudstikker's masculine one. See Joan Riviere, "Womanliness as a Masquerade," in *Formations of Fantasy,* ed. Victor Burgin, James Donald, and Cora Kaplan (London: Methuen, 1986); Martin, *Woman and Modernity,* 237–38.

36. Bülow's letters addressed Salomé as "Beloved Lou-child" and ended "Your brown boy." Welsch and Wiesner, *Lou Andreas Salomé,* 118–19; Binion, *Frau Lou,* 177, 216.

37. Salomé, whose father was an official at the Tsar's court, grew up in the highest social circles in St. Petersburg. She was among the early women students in Zurich.

38. Martin, *Woman and Modernity,* 4.

39. Ibid., 5–6, 41–43.

40. Ibid., 6.

41. Binion, *Frau Lou,* 184, 198, 204. Welsch and Wiesner interpret Salomé's work to imply that Rilke was her first sexual partner, Welsch and Wiesner, *Lou Andreas-Salomé,* 163–66.

42. Streiter, "Nachwort," 245.

43. In addition to Martin, *Woman and Modernity,* cited above, Binion, *Frau Lou,* 212–13; and Welsch and Wiesner, *Lou Andreas-Salomé,* 135–36. Neither Martin nor Welsch and Wiesner include an interpretation of "Mädchenreigen," the story analyzed below.

44. All but Goudstikker were major figures in the national feminist leadership. Not long after the photo was taken, the other four affiliated with rival organizational sections of the women's movement. These splits involved painful personal as well as philosophical differences. See Amy Hackett, "The Politics of Feminism in Wilhelmine Germany," PhD thesis (New York: Columbia University, 1976), ch. 3.

45. Women's contributions to periodicals at this period were more frequently essays or literary sketches than reports on news events.

46. The second photograph is reproduced in Herz and Bruns, *Hof-Atelier Elvira*, 198.

47. A second photograph from the occasion is reproduced in Herz and Bruns, *Hof-Atelier Elvira*, 112.

48. Lou Andreas-Salomé, "Mädchenreigen," in *Werde die du bist! Zwischen Anpassung und Selbstbestimmung: Texte deutschsprachiger Schriftstellerinnen des 19. Jahrhunderts*, ed. Gisela Henckmann (Munich: Goldmann Verlag, 1993), 340, 331–32.

49. Ibid., 336–38.

50. Bülow, "Laß mich nun vergessen," 75.

51. Ibid., 92.

52. Bülow's sister had drowned trying to save a boy who had fallen through the ice. Perhaps death by drowning had a particular meaning for Bülow. Streiter, *Die schönsten Novellen*, 70.

53. Bülow, "Laß mich nun vergessen," 114–16.

54. Ibid., 139.

55. Ibid., 136–37.

56. The gender confusion in each story is connected by implication with orphan status and mixed ethnic heritage. Orphan Hans's father was Belgian but "my mother was from the south [*Südländerin*]" (340). Her passion is attributed to her "hot Southern blood" (348). Senta's father was "a Neapolitan revolutionary, her mother a German of the old aristocracy. From her father, she inherited her temperament and beauty, from her mother the iron strength of her will. She had lost both parents early" (76). Box, product of a Jewish-Protestant marriage, had already inherited and improved the family business.

57. On narrative patterns in nineteenth-century bourgeois novels, see Regenia Gagnier, *Subjectivities: A History of Self-Representation in Britain, 1832–1920* (New York: Oxford University Press, 1991), 27–28.

58. Sabine Streiter's gloss suggests parallels generally between Gunhild and Bülow, specifically, Bülow's obsessive love for Carl Peters. Streiter, "Nachwort," 246.

59. Bülow, "Laß mich nun vergessen," 83–85.

60. Ibid., 92–93.

61. Courtly love images may be suggested by the popularity of the *Hosenrolle* in nineteenth-century German theater. See Katie Sutton, *The Masculine Woman in Weimar Germany* (New York: Berghahn, 2011), 128.

62. Bülow, "Laß mich nun vergessen," 139.

63. This reading is suggested by Streiter's claim, apparently based on Bülow's diaries and letters, that "Frieda von Bülow was even in love with this spirited, passionate, self confident woman for a short time at one point." Streiter, "Nachwort," 245. Triangulating homoerotic attraction through a heterosexual relationship is similar to the analysis employed so productively by Eve Sedgwick. Eve Sedgwick, *Between Men: English Literature and Male Homosocial Desire* (New York: Columbia University Press, 1985).

64. Salomé's biographers disagree about when the story was written and what biographical incidents inspired it. The similarities between Hans and the other characters discussed here are strong evidence that it was partially based on Salomé's encounter with Goudstikker. Binion dates the story to the winter of 1896–97, before the time spent with Goudstikker. He interprets it as a representation of the relationship between Salomé (Hans) and Richard Beer-Hoffmann (Alex), an affair that had recently ended unhappily. Binion, *Frau Lou*, 199–200, 212. Streiter dates it from 1897. Streiter, "Nachwort," 245.

65. Andreas-Salomé, "Mädchenreigen," 350–51.

66. As one of the anonymous reviewers of the manuscript suggested, there are other readings of these narratives. One is that the authors were engaged in a critique of heterosexuality, perhaps using a female lover to think a through alternative possibilities for heterosexual love.

67. On Wolzogen, see Jelavich, *Berlin Cabaret* (Cambridge: Harvard University Press, 1993), ch. 2; Bruns, "Das dritte Geschlecht von Ernst von Wolzogen," in *Hof-Atelier Elvira*; Wolzogen, *Wie ich mich ums Leben brachte*.

68. Bruns, "Das dritte Geschlecht," 177.

69. Diethe claims, "The portrayal of feminists as homosexuals in the plot is probably a transparent allusion to the relationship between Lida Gustava Heymann and Anita Augspurg." Further, she asserts, "Any woman who tried to make her own way in any profession risked the slur of lesbianism." Diethe, *Nietzsche's Women*, 114–15. Her argument requires the assumption that Wolzogen would have connected masculinity, independence, and feminism with female homosexuality.

70. Wolzogen, *Das dritte Geschlecht*, 24.

71. Ibid., 23.

72. Ibid., 23–24.

73. Ibid., 29–30.

74. As claimed in Diethe, *Nietzsche's Women*, 114.

75. Martin, *Woman and Modernity*, 238–39; Streiter, "Nachwort," 245–46.

76. Frank Wedekind, *Lulu: Erdgeist, Die Büchse der Pandora*, ed. Erhard Weidl (Stuttgart: Philipp Reclam, jun., 1989).

77. Salomé had been intimately involved with Schnitzler's circle during an 1895 stay in Vienna. The play was seen in Munich at private performances and in excerpts included in cabaret shows; it could not pass the Munich theater censors. Jelavich, *Munich and Theatrical Modernism*, 181, 183.

78. Whitinger titles it "Maidens' Roundelay." Other English titles include "Circle of Girls" and "Dance of Girls." See Raleigh Whitinger, "Introduction," in Lou Andreas Salomé, *The Human Family* (Lincoln: University of Nebraska, 2005), xv–xvi.

79. Andreas-Salomé, "Mädchenreigen," 338.

80. Ibid., 339.

81. Ibid., 343–44.

82. As Kennedy and Davis describe in their ethnography of mid-twentieth-century working-class lesbian culture in Buffalo, the masculine woman gives sexual pleasure to her partner, while the feminine partner is not allowed to touch her partner sexually.

The butch experiences sexual satisfaction vicariously through the partner's pleasure. Elizabeth Lapovsky Kennedy and Madeline Davis, *Boots of Leather, Slippers of Gold: The History of a Lesbian Community* (New York: Routledge, 1993), 191.

83. Andreas-Salomé, "Mädchenreigen," 346–47.

84. In the 1890s, certain intellectuals revived German Hellenism as an alternative to Christianity and the (female-dominated) family. A wing of the youth movement and Adolf Brand's homosexual group built on this ideology. The sexual was usually subordinated to ideal Eros or ruled out completely. See Harry Oosterhuis, "Homosexual Emancipation in Germany Before 1933: Two Traditions," and "Eros and Male-Bonding in Society: Introduction" in *Homosexuality and Male-Bonding in Pre-Nazi Germany*, ed. Harry Oosterhuis and Hubert Kennedy (New York: Harrington Park Press, 1991), 3, 9, 16, 121–24. Hellenism was also influential through much of the nineteenth century in Britain, and shaped both male and female notions of homosexuality. See Linda C. Dowling, *Hellenism and Homosexuality in Victorian Oxford* (Ithaca: Cornell University Press, 1994). The classical influence does not seem to have been as widespread among German women, at least until the 1920s.

85. See Margit Göttert, *Macht und Eros: Frauenbeziehungen und weibliche Kultur um 1900: eine neue Perspektive auf Helene Lange und Gertrude Bäumer* (Königstein/Taunus: Ulrike Helmer Verlag, 2000), 39–44.

86. Andreas-Salomé, "Mädchenreigen," 347.

87. Ibid., 345–46.

88. Ibid., 355.

89. Bülow, "Laß mich nun vergessen," 77.

90. Ibid., 104–105.

91. Welsch and Wiesner paraphrase a letter from Bülow to Salomé from that same year reporting that Goudstikker did not "hide her lesbian preferences." Without access to the letter itself, it is impossible to specify the exact words or context for this assertion. Although the letter has been used as evidence of Goudstikker's claiming a homosexual identity, the biographer's choice of words makes it hard to know what exactly prompted Bülow's observation. "Lesbian preferences" refers to sexual orientation in the late twentieth century, but may mean something different in the earlier period. In any case, it is significant that Bülow made this point two years after Salomé and Bülow spent several months on intimate terms with Goudstikker. This may be further evidence that the notion of homosexuality came into broader circulation right around 1900. Bülow may have been interpreting Goudstikker's erotic performances anew using a conceptual vocabulary not available during the earlier visit. Welsch and Wiesner, *Lou Andreas-Salomé*, 135.

92. Frieda von Bülow, "Sie und er," in *Die schönsten Novellen*, ed. Streiter, 211. "As if these arrangements had been there before the people who made them for themselves according to their needs at the time."

93. Ibid., 210.

94. As Streiter claims. Streiter, "Nachwort," 245–46.

95. Among these are Gabriele Reuter, *Aus guter Familie: Leidensgeschichte eines Mädchens* (Berlin: S. Fischer, 1906, orig. 1895); Franziska, Gräfin zu Reventlow,

Ellen Olestjerne; Elisabeth Dauthendey, *Vom neuen Weib und seiner Liebe: Ein Buch für reife Geister* (Berlin and Leipzig: Schuster u. Loeffler, 1901, orig. 1900); see also Lillian Faderman and Brigitte Ericksson, *Lesbians in Germany: 1890's–1920's* (Tallahassee: Naiad, 1980).

96. Halberstam, *Female Masculinity,* 73. The internal quote refers to Carroll Smith-Rosenberg's seminal article "The Female World of Love and Ritual: Relations between Women in Nineteenth Century America," *Signs* 1 (1975).

97. Göttert, *Macht und Eros,* 37–44.

98. In this case a circuit can be completed connecting Lange-Bäumer-Freudenberg-Goudstikker-Bülow-Lange.

99. These observations are taken from Göttert, *Macht und Eros,* 166–70.

100. Bäumer, letter to Marianne Weber, 26 December 1907. Quoted in Göttert, *Macht und Eros,* 169. Freudenberg suffered from cancer from 1906 to 1912. The obituary for Goudstikker claimed, "Ika Freudenberg could not have devoted her energy to her high calling had not her friend prepared the carefree domestic life and the pleasant, comfortable environment that her intellectual production required. Sophia Goudstikker was a also an excellent housewife." Quoted in Streiter, "Nachwort," 248.

101. Bäumer, letter to Weber, 2 January 1910. Quoted in Göttert, *Macht und Eros,* 169.

102. Bäumer, letter to Weber, 29 January 1908. Quoted in ibid., 169. The original version of this quotation begins with "he" in reference to "*der Meeschter*" (dialect for "the master") a term she often used to refer jokingly to Lange in her letters to Weber (129).

103. Friedrich Naumann, letter to Bäumer, originally published in Bäumer's 1933 memoir, here quoted from ibid., 170.

104. Fritz, *Die Erotische Rebellion,* 30, 71–77.

105. Marianne Weber, *Die Frauen und die Liebe* (Leipzig: K. R. Langewiesche, 1936), quoted in Fritz, *Die Erotische Rebellion,* 85. It should be noted that Weber's book was published during the Nazi period.

106. Franziska zu Reventlow, "*Viragines* oder Hetären?" quoted in Bruns, "Das dritte Geschlecht," 182–83.

107. Fritz, *Die erotische Rebellion,* 12–18, 72.

108. Irene Hardach-Pinke, "Managing Girls' Sexuality among the German Upper Classes," in *Secret Gardens, Satanic Mills: Placing Girls in European History, 1750–1960,* ed. Mary Jo Maynes, Birgitte Søland, and Christina Benninghaus (Bloomington: Indiana University Press, 2005).

109. Ika Freudenberg, "Moderne Sittlichkeitsprobleme," in *Frauenbewegung und Sexualethik: Beiträge zur Modernen Ehekritik* (Heilbronn, 1909), here quoted from Stoehr, "Fraueneinfluß oder Geschlechterversöhnung?" 159.

110. Lou Andreas-Salomé, *Die Erotik* (Frankfurt: Rütten u. Loening, 1910), 9.

111. Wolzogen described an influential sexual experience during the 1890s in Munich. "I was 38 years old without ever having experienced a woman's ecstasy or having enjoyed the wonderful exultation which inflames a man in the proud consciousness that he is in a position to make a woman blissful. . . . I was drunk as

if on young wine." Ernst von Wolzogen, *Verse zu meinem Leben,* quoted in Bruns, "Das dritte Geschlecht," 181.

112. This is not to argue that alternative sexual practices were unknown or taboo. However, sexological discourse suggests the hegemonic view that they properly led to intercourse. For example, Sigmund Freud, *Three Essays on the Theory of Sexuality,* trans. James Strachey (New York: Basic Books, 1962), 15–26.

113. See Dagmar Herzog, *Sex After Fascism: Memory and Morality in Twentieth Century Germany* (Princeton: Princeton University Press, 2005); Atina Grossmann, *Reforming Sex: The German Movement for Birth Control and Abortion Reform, 1920–1950* (New York: Oxford University Press, 1995); Cornelie Usborne, *The Politics of the Body in Weimar Germany: Women's Reproduction Rights and Duties* (Ann Arbor: University of Michigan Press, 1992); Erica Carter, *How German Is She? Postwar West German Reconstruction and the Consuming Woman* (Ann Arbor: University of Michigan Press, 1997); Uta Poiger, *Jazz, Rock, and Rebels: Cold War Politics and American Culture in a Divided Germany* (Berkeley: University of California Press, 2000).

Chapter 3. Asserting Sexual Subjectivity in Berlin

1. Elisabeth Dauthendey, *Vom neuen Weibe und seiner Liebe: Ein Buch für reife Geister* (Berlin: Schuster u. Loeffler, 1901), 101–103.

2. See Elena Mancini, *Magnus Hirschfeld and the Quest for Sexual Freedom: A History of the First International Sexual Freedom Movement* (New York: Palgrave Macmillan, 2010); James Steakley, "Per Scientiam ad Justitiam: Magnus Hirschfeld and the Sexual Politics of Innate Homosexuality, in *Science and Homosexualities,* ed. Vernon Rosario (New York: Routledge, 1997).

3. Magnus Hirschfeld, *Was soll das Volk vom dritten Geschlecht wissen? Eine Aufklarungsschrift über gleichgeschlechtliche (homosexuell) empfindende Menschen* (Leipzig: Max Spohr Verlag, 1901).

4. The important German work focuses on one or the other, see Heike Schader, *Virile, Vamps und wilde Veilchen: Sexualität, Begehren und Erotik in den Zeitschriften homosexueller Frauen im Berlin der 1920er Jahre* (Königstein: Ulrike Helmer Verlag, 2004); Ilse Kokula, *Weibliche Homosexualität um 1900 in Zeitgenossischen Dokumente* (Kiel: Frühlings Erwachen, 1986); Mecki Pieper, "Die Frauenbewegung und ihre Bedeutung für lesbische Frauen," and Ilse Kokula, "Lesbisch Leben von Weimar bis zur Nachkriegzeit," in *Eldorado: Homosexuelle Frauen und Männer in Berlin 1850–1950: Geschichte, Kultur, Alltag* (Berlin: Edition Hentrich, 1992). The major exception to this approach is Hanna Hacker, *Frauen und Freundinnen: Studien zur "weiblichen Homosexualität" am Beispiel Österreich 1870–1938* (Weinheim: Beltz Verlag, 1987).

5. Th. Ramien [Magnus Hirschfeld], *Sappho und Sokrates: wie erklärt sich die Liebe der Männer und Frauen zu Personen des eigenen Geschlechts?* (Leipzig: M. Spohr, 1896).

6. Mark Lehmstedt, *Bücher für das "dritte Geschlecht": der Max Spohr Verlag in Leipzig: Verlagsgeschichte und Bibliographie (1881–1941)* (Wiesbaden: Harrassowitz, 2002).

7. E. Krause, "Die Wahrheit über mich," and M. F. "Wie ich es sehe," both in *Jahrbuch für sexuelle Zwischenstufen* 3 (1901).

8. Magnus Hirschfeld, *Berlins drittes Geschlecht* (Berlin: Hermann Seemann's Nachfolger, 1905).

9. Peter Fritzsche, "Vagabond in the Fugitive City: Hans Ostwald, Imperial Berlin and the Grossstadt-Dokumente," *Journal of Contemporary History* 29 (1995).

10. Hirschfeld, *Berlins drittes Geschlecht*, 56–57.

11. Ibid., 65–66.

12. Wilhelm Hammer, *Die Tribadie Berlins: Zehn Fälle weibweiblicher Geschlechtsliebe aktenmäßig dargestellt nebst zehn Abhandlungen über die gleichgeschlechtliche Frauenliebe* (Berlin: Verlag Hermann Seemann Nachfolger, 1906).

13. Ibid., 11.

14. Ibid., 14–15.

15. Ibid., 92.

16. Ibid., 110–11.

17. Quoted in ibid., 50.

18. Ibid., 80.

19. Ibid., 66–67.

20. Ibid., 68, 85.

21. Ibid., 20–21.

22. Ibid., 97.

23. Ibid., 101.

24. See Christiane Leidinger, *Keine Tochter aus gutem Hause: Johanna Elberskirchen (1864–1943)* (Konstanz: UVK Verlag, 2008).

25. Johanna Elberskirchen, *Die Liebe des dritten Geschlechts: Homosexualität, eine bisexuellen Varietät, keine Entartung, keine Schuld* (Leipzig, Spohr Verlag, 1904).

26. Johanna Elberskirchen, *Was hat der Mann aus Weib, Kind, und sich gemacht? Revolution und Erlösung des Weibes: Eine Abrechnung mit dem Mann—Ein Wegweiser in die Zukunft!* (Leipzig: Magazin-Verlag, 1904), 98–99.

27. The major texts are Carroll Smith-Rosenberg, "Discourses of Sexuality and Subjectivity: The New Woman, 1870–1936," in *Hidden From History: Reclaiming the Gay and Lesbian Past*, ed. Martin Duberman, Martha Vicinus, and George Chauncey Jr. (New York: Penguin Meridian, 1989); Lillian Faderman, *Surpassing the Love of Men: Romantic Friendship and Love Between Women from the Renaissance to the Present* (New York: William Morrow, 1981); Sheila Jeffreys, *The Spinster and Her Enemies: Feminism and Sexuality 1880–1930* (London: Pandora, 1985).

28. On similar theorizing in Britain, see Lucy Bland, *Banishing the Beast: Feminism, Sex and Morality* (London: Tauris Parke, 2002).

29. Hammer, *Die Tribadie Berlins*, 101.

30. This was a commonly held antifeminist view at the time. In the German history of homosexuality it is connected with the "masculinists"—a group of writers that also rejected the medical view of homosexuality. For a convenient summary of the contrasting ideas of the "third-sexers" (Hirschfeld and the WhK) and the "masculinists" (Adolf Brand, Benedikt Friedländer, and other writers), see Harry Oosterhuis, "Homosexual Emancipation in Germany Before 1933: Two Traditions," in *Homosexuality and Male-Bonding in Pre-Nazi Germany*, ed. Harry Oosterhuis and Hubert Kennedy (New York: Harrington Park Press, 1991).

31. Hammer, *Die Tribadie Berlins*, 100.

32. Ibid., 97–102.

33. Elberskirchen, *Die Liebe des dritten Geschlechts*, 26.

34. Ella Mensch, *Bildstürmer in der Berliner Frauenbewegung* (Berlin: Hermann Seemann Nachfolger, 1906), 71–75, quote, 71.

35. See Margit Göttert, *Macht und Eros: Frauenbeziehungen und weibliche Kultur um 1900: eine neue Perspektive auf Helene Lange und Gertrud Bäumer* (Königstein/Taunus: Ulrike Helmer Verlag, 2000), 247–48.

36. Mensch, *Bildstürmer*, 31–34. Mensch's text fit into the series through its exposé of the "erotic epidemic" Mensch saw as infecting certain sectors of women's emancipation (11).

37. Ibid., 54, 37.

38. Ibid., 75.

39. Anna Rühling, "Welches Interesse hat die Frauenbewegung an der Lösung des homosexuellen Problems?" *Jahrbuch für sexuelle Zwischenstufen* 7 (1905).

40. Ibid., 140.

41. Ibid., 133.

42. Ibid., 144.

43. Victoria Harris, *Selling Sex in the Reich: Prostitutes in German Society, 1914–1945* (Oxford: Oxford University Press, 2010) makes this point about prostitutes generally.

44. Despite my connection of the confrontation with sexual subjectivity to "younger women," the authors discussed in this chapter were in their thirties and forties when they wrote their texts: Johanna Elberskirchen, b. 1864; Elisabeth Dauthendey, b. 1854; Elsa Asenijeff, b. 1867.

45. Christine Leidinger, "Johanna Elberskirchen (1864–1943)." Lesbengeschichte, accessed January 15, 2012. http://www.lesbengeschichte.de/bio_elberskirchen_d.html;

46. Elberskirchen, *Was hat der Mann*, 79–80.

47. Ibid., 87–88.

48. Dauthendey, *Die Neue Frau*, 118–19.

49. Ibid., 45, 51–52.

50. Ibid., 62.

51. Ibid., 57–58.

52. Elsa Asenijeff, *Aufruhr der Weiber und das Dritte Geschlecht* (Leipzig: Friedrich, 1898).

53. Ibid., 73.

54. Ibid., 88.

55. Ibid., 90.

56. Ibid., 118.

57. Elberskirchen, *Was hat der Mann*, 85.

58. Ibid., 63, 66.

59. Ibid., 75.

60. Ibid., 10–12.

61. Asenijeff, *Aufruhr*, 59.

62. Ibid., 22, 61.

63. Ibid., 86–88.

64. Ibid., 109.

65. Ibid., 64.

66. Johanna Elberskirchen, *Geschlechtsleben und Geschlechtsenthaltsamkeit des Weibes* (Munich: Seltz und Schauer, 1905).

67. Ibid., 33–34.

68. Ibid., 8.

69. Dauthendey, *Die Neue Frau*, 66.

70. Ibid., 72.

71. Ibid., 80.

72. Ibid., 92.

73. Ibid., 100–102.

74. Elisabeth Dauthendey, "Die urnische Frage und die Frau," *Jahrbuch für sexuelle Zwischenstufen* 8 (1906): 298.

75. BArch, R 8034 II, No. 6965-6966 Censorship; John Fout, "Sexual Politics in Wilhelmine Germany: The Male Gender Crisis, Moral Purity, and Homophobia," *Journal of the History of Sexuality* 2 (1992).

76. On the scandals, see James Steakley, "Iconography of a Scandal: Political Cartoons and the Eulenburg Affair in Wilhelmin Germany," in *Hidden from History: Reclaiming the Gay and Lesbian Past*, ed. Martin Duberman, George Chauncey Jr., and Martha Vicinus (New York: Meridian, 1989); Susanne zur Nieden, ed., *Homosexualität und Staatsräson: Männlichkeit, Homophobie und Politik in Deutschland 1900–1945* (Frankfurt: Campus Verlag, 2005).

77. The genre dates back to Renaissance and Enlightenment mobilizations of the middle classes against royalty and aristocracy. See Lynn Hunt, "Introduction," in *The Invention of Pornography: Obscenity and the Origins of Modernity, 1500–1800* (Cambridge: MIT Press, 1993).

78. "Ein perverses Stiftskind," *Große Glocke*, 8 April 1908.

79. "Homosexuelle Frauen," *Große Glocke*, 15 April 1908.

80. "Der 'Damenklub,'" *Berliner Tageblatt*, 22 April 1909.

81. Felix Wolff, "Homosexuelle Frauen," *Große Glocke*, 28 April 1909.

82. "Der Homosexuellen-Klub 'Neue Damengemeinschaft," *Große Glocke*, 20 January 1909.

83. Wolff, "Homosexuelle Frauen."

84. "Der 'Damenklub.'"

85. "Ein Damenklub vor Gericht," *Berliner Lokal-Anzeiger*, 22 April 1909. The *Lokal-Anzeiger* was published by the Scherl media corporation, controlled in the Weimar period by the radical nationalist Alfred Hugenburg and allied with his party, the DNVP.

86. "Homosexuellenquartier im Bayrischen Viertel," *Große Glocke*, 11 May 1910.

87. I am indebted to one of the anonymous reviewers of the manuscript for this connection.

88. "Ein neuer Klub der weiblichen Homosexuellen in der Lutherstraße," *Große Glocke*, 22 June 1910. Ellipsis in original.

89. "Ein homosexueller Damen-Kegelklub," *Große Glocke*, 21 December 1910.

90. "Die neueste Homosexuellen-Skandale," *Große Glocke*, 1 February 1911.

91. Ibid.

92. "Feminismus," *Große Glocke*, 22 March 1911. Emphasis in original. The second article was Felix Wolff, "Antifeministen," *Große Glocke*, 19 June 1912. "The woman should pay more attention to the protection of her dignity than to the extension of her rights, which are already equal to those of the man."

93. BArch 30.01, Nr. 5806, Bl. 12; Kai Sommer, *Die Strafbarkeit der Homosexualität von der Kaiserzeit bis zum Nationalsozialismus: Ein Analyse der Straftatbestände im Strafgesetzbuch und in den Reformentwürfen* (Frankfurt: Peter Lang, 1998), 144–45.

94. Felix Wolff, "Das Recht auf Homosexualität??" *Große Glocke*, 15 February 1911.

95. The new draft numbered this section §250. However, for simplicity, I will continue to refer to it as §175. The existing number was commonly referred to in the discussion cited here.

96. Sommer, *Die Strafbarkeit der Homosexualität*, 143.

97. *Begründung zu Abschnitt 13. Vorentwurf,* 1909, BArch R30.01, No. 5871, Bl. 168–70.

98. Sabine Hark, " 'Welches Interesse hat die Frauenbewegung an der Lösung des homosexuellen Problems?' Zur Sexualpolitik der bürgerliche Frauenbewegung im Deutschland des Kaiserreich: Sexualität und Sexualmoral im Wilhelminischen Deutschland," in *Industrializierung und Frauenbewegung: Zum weiblichen Alltag 1870–1933,* ed. Ulrike Prokop (Frankfurt: Fischer, 1990), 24–25; Kokula, *Weibliche Homosexualität,* 30.

99. Margit Göttert, "Zwischen Betroffenheit, Abscheu und Sympathie: Die alte Frauenbewegung und das 'heikle' Thema Homosexualität," *Ariadne* 29 (1996), 20.

100. Antrag Nr. B556, Wilhelm Kahl, 11 July 1912, BArch, R30.01, Nr. 6341. The illegible word makes a strange metaphor for the difficulty of finding language and the refusal to specify when it came to female homosexual acts.

101. F. B. [Friedrich Bechly], "Was heißt widernatürliche Unzucht beim weiblichen Geschlecht?" *Geschlecht und Gesellschaft* 6 (1911), reprinted in Kokula, *Weibliche Homosexualität.*

102. Friedrich Bechly, "Über die Ausdehnung des Homosexualitäts-Paragraphen (§ 175) auf die Frau," *Sexualreform: Beiblatt zu "Geschlecht und Gesellschaft*," February 1911, reprinted in Kokula, *Weibliche Homosexualität*, 251.

103. See also Tracy Matysik, "In the Name of the Law: The 'Female Homosexual' and the Criminal Code in Fin-de-Siécle Germany," *Journal of the History of Sexuality* 13, no. 1: 2004.

104. Helene Stöcker, "Die beabsichtigte Ausdehnung des 175 auf die Frau," *Neue Generation* 7 (1911), reprinted in Kokula, *Weibliche Homosexualität*, 267–78, quotes 267, 276.

105. Visiting card, letter, and article from the *Monatschrift für Kriminalpsychologie und Strafrechtreform,* 1911, BArch, R30.01, Nr. 5961, unpaged. Krukenberg, Schirmacher, and Mensch contributed to the debates about women students, see chapter 1. Mensch wrote an article during the Eulenberg scandals giving a woman's perspective on §175. In it she connected male homosexuality to rejection and maltreatment of women, but did not comment on female homosexuality. Ella Mensch, "Eine Frau über §175," *Große Glocke,* 21 November 1907.

106. Elspeth Krukenberg, "§175," BArch, R30.01, Nr. 5961. This was a published article: *Monatschrift für Kriminalpsychologie und Strafrechtsreform,* 7 (1911), reprinted in Kokula, *Weibliche Homosexualität*, 256.

107. On responses of the mainstream women's movement to Krukenberg's effusions, see Margit Göttert, *Zwischen Betroffenheit*, 17.

108. Anna Pappritz, "Zum §175," *Der Abolitionist,* 1 February 1911, reprinted in Kokula, *Weibliche Homosexualität*; Dr. Helene Stöcker, "Die beabsichtigte Ausdehnung des § 175."

109. Dr. Käthe Schirmacher, "§175 des deutschen Strafgesetzes," *Der Abolitionist,* 1 January 1911, reprinted in Kokula, *Weibliche Homosexualität*. Her terminology was "geschlechtliche Beziehungen."

110. Pappritz was an activist in the antiprostitution and venereal disease movement. She may have been more aware of alternative sexual expression through this work. Also interesting in this respect is correspondence between Pappritz and Helene Stöcker in which Pappritz accused Stöcker of slandering a woman of their acquaintance. See Margot Göttert, "Zwischen Betroffenheit," 15.

111. Strafrecht Kommission Protokolle, 30 September 1912, BArch, R30.01, Nr. 5926, 18.

112. This is parallel to, but much more limited than such efforts by men. See Oosterhuis, "Two Traditions."

113. Ibid.

Chapter 4. Denying Desire

1. Anna Philipps, *Um Ehre und Recht: Mein Kampf gegen das Provinzial-Schulkollegium Hannover und das Ministerium für Wissenschaft, Kunst, und Volksbildung,* unpublished printed manuscript (Neuminster, [1932 ?]), 4. The book

is probably Magnus Hirschfeld, *Homosexualität des Mannes und des Weibes* (Berlin: L. Marcus, 1914). On the film, see, James D. Steakley, "Cinema and Censorship in the Weimar Republic: The Case of *Anders als die Anderen*," *Film History* 11 (1999).

2. Philipps, *Um Ehre und Recht*, 23. The book manuscript, intended as an exposé, was published after she was dismissed from her teaching position. It included a biographical narrative and documents from her disciplinary file. Note the subtitle.

3. I am indebted to the scholars who made me aware of the cases. Ursula Nienhaus told me about the Erkens case when I met her in Berlin in 2000. Her thorough reconstruction of the events of Erkens's career (but not the disciplinary case) is found in Ursula Nienhaus, *"Nicht für eine Führungsposition geeignet . . .": Josefine Erkens und die Anfänge weiblicher Polizei in Deutschland 1923–1933* (Münster: Westfälisches Dampfboot, 1999). Archivist Heino Rose at the Staatsarchiv Hamburg called my attention to the seventeen volumes of the disciplinary case. The Philipps case is discussed in Kirsten Plötz's book on Weimar female homosexuality in provincial Germany. Kirsten Plötz, *Einsame Freundinnen: Lesbisches Leben während der zwanziger Jähre in der Provinz* (Hamburg: Männerschwarmskript, 1999). I learned of the files on Schwester Hedwig Atteln from Ute Schumacher, archivist at the Frankfurt Institut für Stadtgeschichte.

4. Atina Grossmann, "*Girlkultur* or Thoroughly Rationalized Female: A New Woman in Weimar Germany?" in *Women in Culture and Politics: A Century of Change*, ed. Judith Friedlander (Bloomington: Indiana University Press, 1986); Lynne Frame, "Gretchen, Girl, Garçonne? Weimar Science and Popular Culture in Search of the Ideal New Woman," in *Women in the Metropolis: Gender and Modernity in Weimar Culture*, ed. Katharina von Ankum (Berkeley: University of California Press, 1997); Patrice Petro, *Joyless Streets: Women and Melodramatic Representations in Weimar Germany* (Princeton: Princeton University Press, 1989).

5. Ute Frevert, *Women in German History: From Bourgeois Emancipation to Sexual Liberation*, trans. Stuart McKinnon Evans (New York: Berg, 1989) 197–98; Young Sun Hong, *Welfare, Modernity, and the Weimar State, 1919–1933* (Princeton: Princeton University Press, 1998), 149–58; David Crew, *Germans on Welfare: From Weimar to Hitler* (New York: Oxford University Press, 1998), 50–54.

6. The Erkens case files are found in the Stadtarchiv Hamburg (StAH): Senatsakten, Einrichtung einer weiblichen Kriminalpolizei, Cl. VII Lit. Lb, No. 28a2 Vol. 120, Fasc. 5 and 5b; Weibliche Kriminalpolizei, Polizeibehörde I, Arb. Sig. 314 and 338; Personalakten Josefine Erkens, Polizei-Personalakten 316, Bd. 1–2; Staatliche Pressestelle, Nr. 4011 and 4031; Dizsiplinärkammer, 221-10, D 8/31 Bd. 1–17, Sonderakt (DK Erkens).

7. Josefine Erkens, "Grundsätzliches zur Frage der Weiblichen Polizei," in *Weibliche Polizei: Ihr Werden, ihre Ziele und Arbeitsformen als Ausdruck eines neuen Wollens auf dem Gebiete der Polizei* (Lübeck: Deutscher Polizei-Verlag, 1925), 31.

8. Richard W. McCormick, *Gender and Sexuality in Weimar Modernity: Film, Literature, and "New Objectivity"* (New York: Palgrave, 2001), ch. 1 and 117–21; Stephen Brockmann, "Weimar Sexual Cynicism," in *Dancing on the Volcano: Essays*

on the Culture of the Weimar Republic, ed. Thomas Kniesche and Stephen Brockman (Columbia, SC: Camden House, 1994).

9. This is the approach in Ursula Nienhaus, *"Nicht für eine Führungsposition geeignet."* See Young Sun Hong, *Welfare, Modernity, and the Weimar State,* ch. 5, for an extended discussion of the many points of tension between male administrators and female social workers.

10. See Lillian Faderman, *Surpassing the Love of Men: Romantic Friendship and Love Between Women from the Renaissance to the Present* (New York: William Morrow, 1981) esp. 314–31; Sheila Jeffreys, *The Spinster and Her Enemies: Feminism and Sexuality, 1880–1930* (London: Pandora, 1985), esp. 128–46; Carroll Smith-Rosenberg, "Discourses of Sexuality and Subjectivity: The New Woman, 1870–1936," in *Hidden from History: Reclaiming the Gay and Lesbian Past,* ed. Martin Duberman, Martha Vicinus, and George Chauncey Jr. (New York: Penguin/Meridian, 1989).

11. This is not to deny that such stereotypes were used by antifeminist cultural pessimists in the same period. See Anton Schuecker, *Zur Psychopathologie der Frauenbewegung* (Leipzig: C. Kabitsch, 1931) and E. F. W. Eberhardt, *Feminismus und Kulturuntergang: die Erotischen Grundlagen der Frauenemanzipation* (Leipzig: Braumueller, 1927).

12. See the fuller discussion in Julia Roos, *Weimar through the Lens of Gender: Prostitution Reform, Women's Emancipation, and German Democracy, 1919–1933* (Ann Arbor: University of Michigan Press, 2010), 101–107.

13. See Laura Tate, "The Culture of Literary *Bildung* in the Bourgeois Women's Movement in Imperial Germany," *German Studies Review* 24 (2001).

14. Sickermann statement, printed in Anna Philipps, *Um Ehre und Recht,* 57.

15. On ideas about masculine erotic pedagogy in the era, see Harry Oosterhuis, "Eros and Male Bonding in Society: Introduction," in *Homosexuality and Male Bonding in Pre-Nazi Germany: The Youth Movement, the Gay Movement, and Male Bonding before Hitler's Rise,* ed. Harry Oosterhuis and Hubert Kennedy (New York: Harrington Park Press, 1991).

16. Fricke statement, printed in Philipps, *Um Ehre und Recht,* 53.

17. Philipps, *Um Ehre und Recht,* 5.

18. The case is found in Institut für Stadtgeschichte Frankfurt, Personalakt Hedwig Atteln, Personalakten 52.667 (ISGF Atteln).

19. Since Atteln took the initiative to prepare the applications, it seems plausible that she was the more invested in moving away from her family to a location where she and Westheider could live together. A 1929 request for leave to help her aging parents move was denied. The timing suggests that this was a trigger in her workplace and relationship troubles, which were constant from 1930–33.

20. Head Sister's Report [on investigation of complaints against Atteln], 28 July 1930, ISGF Atteln.

21. The 1927 Law for Combatting Venereal Diseases outlawed the old style Morals Police and encouraged the development of Women Police Units. Women police officers were not integrated into the ranks of existing police. Their positions were

part of a special women's unit that worked primarily with young female offenders, family violence, and sex crimes. Whether they would patrol the streets or simply work with suspects and victims referred to them by male police officers was a matter of controversy. See accounts in Nienhaus, *Nicht für eine Führungsposition*; Roos, *Weimar through the Lens,* 122–23.

22. Maria Fischer volunteered for war work in 1914. After the war she worked in various small towns as child welfare worker. During the war, Theresa Dopfer trained as a childcare worker in Frankfurt. One of her childcare positions brought her together with Fischer. They lived together on and off during the period 1923–25. Because of illness and unemployment, each lived for a time with relatives. In 1925 they set up a joint household in Frankfurt. The following year Dopfer got a job with the Women's Police; Fischer was unemployed. Dopfer apparently agreed to move to Hamburg on condition that Fischer would also get a job in the new service.

23. Erkens letter to Wieking, 30 April 1931, StAH, DK Erkens, Bd. 3, Bl. 359–360. Wieking was head of the Berlin Women's Police.

24. Maria Fischer letter to "Gretel," 10 November 1930, StAH, DK Erkens, Bd. 3, Bl. 389.

25. "Die Frauentragödie im Hamburger Polizei-Präsidium," *BZ am Mittag,* 11 July 1931.

26. Theresa Dopfer letter to Antonie Storbeck, 31 March 1931, StAH, DK Erkens, Bd. 3, Bl. 351.

27. StAH, DK Erkens, Bd. 3, Bl. 359–360.

28. See Modern Girl Around the World Research Group, "The Modern Girl around the World: A Research Agenda and Preliminary Findings," *Gender & History* 17 (2005).

29. On generations in the women's movement see Elizabeth Harvey, "The Failure of Feminism? Young Women and the Bourgeois Feminist Movement in Weimar Germany," *Central European History* 28 (1995); and Margit Göttert, *Macht und Eros: Frauenbeziehungen und weibliche Kultur um 1900: Eine neue Perspektive auf Helene Lange und Gertrud Bäumer* (Königstein: Ulrike Helmer Verlag, 2000), 45–111.

30. Ute Frevert, *Women in German History,* 185; Renate Bridenthal and Claudia Koonz, "Beyond *Kinder, Küche, Kirche*: Weimar Women in Politics and Work," in *When Biology Became Destiny: Women in Weimar and Nazi Germany,* ed. Renate Bridenthal, Atina Grossmann, and Marion Kaplan (New York: Monthly Review Press, 1984), 44–45, 53.

31. See Roos, *Weimar through the Lens,* ch. 3; Hong, *Weimar, Modernity, and the Welfare State,* 142–45; Irene Stoehr, " 'Organizierte Mütterlichkeit': Zur Politik der deutschen Frauenbewegung um 1900," in *Frauen suchen ihre Geschichte,* ed. Karin Hausen (Munich: Beck, 1983); Christof Sachße, *Mütterlichkeit als Beruf: Sozialarbeit, Sozialreform und Frauenbewegung* (Frankfurt: Suhrkamp, 1986).

32. See Young Sun Hong, "Femininity as Vocation: Gender and Class Conflict in the Professionalization of German Social Work," in *The German Professions 1800–1950,* ed. Geoffrey Cocks and Konrad Jarausch (New York: Oxford University Press, 1990); Young Sun Hong, *Welfare Modernity and the Weimar State, 1919–1933,* ch. 5; Atina

Grossman, *Reforming Sex: The German Movement for Birth Control and Abortion Reform, 1920–1950* (New York: Oxford University Press, 1995), ch. 3. On women in state employment, see Elisabeth Lembeck, *Frauenarbeit bei Vater Staat: Weibliche Behördenangestellte in der Weimarer Republik* (Pfaffenweiler: Centaurus, 1993).

33. Gertrud Bäumer, "Schicksalsfragen der weiblichen Polizei." *Vossische Zeitung,* July 18, 1931.

34. Göttert, *Macht und Eros.*

35. Roos, *Weimar through the Lens.* On the roots of these ideas in the German Women's Movement, see Edward Ross Dickinson, "Dominion of the Spirit over the Flesh: Religion, Gender, and Sexual Morality in the German Women's Movement before World War I," *Gender & History* 17 (2005).

36. See, for example, the chilling case study of one of Erkens's successors in managing prostitution in Hamburg in Victoria Harris, *Selling Sex in the Reich: Prostitutes in German Society, 1914–1945* (Oxford: Oxford University Press, 2010) 175–83. A more benign view is found in Roos, *Weimar through the Lens,* 129–33.

37. Nursing obviously does not fit this pattern as well as teaching and social work. However, the roots of the gendered ideology find early expression in Florence Nightingale's vision for nursing as analyzed in Mary Poovey, "A Housewifely Woman: The Social Construction of Florence Nightingale," in *Uneven Developments: The Ideological Work of Gender in Mid-Victorian England* (Chicago: University of Chicago Press, 1988).

38. Roos, *Weimar through the Lens,* 121–22.

39. Erkens, "Grundsätzliches zur Frage der Weiblichen Polizei," 31.

40. Roos, *Weimar through the Lens,* 114–21.

41. Josefine Erkens, "Entwicklung und Aufgabegebiete der deutschen Frauenpolizei," *Deutsche Zeitschrift für Wohlfahrtspflege* (1928), 400; Elisabeth Cleuver, "Tätigkeitsbericht der Frauen-Wohlfahrtspolizei, Cöln," in *Weibliche Polizei,* ed. Josefine Erkens, 76.

42. F. O'Mon, "Zwischen Beruf und Leben: Was lehrt die Tragödie in Hamburgs Frauenpolizei?" *Vossische Zeitung,* July 15, 1931. "The Hamburg tragedy, in which really unique things play a role, raises the question of whether marriage is not almost indispensable for the female officer."

43. On the German women's police see Erika S. Fairchild, "Women Police in Weimar: Professionalism, Politics, and Innovations in Police Organizations," *Law & Society Review* 21 (1987); Elisabeth Meyer-Renschhausen, "Die Männerhaß der Polizeimatronen," in *Documentation 4. Historikerinnentreffen* (Berlin: Technische Universität, 1983); Friedrike Wieking, *Die Entwicklung der weiblichen Kriminalpolizei in Deutschland von den Anfängen bis zur Gegenwart* (Lübeck: Verlag für polizeiliches Fachschrifttum, 1958); Lothar Barck, *Ziele und Aufgaben der weiblichen Polizei in Deutschland* (Berlin: Deutscher Polizei-Verlag, 1928); Josefine Erkens, *Weibliche Polizei.* Several historical works have recently examined the British Women's Police in this period. Philippa Levine, " 'Walking the Streets in a Way No Decent Woman Should': Women Police in World War I," *Journal of Modern History* 66 (1994); R. M. Douglas, *Feminist Freikorps: The British Voluntary Women Police, 1914–1940* (Westport CT:

Praeger, 1999); Laura Doan, *Fashioning Sapphism: The Origins of a Modern English Lesbian Culture* (New York: Columbia University Press, 2001), ch. 3.

44. This was also a broad trend in progressive criminology of the period. See Christian Müller, *Verbrechungsbekämpfung im Anstaltstaat: Psychiatrie, Kriminologie und Strafrechtsreform in Deutschland, 1871–1933* (Göttingen: Vandenhoeck u. Ruprecht, 2004); Richard Wetzell, *Inventing the Criminal: A History of German Criminology, 1880–1945* (Chapel Hill: University of North Carolina Press, 2000).

45. Erkens, "Entwicklung und Aufgabengebiete," 398.

46. Quoted in Wieking, *Die Entwicklung der weiblichen Kriminalpolizei,* 43.

47. One list of invitees to a committee meeting gives three of them the title "*Frau*" and the others "*Fräulein*." "Liste der Einladungs-Empfänger zu der Aussprache am Mittwoch den 5.1. über die Einordnung der weiblichen beamteten Kräfte in die Polizei," Landesarchiv Berlin, Helene Lange Archiv (HLA), Nr. 33/170. Among the twelve members of the *BdF* police committee, three (Gertrud Bäumer, Anna Pappritz, and Martha Mosse) can be shown to have lived in long-term couple arrangements. See Margit Göttert, *Macht und Eros,* 178–88, for Bäumer and Pappritz; for Mosse, see Elisabeth Kraus, *Die Familie Mosse: Deutsch-jüdisches Bürgertum im 19. und 20. Jahrhundert* (Munich: C. H. Beck Verlag, 1999), 590. There is thinner evidence for Wieking having a partner. The documents refer to her traveling with her "girlfriend," an ambiguous term. Landesarchiv Berlin, Pr. Br. Rep. 30, Acc. 3981, Nr. 1094, 42.

48. Jaeger, letter to committee, HLA, 33/176; Protokoll der von Bund deutscher Frauenvereine veranstalteten Sachverständigen-Aussprache in kleinem Kreise über die Frage der Einordnung weiblicher beamteter Kräfte in die Polizei am 6 Januar 1926, HLA No. 33/173.

49. HLA, 33/188.

50. HLA, 33/173, 1–2.

51. Erkens, "Grundsätzliches zur Frage der weiblichen Polizei," 58–60.

52. Roos, *Weimar through the Lens,* 133–35.

53. As used by historians of male and female same-sex intimacy, the term refers most precisely to sustaining friendships between people who were otherwise embedded in family networks where intimacy involved different obligations. George Mosse argued that intimate same-sex friendships were stigmatized through the nationalist orientation of families in the nineteenth century. George Mosse, *Nationalism and Sexuality: Respectability and Abnormal Sexuality in Modern Europe* (New York: Howard Fertig, 1985). When considering women's relationships, perhaps a different term should be used when discussing the female couples who began to become more numerous, especially in the Anglo-American context, in the second half of the nineteenth century. See Sharon Marcus, *Between Women: Friendship, Desire, and Marriage in Victorian England* (Princeton: Princeton University Press, 2007). Relationships in the 1920s were different yet again, since middle-class career women began to emulate the patterns of nineteenth-century women who were closer to the social elite.

54. *Duzen* means to use the familiar form of the second person pronoun. This usage was only proper with family and very close friends. In some novels, its use indicates that a couple has become sexually intimate.

55. Sickermann statement, 28 April 1922, printed in Philipps, *Um Ehre und Recht*, 65–66.

56. Erkens statement, 18 June 1931, StAH, DK Erkens, Bd. 4, Bl. 20.

57. Dopfer statement, 15 June 1931, StAH, DK Erkens, Bd. 4, Bl. 8.

58. Fischer statement, 15 June 1931, StAH, DK Erkens, Bd. 4. Bl. 10. Erkens responded, "It is also possible that I occasionally called her by her first name, but I didn't use *Du*. On her side she repeatedly suggested that I use *Du* with her, since she used it with me. There she came up against decided resistance from me." Erkens statement, 18 June 1931, StAH, DK Erkens, Bd. 4, Bl. 20.

59. Paula Valk statement, 26 September 1931, StAH, DK Erkens, Bd. 4, Bl. 59–60.

60. Frau Dr. de Lemos statement, 10 October 1931, StAH, DK Erkens, Bd. 4, Bl.83.

61. Galuschky statement, 24 September 1931, StAH, DK Erkens, Bd. 4, Bl. 48.

62. Mergard statement, 27 April 1932, StAH, DK Erkens, Bd. 4, Bl. 197.

63. Theresa Dopfer statement, 15 June 1931, StAH, DK Erkens, Bd. 4, Bl. 7.

64. Erkens statement, 5 October 1931, StAH, DK Erkens, Bd. 4, Bl. 91–92.

65. Letter to (Police Chief) Schlanbusch from Friedrichs, Stahl, Rück, Meyer, Mergard, 15 September 1931, StAH, DK Erkens, Bd. 17, Bl. 28.

66. Otto Dopfer statement, 2 March 1932, StAH, DK Erkens, Bd. 3, Bl. 297.

67. Georg Fischer statement, 16 March 1932, StAH, DK Erkens Bd. 3, Bl. 390–391.

68. Hans Dopfer statement, 18 March 1932, StAH, DK Erkens, Bd. 3, Bl. 317.

69. Theodor Spira letter to (Judge) Baritsch, 9 April 1932, StAH, DK Erkens, Bd. 3, Bl. 415.

70. Berta Esser statement, 11 May 1932, StAH, DK Erkens, Bd. 3, Bl. 284.

71. Maria Korr statement, 11 May 1932, StAH, DK Erkens, Bd. 3, Bl. 285.

72. Berta Esser statement, 11 May 1932.

73. Hardrat statement, in Philipps, *Um Ehre und Recht*, 49.

74. Sickermann statement, in Philipps, *Um Ehre und Recht*, 56–57.

75. Hardrat statement, in Philipps, *Um Ehre und Recht*, 49.

76. Fricke statement, in Philipps, *Um Ehre und Recht*, 53.

77. According to hearsay testimony, Philipps had said, "What she had to tell was so damaging that she had to write it rather than say it aloud." Hardrat statement, n. d., in Philipps, *Um Ehre und Recht*, 53.

78. Philipps, *Um Ehre und Recht*, 6.

79. Justiziar Büchsel to the Ministry, n. d., printed in Philipps, *Um Ehre und Recht*, 72.

80. Staatsanwaltschaft, Wesermünde—Geestemünde to Philipps, 21 September 1926, in Philipps, *Um Ehre und Recht*, 16.

81. Philipps, *Um Ehre und Recht*, 23.

82. Plötz, *Einsame Freundinnen*, 102.

83. Philipps, *Um Ehre und Recht*, 109.

84. Suspicion of homosexual conspiracies that threatened the state was not a new invention. She referred to the scandals of the decades before World War I. See Susanne zur Nieden, ed., *Homosexualität und Staatsräson: Männlichkeit, Homophobie,*

und Politik in Deutschland 1900–1945 (Frankfurt: Campus Verlag, 2005); James Steakley, "Iconography of a Scandal: Political Cartoons and the Eulenburg Affair in Wilhelmin Germany," in *Hidden from History: Reclaiming the Gay and Lesbian Past,* ed Martin Duberman, Martha Vicinus, and George Chauncey Jr. (New York: Meridian, 1989).

85. Plötz, *Einsame Freundinnen,* 100.

86. Atteln suicide letter, ISGF Atteln.

87. Report of a meeting with Hedwig Atteln, written by the Head Sister, ISGF Atteln.

88. Atteln letters to Westheider, apparently late January 1933, ISGF Atteln.

89. Atteln suicide letter, ISGF Atteln.

90. Josefine Erkens statement, 18 June 1931, StAH, DK Erkens, Bd. 4, Bl. 20.

91. Josefine Erkens statement, 5 April 1932, StAH, DK Erkens, Bd. 5, Bl. 41.

92. M. Lohse statement, 18 April 1932, StAH, DK Erkens, Bd. 5, Bl. 121. In the quotation I translate both words as "queer" to capture the overlap in meaning between "*schwül*" meaning "humid" or "sultry" and the slang term "*schwul.*"

93. O. Lohse statement, 18 April 1932, StAH, DK Erkens, Bd. 5, Bl. 121.

94. Verdict, 8 October 1932, StAH, DK Erkens, Bd. 15.

95. This sentiment was expressed in the ultranationalist *Hamburger Warte,* April 1932. StAH, Personalakten, 316, Bd. 2. Similar formulations appeared in opinions from the judge to the Senat, April and May, 1932. StAH, Personalakten, 316, Bd. 1.

96. The law disqualified most Jews and allowed the regime to dismiss civil servants for questionable loyalty. The Gestapo investigated Erkens in 1934 when she applied to emigrate to the United States. She did eventually emigrate and spent 1936 through 1939 working for a welfare agency in Pittsburgh. She returned to Germany in 1939, settling in Düsseldorf. She immediately began petitioning the government for reinstatement of her pension. After the war she continued to press for pension rights and for compensation as a victim of the National Socialists. She had limited success with the former, although she was unsatisfied with the amount. She never gained recognition as a Nazi victim. She died on 6 May 1974. Nienhaus, *Nicht für eine Führungsposition,* 81, 99–102.

97. Michel Foucault, *The History of Sexuality,* vol. 1 *An Introduction,* trans. Robert Hurley (New York: Vintage, 1978), 92–102.

98. Oberarzt Dr. Peter, statement, 24 September 1931, StAH, DK Erkens, Bd. 4, Bl. 52–53.

99. Erkens statement, 3 April 1932, StAH, DK Erkens, Bd. 2, Bl. 114. Erkens named three other doctors who should be asked to testify about Peter's competence, claiming "apparently in all his previous positions he was judged a professionally and personally doubtful personality." Erkens statement, 7 April 1932, StAH, DK Erkens, Bd. 5, Bl. 77.

100. Rautenberg letter to Baritsch, 6 May 1932, StAH, DK Erkens, Bd. 3, Bl. 273.

101. See sketch in *Goodbye to Berlin: 100 Jahre Schwulenbewegung* (Berlin: Verlag Rosa Winkel, 1997), 32. His book on homosexuality was Albert Moll, *Die*

konträre Sexualempfindung: Mit Benutzung amtlichen Materials (Berlin: Fischers Medizinische Buchhandlung, 1893).

102. Laura Doan, "'Acts of Female Indecency': Sexology's Intervention in Legislating Lesbianism," in *Sexology and Culture: Labelling Bodies and Desires,* ed. Lucy Bland and Laura Doan (Chicago: University of Chicago Press, 1998), 205.

103. Letter from Oppenheimer law firm to Disziplinarkammer, 27 August 1932, StAH, DK Erkens, Bd. 11, Bl. 157–161.

104. Letter from Disziplinarkammer to Oppenheimer law firm, date unknown, StAH, DK Erkens, Bd. 11, Bl. 184.

105. Medical report by Dr. D. Fünfgeld, 23 June 1933, ISGF Atteln.

106. Kreisärztliches Attest vom 15 February 1927, in Philipps, *Um Ehre und Recht,* 74.

107. Abschrft des ärztlichen Gutachtens des Sanitätsrat Dr. Hirschfeld, in Philipps, *Um Ehre und Recht,* 79.

108. Doan, *Fashioning Sapphism,* 96–99; Katie Sutton, *The Masculine Woman in Weimar Germany* (New York: Berghahn, 2011), 62.

Chapter 5. Emancipation and Desire in Weimar Berlin's Female Homosexual Public Sphere

1. Ute Daniel, *The War from Within: German Working-Class Women in the First World War,* trans. Margaret Ries (Oxford: Berg, 1997), 182; Roger Chickering, *Imperial Germany and the Great War, 1914–1918* (Cambridge: Cambridge University Press, 2004), 118.

2. Lotte Hahm, "Mondschein-Dampferpartie von 'Violetta,'" *Die Freundin,* 2 July 1930, 5.

3. Lotte Hahm, "Mondscheinfahrt für unsere Frauen!" *Die Freundin,* 25 June 1930, 6.

4. Ilse Kokula, "Die 'Goldenen Zwanziger' in Berlin—von unten gesehen: Brief von G. M.," in *Jahre des Glücks, Jahre des Leids: Gespräche mit älterer lesbischen Frauen: Dokumente* (Kiel: Frühlings Erwachen, 1986), 92.

5. Charlotte Wolff, *Hindsight: An Autobiography* (London: Quartet Books, 1980), 66.

6. Ute Scheub, *Verrückt nach Leben: Berliner Szenen in den zwanziger Jahren* (Reinbek: Rowohlt, 2000); Birgit Haustedt, *Die wilden Jahre in Berlin: eine Klatsch- und Kulturgeschichte der Frauen* (Berlin: Edition Ebersbach, 1999).

7. Michael Warner, "Publics and Counterpublics," *Public Culture* 14 (2002); Michael Warner, ed., *Fear of a Queer Planet: Queer Politics and Social Theory* (Minneapolis: University of Minnesota Press, 1993); Lauren Berlant, *The Queen of America Goes to Washington City: Essays on Sex and Citizenship* (Durham: Duke University Press, 1997); Lauren Berlant and Michael Warner, "Sex in Public," *Critical Inquiry* 24 (1998).

8. Klaus Petersen, "The Harmful Publications (Young Persons) Act of 1926: Literary Censorship and the Politics of Morality in the Weimar Republic," *German Studies Review* 15 (1992); Margaret Stieg, "The 1926 German Law to Protect Youth against Trash and Dirt: Moral Protectionism in a Democracy," *Central European History* 23 (1990).

9. Letter from Cecilia F., "Briefe, die man der 'Freundin' schreibt . . . ," *Die Freundin*, 12 December 1927, 5.

10. Mel Gordon, *Voluptuous Panic: The Erotic World of Weimar Berlin* (Venice, CA: Feral House, 2000), 107. Gordon quotes Magnus Hirschfeld's 1930 estimate of a Berlin lesbian population of four hundred thousand. Gordon is rightly skeptical of the number, arrived at by taking a percentage of the population as a whole. However, he gives his own estimate at eighty-five thousand. In my view, specific numbers do not make sense because of the great diversity of women who might be considered "lesbian." Clubs claimed to have thousands of members and attendance at events was counted in the hundreds. Multiplied by ten and twenty venues, this gives us a sense of the numbers actively participating in social organizations and nightlife. Many women would have been unable to afford to participate and others found the bar atmosphere uncongenial.

11. Detlev Peukert, *The Weimar Republic: The Crisis of Classical Modernity*, trans. Richard Deveson (New York: Hill and Wang, 1989), 96–97; David Blackbourn, "The *Mittelstand* in German Society and Politics 1871–1914," *Social History* 2 (1977).

12. According to Childers, one-quarter of white collar employees came from working-class backgrounds, while women made up one-third of the category. Thomas Childers, "The Social Language of Politics in Germany: The Sociology of Political Discourse in the Weimar Republic," *American Historical Review* 95 (1990): 350.

13. Ute Frevert, *Women in German History: From Bourgeois Emancipation to Sexual Liberation,* trans. Stuart McKinnon-Evans (Oxford: Berg, 1988), 183–84.

14. Eberhard Kolb, *The Weimar Republic,* trans. P. S. Falla and R. J. Park (New York: Routledge, 2005), 87.

15. Adele Meyer, ed., *Lila Nächte: die Damenklubs im Berlin der zwanziger Jahre* (Berlin: Edition Lit.Europe, 1994), 49–50. Reprinted from Ruth Margarete Roellig, *Berlins lesbische Frauen* (Leipzig: Bruno Gebauer Verlag, 1928).

16. Gordon, *Voluptuous Panic,* 243.

17. Claire Waldoff, *Weeste noch . . . ? Errinerungen und Dokumente* (Berlin: Parthas Verlag, 1997), 60–61.

18. Curt Moreck, *Führer durch das 'lasterhafte' Berlin* (Leipzig: Verlag moderner Stadtführer, 1931), 158–60.

19. Gordon, *Voluptuous Panic,* 245.

20. Wolff, *Hindsight,* 75.

21. Ibid., 77–78.

22. Ilse Kokula, " 'Da hab' ich jeden Kontakt zu Lesben verloren: Gespräch mit Gerda Madsen," *Jahre des Glücks,* 79. "Gerda Madsen" is a pseudonym.

23. Gordon, *Voluptuous Panic,* 244; Meyer, ed., *Lila Nächte,* 37–38.

24. *Die Freundin*, 1 October 1924, 7, lists the following clubs: Pyramide, Tatjana, Goldene Kugel, Lustige Neun, Theater- und Sparverein Goldregen, Sparverein Kleeblatt, Sparverein Altes Geld, and Theaterverein Hand in Hand.

25. R., "Das 17 jährige Stiftungsfest," *Die Freundin*, 27 November 1929, 6. Goldene Kugel celebrated its twenty-fifth anniversary in early 1930. Advertisement, *Die Freundin*, 11 December 1929, 7.

26. Maximiliane Ackers, *Freundinnen: Ein Roman unter Frauen* (Maroldsweisach: Feministischer Buchverlag, 1995, orig. 1923).

27. Ibid., 138.

28 At its peak the BfM claimed to have one hundred thousand members. The vast majority were men. See Stefan Micheler, "Kampf, Kontakt, Kultur: Die Freundschaftsverbände gleichgeschlechtlich begehrender Männer und Frauen in der Weimarer Republik in Norddeutschland," in *Querschnitt—Gender Studies: ein interdisziplinärer Blick nicht nur auf Homosexualität*, ed. Paul M. Hahlbohm and Till Hurlin (Kiel: Verlag Ludwig, 2001), 51–52. An infamous member of the BfM was Ernst Röhm, the leader of the National Socialist SA, executed by the SS in 1934.

29. Little has been written on these groups in English. German monographs using them have appeared only recently: Stefan Micheler, *Selbstbilder und Fremdbilder der "Anderen": eine Geschichte männerbegehrende Männer in der Weimarer Republik und der NS-Zeit* (Konstanz: UVK Verlagsgesellschaft, 2005); Heike Schader, *Virile, Vamps und wilde Veilchen: Sexualtät, Begehren, und Erotik in den Zeitschriften homosexueller Frauen im Berlin der 1920er Jahre* (Königstein, Ulrike Helmer Verlag, 2004).

30. On the print sphere and belonging, see Benedict Anderson, *Imagined Communities* (London: Verso, 1991).

31. Heike Schader's bibliography lists 1924 and 1925 issues that were not on the microfilm I consulted. The microfilms are mostly complete from September 1927 through March 1933. Schader, *Virile, Vamps, und wilde Veilchen*, 290.

32. *Die Freundin*, 15 September 1924, 2. When *Die Freundin* was put on the *Schund und Schmutz* list, prohibiting stores and kiosks from displaying it openly for sale, the Radszuweit Verlag replaced it with the title *Ledige Frauen*.

33. Radszuweit probably employed male associates to produce *Die Freundin* along with the other BfM titles. Killmer and a few other women continued to publish fiction, poetry, and opinion pieces for most of the periodical's run; however, it is not clear whether they worked together or simply submitted manuscripts.

34. Title changes complicate references to *Frauenliebe*. In 1930, *Frauenliebe* became *Garçonne*. I use *Frauenliebe* to refer to the periodicals of the Bergmann Verlag.

35. In the records of a censorship hearing, she was identified as Käthe André-Karen. In the periodical she was only Karen. Report of the Leipzig Prüfstelle, 22 May 1931, Geheimes Staatsarchiv Preussischer Kulturbesitz (GSPK), Rep. 77, Tit. 2772, Nr. 3g, Bl. 22.

36. Patrice Petro, *Joyless Streets: Women and Melodramatic Representation in Weimar Germany* (Princeton: Princeton University Press, 1989), 90.

37. *Die Freundin*, 15 October 1924, 1.

38. Kokula, "Interview mit Branda," *Jahre des Glücks*, 95.

39. Fredy Thoma, "Garçonne und ihr Aushängverbot," *Garçonne*, 1931, no. 21, 2.

40. Ikarus, "Autoren-Abend im Dorian Gray," *Garçonne*, 1930, no. 5, 7.

41. "Bericht von der Mitglieder-Versammlung," *Frauenliebe* 3, no. 43 (1928), 5.

42. References to literature and philosophy, as well as sexology, were more frequent.

43. *Die Freundin* published continuously, except for a year on the restricted list, from 1927 until the Nazis closed down the BfM.

44. V. R., "An Jlse Schwarze," *Garçonne*, 1931, no. 1, 7.

45. D., "Sappho-Gedenkfeier," *Garçonne*, 1931, no. 17, 4.

46. Harry Oosterhuis, "Homosexual Emancipation in Germany before 1933: Two Traditions," in *Homosexuality and Male-Bonding in Pre-Nazi Germany*, ed. Harry Oosterhuis and Hubert Kennedy (New York: Harrington Park Press, 1991), 4–5.

47. "Ein Maskenball im Damenklub Violetta, Kolosseum, Kommendantenstraße 62," *Frauenliebe* 2, no. 8 (1927), 3.

48. On Zauberflöte, see Curt Moreck, *Führer*, 144.

49. Kokula, "Lesben in der Nazi-Zeit," *Jahre des Glücks*, 66–72.

50. Lu Bilse, "Apachenball!" *Die Freundin*, 21 October 1931, 5.

51. L. W., "Berlins Damenklub Monbijou," *Frauenliebe* 5, no. 25 (1930), 2.

52. Selli Engler, "V i e l e Stimmen und e i n Ziel," *Die Freundin*, 21 May 1930, 2.

53. G. D., "Bericht von der Mitglieder Versammlung," *Frauenliebe* 3, no. 49 (1928), 5.

54. "Der Verrat des mann-männlichen Damenklub 'Violetta,'" *Frauenliebe* 4, no. 1 (1929), 2.

55. Cover photo, *Die Freundin*, 2 July 1929, 1.

56. Lotte Hahm, "Damenklub 'Monbijou' and Damenklub 'Violetta haben sich vereinigt," *Die Freundin*, 11 September 1929, 2.

57. Selli Engler, "Selli Engler erklärt," *Die Freundin*, 18 September 1929, 3.

58. Advertisement, *Die Freundin*, 11 May 1932, 8.

59. Warner, "Publics and Counterpublics," 88; Lauren Berlant and Elizabeth Freeman, "Queer Nationality," in *The Queen of America Goes to Washington City*, 218–21.

60. Kolb, *The Weimar Republic*, 27, 210–11; His-Huey Liang, *Die Berliner Polizei in der Weimarer Republik* (Berlin: de Gruyter, 1977).

61. Paul Weber, quoting the police decree. "Ausnahmebestimmung gegen Homosexuelle," *Die Freundin*, 12 October 1932, 2.

62. Mel Gordon's titillating reconstruction of lesbian bar culture of the period named eight different "types." Some of his conclusions seem questionable in light of other sources. He also maintains that a general term for female homosexuals was "Hot Sisters," a term I have never encountered elsewhere. Gordon, *Voluptuous Panic*, 104. The regulars in the bar environment likely engaged in their own taxonomic practices parallel to the sexologists. The term *Freundinnen* (girlfriends) was ubiquitous in sources.

63. Elsbeth Killmer, "Zum wahren Volkswohl," *Die Freundin,* 2 October 1929, 2.

64. Elsbeth Killmer, "Aufruf an alle Frauen und Mütter," *Die Freundin,* 23 October 1929, 2.

65. Elsbeth Killmer, "Wahrheiten," *Die Freundin,* 30 October 1929, 2–3.

66. Austrian law criminalized both male and female homosexuality. Lou Steffen and Edith Weymer, "Tanzende Frauen," *Ledige Frauen* 1928, no. 12, 6.

67. Lotte Hahm, "Die lesbische Liebe," *Die Freundin,* 12 February 1930, 2.

68. "Ist Homosexualität ein Laster?" *Frauenliebe* 3, no. 1 (1928), 3–4.

69. Karen, "An Alle (Ein kleines moralisches Traktat)," *Frauenliebe* 3. no. 4 (1928), 3–4.

70. Cläre, "Meinungsaustausch," *Frauenliebe* 3 no. 4 (1928), 8; "Meinungsaustausch," *Frauenliebe* 3, no, 6–10 (1928).

71. A similar series of harshly condemning letters on bisexual women appeared in *Die Freundin.* "There must be a selection process from the very beginning to keep out all shady elements, because bisexual women drag our humanity through the mud. Because these kinds of people are only interested in us as long as they find sensual and material satisfaction." S. S., "Unsere Leserinnen haben das Wort," *Die Freundin,* 4 December 1929, 4. Replies appeared in *Die Freundin,* 8 January, 26 February, and 9 April 1930.

72. Hanni Schulz, "Meinungsaustausch," *Frauenliebe* 3, no. 7 (1928), 8.

73. G. B., "Meinungsaustausch," *Frauenliebe* 3, no. 6 (1928), 8.

74. For example, R. von Krafft-Ebing, *Psychopathia Sexualis, with especial reference to Contrary Sexual Instinct,* trans. Charles Gilbert Chaddock (Philadelphia: F. A. Davis, 1899), 188–232. Karen, "Gedanken über den Vortrag 'Was zieht das Weib zum Weibe,'" *Frauenliebe* 2, no. 43 (1927), 3–4; Cläre, "Meinungsaustausch," *Frauenliebe* 3, no. 12 (1928), 7–8. See Merl Storr, "Transformations: Subjects, Categories and Cures in Krafft-Ebing's Sexology," in *Sexology in Culture: Labeling Bodies and Desires,* ed. Lucy Bland and Laura Doan (Chicago: University of Chicago Press, 1998).

75. Marie Rudolph, "Meinungsaustausch," *Frauenliebe* 3, no. 7 (1928), 8–9.

76. Cläre, "Meinungsaustausch," *Frauenliebe* 3, no. 12 (1928), 7–8.

77. Karen, "Betrifft: Meinungaustausch Cläre," *Frauenliebe* 3, no. 5 (1928), 8.

78. Hortensee [*sic*] Hohensee, "Die lesbische Frau," *Frauenliebe,* 27 October 1926, 2.

79. Annette Eick, "Was Frauen den Weg zum eignen Geschlecht finden läßt," *Frauenliebe* 5, no. 19 (1930), 1–3. For Eick's biography, see Claudia Schoppmann, *Days of Masquerade: Life Stories of Lesbians during the Third Reich* (New York: Columbia University Press, 1996), 102–109, quote on 107. Eick was only twenty-one and one of the younger women among the *Frauenliebe* writers when she wrote the essay.

80. Elsbeth Killmer, "Wahrheiten," *Die Freundin,* 30 October 1929, 2–3.

81. Otto Weininger, *Geschlecht und Charakter* (Munich: Matthes u. Seitz, 1980 repr.).

82. Judy Greenway, "It's What You Do with It That Counts: Interpretations of Otto Weininger," in *Sexology in Culture.*

83. Otto Weininger, "Geschlecht und Charakter: 'Die emancipierte Frau,'" *Die Freundin*, 14 January 1931, 2–3.

84. "Vom Schamgefühl der Frau," *Die Freundin*, 13 August 1930, 2. This lead article was unsigned and unattributed. It used the scientific language of nineteenth-century gender theorists such as Italian anthropologist Paolo Mantegazza. On Mantegazza, see Thomas Medicus, *"Die große Liebe": Ökonomie und Konstruktion der Körper im Werk von Frank Wedekind* (Marburg: Verlag Guttandin u. Hoppe, 1982), 1–15. A 1933 article reiterated the conflation of femininity and eroticism. "For women, the erotic rules the whole being, the thoughts, the deeds." Dr. K., "Die körperliche und seelische Struktur des Homosexuellen," *Die Freundin*, 15 February 1933, 2.

85. Herta Laser, "Was sagt Weininger über die Frau," *Frauenliebe* 2, no. 28 (1927), 3–4. See also Herta Laser, "Über die Einsamkeit," *Frauenliebe* 2, no. 13 (1927), 2.

86. Annette Eick. "Was Frauen den Weg zum eigenen Geschlecht finden läßt," 1–3.

87. Early scholars preferred to write about the politically active Scientific Humanitarian Committee of Magnus Hirschfeld or the literary and militant Adolf Brand and his coterie. They seem to take contemporary criticism of the mass organizations as "just social clubs" with no value for homosexual emancipation at face value.

88. Friedrich Radszuweit, "Die homosexuellen Frauen und unsere Bewegung," *Ledige Frauen* 4, no. 1 (1929), 1–2. Radszuweit's lobbying is documented in Bundesarchiv Deutschland, R30.01, Nr. 5774-5775, Anträge auf Beiseitigung des 175, vol. 2–3.

89. Frevert, *Women in German History*, 174–68; Elizabeth Harvey, "Serving the Volk, Saving the Nation: Women in the Youth Movement and the Public Sphere in Weimar Germany," in Larry Eugene Jones and James Retallack, *Elections, Mass Politics, and Social Change in Modern Germany: New Perspectives* (Cambridge: Cambridge University Press, 1992).

90. Katharina Vogel, "Zum Selbstverständnis lesbischer Frauen in der Weimarer Republik: eine Analyse der Zeitschrift 'Die Freundin' 1924–1933," in *Eldorado: Homosexuelle Frauen und Männer in Berlin 1850–1950: Geschichte, Alltag, Kultur* (Berlin: Edition Hentrich, 1992), 166, 169.

91. Irene von Behlau, "Die homosexuelle Frau und die Reichstagswahl," *Die Freundin*, 14 May 1928, 2.

92. Karen, "Oeffentlicher Brief an die Oberprüfstelle in Leipzig," *Garçonne* 1931, no. 12, 1–2.

93. Childers, "The Social Language of Politics in Germany," 356–57.

94. Rita Volker, "Ein Sapphisches Pamphlet," *Garçonne* 1932, no. 2, 3–6. Emphasis in original.

95. Engler, "V i e l e Stimmen und e i n Ziel." Engler's last nonfiction article in *Die Freundin* harangued her readers to show more political consciousness. She also focused on female masculinity as characteristic of businesswomen, who had "more business talent than normal men." She ridiculed homosexual women who wore

high-heeled shoes and rose-strewn hats to hide their identities. Selli Engler, "An die selbstständigen homosexuellen Frauen!" *Die Freundin,* 8 April 1931, 2.

96. G. Fü., "Worte an meine Mitschwestern," *Frauenliebe* 2, no. 34 (1927), 3.

97. Herta Laser, "Aus der Bewegung," *Frauenliebe* 2, no. 38 (1927), 3–4.

98. Hanna Blumenthal, "Die Stellung des Homoeroten in der Gesellschaft," *Frauenliebe* 2, no. 47 (1927), 3–4. Benedict Friedländer was an antifeminist writer prominent in Brand's publication. Gustav Wynecken and Hans Blüher wrote about pedagogical Eros in education and the youth movement.

99. On education as the site of feminist belonging, see Laura Tate, "The Culture of Literary *Bildung* in the Bourgeois Women's Movement in Imperial Germany," *German Studies Review* 24 (2001).

100. Jürgen Habermas, *The Structural Transformation of the Public Sphere: An Inquiry into a Category or Bourgeois Society,* trans. Thomas Burger (Cambridge: MIT Press, 1989, orig. 1962), 46.

101. Examples are Jim Steakley, *The Homosexual Emancipation Movement in Germany* (New York: Arno Press, 1975) and Hanna Hacker, *Frauen und Freundinnen: Studien zur "weiblichen Homosexualität" am Beispiel Österreich 1870–1938* (Weinheim: Beltz, 1987).

102. Habermas argued that the novel represented and reproduced the private sphere. Habermas, *The Structural Transformation of the Public Sphere,* 50.

103. Selli Engler, "Die Frauen der Bianca Torsten," *Die Freundin* 5, no. 16-6, no. 1 (1929–1930).

104. Engler, "Die Frauen der Bianca Torsten, *Die Freundin,* 16 October 1929, 3.

105. Engler, "Die Frauen der Bianca Torsten, *Die Freundin,* 6 November 1929, 3.

106. Engler, "Die Frauen der Bianca Torsten," *Die Freundin,* 18 December 1929, 4.

107. Marry, an actress whom Bianca meets during the filming of a script she wrote, expresses the cultural ambivalence of the 1920s: "I see so little of naturalness and truth in the studio. . . . All of the lesser aspects are saturated with too much envy of colleagues, too much illusion, with too little pay . . . so that one finally begins to dream about a house in the country, a little garden, and an unmade-up face." Engler, "Die Frauen der Bianca Torsten," *Die Freundin,* 11 December 1929, 5. Blending an outdated ideal with the latest in popular media is characteristic.

108. Engler, "Die Frauen der Bianca Torsten," *Die Freundin,* 6 November 1929, 5.

109. See Irene Hardach-Pinke, "Managing Girls' Sexuality among the German Upper Classes," in *Secret Gardens, Satanic Mills: Placing Girls in European History, 1750–1960,* ed. Mary Jo Maynes, Birgitte Søland, and Christina Benninghaus (Bloomington: Indiana University Press, 2005). For a vivid fictional portrait of inculcation of sexual shame, see Gabriele Reuter, *From a Good Family,* trans. Lynne Tatlock (Rochester, NY: Camden House, 1999).

110. The vulnerability of heterosexual relations is analyzed thoroughly in Kerstin Barndt, *Sentiment und Sachlichkeit: Der Roman der Neuen Frau in der Weimarer Republik* (Cologne: Böhlau, 2003).

111. Ikarus, "Von der Sehnsucht," *Garçonne* 1931, no. 6, 6.

112. See Niklas Luhmann, *Liebe als Passion: zur Codierung von Intimität* (Frankfurt: Suhrkamp, 1982), 172. Many of the puzzling excesses of the homosexual stories match Luhmann's description of love in works from *Sturm und Drang* and German Romanticism—self-torture, oscillation between passion and friendship, the ideal as resolving the paradox of autonomy and submission, the important role of accident or fate, and romantic love as the privileged site of personal happiness and fulfillment.

113. Ikarus, "Von der Sehnsucht."

114. Ikarus, "Gerechtigkeit—und unsere Liebe," *Frauenliebe* 1931, no. 9, 7–8.

115. Ilse Schwarze, "Das Opfer," *Die Freundin*, 5 February 1930, 4–6.

116. "Meinungsaustausch über Tagesfragen: Zusammenleben oder nicht?" *Die Freundin*, 5 September 1927, 6–7. The discussion continued in *Die Freundin* issues 19 September, 3 and 31 October, and 14 November.

117. "Meinungsaustausch über Tagesfragen: Zusammenleben oder nicht?" *Die Freundin*, 3 October 1927, 6.

118. "Meinungsaustausch über Tagesfragen: Zusammenleben oder nicht?" *Die Freundin*, 14 November 1927, 6.

119. Meyer, ed., *Lila Nächte*, 48.

120. Ibid., 55.

121. Käthe Wundram, "Die Treue der maskulinen und der femininen Frau," *Garçonne* 1931 no. 15, 1–2. The debate continued in issues 17, 18, 19, 20, 21, 22, 23, 24, and 26 of 1931 and 1 of 1932.

122. Käthe Wundram, "Kameradschaft und Liebesfreundschaft," *Garçonne* 1931, no. 24, 1–2, quotes on 1. The idea that feminine women were incapable of friendship because of their fickleness and obsession with romantic love was also expressed in an earlier debate on friendship in *Die Freundin*. "Ist die Frau der Freundschaft fähig?" *Die Freundin*, 10 Oktober 1924, 5 (reprinted from Nord Badische Landeszeitung); Maria Ziebarth, "Ist die Frau der Freundschaft fähig?" *Die Freundin*, 1 November 1924, 5.

123. Karen, "Zum Artikel: 'Die Treue der maskulinen und die der femininen Frau,'" *Garçonne* 1931, no. 17, 1.

124. Ilse Schwarze, "Ist Männlichkeit gleichbedeutend mit Intelligenz?" *Garçonne* 1931, no. 20, 1–2.

125. Ilse Schwarze, "Offener Brief an Thea Neumann," *Garçonne* 1931, no. 24, 3.

126. Lo Hilmar, "Treue gehört zur Liebe," *Garçonne* 1931, no. 18, 2.

127. Ibid., 1–2.

128. Thea Neumann, "Diskussion und Widerspruchsgeist," *Garçonne* 1931, no. 22, 1.

129. Karla Mayburg, "Besuchsanzeige," *Garçonne* 1931, nos. 17, 18, 19, and 20.

130. Karla Mayburg, "Besuchsanzeige," *Garçonne* 1931, no. 17, 2.

131. Karla Mayburg, "Männlich—weiblich," *Garçonne* 1931, no. 19, 1–2.

132. Käthe W., "Definition der Liebe," *Garçonne* 1932, no. 4, 3.

133. Kirsten Plötz, "Bubis und Damen: die zwanziger Jahre," in *Butch-Femme: eine Erotische Kultur*, ed. Stephanie Kuhnen (Berlin: Querverlag, 1997); Schader, *Virile, Vamps, und wilde Veilchen*, 102–106; Heike Schader, "Virile homosexuelle

Frauen im Spiegel ihrer Zeitschriften im Berlin der zwanziger Jahre," in *Verqueere Wissenschaft? Zum Verhältnis von Sexualwissenschaft und Sexual Reformbewegung in Geschichte und Gegenwart,* ed. Ursula Ferdinand, Andreas Pretzel, and Andreas Seeck (Münster: LIT, 1998); Heike Schader, "Konstruktionen weiblicher Homosexualität in Zeitschriften homosexueller Frauen in den 1920er Jahre," *Invertito* 2 (2000); Heike Schader analyzed the debate as a two-sided argument between opposed groups within the female homosexual community. Schader provided biographical sketches of the authors in an appendix to *Virile, Vamps und wilde Veilchen,* 236–46.

134. Studies of lesbian relationships in the United States differentiate between middle-class romantic friendship and working-class butch/femme cultures. See Sue Ellen Case, "Toward a Butch-Femme Aesthetic," in *The Lesbian and Gay Studies Reader,* ed. Henry Abelove, Michele Aina Barale, and David Halperin (New York: Routledge, 1993); Leila Rupp, " 'Imagine My Surprise': Women's Relationships in Mid-Twentieth Century America," in *Hidden from History: Reclaiming the Gay and Lesbian Past,* ed. Martin Duberman, George Chauncey Jr., and Martha Vicinus (New York: Meridian 1989), esp. 398.

135. Three of the contributors to the debate, Karen, Käthe Wundram, and Ilse Schwarze, appeared together on the program of a writer's event about a year earlier. Ikarus, "Autoren-Abend im Dorian Gray," *Garçonne* 1930, no. 5, 7.

136. Claudia Schoppmann, *Days of Masquerade,* 139 (Roellig), 109 (Eick), 71, 50–52 (Hahm and homosexual spaces after 1933). Heike Schader, *Virile, Vamps und wilde Veilchen,* 74–76 (Engler), 76–77 (Hahm), 80 (Reinhard), 80–81 (Killmer).

137. Claudia Schoppmann, *Days of Masquerade,* 45–47. "Johnny" remembered Dr. Hilde Lemke as being in her early forties and having "black hair cut in a man's hairstyle." "She was married, had two children, but she also had a girlfriend on the side."

Conclusion

1. For an exploration of marginality in German history, see Neil Gregor, Nils Roemer, and Mark Roseman, eds., *German History from the Margins* (Bloomington: Indiana University Press, 2006). Emancipated middle-class women are marginal in a different way than minorities, living and having been socialized in the "center."

2. Carroll Smith-Rosenberg, "Discourses of Sexuality and Subjectivity: The New Woman, 1870–1936," in *Hidden from History: Reclaiming the Gay and Lesbian Past,* ed. Martin Duberman, Martha Vicinus, and George Chauncey Jr. (New York: Penguin/Meridian, 1989).

3. On the continuing strength of natalism in the Weimar period, see Erik Jensen, *Body by Weimar: Athletes, Gender, and German Modernity* (Oxford: Oxford University Press, 2010).

4. Michael Warner, "Publics and Counterpublics," *Public Culture* 14 (2002).

5. Adele Meyer, ed., *Lila Nächte: Die Damenklubs im Berlin der zwanziger Jahre* (Berlin: Edition Lit.Europe, 1994), 48, 55.

6. See Dagmar Herzog, *Sex After Fascism: Memory and Morality in Twentieth Century Germany* (Princeton: Princeton University Press, 2005).

Bibliography

Archival Sources

Bundesarchiv Berlin
Justiz Ministerium R 3001, No. 5773-5915, 6330-6348
  Pressestelle R 8034 II, No. 6965-6966
Bundesarchiv Filmarchiv, Berlin
  "Film Zd: 15.09.1928." 1928. (Women Police)
  "Film Zd: 17.06.29." 1929. (Women Police)
Landesarchiv Berlin
  Polizei Präsidium A Pr. Br. Rep. 030, Tit. 121, Nr. 16965; Tit. 185, Nr. 20431;
    Acc. 3981, Nr. 1094, A Pr. Br. Rep. 031–03
  Helene Lange Archiv No. 6, 25, 45–46, 62, 88
Geheimes Staatsarchiv Preußischer Kulturbesitz (Berlin)
  Ministerium des Innern HA I, Rep. 77, Tit. 2772, Nr. 2–8, 11; Tit. 423
Institut für Stadtgeschichte Frankfurt
  Personalakten 52.667
Staatsarchiv Hamburg
  Disziplinärkammer, D 8/32, Bd. 1–17
Senatsakten Fasc. 5–5b
  Polizeibehörde, No. 314, 338
  Polizei Personalakten, No. 316.1, 316.2
  Staatliche Pressestelle, No. 4011, 4031
Stadtarchiv München
  Polizeidirektion, Nr. 397 (348)
Staatsarchiv München
  Oberbayern Kammer des Innern, RA Fasz. 3795 Nr. 57852, 57851
  München Polizeidirektion, Nr. 520, No. 592, No. 7419

Selected Periodicals

Frauenliebe (1926–1930)
Die Freundin (1924, 1927–1933)

Garçonne, die Junggesellin (1930–32)
Große Glocke (1906–1922)
Ledige Frauen (1928–29)

Selected Published and Manuscript Sources

Ackers, Maximiliane. *Freundinnen: Ein Roman unter Frauen.* Maroldsweisach: Feministischer Buchverlag, 1995.

Albisetti, James. *Schooling German Girls and Women: Secondary and Higher Education in the Nineteenth Century.* Princeton: Princeton University Press, 1988.

Allen, Ann Taylor. *Feminism and Motherhood in Germany, 1800–1914.* New Brunswick: Rutgers University Press, 1991.

———. "Mothers of the New Generation: Adele Schreiber, Helene Stöcker and the Evolution of a German Idea of Motherhood, 1900–1914." *Signs* 10 (1985): 418–38.

Althusser, Louis. "Ideology and Ideological State Apparatuses (Notes Toward an Investigation)." In *Lenin and Philosophy and Other Essays,* translated by Ben Brewster, 127–86. New York: Monthly Review Press, 1971.

Anderson, Susan C. "Otto Weininger's Masculine Utopia." *German Studies Review* 19 (1996): 433–53.

Andreas-Salomé, Lou. *The Human Family.* Edited by Raleigh Whitinger. Lincoln: University of Nebraska Press, 2005.

———. "Ketzereien gegen die moderne Frau." *Die Zukunft* 7 (1898–99): 237–40.

———. *Looking Back: Memoirs.* Translated by Breon Mitchell. Edited by Ernst Pfeiffer. New York: Marlow, 1995.

Ankum, Katharina von, ed. *Women in the Metropolis: Gender and Modernity in Weimar Culture.* Berkeley: University of California Press, 1997.

Asenieff, Elsa. *Aufruhr der Weiber und das dritte Geschlecht.* Leipzig: W. Friedrich, 1898.

Augspurg, Anita. "Reformgedanken zur Sexuellen Moral." In *Ehe? Zur Reform der sexuellen Moral,* 19–35. Berlin: Internationale Verlagsanstalt für Kunst und Literatur, 1911.

———. "Ein typischer Fall der Gegenwart [gesetzliche oder freie Ehe] Offener Brief." In *Frauen und Sexualmoral,* edited by Marielouise Janssen-Jurreit, 101–107. Frankfurt: Fischer Taschenbuch Verlag, 1986.

B., F. "Was heißt widernatürliche Unzucht beim weiblichen Geschlecht?" *Geschlecht und Gesellschaft* 6 (1911): 269–76.

Barck, Lothar. *Ziele und Aufgaben der weiblichen Polizei in Deutschland.* Berlin: Deutscher Polizei-Verlag, 1928.

Barndt, Kerstin. "Frauen-Litteratur um 1900." Paper presented at the annual meeting for the German Studies Association, Atlanta, Georgia, October 4–7, 1999.

———. *Sentiment und Sachlichkeit: Der Roman der neuen Frau in der Weimarer Republik.* Cologne: Böhlau, 2003.

Bäumer, Gertrud. "Schicksalsfragen der weiblichen Polizei." *Vossische Zeitung*, July 18, 1931.

Baumgart, Manfred. "Die homosexuellen Bewegung bis zum Ende des ersten Weltkriegs." In *Eldorado: Homosexuelle Frauen Und Männer in Berlin, 1850–1950: Geschichte, Alltag, und Kultur*, 17–27. Berlin: Edition Hentrich, 1992.

Bechly, Friedrich. "Über die Ausdehnung des Homosexualitäts-Paragraphen (§175) auf die Frau." *Sexualreform: Beiblatt zu "Geschlecht und Gesellschaft"* (1911).

Bennett, Judith M. "'Lesbian-Like' and the Social History of Lesbianism." *Journal of the History of Sexuality* 9 (2000): 1–24.

Benninghaus, Christina. *Die andere Jügendlichen: Arbeitermädchen in der Weimarer Republik*. Frankfurt: Campus Verlag, 1999.

Berlant, Lauren. *The Queen of America Goes to Washington City: Essays on Sex and Citizenship*. Durham: Duke University Press, 1997.

———, and Elizabeth Freeman. "Queer Nationality." In Lauren Berlant, *The Queen of America Goes to Washington City: Essays on Sex and Citizenship*, 145–73. Durham: Duke University Press, 1997.

———, and Michael Warner. "Sex in Public." *Critical Inquiry* 24 (1998): 547–66.

Bhabha, Homi. "Of Mimicry and Man: The Ambivalence of Colonial Discourse." In *Tensions of Empire: Colonial Cultures in a Bourgeois World*, edited by Frederick Cooper and Ann Laura Stoler, 152–60. Berkeley: University of California Press, 1997.

Binion, Rudolph. *Frau Lou: Nietzsche's Wayward Disciple*. Princeton: Princeton University Press, 1968.

Blackbourn, David. "The *Mittelstand* in German Society and Politics 1871–1914." *Social History* 2 (1977): 409–33.

Blackbourn, David, and Geoff Eley. *The Peculiarities of German History: Bourgeois Society and Politics in Nineteenth Century Germany*. Oxford: Oxford University Press, 1984.

Bland, Lucy, and Laura Doan, eds. *Sexology in Culture: Labelling Bodies and Desires*. Chicago: University of Chicago Press, 1998.

Bosch, Mineke, with Annemarie Kloosterman, ed. *Politics and Friendship: Letters from the International Woman Suffrage Alliance, 1902–1942*. Columbus: Ohio State University Press, 1990.

Brentjes, Sonja, and Karl-Heinz Schlote. "Zum Frauenstudium an der Universität Leipzig in der Zeit von 1870 bis 1910." *Jahrbuch für Regionalgeschichte und Landeskunde* 19 (1993): 57–75.

Bridenthal, Renate, Atina Grossmann, and Marion Kaplan, eds. *When Biology Became Destiny: Women in Weimar and Nazi Germany*. New York: Monthly Review Press, 1984.

Bristow, Joseph. "Remapping the Sites of Modern Gay History: Legal Reform, Medico-Legal Thought, Homosexual Scandal, Erotic Geography." *Journal of British Studies* 46 (2007): 116–43.

———. "Symonds's History, Ellis's Heredity: *Sexual Inversion.*" In *Sexology in Culture: Labelling Bodies and Desires,* edited by Lucy Bland and Laura Doan, 79–99. Chicago: University of Chicago Press, 1998.

Bruns, Brigitte. "Das dritte Geschlecht von Ernst von Wolzogen." In *Hof-Atelier Elvira, 1887–1928: Ästheten, Emanzen, Aristokraten,* edited by Rudolf Herz and Brigitte Bruns, 171–90. Munich: Münchener Stadtmuseum, 1985.

———. "Weibliche Avantgarde um 1900." In *Hof-Atelier Elvira, 1887–1928: Ästheten, Emanzen, Aristokraten,* edited by Rudolf Herz and Brigitte Bruns, 191–219. Munich: Münchener Stadtmuseum, 1985.

Bülow, Frieda von. "Männerurtheil über Frauendichtung," *Die Zukunft* 7, no. 26 (1898–99): 26–29.

———. *Die schönsten Novellen der Frieda von Bülow über Lou Andreas-Salomé und andere Frauen.* Edited by Sabine Streiter. Frankfurt: Ullstein Taschenbuch, 1990.

Butler, Judith. *Bodies That Matter: On the Discursive Limits of "Sex."* New York: Routledge, 1993.

———. *Gender Trouble: Feminism and the Subversion of Identity.* New York: Routledge, 1999.

———. "Imitation and Gender Insubordination." In *Inside/Out: Lesbian Theories, Gay Theories,* edited by Diana Fuss, 13–31. New York: Routledge, 1991.

Calhoun, Cheshire. "The Gender Closet: Lesbian Disappearance under the Sign 'Woman.'" In *Lesbian Subjects: A Feminist Studies Reader,* edited by Martha Vicinus, 209–32. Bloomington: Indiana University Press, 1996.

Calhoun, Craig, ed. *Habermas and the Public Sphere.* Cambridge: MIT Press, 1992.

Canning, Kathleen. "Claiming Citizenship: Suffrage and Subjectivity in Germany after the First World War." In *Gender History in Practice: Historical Perspectives on Bodies, Class, and Citizenship,* 212–37. Ithaca: Cornell University Press, 2006.

———. "Gender History: Meanings, Methods, and Metanarratives." In *Gender History in Practice: Historical Perspectives on Bodies, Class, and Citizenship,* 3–62. Ithaca: Cornell University Press, 2006.

Case, Sue-Ellen. "Toward a Butch-Femme Aesthetic." In *The Lesbian and Gay Studies Reader,* edited by Henry Abelove, Michele Aina Barale and David Halperin, 294–306. New York: Routledge, 1993.

Castle, Terry. *The Apparitional Lesbian: Female Homosexuality and Modern Culture.* New York: Columbia University Press, 1993.

Chauncey, George. "From Sexual Inversion to Homosexuality: Medicine and the Changing Conceptualization of Female Deviance." *Salmagundi* 58–59 (1983): 114–46.

———. *Gay New York: Gender, Urban Culture, and the Making of the Gay Male World, 1890–1940.* New York: Basic Books, 1994.

Chickering, Roger. "'Casting Their Gaze More Broadly': Women's Patriotic Activism in Imperial Germany." *Past & Present* 118 (1988): 156–85.

Childers, Thomas. "The Social Language of Politics in Germany: The Sociology of Political Discourse in the Weimar Republic." *American Historical Review* 95 (1990): 331–58.

Choquette, Leslie. "Paris-Lesbos: Lesbian Social Space in the Modern City, 1870–1940." *Proceedings of the Western Society for French History* 26 (1998): 122–32.

Dauthendey, Elisabeth. *Vom neuen Weibe und seiner Liebe: Ein Buch für reifer Geister.* Berlin: Schuster u. Loeffler, 1901.

Dickinson, Edward Ross. "Dominion of the Spirit over the Flesh: Religion, Gender and Sexual Morality in the German Women's Movement before World War I." *Gender & History* 17 (2005): 378–408.

Delap, Lucy. *The Feminist Avant-Garde: Transatlantic Encounters of the Early Twentieth Century.* Cambridge: Cambridge University Press, 2007.

Diethe, Carol. *Nietzsche's Women: Beyond the Whip.* Berlin: Walter de Gruyter, 1996.

Doan, Laura. " 'Acts of Female Indecency': Sexology's Intervention in Legislating Lesbianism." In *Sexology and Culture: Labelling Bodies and Desires,* edited by Lucy Bland and Laura Doan, 199–213. Chicago: University of Chicago Press, 1998.

———. *Fashioning Sapphism: The Origins of a Modern English Lesbian Culture.* New York: Columbia University Press, 2001.

———. "Topsy-Turvydom: Gender Inversion, Sapphism, and the Great War." *GLQ: A Journal of Lesbian and Gay Studies* 14 (2006): 517–42.

Dobler, Jens. "Zensur von Büchern und Zeitschriften mit homosexueller Thematik in der Weimarer Republik." *Invertito* 2 (2000): 85–104.

Donoghue, Emma. *Passions between Women: British Lesbian Culture, 1668–1801.* London: Scarlet Press, 1993.

Duberman, Martin, Martha Vicinus, and George Chauncey Jr. "Introduction." In *Hidden from History: Reclaiming the Gay and Lesbian Past,* edited by Martin Duberman, Martha Vicinus, and George Chauncey Jr., 1–13. New York: Meridian, 1989.

Duc, Aimée [Minna Wettstein-Adelt]. *Sind es Frauen? Roman über das dritte Geschlecht.* Berlin: Amazonen Frauenverlag, 1976.

Duensing, Frieda. *Frieda Duensing: Ein Buch der Erinnerung.* Edited by Marie Baum, Ricarda Huch, Ludwig Curtius, and Anton Erkelenz. Berlin: F. A. Herbig, 1926.

Duggan, Lisa. "The Trials of Alice Mitchell: Sensationalism, Sexology, and the Lesbian Subject in Turn-of-the-Century America." *Signs: Journal of Women in Culture and Society* 18 (1993): 791–814.

Elberskirchen, Johanna. *Geschlechtsleben und Geschlechtsenthaltsamkeit des Weibes.* Munich: Seltz und Schauer, 1905.

———. *Die Liebe des dritten Geschlechts: Homosexualität, eine bisexuellen Varietät; Keine Entartung, keine Schuld.* Leipzig: Spohr Verlag, 1904.

———. *Was hat der Mann aus Weib, Kind und sich gemacht: Revolution und Erlösung des Weibes: Eine Abrechnung mit dem Mann, ein Wegweiser in die Zukunft!* Leipzig: Magazin Verlag, 1904.

Eldorado: Homosexuelle Frauen und Männer in Berlin, 1850–1950: Geschichte, Alltag und Kultur. Berlin: Edition Hentrich, 1992.

Eley, Geoff. "How and Where Is German History Centered?" In *German History from the Margins,* edited by Neil Gregor, Nils Roemer and Mark Roseman, 268–86. Bloomington: Indiana University Press, 2006.

————. "Politics, Culture, and the Public Sphere." *positions* 10 (2002): 219–36.

————. *Reshaping the German Right: Radical Nationalism and Political Change after Bismarck.* Ann Arbor: University of Michigan Press, 1991.

Erkens, Josefine. "Entwicklung und Aufgabengebiete der deutschen Frauenpolizei." *Deutsche Zeitschrift für Wohlfahrtspflege* (1928): 398–401.

————. "Kriminalpolizei und soziale Gerichtshilfe." *Kriminalistische Monatshefte* 2 (1928): 193–96.

————. "Personlichkeit und Ausbildung der Polizeibeamtin." *Arbeit und Beruf* (1927): 242–44.

————. *Weibliche Polizei: Ihr Werden, ihre Ziele und Arbeitsformen als Ausdruck eines neuen Wollens auf dem Gebiete der Polizei.* Lübeck: Deutscher Polizei-Verlag, 1925.

Ewing, E. Thomas. "Personal Acts with Public Meanings: Suicides by Soviet Women Teachers in the Early Stalin Era." *Gender & History* 14 (2002): 117–37.

Faderman, Lillian. *Surpassing the Love of Men: Romantic Friendship and Love between Women from the Renaissance to the Present.* New York: William Morrow, 1981.

————, and Brigitte Ericksson, eds. *Lesbians in Germany: 1890's–1920's.* Tallahassee: Naiad, 1980.

Fairchild, Erika S. "Women Police in Weimar: Professionalism, Politics, and Innovations in Police Organizations." *Law & Society Review* 21 (1987): 375–402.

Ferdinand, Ursula, Andreas Pretzel, and Andreas Seeck, eds. *Verqueere Wissenschaft? Zum Verhältnis von Sexualwissenschaft und Sexualreformbewegung in Geschichte und Gegenwart.* Münster: LIT Verlag, 1998.

"Fluch, Vergnügen oder . . . ? Facetten weiblicher Homosexualität." Special Issue. *Ariadne: Almanach des Archivs der deutschen Frauenbewegung* 29 (1996).

Foucault, Michel. *The History of Sexuality,* Vol. 1 *An Introduction.* Translated by Robert Hurley. New York: Vintage, 1990.

Fout, John C. "Sexual Politics in Wilhelmine Germany: The Male Gender Crisis, Moral Purity, and Homophobia." *Journal of the History of Sexuality* 2 (1992): 388–421.

Frame, Lynne. "Gretchen, Girl, Garçonne? Weimar Science and Popular Culture in Search of the Ideal New Woman." In *Women in the Metropolis: Gender and Modernity in Weimar Culture,* edited by Katharina von Ankum, 12–40. Berkeley: University of California Press, 1997.

Fraser, Nancy. "What's Critical About Critical Theory? The Case of Habermas and Gender." In *Feminism as Critique: On the Politics of Gender,* edited by Seyla Benhabib and Drucilla Cornell, 31–56. Minneapolis: University of Minnesota Press, 1987.

Freunde eines Schwulen-Museums in Berlin, ed. *Die Geschichte des Paragraph 175: Strafrecht gegen Homosexuelle. Katalog zur Ausstellung in Berlin und in Frankfurt am Main.* Berlin: Rosa Winkel, 1990.

Frevert, Ute. "Vom Klavier zur Schreibmaschine: Weiblicher Arbeitsmarkt und Rollenzuweisungen am Beispiel der weiblichen Angestellten in der Weimarer Republik." In *Frauen in der Geschichte,* edited by Annette Kuhn and Gerhard Schneider, 82–112. Düsseldorf: Schwann, 1979.

————. *Women in German History: From Bourgeois Emancipation to Sexual Liberation.* Translated by Stuart McKinnon-Evans. New York: Berg, 1989.

Fritz, Helmut. *Die erotische Rebellion: Das Leben der Franziska Gräfin zu Reventlow.* Frankfurt: Fischer Taschenbuch Verlag, 1980.

Fritzsche, Peter. "Did Weimar Fail?" *Journal of Modern History* 68 (1996): 629–56.

Gagnier, Regenia. *Subjectivities: A History of Self-Representation in Britain, 1832–1920.* New York: Oxford, 1991.

Garber, Marjorie. *Vested Interests: Cross-dressing and Cultural Anxiety.* New York: Routledge, 1997.

Goodbye to Berlin? 100 Jahre Schwulenbewegung. Berlin: Rosa Winkel, 1997.

Gordon, Mel. *Voluptuous Panic: The Erotic World of Weimar Berlin.* Venice, CA: Feral House, 2000.

Göttert, Margit. "'Chloe liebt Olivia . . .': Frauenbeziehungen als Gegenstand historischer Forschung." In *Frauengeschichte: Gesucht—Gefunden?Auskunft zum Stand der historischen Frauenforschung,* edited by Beate Fieseler und Birgit Schulze, 92–111. Cologne: Böhlau, 1991.

————. *Macht und Eros: Frauenbeziehungen und weibliche Kultur um 1900: eine neue Perspektive auf Helene Lange und Gertrud Bäumer.* Königstein/Taunus: Ulrike Helmer Verlag, 2000.

————. "Zwischen Betroffenheit, Abscheu und Sympathie: Die alte Frauenbewegung und das 'heikle Thema' Homosexualität." *Ariadne* 29 (1996): 14–21.

Gregor, Neil, Nils Roemer, and Mark Roseman. "Introduction." In *German History from the Margins,* edited by Neil Gregor, Nils Roemer and Mark Roseman, 1–26. Bloomington: Indiana University Press, 2006.

Grossmann, Atina. "Girlkultur or Thoroughly Rationalized Female: A New Woman in Weimar Germany?" In *Women in Culture and Politics: A Century of Change,* edited by Judith Friedlander, Blanche W. Cook, Alice Kessler-Harris, and Carroll Smith-Rosenberg, 62–80. Bloomington: Indiana University Press, 1986.

————. "The New Woman and the Rationalization of Sexuality in Weimar Germany." In *Powers of Desire: The Politics of Sexuality,* edited by Ann Snitow, Christine Stansell, and Sharon Thompson, 153–71. New York: Monthly Review Press, 1983.

Habermas, Jürgen. *The Structural Transformation of the Public Sphere: An Inquiry into a Category of Bourgeois Society.* Translated by Thomas Burger. Cambridge: MIT Press, 1989.

Hacker, Hanna. "Eigensinn und Doppelsinn in frauenbezogenen und lesbischen literarischen Texten österreichischer Autorinnen 1900-1939." *Kulturjahrbuch* 2 (1983): 264–81.

————. *Frauen und Freundinnen: Studien zur "weiblichen Homosexualität" am Beispiel Österreich 1870–1938.* Weinheim: Beltz, 1987.

Hackett, Amy. "Helene Stöcker: Left-Wing Intellectual and Sex Reformer." In *When Biology Became Destiny: Women in Weimar and Nazi Germany,* edited by Atina Grossmann, Renate Bridenthal, and Marion Kaplan, 109–30. New York: Monthly Review Press, 1984.

———. "The Politics of Feminism in Wilhelmine Germany." PhD diss., Columbia University, 1976.

Halberstam, Judith. *Female Masculinity*. Durham: Duke University Press, 1998.

Hallett, Nicky. *Lesbian Lives: Identity and Auto/Biography in the Twentieth Century*. London: Pluto Press, 1999.

Hammer, Wilhelm. *Die Tribadie Berlins: Zehn Fälle weibweiblicher Geschlechtsliebe aktenmäßig dargestellt nebst zehn Abhandlungen über die gleichgeschlechtliche Frauenliebe*. Berlin: Verlag Hermann Seemann, 1906(?).

Hardach-Pinke, Irene. "Managing Girls' Sexuality among the German Upper Classes." In *Secret Gardens, Satanic Mills: Placing Girls in European History, 1750–1960*, edited by Mary Jo Maynes, Birgitte Søland, and Christina Benninghaus, 101–14. Bloomington: Indiana University Press, 2005.

Hark, Sabine. *Deviante Subjekte: Die paradoxe Politik der Identität*. Opladen: Leske u. Budrich, 1996.

Harris, Victoria. *Selling Sex in the Reich: Prostitutes in German Society, 1914–1945*. Oxford: Oxford University Press, 2010.

Harvey, Elizabeth. "The Failure of Feminism? Young Women and the Bourgeois Feminist Movement in Weimar Germany, 1918–1933." *Central European History* 28 (1995): 1–28.

———. "Serving the Volk, Saving the Nation: Women in the Youth Movement and the Public Sphere in Weimar Germany." In *Elections, Mass Politics, and Social Change in Modern Germany*, edited by Larry Eugene Jones and James Retallack, 201–21. Cambridge: Cambridge University Press, 1992.

———. "Visions of the Volk: German Women and the Far Right from Kaiserreich to Third Reich." *Journal of Women's History* 16 (2004): 152–69.

Hausen, Karin. "Family and Role-Division: The Polarization of Sexual Stereotypes in the Nineteenth Century." In *The German Family: Essays on the Social History of the Family in Nineteenth and Twentieth Century Germany*, edited by Richard J. Evans and W. R. Lee. Totowa, NJ: Barnes and Noble, 1981.

Haustedt, Birgit. *Die wilden Jahre in Berlin: Eine Klatsch- und Kulturgeschichte der Frauen*. Dortmund: Edition Ebersbach, 1999.

Hekma, Gert. "A Female Soul in a Male Body: Sexual Inversion as Gender Inversion in Nineteenth Century Sexology." In *Third Sex, Third Gender: Beyond Sexual Dimorphism in Culture and History*, edited by Gilbert Herdt, 213–39. New York: Zone Books, 1994.

Henckmann, Gisela, ed. *Werde die du bist! Zwischen Anpassung und Selbstbestimmung: Texte deutschsprachiger Schriftstellerinnen des 19. Jahrhunderts*. Munich: Goldmann Verlag, 1993.

Herz, Rudolf. "Das Fotoatelier Elvira (1887–1928): Seine Fotografinnen, seine Kundschaft, seine Bilder." In *Hof-Atelier Elvira, 1887–1928: Ästheten, Emanzen, Aristokraten*, edited by Rudolf Herz and Brigitte Bruns, 63–127. Munich: Münchener Stadtmuseum, 1985.

———, and Brigitte Bruns, eds. *Hof-Atelier Elvira, 1887–1928: Ästheten, Emanzen, Aristokraten*. Munich: Münchener Stadtmuseum, 1985.

Herzer, Manfred. "Adolf Brand und *Der Eigene*." In *Goodbye to Berlin? 100 Jahre Schwulenbewegung*, 49–53. Berlin: Rosa Winkel, 1997.

———. "Dichtung und Wahrheit der Berliner Schwulen im ersten Jahrhundertdrittel." In *Eldorado: Homosexuelle Frauen und Männer in Berlin, 1850–1950: Geschichte, Alltag, und Kultur*, 97–101. Berlin: Edition Hentrich, 1992.

———. "Das Jahr 1869." In *Eldorado: Homosexuelle Frauen und Männer in Berlin, 1850–1950: Geschichte, Alltag und Kultur*, 10–12. Berlin: Edition Hentrich, 1992.

———. "Das Wissenschaftlich-humanitäre Komitee." In *Goodbye to Berlin? 100 Jahre Schwulenbewegung*, 37–48. Berlin: Rosa Winkel, 1997.

Herzog, Dagmar. *Sex after Fascism: Memory and Morality in Twentieth Century Germany*. Princeton: Princeton University Press, 2005.

Heymann, Lida Gustava, and Anita Augspurg. *Erlebtes—Erschautes: Deutsche Frauen kämpfen für Freiheit, Recht und Frieden, 1850–1940*. Edited by Margit Twellmann. Meisenheim am Glan: Verlag Anton Hain, 1972.

Hirschfeld, Magnus. *Berlins drittes Geschlecht*. Berlin: Hermann Seemann's Nachfolger, 1905.

———. *Was soll das Volk vom dritten Geschlecht wissen? Eine Aufklärungsschrift über gleichgeschlechtlich (homosexuell) empfindende Menschen*. Leipzig: Max Spohr Verlag, 1901.

Hong, Young Sun. "Femininity as a Vocation: Gender and Class Conflict in the Professionalization of German Social Work." In *The German Professions, 1800–1950*, edited by Geoffrey Cocks and Konrad H. Jarausch, 251–98. New York: Oxford University Press, 1990.

———. *Welfare Modernity and the Weimar State*. Princeton: Princeton University Press, 1998.

Huch, Ricarda. *Erinnerung an das eigenen Leben*. Cologne: Kiepenheuer u. Witsch, 1980.

———. *Frühling in der Schweiz: Jugenderinnerungen*. Zurich: Atlantis Verlag, 1938.

Isherwood, Christopher. *Berlin Stories*. New York: New Directions, 1935.

———. *Christopher and His Kind, 1929–1939*. New York: Farrar, Straus, and Giroux, 1976.

Jagose, Annemarie. *Queer Theory: An Introduction*. New York: New York University Press, 1996.

Janssen-Jurreit, Marielouise, ed. *Frauen und Sexualmoral*. Frankfurt: Fischer Taschenbuch Verlag, 1986.

Jeffreys, Sheila. *The Spinster and Her Enemies: Feminism and Sexuality, 1880–1930*. London: Pandora, 1985.

Jelavich, Peter. *Berlin Cabaret*. Cambridge: Harvard University Press, 1993.

———. *Munich and Theatrical Modernism: Politics, Playwriting, and Performance, 1890–1914*. Cambridge: Harvard University Press, 1985.

Jensen, Erik N. *Body by Weimar: Athletes, Gender, and German Modernity*. New York: Oxford, 2010.

Kennedy, Elizabeth Lapovsky, and Madeline Davis. *Boots of Leather, Slippers of Gold: The History of a Lesbian Community*. New York: Routledge, 1993.

Kennedy, Hubert. "Karl Heinrich Ulrichs: First Theorist of Homosexuality." In *Science and Homosexualities*, edited by Vernon Rosario, 26–45. New York: Routledge, 1997.

Kleemann, Elisabeth. *Zwischen symbolischer Rebellion und politischer Revolution: Studien zur deutschen Boheme zwischen Kaiserreich und Weimarer Republik—Else Lasker-Schüler, Franziska Gräfin Reventlow, Frank Wedekind, Ludwig Derleth, Arthur Moeller van den Bruck, Hanns Johst, Erich Mühsam*. Frankfurt: Verlag Peter Lang, 1985.

Kokula, Ilse. *Jahre des Glücks, Jahre des Leids: Gespräche mit älteren lesbischen Frauen: Dokumente*. Kiel: Frühlings Erwachen, 1986.

———. "Lesbisch Leben von Weimar bis zur Nachkriegzeit." In *Eldorado: Homosexuelle Frauen und Männer in Berlin 1850–1950: Geschichte, Alltag, und Kultur*, 149–61. Berlin: Edition Hentrich, 1992.

———. *Weibliche Homosexualität um 1900 in zeitgenössischen Dokumenten*. Munich: Frauenoffensive, 1981.

Krüger, Hanna. *Die unbequeme Frau: Käthe Schirmacher im Kampf für die Freiheit der Frau und die Freiheit der Nation, 1865–1930*. Berlin: Hans Bott Verlag, 1936.

Krukenberg, Elspeth. "Paragraph 175." *Monatschrift für Kriminalpsychologie und Strafrechtsreform* 7 (1911): 612.

Krukenberg-Conze, Elspeth. *Über Studium und Universitätsleben der Frauen*. Gebhardshagen: J. H. Maurer-Greiner Nachf., 1903.

Lehmstedt, Mark. *Bücher für das dritte Geschlecht: Der Max Spohr Verlag in Leipzig: Verlagsgeschichte und Bibliographie (1881–1941)*. Wiesbaden: Harrassowitz, 2001.

Lembeck, Elisabeth. *Frauenarbeit bei Vater Staat: Weibliche Behördenangestellte in der Weimarer Republik*. Pfaffenweiler: Centaurus, 1993.

Lengerke, Christiane von. " 'Homosexuelle Frauen': Tribaden, Freundinnen, Urninden." In *Eldorado: Homosexuelle Frauen und Männer in Berlin 1850–1950: Geschichte, Alltag, und Kultur*, 125–48. Berlin: Edition Hentrich, 1992.

Lenman, Robin. "Art, Society, and the Law in Wilhelmine Germany: The Lex Heinze," *Oxford German Studies* 8 (1974): 86–113.

———. "Politics and Culture: The State and the Avant-garde in Munich, 1886–1914." In *Society and Politics in Wilhelmine Germany*, edited by Richard Evans, 91–111. London: Croom Helm, 1978.

Lesbengeschichte. Website, edited by Ingeborg Boxhammer and Christiane Leidinger. Accessed June 18, 2012. http://www.lesbengeschichte.de.

Leuenberger, Robert. "Politik und Wissenschaft in der Anfangzeit der Zürcher Universität." *Schweizer Monatshefte: Zeitschrift für Politik, Wirtschaft und Kultur* 61 (1981): 579–84.

Levine, Phillippa. " 'Walking the Streets in a Way No Decent Woman Should': Women Police in World War I." *Journal of Modern History* 66 (1994): 34–78.

Liang, His-Huey. *Die Berliner Polizei in der Weimarer Republik*. Berlin: DeGruyter, 1977.

Lindemann, Renate. *100 Jahre Verein für Fraueninteressen*. Munich: Verein für Fraueninteressen, 1994.

Luhmann, Niklas. *Liebe als Passion: Zur Codierung von Intimität.* Frankfurt: Suhrkamp, 1982.

Mak, Geertje. "Hirschfeld und Transvestitinnen: Warum es nie etwas geworden ist zwischen Frauen in Männerkleidung und der Sexualwissenschaft." In *100 Jahre Schwulenbewegung,* edited by Manfred Herzer, 157–69. Berlin: Verlag Rosa Winkel, 1998.

———. "Sandor/Sarolta Vay: From Passing Woman to Sexual Invert." *Journal of Women's History* 16 (2004): 54–77.

Marcus, Sharon. *Between Women: Friendship, Desire, and Marriage in Victorian England.* Princeton: Princeton University Press, 2007.

Martin, Biddy. "Sexual Practice and Changing Lesbian Identities." In *Destabilizing Theory: Contemporary Feminist Debates,* edited by Michele Barrett and Anne Phillips, 93–119. Stanford: Stanford University Press, 1992.

———. "Sexualities without Genders and Other Queer Utopias." *Diacritics* 24 (1994): 104–21.

———. *Woman and Modernity: The (Life)Styles of Lou Andreas-Salomé.* Ithaca: Cornell University Press, 1991.

Martin, Luther H., Huck Gutman, and Patrick Hutton, eds. *Technologies of the Self: A Seminar with Michel Foucault.* Amherst: University of Massachusetts Press, 1988.

Matysik, Tracie. *Reforming the Moral Subject: Ethics and Sexuality in Central Europe, 1890–1930.* Ithaca: Cornell University Press, 2008.

Mazón, Patricia. *Gender and the Modern Research University: The Admission of Women to German Higher Education, 1865–1914.* Stanford: Stanford University Press, 2003.

McCormick, Richard W. *Gender and Sexuality in Weimar Modernity: Film, Literature, and the "New Objectivity."* New York: Palgrave, 2001.

Medicus, Thomas. *"Die große Liebe," Ökonomie und Konstruktion der Körper im Werke von Frank Wedekind.* Marburg: Verlag Guttandin u. Hoppe, 1982.

Mensch, Ella. *Auf Vorposten: Roman aus meiner Züricher Studentenzeit.* Leipzig: Verlag der Frauenrundschau, 1903.

———. *Bildstürmer in der Berliner Frauenbewegung.* Berlin: Hermann Seemann Nachfolger, 1906.

Meyer, Adele, ed. *Lila Nächte: Die Damenklubs im Berlin der zwanziger Jahre.* Berlin: Edition Lit.Europe, 1994.

Meyer-Renschhausen, Elisabeth. "Die Männerhaß der Polizeimatronen." In *Dokumentation 4. Historikerinnentreffen,* 240–65. Berlin: Technische Universität Berlin, 1983.

———. "Zur Geschichte der Gefühle: Das Reden von 'Scham' und 'Ehre' innerhalb der Frauenbewegung um die Jahrhundertwende." In *Unter allen Umständen: Frauengeschichte(N) in Berlin,* edited by Christiane Eifert and Susanne Rouette, 99–122. Berlin: Rotation Verlag, 1986.

Micheler, Stefan. "Kampf, Kontakt, Kultur: Die Freundschaftsverbände gleichgeschlechtlich begehrender Männer und Frauen in der Weimarer Republik in Norddeutschland." In *Querschnitt—Gender Studies: Ein interdisziplinärer Blick nicht nur auf Homosexualität,* edited by Paul M. Hahlbohm and Till Hurlin, 42–82. Kiel: Verlag Ludwig, 2001.

———. *Selbstbilder und Fremdbilder der "Anderen": Eine Geschichte männer-begehrende Männer in der Weimarer Republik und der NS-Zeit.* Konstanz: UVK Verlagsgesellschaft, 2005.

Moreck, Curt. *Führer durch das 'lasterhafte' Berlin.* Leipzig: Verlag moderner Stadtführer, 1931.

Nestle, Joan. "Butch-Fem Relationships: Sexual Courage in the 1950s." *Heresies* 12 (1981): 21–24.

Newton, Esther. "The Mythic Mannish Lesbian: Radclyffe Hall and the New Woman." In *Hidden from History: Reclaiming the Gay and Lesbian Past,* edited by Martin Duberman, Martha Vicinus, and George Chauncey Jr., 281–93. New York: Meridian, 1989.

Nieden, Susanne zur, ed. *Homosexualität und Staatsräson: Männlichkeit, Homophobie und Politik in Deutschland 1900–1945.* Frankfurt: Campus Verlag, 2005.

Nienhaus, Ursula. *"Nicht für eine Führungsposition geeignet": Josefine Erkens und die Anfänge weiblicher Polizei in Deutschland, 1923–1933.* Münster: Westfälisches Dampfboot, 1999.

Oosterhuis, Harry. "Eros and Male-Bonding in Society: Introduction." In *Homosexuality and Male-Bonding in Pre-Nazi Germany,* edited by Harry Oosterhuis and Hubert Kennedy, 119–25. New York: Harrington Park Press, 1991.

———. "Homosexual Emancipation in Germany before 1933: Two Traditions." In *Homosexuality and Male-Bonding in Pre-Nazi Germany,* edited by Harry Oosterhuis and Hubert Kennedy, 1–27. New York: Harrington Park Press, 1991.

———. "Richard Krafft-Ebing's 'Step-Children of Nature': Psychiatry and the Making of Homosexual Identity." In *Science and Homosexualities,* edited by Vernon Rosario, 67–88. New York: Routledge, 1997.

———, and Hubert Kennedy, eds. *Homosexuality and Male-Bonding in Pre-Nazi Germany.* New York: Harrington Park Press, 1991.

Oram, Alison. *Her Husband was a Woman!: Women's Gender-Crossing in Modern British Popular Culture.* New York: Routledge, 2008.

Pappritz, Anna. "Zum Paragraph 175." *Der Abolitionist,* 1 February 1911.

Pateman, Carole. *The Sexual Contract.* Stanford: Stanford University Press, 1988.

Perret, Roger. " 'Ernst, Würde und Glück des Daseins.' " In Annemarie Schwarzenbach, *Lyrische Novelle.* Basel: Lenos Verlag, 1999.

Petersen, Klaus. "The Harmful Publications (Young Persons) Act of 1926: Literary Censorship and the Politics of Morality in the Weimar Republic." *German Studies Review* 15 (1992): 505–25.

———. *Zensur in der Weimarer Republik.* Stuttgart: Verlag J. B. Metzler, 1995.

Petersen, Vibeke. *Women and Modernity in Weimar Germany: Reality and Representation in Popular Fiction.* Oxford: Berghahn, 2001.

Petro, Patrice. *Joyless Streets: Women and Melodramatic Representation in Weimar Germany.* Princeton: Princeton University Press, 1989.

———. "Perceptions of Difference: Woman as Spectator and Spectacle." In *Women in the Metropolis: Gender and Modernity in Weimar Culture,* edited by Katharina von Ankum, 41–66. Berkeley: University of California, 1997.

Peukert, Detlef. *The Weimar Republic: The Crisis of Classical Modernity.* Translated by Richard Deveson. New York: Hill and Wang, 1989.

Philipps, Anna. *Um Ehre und Recht: Mein Kampf gegen das Provinzial-Schulkollegium Hannover und das Ministerium für Wissenschaft, Kunst und Volksbildung.* Unpublished printed manuscript, Neuminster, 1931(?).

Pieper, Mecki. "Die Frauenbewegung und ihre Bedeutung für lesbische Frauen." In *Eldorado: Homosexuelle Frauen und Männer in Berlin 1850–1950: Geschichte, Alltag, und Kultur,* 116–24. Berlin: Edition Hentrich, 1992.

Plötz, Kirsten. "Anders als die Anderen? Lesbische Frauen in der Weimarer Republik." In *Außer Haus: Frauengeschichte in Hannover,* edited by Christiane Schröder and Monika Sonneck, 69–74. Hanover: Reichold Verlag, 1994.

———. *Einsame Freundinnen: Lesbisches Leben während der zwanziger Jahre in der Provinz.* Hamburg: Männerschwarmskript, 1999.

———. "Bubis und Damen: Die zwanziger Jahre." In *Butch-Femme: Eine erotische Kultur,* edited by Stephanie Kuhnen, 35–47. Berlin: Querverlag, 1997.

Poovey, Mary. *Uneven Developments: The Ideological Work of Gender.* Chicago: University of Chicago Press, 1988.

Porter, Roy, and Mikulas Teich, eds. *Sexual Knowledge, Sexual Science: The History of Attitudes to Sexuality.* Cambridge: Cambridge University Press, 1994.

Ramien, Th. (Magnus Hirschfeld). *Wie erklärt sich die Liebe der Männer und Frauen zu Personen des eigenen Geschlechts?* Leipzig: Verlag Max Spohr, 1896.

Reagin, Nancy. *A German Women's Movement: Class and Gender in Hanover, 1880–1933.* Chapel Hill: University of North Carolina Press, 1995.

Reuter, Gabriele. *Aus guter Familie: Leidensgeschichte eines Mädchens.* Berlin: S. Fischer, 1906.

———. *From a Good Family.* Translated by Lynne Tatlock. Rochester, NY: Camden House, 1999.

———. *Vom Kinde zum Menschen: die Geschichte meiner Jugend.* Berlin: Fischer Verlag, 1921.

Reventlow, Franziska von. *Ellen Olestjerne.* Munich: Buch u. Media, 2002.

Riviere, Joan. "Womanliness as Masquerade." In *Formations of Fantasy,* edited by Victor Burgin, James Donald, and Cora Kaplan, 35–44. London: Methuen, 1986.

Roberts, Mary Lou. *Civilization without Sexes: Reconstructing Gender in Postwar France, 1917–1927.* Chicago: University of Chicago Press, 1994.

———. *Disruptive Acts: The New Woman in Fin-de-Siècle France.* Chicago: University of Chicago Press, 2002.

Rogoff, Irit. "Tiny Anguishes: Reflections on Nagging, Scholastic Embarrassment, and Feminist Art History." *differences: A Journal of Feminist Cultural Studies* 4 (1992): 38–65.

Roos, Julia. *Weimar through the Lens of Gender: Prostitution Reform, Woman's Emancipation, and German Democracy, 1919–33*. Ann Arbor: University of Michigan Press, 2010.

Rosario, Vernon, ed. *Science and Homosexualities*. New York: Routledge, 1997.

Rosenhaft, Eve. "Women, Gender, and the Limits of Political History in the Age of 'Mass' Politics." In *Elections, Mass Politics, and Social Change in Modern Germany*, edited by Larry Eugene Jones and James Retallack, 149–73. Cambridge: Cambridge University Press, 1992.

Rubin, Gayle. "Thinking Sex: Notes for a Radical Theory of the Politics of Sexuality." In *Pleasure and Danger: Exploring Female Sexuality*, edited by Carole Vance, 267–319. Boston: Routledge and Kegan Paul, 1984.

Rühling, Anna. "Welches Interesse hat die Frauenbewegung an der Lösung des Homosexuellen Problems?" *Jahrbuch für sexuelle Zwischenstufen* 7 (1905): 131–51.

Rupp, Leila. *Sapphistries: A Global History of Love between Women*. New York: New York University Press, 2009.

———. "Sexuality and Politics in the Early Twentieth Century: The Case of the International Women's Movement." *Feminist Studies* 23 (1997): 577–605.

Ryan, Marynel. "Different Paths to the Public: European Women, Educational Opportunity, and Expertise, 1890–1930." *Continuity and Change* 19 (2004): 367–386.

Schader, Heike. "Konstructionen weiblicher Homosexualität in Zeitschriften homosexueller Frauen in den 1920er Jahren." *Invertito* 2 (2000): 8–33.

———. "Virile homosexuelle Frauen im Spiegel ihrer Zeitschriften im Berlin der zwanziger Jahre." In *Verqueere Wissenschaft? Zum Verhältnis von Sexualwissenschaft und Sexualreformbewegung in Geschichte und Gegenwart*, edited by Ursula Ferdinand, Andreas Pretzel, and Andreas Seeck, 137–46. Münster: LIT, 1998.

———. *Virile, Vamps und wilde Veilchen: Sexualität, Begehren und Erotik in den Zeitschriften homosexueller Frauen im Berlin der 1920er Jahre*. Königstein: Ulrike Helmer Verlag, 2004.

Schaser, Angelika. "Gertrud Bäumer—'Eine der wildesten Demokratinnen' oder verhinderte Nationalsozialistin?" In *Zwischen Karriere und Verfolgung: Handlungsräume von Frauen im nationalsozialistischen Deutschland*, edited by Kirsten Heinsohn, Barbara Vogel, and Ulrike Weckel, 24–43. Frankfurt: Campus Verlag, 1997.

Scheub, Ute. *Verrückt nach Leben: Berliner Szenen in den zwanziger Jahren*. Reinbek, Rowohlt, 2000.

Schirmacher, Käthe. *Flammen: Erinnerungen aus mein Leben*. Leipzig: Dürr u. Weber, 1921.

———. *Die Libertad: Novelle*. Zurich: Verlags-Magazin, 1891.

———. "Paragraph 175 des deutschen Strafgesetzes." *Der Abolitionist*, 1 January 1911.

———. *Züricher Studentinnen*. Leipzig and Zurich: Verlag von Th. Schröter, 1896.

Schoppmann, Claudia. *Days of Masquerade: Life Stories of Lesbians During the Third Reich*. New York: Columbia University Press, 1996.

—————. "National Socialist Policies Towards Female Homosexuality." In *Gender Relations in German History: Power, Agency, and Experience from the Sixteenth to the Twentieth Century*, edited by Lynn Abrams and Elizabeth Harvey, 177–87. Durham: Duke University Press, 1997.

—————. *Nationalsozialistische Sexualpolitik und weibliche Homosexualität*. Pfaffenweiler: Centaurus, 1991.

Schorske, Carl. *Fin-de-Siècle Vienna Politics and Culture*. New York: Vintage, 1981.

Schubert, Werner, ed. *Protokolle der Kommission für die Reform des Strafgesetzbuches (1911–1913)*, 4 vols. Frankfurt: Keip Verlag, 1990.

Schwartz, Gudrun. "'Mannweiber' in Männertheorien." In *Frauen suchen ihre Geschichte: Historische Studien zum 19. und 20. Jahrhundert*, edited by Karin Hausen, 62–80. Munich: C. H. Beck, 1983.

Schweizerischer Verband der Akademikerinnen. *Das Frauenstudium an den schweizer Hochschulen*. Zurich: Rascher u. Cie., 1928.

Scott, Joan Wallach. "Gender: A Useful Category of Analysis." *American Historical Review* 91 (1986): 1053–75.

—————. *Only Paradoxes to Offer: French Feminists and the Rights of Man*. Cambridge: Harvard University Press, 1996.

Sedgwick, Eve Kosofsky. *Between Men: English Literature and Male Homosocial Desire*. New York: Columbia University Press, 1985.

—————. *Epistemology of the Closet*. Berkeley: University of California Press, 1990.

Sengoopta, Chandak. *Otto Weininger: Sex, Science, and Self in Imperial Vienna*. Chicago: University of Chicago Press, 2000.

—————. "The Unknown Weininger." *Central European History* 29 (1997): 453–93.

Showalter, Elaine. *Sexual Anarchy: Gender and Culture at the Fin-de-Siècle*. New York: Viking, 1990.

Smith, Sidonie, and Julia Watson. "Introduction: Situating Subjectivity in Women's Autobiographical Practices." In *Women/Autobiography/Theory: A Reader*, edited by Sidonie Smith and Julia Watson, 3–52. Madison: University of Wisconsin Press, 1998.

Smith-Rosenberg, Carroll. "Discourses of Sexuality and Subjectivity: The New Woman, 1870–1936." In *Hidden from History: Reclaiming the Gay and Lesbian Past*, edited by Martin Duberman, Martha Vicinus, and George Chauncey Jr., 264–80. New York: Meridian, 1989.

—————. "The Female World of Love and Ritual: Relations between Women in Nineteenth Century America." *Signs* 1 (1975): 1–29.

Sommer, Kai. *Die Strafbarkeit der Homosexualität von der Kaiserzeit bis zum Nationalsozialismus: Ein Analyse der Straftatbestände im Strafgesetzbuch und in den Reformentwürfen*. Frankfurt: Peter Lang, 1998.

Spector, Scott. "Edith Stein's Passing Gestures: Intimate Histories, Empathic Portraits." *New German Critique* 75 (1998): 28–56.

—————. "Where Personal Fate Turns to Public Affair: Homosexual Scandal and Social Order in Vienna, 1900–1910." *Austrian History Yearbook* 38 (2007): 15–24.

―――. "The Wrath of the 'Countess Merviola': Tabloid Exposé and the Emergence of Homosexual Subjects in Vienna in 1907." In *Sexuality in Austria,* edited by Günter Bischof, Anton Pelinka, and Dagmar Herzog, 31–47. New Brunswick: Transaction, 2006.

Springer, Jenny. "Die deutsche Studentin." *Die Woche* 1907, no. 13, 563–66.

Steakley, James. *The Homosexual Emancipation Movement in Germany.* New York: Arno Press, 1975.

―――. "Iconography of a Scandal: Political Cartoons and the Eulenburg Affair in Wilhelmin Germany." In *Hidden from History: Reclaiming the Gay and Lesbian Past,* edited by Martin Duberman, Martha Vicinus, and George Chauncey Jr., 233–57. New York: Meridian, 1989.

―――. "*Per Scientiam Ad Justitiam*: Magnus Hirschfeld and the Sexual Politics of Innate Homosexuality." In *Science and Homosexualities,* edited by Vernon Rosario, 131–54. New York: Routledge, 1997.

Stieg, Margaret. "The 1926 German Law to Protect Youth against Trash and Dirt: Moral Protectionism in a Democracy." *Central European History* 23 (1990): 22–56.

Stöcker, Helene. "Die beabsichtigte Ausdehnung des Paragraph 175 auf die Frau." *Neue Generation,* 14 March 1911.

―――. *Liebe: Roman.* Berlin: Verlag der Neuen Generation, 1925.

Stoehr, Irene. "Fraueneinfluß oder Geschlechterversöhnung? Zur 'Sexualitätsdebatte' in der deutschen Frauenbewegung um 1900." In *Frauenkörper/Medizin/Sexualität: Auf dem Wege zu einer neuen Sexualmoral,* edited by Johanna Geyer-Kordesch and Annette Kuhn, 159–90. Düsseldorf: Schwann, 1986.

Storr, Merl. "Transformations: Subjects, Categories, and Cures in Krafft-Ebing's Sexology." In *Sexology in Culture: Labelling Bodies and Desires,* edited by Lucy Bland and Laura Doan, 11–26. Chicago: University of Chicago Press, 1998.

Streiter, Sabine. "Nachwort." In *Die schönsten Novellen der Frieda von Bülow über Lou Andreas-Salomé und andere Frauen,* by Frieda von Bülow, edited by Sabine Streiter, 236–52. Frankfurt: Verlag Ullstein, 1990.

Sutton, Katie. *The Masculine Woman in Weimar Germany.* New York: Berghahn, 2011.

Tate, Laura. "The Culture of Literary *Bildung* in the Bourgeois Women's Movement in Imperial Germany." *German Studies Review* 24 (2001): 267–81.

Teich, Mikulas, and Roy Porter, eds. *Fin de Siècle and Its Legacy.* Cambridge: Cambridge University Press, 1990.

Theis, Wolfgang, and Andreas Sternweiler. "Alltag im Kaiserreich und in der Weimarer Republik." In *Eldorado: Homosexuelle Frauen und Männer in Berlin, 1850–1950: Geschichte, Alltag und Kultur,* 48–73. Berlin: Edition Hentrich, 1992.

Tiburtius, Franziska. *Erinnerungen einer Achtzigjährigen.* Berlin: C. A. Schwetschke und Sohn, 1929.

Traub, Valerie. "Psychomorphology of the Clitoris." *GLQ* 2 (1996): 81–113.

―――. *The Renaissance of Lesbianism in Early Modern England.* New York: Cambridge University Press, 2002.

Trumbach, Randolph. "London's Sapphists: From Three Sexes to Four Genders in the Making of Modern Culture." In *Third Sex, Third Gender: Beyond Sexual*

Dimorphism in Culture and History, edited by Gilbert Herdt, 111–36. New York: Zone Books, 1994.

Usborne, Cornelie. "The New Woman and Generational Conflict: Perceptions of Young Women's Sexual Mores in the Weimar Republic." In *Generations in Conflict: Youth Revolt and Generation Formation in Germany 1770–1968,* edited by Mark Roseman, 137–63. Cambridge: Cambridge University Press, 1995.

———. *The Politics of the Body in Weimar Germany: Women's Reproductive Rights and Duties.* Ann Arbor: University of Michigan Press, 1992.

Vicinus, Martha. *Independent Women: Work and Community for Single Women, 1850–1920.* Chicago: University of Chicago Press, 1985.

———. *Intimate Friends: Women Who Loved Women, 1778–1928.* Chicago: University of Chicago Press, 2004.

———. "Lesbian History: All Theory and No Facts or All Facts and No Theory." *Radical History Review* 60 (1994): 57–75.

———. " 'They Wonder to Which Sex I Belong': The Historical Roots of the Modern Lesbian Identity." *Feminist Studies* 18 (1992): 467–97.

———. "Turn-of-the-Century Male Impersonation: Rewriting the Romance Plot." In *Sexualities in Victorian Britain,* edited by Andrew H. Miller and James Eli Adams, 187–213. Bloomington: Indiana University Press, 1996.

Vogel, Katharina. "Zum Selbstverständnis lesbischer Frauen in der Weimarer Republik: Eine Analyse der Zeitschrift 'Die Freundin' 1924–1933." In *Eldorado: Homosexuelle Frauen und Männer in Berlin 1850–1950: Geschichte, Alltag, und Kultur,* 162–68. Berlin: Edition Hentrich, 1992.

Waldoff, Claire. *Weeste Noch . . . ? Erinnerungen und Dokumente.* Edited by Volker Kühn. Berlin: Parthas Verlag, 1997.

Walzer, Anke. *Käthe Schirmacher: Eine deutsche Frauenrechtlerin auf dem Wege vom Liberalismus zum konservativen Nationalismus.* Pfaffenweiler: Centaurus-Verlagsgesellschaft, 1991.

Warner, Michael, ed. *Fear of a Queer Planet: Queer Politics and Social Theory.* Minneapolis: University of Minnesota Press, 1993.

———. "Publics and Counterpublics." *Public Culture* 14 (2002): 49–90.

Wedekind, Frank. *Frank Wedekind: Diary of an Erotic Life.* Translated by W. E. Yuill. Edited by Gerhard Hay. Cambridge, MA: Blackwell, 1990.

———. *Lulu: Erdgeist, Die Büchse der Pandora.* Edited by Erhard Weidl. Stuttgart: Philipp Reclam jun., 1989.

Weeks, Jeffrey. *Making Sexual History.* Cambridge: Polity Press, 2000.

Weininger, Otto. *Geschlecht und Charakter: Eine prinzipielle Untersuchung.* Vienna: Braunmüller, 1903.

Weitz, Eric. "Man and the Ever-Changing Woman: Gender and Politics in European Communism." In *Gender and Class in Modern Europe,* edited by Laura Frader and Sonya Rose, 311–51. Ithaca: Cornell University Press, 1996.

Welsch, Ursula, and Michaela Wiesner. *Lou Andreas-Salomé: Vom "Lebensgrund" zur Psychoanalyse.* Munich: Internationale Psychoanalyse, 1990.

Wetzell, Richard. *Inventing the Criminal: A History of German Criminology, 1880–1945.* Chapel Hill: University of North Carolina Press, 2000.

Weydmann, Joseph. "Polizeiassistentinnen und Polizeipflegerinnen in Deutschland." *Soziale Kultur,* February 1913: 81–88.

Wieking, Friedrike. *Die Entwicklung der weiblichen Kriminalpolizei in Deutschland von den Anfängen bis zur Gegenwart.* Lübeck: Verlag für polizeiliches Fachschrifttum, 1958.

Wolfe, Georg Jakob. *Die Münchnerin: Kultur und Sittenbilder aus dem alten und neuen München.* Munich: Fran Hanfstaengl, 1924.

Wolff, Charlotte. *Hindsight: An Autobiography.* London: Quartet Books, 1980.

———. *Magnus Hirschfeld: A Portrait of a Pioneer in Sexology.* London: Quartet Books, 1986.

Wolzogen, Ernst von. *Das dritte Geschlecht.* Berlin: Richard Ecksten Nachf., 1901.

———. *Verse zu meinem Leben.* Berlin: F. Fontane, 1907.

———. *Wie ich mich ums Leben brachte: Erinnerungen und Erfahrungen.* Braunschweig and Hamburg: Verlag von Georg Westermann, 1922.

Index

Friendships *(continued)*
  importance of extreme discretion to, 134
  intimacy and eroticism in, 58
  levels of, 36, 38
  with professional women, 130–139
  pure, 138
  reinterpreted by accusers, 131
  rejection and, 131
  romantic, 131, 228*n53*, 239*n134*
  special, 131
  true, 141
  use of *Du* as metaphor of intimacy, 131
  as vulnerabilities, 131
Funny Nine (club), 158

Garçonne (periodical), 162, 163, 182, 185, 186
Gender
  ambiguity, 74, 186
  binary, 28, 30, 50, 51, 53, 84, 170
  change, 38, 50, 51, 81
  changelings, 47
  confusion, 214*n56*
  constraints, 14
  construction, 21
  continuum, 18, 172
  contrast, 61, *62*
  destiny, 67
  deviance, 23, 102
  difference, 21, 46, 53
  effect on desire, 74
  emancipation, 3, 12, 13, 155, 192
  equity, 21, 108–115
  essentialism, 80
  expectations, 149
  ideology, 72, 95
  injustice of roles, 53
  inversion, 18, 74, 93, 150
  medicalization of, 67
  mimicry, 49–53
  nonconformity, 75, 182
  normative order of, 3

  norms, 53, 85
  opposition, 182, 185
  polarity, 5, 72, 190
  polarized concepts of, 5
  politics, 166
  as primary determinant of character, 18
  recognition of desire and, 3
  reform, 36, 51
  relationship to sexuality, 4
  rethinking, 21
  revised meaning of, 21
  roles, 72, 84, 94, 137, 182, 186
  sameness, 43
  segregation, 155
  social construction of roles, 46, 75
  solidarity, 94, 173, 176
  stereotypes, 183
  style, 18
  unclear, 23
George, Stefan, 54, 55
German Friendship Association (DFV), 151, 154, 159, 161, 163
  commitment to ideas about etiology and meaning of homosexuality, 168
  political involvement, 174
  publishes *Frauenliebe*, 159
German National People's Party (DNVP), 44, 45
  feel women have sacred position in family, 44
German Women for Reform, 55
  police surveillance of, 56
  renamed Society for Women's Interests, 57
Germany
  end of Bismarck system of antisocialist rule, 5
  female homosexuality in interwar years in, 156–168
  "gay life" retreat to discreet subcultural forms, 187, 188
  governmental measures to clean up streets of Berlin, 166, 167